CALIFORNIA

MAX Moenssen P1

Biology Foundations

Reading and Study Guide

Miller & Levine •

Experience Biology

The Living Earth

Savvas Learning Company LLC, 15 East Midland Avenue, Paramus, NJ 07652

Front cover: Anatolii/Fotolia; Bkgd: Ftotti1984/Fotolia; Back cover, Spine: Daniel Prudek/Shutterstock

ISBN-13: 978-1-4183-2955-6
ISBN-10: 1-4183-2955-X
8 23

CHAPTER 1

LESSON 1

Introduction to Global Systems

READING TOOL **Make Connections** The chart below shows key terms from the lesson with their definitions. As you read, complete the chart by writing a strategy to help you remember the meaning of each term. Two examples have been filled in for you.

Term	Definition	How I'm Going to Remember the Meaning
Biosphere	consists of all life on Earth and all parts of Earth in which life exists	
Ecology	the scientific study of the interactions between organisms and between organisms and their surroundings	
Species	group of organisms that breed and produce offspring	
Population	a group of individuals that belong to the same species and live in the same area	
Community	a group of different populations that live together in a defined area	
Ecosystem	all of the organisms that live in a place, together with their physical environment	an ecosystem includes the organisms exchanging energy in an environment
Biotic factor	any living part of the environment	
Abiotic factor	any nonliving part of the environment	the prefix a- means "without," and bio- means "life": *abiotic* = nonliving
Atmosphere	a layer of all the gases that surround Earth	
Hydrosphere	all the water of the Earth's surface as well as the water vapor and rain in the atmosphere and water underground	
Geosphere	solid earth which consists of rocks, continents, and the ocean floor	

Lesson Summary

As you read, circle the answers to each Key Question. Underline any words you do not understand.

BUILD Vocabulary

biosphere part of Earth in which life exists including land, water, and air or atmosphere

ecology scientific study of interactions among organisms and between organisms and their environment

species a group of similar organisms that can breed and produce fertile offspring

population group of individuals of the same species that live in the same area

community assemblage of different populations that live together in a defined area

ecosystem all the organisms that live in a place, together with their nonliving environment

Understand Prefixes The prefix *bio-* means "life." **Which vocabulary words in this lesson contain this prefix and what are their meanings?**

____

____

____

____

____

____

Ecology: Studying Our Living Planet

KEY QUESTION *Why is ecology important?*

The **biosphere** includes all parts of Earth in which life exists, underground, on land, and in the water and air. The biosphere therefore includes humans and all other living things.

The Science of Ecology All forms of life interact with each other and with their environments. **Ecology** is the scientific study of interactions among organisms, populations, and communities and their interactions with their environment.

Why Study Ecology? When human populations were small and scattered, humans only had local effects on the environment. As human populations have grown and the power of technology has increased, human impact on the environment has increased. Humans depend on healthy ecological systems for clean water and good soil for growing food. We need to understand ecology so that human activity does not continue to damage the environment.

Levels of Ecological Organization Ecologists study organisms and their environment at different levels. A **species** is a group of similar organisms that produce offspring together. A **population** is a group of individuals that belong to the same species and live in the same area. Different populations that live in the same area form a **community**. A community and its physical environment form an **ecosystem**. Similar ecosystems around the world form a biome. The biosphere is all living things on Earth.

Gathering Ecological Data

KEY QUESTION *What methods are used in ecological studies?*

Ecologists generally rely on three main approaches, all of which are part of scientific methodology: observation, experimentation, and modeling. Many studies involve all three approaches. Ecologists may use tools ranging from DNA analysis to data gathered from satellites.

Observation Observation is often the first step in asking ecological questions. Questions can lead to new scientific hypotheses that can be tested during experimentation.

Experimentation Experiments are designed to test hypotheses. Experiments gather data that support or reject hypotheses. In some experiments, ecologists may carefully alter conditions in parts of natural environments. Or ecologists may design artificial environments. In these experiments, ecologists examine how organisms react to changes in the environment.

Modeling Many ecological models consist of mathematical formulas. These formulas are based on data that have been collected through observation and experimentation. Useful models can lead to new hypotheses and new experiments to test them.

READING TOOL

Connect to Visuals
Study Figure 1-3 in your textbook. Think about the biotic factors, the abiotic factors, and the factors that are both biotic and abiotic in the pond ecosystem shown. ☑ **What factors can be both abiotic and biotic? How so?**

____

____

____

____

____

Biotic and Abiotic Factors

KEY QUESTION *What are biotic and abiotic factors?*

An organism's environment consists of all the conditions, or factors, around the organism that affect it in any way. These factors are divided into biotic factors and abiotic factors.

Biotic Factors Living things affect one another. A **biotic factor** is any other living thing with which an organism might interact. Biotic factors include animals, plants, mushrooms, and bacteria.

Abiotic Factors Physical factors also affect living organisms. An **abiotic factor** is any nonliving part of the environment, such as sunlight, heat, precipitation, humidity, wind or water currents, and soil type.

Biotic and Abiotic Factors Together Biotic factors can influence abiotic factors. For example, soils contain decomposing plant and animal material. Decomposing plant matter can make soil more or less acidic. Plants can affect how much sunlight reaches the ground.

BUILD Vocabulary

biotic factor any living part of the environment with which an organism might interact

abiotic factor physical, or nonliving, factor that shapes an ecosystem

atmosphere relatively thin layer of gases that form Earth's outermost layer

hydrosphere portion of Earth that consists of water in any of its forms, including oceans, glaciers, rivers, lakes, groundwater, and water vapor

geosphere the densest parts of Earth, which includes the crust, mantle, and core

Related Words Think of other words that start with *geo-*. such as *geography*. This prefix comes from the Greek word meaning "earth." ☑ **What field of science studies the rocks and solid materials that make up our planet?**

____

Modeling Global Systems

KEY QUESTION *How can we model global systems?*

One way to understand global systems is to develop a model that shows those systems, the processes that operate within each system, and the ways those systems and processes interact. One model, that is shown in Figure 1-4 of your textbook, begins with the four major global systems. The biosphere includes all living organisms and the environments they live in. The **atmosphere** includes all the gases that surround Earth. The **hydrosphere** consists of all Earth's fresh and salt water, including the water vapor and rain in the atmosphere and the water underground. The **geosphere** includes the rocks, continents, ocean floor, and the interior of the planet.

Global Systems and Change Our model of Earth systems has three main parts, or rings. Each ring represents an ecological category.

The outer ring, "Causes of Global Change," represents human and non-human causes of change in global systems.

The middle ring, "How the Earth System Works," represents processes within each of the four global systems. It includes the global climate system, cycles of matter, energy flow, and interactions of organisms.

The inner ring, "Measurable Changes in the Earth System," represents changes in global systems that can scientists can measure.

Building and Using the Model You will learn about many events, processes, and interactions in this unit. Alone, these facts are like pieces in a jigsaw puzzle. The Understanding Global Change model organizes this information so that you can see how the pieces fit together. You will be able to use the model to explore connections among causes and effects in global change.

Visual Reading Tool: Modeling Global Systems

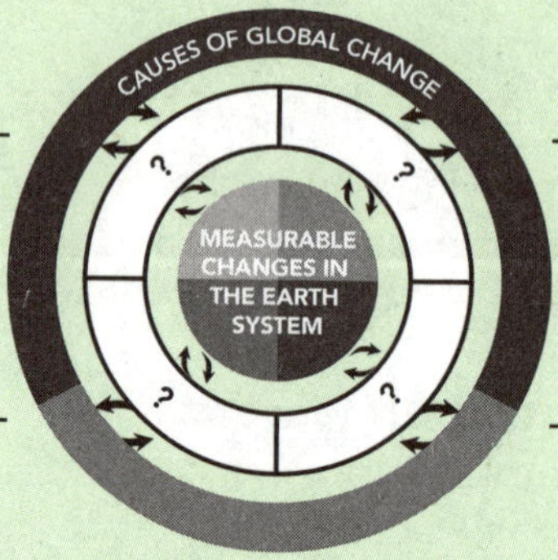

Adapted from *Understanding Global Change*, UC Berkeley

1. Label Earth's four global systems on the circle diagram above and color in each with a different color. Use the same colors to highlight the definitions of these spheres on the previous page.
2. How do the global systems interact to affect ecosystems?

3. What features of the geosphere could affect ecosystems?

CHAPTER 1

LESSON 2

Climate, Weather, and Life

READING TOOL **Cause and Effect** As you read your textbook, identify the cause-and-effect relationships that the text describes. Record your work in the table.

Cause →	Effect
Sunlight, carbon dioxide, water vapor, methane	
Earth's curvature and tilt	
Uneven heat distribution	
Winds, surface current	
Slow climate change	
Giant meteorite hits Earth	
Rapid climate change	

Lesson Summary

Climate and Weather

KEY QUESTION *What is the difference between weather and climate?*

Climate is defined by patterns and averages of temperature, precipitation, clouds, and wind over many years. It also includes the frequency of extreme weather events such as heat waves, droughts, and floods. **Weather** consists of short-term changes in temperature, precipitation, clouds, and wind from day to day, or minute to minute. Weather can change rapidly and can be difficult to predict. Climate is usually more predictable. Short-term changes in weather and long-term changes in climate determine whether food crops succeed or fail. Weather and climate also shape natural populations, communities, and ecosystems.

As you read, circle the answers to each Key Question. Underline any words you do not understand.

BUILD Vocabulary

climate average year-to-year conditions of temperature and precipitation in an area over a long period of time

weather day-to-day conditions of the atmosphere, including temperature, precipitation, and other factors

BUILD Vocabulary

greenhouse effect the process in which certain gases (carbon dioxide, methane, and water vapor) trap sunlight energy in Earth's atmosphere as heat

Use Prior Knowledge A greenhouse is a enclosed glass or plastic structure used to grow plants. ☑ **How does knowing this help you understand the greenhouse effect?**

____

____

____

____

____

____

____

____

____

____

The Global Climate System

KEY QUESTION *How is Earth's climate and average temperature determined?*

The global climate system is powered and shaped by the total amount of solar energy retained in the biosphere as heat. The global climate system is also shaped by the unequal distribution of that heat between the equator and the poles.

Solar Energy and the Greenhouse Effect Some of the sunlight that strikes Earth is reflected into space, and some is converted to heat. Some of this heat is trapped in the atmosphere. Earth's average temperature is determined by the balance between the amount of heat that stays in the atmosphere and the amount of heat that is lost to space. The amount of heat trapped in the atmosphere is mostly determined by three gases in the atmosphere: carbon dioxide, methane, and water vapor. These gases are called greenhouse gases, because they act like glass in a greenhouse. The greenhouse gases allow light to enter the atmosphere but trap heat. This is called the **greenhouse effect**. Both natural and human-related processes affect the amount of greenhouse gases in the atmosphere.

Latitude and Solar Energy The curvature and the tilt of Earth on its axis affect the angle that sunlight strikes the surface. There is more solar energy and therefore more heat near the equator, where the sun is directly overhead, than at the poles. This distribution of heat creates three main climate zones: tropical, temperate, and polar. The tropical zone, near the equator, has warm or hot temperatures all year. The temperate zone, further from the equator, has hot summers and cold winters. The polar zones have very cold winters and summers that are barely warm.

Differential Heating and Global Winds The unequal distribution of heat between the equator and the poles creates winds and ocean currents. Earth has winds because warm air rises and cool air sinks. Between the places where air sinks and the places where it rises, air travels over Earth's surface, creating winds. Earth's rotation causes winds to blow from west to east over the temperate zones, and from east to west over the tropics and poles.

Ocean Currents

KEY QUESTION *What causes ocean currents?*

Ocean currents are driven and shaped by patterns of warming and cooling, by winds, and by the location of continents.

Winds and Surface Currents Winds blowing over the ocean create surface ocean currents. Currents flowing from the tropics to the temperate zones have a warming effect on nearby coastal areas. Currents flowing from cool regions toward the tropics have a cooling effect. These interactions between atmosphere and hydrosphere affect weather and climate in coastal areas.

Deep Ocean Currents Cold water near the poles sinks but can rise to the surface in places where winds push surface water away from a continent. One such upwelling occurs off the coast of Peru, creating the weather phenomenon called El Niño.

READING TOOL

Connect to Visuals Examine Figure 1-9, Climate Zones, in your textbook. Identify the locations of the three main climate zones on Earth. ☑ **How does the angle of sunlight affect the climate of each of the climate zones?**

____

____

____

____

____

Regional Climate

KEY QUESTION *What factors shape regional climate?*

Regional climates are shaped by latitude, the transport of heat and moisture by winds and ocean currents, and by geographic features such as mountain ranges, large bodies of water, and ocean currents. Temperature and precipitation can be very different on different sides of a mountain range.

Changes in Climate

KEY QUESTION *What does climate change involve?*

Earth's climate has remained relatively stable during recorded human history. But global climate has changed dramatically over the much longer history of life. Climate change involves changes in temperature, clouds, winds, patterns and amounts of precipitation, and the frequency and severity of extreme weather events.

Non-Human Causes of Climate Change Several factors cause long-term changes in global climate. These factors include changes in solar energy and variations in Earth's orbit. Sudden events such as collisions with meteorites have had major effects on climate. The positions of Earth's continents change over millions of years because of plate tectonics, affecting winds and currents. Volcanic activity can change the amount of greenhouse gases in the atmosphere.

Results of Past Changes in Global Climate Non-human causes have produced both warm and cold periods over long periods of time. The most recent cold cycle caused the last major glacial period, which ended about 10,000 years ago. Changes in global climate can occur slowly enough that life on Earth can adapt and survive. At least five times in Earth's history, climate changes happened too fast for organisms to adapt, so many died. These episodes are known as mass extinctions.

CHAPTER 1

LESSON 3

Biomes and Aquatic Ecosystems

READING TOOL **Organize Information** As you read your textbook, note the similarities and differences between the different land biomes and aquatic ecosystems. There will be more than 1 biome that fits into each feature, and each biome can be used more than once. Record your work in the table.

Feature	Biome		Feature	Biome
Year-round precipitation			Warm year-round	
Seasonal precipitation			Warm summers, cool winters	
Low precipitation			Cold year-round	
Nutrient-rich soil			Nutrient-poor soil	

Lesson Summary

Life on Land: Natural Biomes

As you read, circle the answers to each Key Question. Underline any words you do not understand.

KEY QUESTION *What abiotic and biotic factors characterize a biome?*

Biomes are regional climate communities on land. Biomes are described in terms of abiotic factors and biotic factors. A graph called a climate diagram summarizes the seasonal pattern of temperature and precipitation in a biome. The organisms living in a biome can vary, due to differing conditions such as elevation or soil.

Ecologists classify climate communities into roughly ten different biomes.

Tropical Rain Forest Tropical rain forests have more species than all other biomes combined. Tall trees form a dense leafy covering called a **canopy** high above the forest floor. In the shade below, shorter plants form a layer called the **understory**. Organic matter on the forest floor is reused so quickly that the soil is not very rich in nutrients.

Tropical Dry Forest Tropical dry forests grow where there are long periods without rain. Plants and animals are adapted to store water or to use less water.

Tropical Grassland/Savanna/Shrubland This biome receives less rain that a tropical dry forest but more than a desert. Grass is interspersed with small groves of trees and shrubs. Organisms are adapted as in a tropical dry forest.

Desert Deserts receive very little rain and often have extreme temperature changes between day and night. Animals get water from their food and are inactive during the hot daytime.

Temperate Grassland This biome includes plains and prairies dominated by grasses, and has fertile soils. Large animals graze on the grasses and small animals depend on camouflage and burrowing for protection from predators.

Temperate Woodland and Shrubland In this biome large areas of grasses are interspersed with trees, and includes shrubland called chaparral. Woody plants resist water loss and may be fire resistant. Animals use camouflage.

Temperate Forest Temperate forests have cold winters and warm summers. The fertile soil is rich in **humus** formed from decaying leaves and other organic matter. Animals may hibernate or migrate in winter.

Northwestern Coniferous Forest This biome has mild temperatures and abundant rain. Tall conifers such as giant redwoods grow here.

Boreal Forest/Taiga Dense forests of evergreen conifers at the northern edge of the temperate zone are called boreal forests or **taiga**. Winters are very cold, but summers are mild. Animals have extra insulation or migrate in winter.

Tundra The tundra is characterized by **permafrost**, a layer of permanently frozen subsoil. Tundra plants are small because it is hard for them to take root in the permafrost. Animals are adapted to limit heat loss or to migrate to avoid winters.

Polar Regions The polar regions are not one of the biomes, but they border the tundra and are cold all year. Plants are few. Animals include insects and marine mammals that have insulation to survive in the cold waters.

BUILD Vocabulary

biome a group of ecosystems that share similar climates and typical organisms

canopy dense covering formed by the leafy tops of tall rain forest trees

understory layer in a rain forest found underneath the canopy formed by shorter trees and vines

humus material formed from decaying leaves and other organic matter

taiga biome with long cold winters and a few months of warm weather; dominated by coniferous evergreens; also called boreal forest

permafrost layer of permanently frozen subsoil found in the tundra

Root Words Break words into component parts to understand their meanings. For example, *permafrost* combines "permanent" and "frost" to indicate the word's meaning. ☑ **What effect does the permafrost have on plants in the tundra?**

____

____

____

READING TOOL

Cause and Effect Abiotic factors cause aquatic ecosystems to have zones with different characteristics. As you read, note how each abiotic factor causes the characteristics of each zone to be different and how this affects the type of organisms that live in each zone. ☑ **Describe the differences in the abiotic factors of the open ocean photic zone compared to the open ocean aphotic zone.**

____

____

____

____

____

____

____

____

Biomes and Anthromes Biomes are useful for describing large regions with similar climate and types of organisms. However, there are not many natural communities left today. Humans have altered nearly 75 percent of all land outside the steepest mountains, the polar regions, and the deserts. Human-altered biomes are called **anthromes**.

Marine Ecosystems

KEY QUESTION *What factors shape aquatic ecosystems?*

Aquatic ecosystems are described primarily by salinity, depth, temperature, flow rate, and concentrations of dissolved nutrients. There are three main groups of aquatic ecosystems: marine ecosystems, freshwater ecosystems, and estuaries. Ecologists divide the ocean into zones based on depth and distance from shore. Water depth influences life because sunlight doesn't penetrate the water very far. Photosynthesis can occur in the sunlit region near the surface called the **photic zone**. Below the photic zone is the dark **aphotic zone**, where photosynthesis cannot occur. Aquatic food chains are based on **plankton**, which includes floating algae, or phytoplankton, and small animals called zooplankton. Phytoplankton require sunlight and only grow in the photic zone. Zooplankton may swim in or out of the photic zone.

Intertidal Zone Organisms in the intertidal zone are submerged in seawater at high tide and exposed to air and sunlight at low tide. This causes extreme changes in temperature.

Coastal Ocean The coastal ocean extends from the low-tide mark to the outer edge of the continental shelf. The continental shelf is a relatively shallow part of the ocean surrounding the continents. Water here is lit by sunlight and often fed by nutrients in freshwater runoff from land. Kelp forests and coastal reefs flourish here.

Open Ocean More than 90 percent of the world's ocean lies past the edge of the continental shelf. Depths range from 500 meters along the continental slopes to more than 10,000 meters in deep ocean trenches. The open ocean is divided into photic and aphotic zones.

Open Ocean Photic Zone The sunlit top 100 meters of the open ocean supports small species of phytoplankton. Most photosynthesis on Earth occurs here, not in forests.

Open Ocean Aphotic Zone The permanently dark aphotic zone includes the deepest parts of the ocean. Deep ocean organisms are exposed to high pressure, cold temperatures, and total darkness. Deep-sea vents, where hot water boils from cracks in the ocean floor, support entire ecosystems based on chemical energy.

Freshwater Ecosystems

KEY QUESTION *What are the major categories of freshwater ecosystems?*

Only three percent of Earth's surface water is fresh water, but that small percentage provides organisms with drinking water, food, and transportation. Freshwater ecosystems can be divided into three main categories: rivers and streams, lakes and ponds, and freshwater wetlands.

Rivers and Streams Rivers, streams, creeks, and brooks often originate from underground water sources. A chain of rivers and streams may flow through several biomes.

Lakes and Ponds Most life in lakes and ponds depends on plankton, algae, and plants. Water typically enters and leaves lakes and ponds through rivers and streams.

Freshwater Wetlands A **wetland** is an ecosystem in which water either covers the soil or is present at or near the surface for at least part of a year. Freshwater wetlands include freshwater bogs, marshes, and swamps.

Estuaries

KEY QUESTION *Why are estuaries so important?*

An **estuary** (ES tyoo ere e) is a wetland formed where a river meets the sea. Fresh water and salt water often mix here. Estuaries serve as spawning and nursery grounds for many ecologically and commercially important fish and shellfish. Salt marshes are temperate estuaries, and mangrove swamps are tropical estuaries.

BUILD Vocabulary

photic zone sunlit region near the surface of water

aphotic zone dark layer of the oceans below the photic zone where sunlight does not penetrate

plankton microscopic organisms that live in aquatic environments; includes both phytoplankton and zooplankton

anthrome a biome that has been altered by humans

wetland ecosystem in which water either covers the soil or is present at or near the surface for at least part of the year

estuary kind of wetland formed where a river meets the ocean

Prefixes The prefix *a-* can have multiple meanings, but in science terms, it often means "without," or "not." The word *aphotic* means "without light," which is opposite in meaning to *photic*. **What other vocabulary word in this chapter is formed from a vocabulary word with the prefix -a added?**

____

Visual Reading Tool: Climate Diagram

Use the climate diagram to answer the questions. The bar graph data shows the amount of precipitation, and the line graph shows the average temperature.

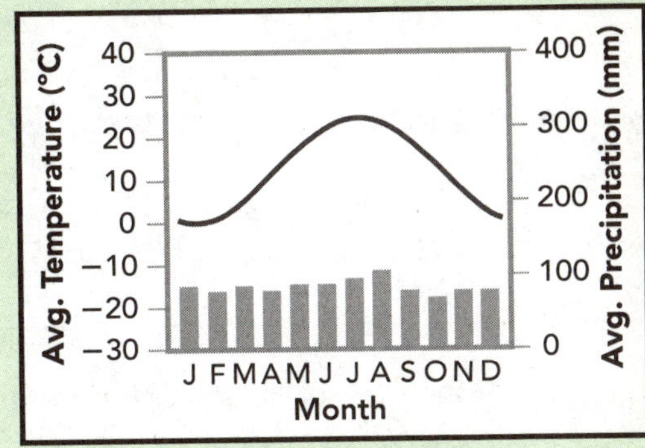

1. Describe the pattern of precipitation in this place. Is it seasonal or year-round?

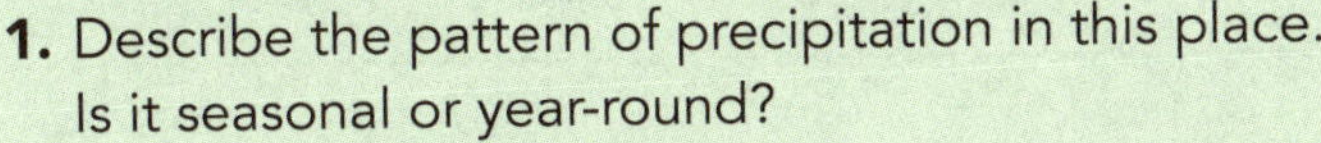

____

____

2. Describe the annual temperature pattern in this place.

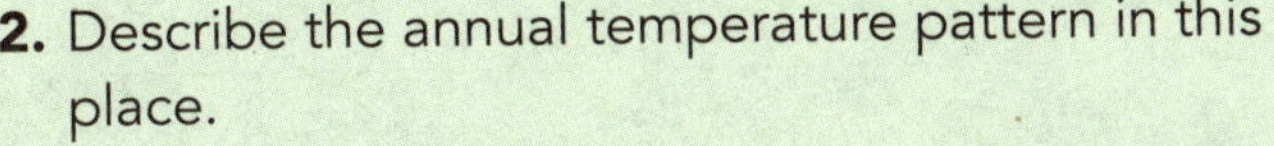

____

3. What makes this chart a climate representation, and not one that shows the weather?

____

1 Chapter Review

Review Vocabulary

Choose the letter of the best answer.

1. The gases in the atmosphere that trap heat produce

A. radiation.

B. solar energy.

C. the greenhouse effect.

D. the hydrosphere.

2. Nonliving factors of an environment are called

A. biotic.

B. bacteria.

C. abiotic.

D. plankton.

Match the vocabulary term to its definition.

3.	______	dense forests of coniferous boreal forests along the northern edge of the temperate zone	a. estuary
4.	______	a wetland formed where a river meets the sea	b. canopy
5.	______	a dense, leafy covering at the tops of tall trees in a rainforest	c. taiga

Review Key Questions

Provide evidence and details to support your answers.

6. How do models help ecologists understand global systems?

____

____

7. What is climate and how does climate change affect ecosystems?

____

____

____

8. What abiotic factors distinguish different biomes?

____

____

9. What factors describe aquatic ecosystems?

____

____

CHAPTER 2

LESSON 1

How Populations Grow

READING TOOL **Cause and Effect** As you read this lesson, use the grapic organizer to take notes on how both types of population growth occur. Make sure to include notes on birth rates, death rates, and growth rates.

Type of Population Growth		Cause	Effect
Exponential Growth		A species is introduced into a new region with plentiful resources and few predators.	
Logistic Growth	Phase 1	A species is introduced into a new region with plentiful resources and few predators.	
	Phase 2	Resources become limited.	
	Phase 3	The carrying capacity of the environment is reached.	

Lesson Summary

Describing Populations

As you read, circle the answers to each Key Question. Underline any words you do not understand.

KEY QUESTION *How do ecologists study populations?*

Ecologists study populations by examining their geographic range, growth rate, density and distribution, and age structure.

Geographic Range The places a population lives make up its geographic range. It is important to know an organism's range today, as well as its historic range. This data helps scientists understand the organism's relationships with other species in its habitat. A population range can vary enormously in size. For example, the population of bacteria in a single rotting vegetable is in a small area. The part of an ocean inhabited by a population of fish can be a very large area. Geographic ranges can grow or shrink over time.

Visual Reading Tool: Patterns of Distribution

Individuals in a population can be spaced out randomly, uniformly, or in clumps.
In each box, draw how 16 individuals would be spaced for each type of distribution pattern.
Draw each individual as a small circle.

Random	Uniform	Clumped

Density and Distribution The number of individuals per unit area is called the **population density**. In a given environment, one species may have very few individuals, or a low density, while another species has a much higher density, with many individuals. **Population distribution** is a description of the way individuals are spaced out across the population's range. There are three distribution patterns: random, uniform, and clumped. In a clumped population, individuals are close together in schools or herds. This may, for example, help protect individuals from predators. In a uniform population, individuals are spaced evenly. This occurs when individuals compete for resources. In a random distribution, individuals are spaced randomly. This occurs when the location of an individual has little effect on another individual.

BUILD Vocabulary

population density number of individuals per unit area

population distribution how individuals are spaced out across their range

age structure the number of males and females of each age in a population

Age Structure To understand a population, ecologists need to know the age of individuals, how many are male, and how many are female. This information describes the **age structure** of the population, which is important because most plants and animals must reach a certain age in order to reproduce. Among animals, only females can produce, and the number of offspring they produce can vary with age.

Population Growth

KEY QUESTION *What factors affect population growth?*

A population will increase or decrease in size depending on how many individuals are added to it or removed from it. Birthrate, death rate, and the rate at which individuals enter or leave a population all affect population growth.

BUILD Vocabulary

immigration movement of individuals into an area occupied by an existing population

emigration movement of individuals out of an area

exponential growth growth pattern in which the individuals in a population reproduce at an increasing rate

Prefixes *Immigration* and *emigration* both have the root word *migration*. The prefix *im-* means "into," and the prefix *e-* means "out of." For some uses, the prefix *ex-* is used instead of *e-*. ☑ **Which word listed below means bringing products into a country from another country? Circle your answer.**

Import

Export

Birthrate and Death Rate Populations can increase if more individuals are born during any time period than die during that same period. In other words, a population can increase when its birthrate is higher than its death rate. If the birthrate equals the death rate, the population may stay the same size. If the death rate is greater than the birthrate, the population will decrease.

Immigration and Emigration A population may increase if individuals move into its range from elsewhere. This is called **immigration**. A surplus of food can cause immigration. A population may decrease if individuals move out of the population's range. This is called **emigration**, which can be caused by a shortage of food or other resources. Immigration and emigration depend in part on how far and how fast individuals can travel, or whether human activity moves them around.

Exponential Growth

KEY QUESTION *What happens during exponential growth?*

If a population has all of the food and space it needs and protection from predators and disease, the population can increase. The rate of population growth increases because each generation contains more individuals than the generation before it. More and more offspring are produced in a situation called **exponential growth**. Under ideal conditions with unlimited resources, a population will increase exponentially. This means the larger the population gets, the faster it grows.

Organisms That Reproduce Rapidly Bacteria can grow very rapidly. If a single bacterium in ideal conditions can divide every 20 minutes, then after 20 minutes there are two bacteria. After another 20 minutes there are four bacteria, and at the end of the first hour, there are eight bacteria cells. After three 20-minute periods, there are $2 \times 2 \times 2$, or $2^3 = 8$ cells. In two hours there are $2^6 = 64$ cells. After one day, there are 4720 quintillion cells. If you plot the bacterial population on a graph, you get a curve shaped like the letter *J* that rises slowly at first and then rises faster and faster. If nothing interfered with this growth, the population would become infinitely large.

Organisms That Reproduce Slowly Most organisms reproduce much more slowly than bacteria. But if exponential growth continued indefinitely, the result would still be an impossible number of individuals.

Invasive Species Sometimes when an organism migrates or is moved to a new location, its population grows exponentially for a time. Its rapidly growing population might devour or destroy native populations.

Logistic Growth

KEY QUESTION *What happens during logistic growth?*

Phases of Growth Natural populations do not grow exponentially for very long. Sooner or later things happen that stop exponential growth. The paragraphs below describe the steps, or phases, that a population's growth follows after a few individuals are introduced into a real-world environment.

Phase 1: Population Grows Rapidly After a short time, the population begins to grow exponentially. It has unrestricted access to necessary resources. Individuals grow and reproduce rapidly. Few individuals die, and many offspring are produced. The population size and growth rate increase more and more rapidly.

Phase 2: Growth Slows Down In real-world populations, at some point exponential growth begins to slow down due to limiting factors, such as competition for resources. This does not mean that the population size decreases. The population still increases, but not as rapidly as before.

Phase 3: Growth Stops At some point the rate of population growth decreases to zero. The size of the population levels off and may remain about the same size for a long time.

The Logistic Growth Curve The logistic growth curve is shaped like the letter *S*. **Logistic growth** occurs when a population's growth slows and then stops, following a period of exponential growth.

Many plant and animal populations follow a logistic growth curve. Growth may slow if the birthrate decreases or if the death rate increases. Changing rates of immigration and emigration also affect population growth.

Carrying Capacity A population stops growing when its birthrate and death rate are the same, and when immigration equals emigration. The population size may rise and fall somewhat, but the changes average out around a certain population size.

The **carrying capacity** is the maximum number of individuals of a particular species that a particular environment can support, if environmental conditions stay relatively constant. Once a population reaches the carrying capacity of its environment, various factors affect the population and help stabilize its size. These factors may include the availability of food, water, and space.

BUILD Vocabulary

logistic growth growth pattern in which a population's growth slows and then stops following a period of exponential growth

carrying capacity largest number of individuals of a particular species that a particular environment can support

Word Origins The word *capacity* comes from the latin word *capax* which means "that can contain." Carrying capacity refers to the number of individuals that a certain environment can support.

☑ **What type of population growth will show a population reaching it's carrying capacity?**

____

CHAPTER 2

LESSON 2

Limits to Growth

READING TOOL **Compare and Contrast** As you read your textbook, complete the Venn diagram to compare and contrast density-dependent limiting factors and density-independent limiting factors.

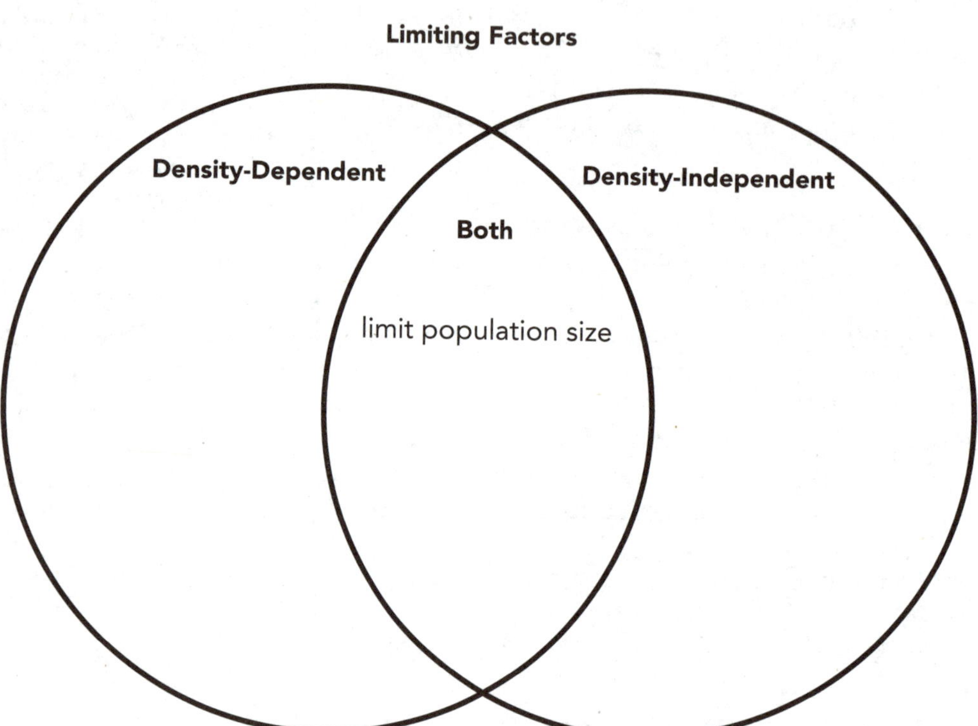

Once you have finished the Venn diagram, categorize the following scenarios as density-dependent and density-independent limiting factors.

Scenario A: A flood wipes out all the plant species that live on a riverbed.

Scenario B: A pack of wolves migrates to a new valley and eats all the deer that inhabit that space.

Scenario C: A large population of zebras is killed due to a contagious virus.

Scenario D: A drought kills many of the deer that live in a valley.

Limiting Factor	Density-Dependent	Density-Independent
Scenario(s)		

Lesson Summary

Limiting Factors

KEY QUESTION *What factors determine carrying capacity?*

The growth of primary producers can be controlled by a limiting nutrient. A limiting nutrient is one example of a limiting factor. A **limiting factor** is any factor that controls the growth of a population. Limiting factors are interactions between members of a population and either biotic or abiotic factors in their environment. Acting separately or together, limiting factors determine the carrying capacity of an environment for a species. Limiting factors produce the pressures of natural selection that are at the heart of Charles Darwin's evolutionary theory.

As you read, circle the answers to each Key Question. Underline any words you do not understand.

BUILD Vocabulary

limiting factor factor that causes population growth to decrease

density-dependent limiting factor limiting factor that depends on population density

Using Prior Knowledge You may have encountered *density* in other classes. It is most commonly used to refer to the mass of material in a given volume. For two objects that are the same size, the denser object will have a greater mass. In population ecology, *population density* can refer to the number of individuals per unit area. Examples include the number of penguins on an island, or the number of bacteria living on a rotting vegetable. **When there is a high population density for a species, what do individuals compete for?**

____

____

Density-Dependent Limiting Factors

KEY QUESTION *What limiting factors depend on population density?*

Limiting factors that operate more strongly when population density is high are called **density-dependent limiting factors**. Such factors do not strongly affect small, scattered populations. Density-dependent limiting factors include competition, stress from overcrowding, parasitism, disease, predation, and herbivory.

Competition When population density is high, individuals may compete for food, water, space, sunlight, and other resources that may be limited. Some individuals may have enough resources to survive and reproduce. Some may have enough to survive, but not to reproduce or to raise offspring. Others may die from lack of resources. Competition for resources can decrease birthrates, increase death rates, or both. Competition is a density-dependent limiting factor because resources can be used up when there are more individuals. Competition can be between members of the same species, or between species. Competition between species often shapes plant and animal communities and is a major force behind evolutionary change.

Parasitism and Disease Parasites and disease-causing organisms weaken their hosts and can cause death. Parasitism and disease are density-dependent factors because they spread from one host to another more easily when populations are dense.

BUILD Vocabulary

density-independent limiting factor limiting factor that affects all populations in similar ways, regardless of the population density

READING TOOL

Connect to Visuals The graph shows the rabbit population in South Australia before and after a virus, myxomatosis, was introduced to reduce the rabbit population. Use the graph and the information presented in this lesson to answer the questions.

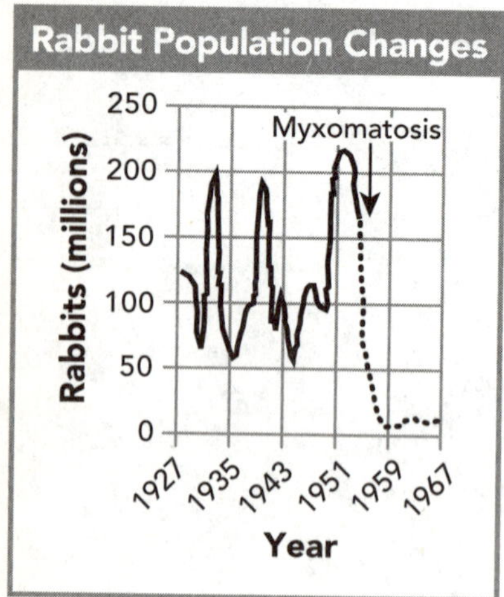

☑ **Was the virus a density-dependent or a density-independent limiting factor?**

____

Stress From Overcrowding Some organisms fight each other if they are overcrowded. Individuals can be weakened and may die. In some species, overcrowding stress can cause animals to neglect or kill their own offspring. Overcrowding stress can lower birthrates, raise death rates, or increase emigration.

Predation and Herbivory The effects of predators on prey or herbivores on plants are density dependent.

Predator-Prey Relationships Populations of predators and prey may rise and fall. When there is plenty of prey, the predators have plenty to eat and may increase in number. This causes the prey death rate to rise higher than its birthrate, so the prey population decreases. As the prey decreases, the predators begin to starve, so the predator population falls. This allows the prey population to start rising again.

Herbivore Effects An herbivore is a predator of a plant. Populations of herbivores and plants cycle up and down, just like populations of predators and prey.

Humans as Predators Human activity may limit populations of other organisms. Hunting is one way that humans can cause large decreases in animal populations.

Density-Independent Limiting Factors

KEY QUESTION *What limiting factors do not typically depend on population density?*

Density-independent limiting factors affect all populations regardless of population size and density. Environmental extremes—including weather extremes such as hurricanes, droughts, or floods, and natural disasters such as wildfires—can act as density-independent limiting factors. Such factors may cause a population to "crash," or reach very small sizes. After a crash, a population may increase again or stay low for a long time. Extreme hot and cold weather and severe drought, along with human-caused environmental damage, can affect populations of plants and animals.

True Density Independence? Bad weather can affect dense populations more than it would affect less dense populations by, for example, making food less available. It is sometimes difficult to say that a limiting factor acts only in a density-independent way.

Controlling Introduced Species The number of individuals of a species can increase rapidly when introduced into a new environment. Artificial density-independent control measures, such as hunting, are not always effective in controlling introduced species. A predator or a pathogen can be introduced to control a population, but if this works, the effect may be only temporary.

Limiting Factors, Global Change, and Extinction

KEY QUESTION *What is the relationship between limiting factors and extinction?*

Limiting factors such as temperature and rainfall can change over time. Human activity can divide natural environments into smaller pieces, reducing available space and carrying capacity. If carrying capacity falls low enough, populations can be wiped out, leading to species extinction. An extinct species has no members remaining.

Visual Reading Tool: Analyzing Changes in Wolf and Moose Populations

Figure 2-9 in your textbook shows the populations of wolves and moose on Isle Royale from 1955–2005. Use the data to answer the questions below.

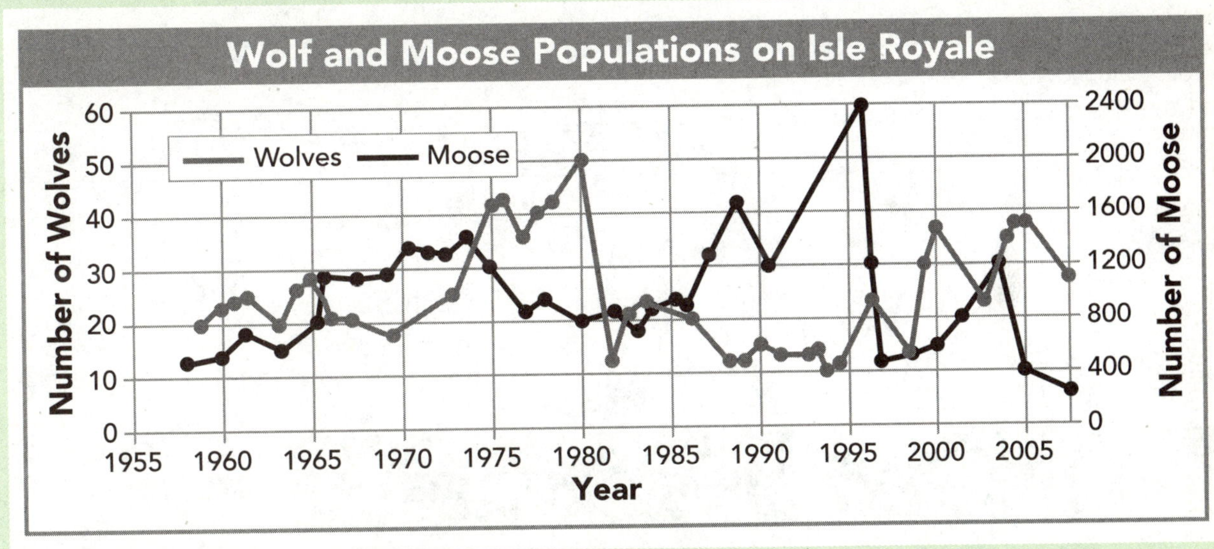

1. Circle the location on the graph where the wolves experienced a steep population decrease. What could have caused this?

____

____

____

2. Why is there a steep increase in moose from 1985–1995?

____

____

____

CHAPTER 2

LESSON 3

Human Population Growth

READING TOOL **Sequence of Events**
As you read this lesson, use your workbook to explain the five stages of The Demographic Transition. Look for words like "next" and "lastly" in the text, and use Figure 2-14 to help you.

Stage 1: ______________________________
____

Stage 2: ______________________________
____

Stage 3: ______________________________
____

Stage 4: ______________________________
____

Stage 5: ______________________________
____

Lesson Summary

Historical Overview

As you read, circle the answers to each Key Question. Underline any words you do not understand.

KEY QUESTION *How has human population size changed over time?*

Human populations can increase, remain the same, or decrease, due to the same factors that affect the population growth of other species. Human populations, like other populations, tend to increase, and the rate of those increases has changed over time. For most of human existence, our population grew slowly because predators and disease were common. These limiting factors caused high death rates. Eventually, civilization advanced, and food supplies became more reliable. The human population began to grow more rapidly.

Exponential Human Population Growth As countries became more developed, better sanitation and medicine reduced death rates. The combination of lower death rates and high birthrates led to exponential growth. It took 123 years for the human population to double from 1 billion in 1804 to 2 billion in 1927. Then it took only 33 years to grow by another billion. That exponential growth continued until around 1999, when growth began to slow down.

The Predictions of Malthus Exponential growth cannot continue forever. Two centuries ago, English economist Thomas Malthus was concerned about exponential human population growth. He argued that the world's carrying capacity for humans is determined by limited resources. Malthus suggested that only war (competition), famine (limited resources), and disease could limit human population growth.

World Population Growth Slows The human population's growth rate rose exponentially from around 1850 until the mid-1960s. After that, the growth rate began to decrease. The total human population continues to grow, but at a slower rate than it did over most of the last two centuries.

READING TOOL

Academic Words

sanitation prevention of disease by removal of sewage and trash

☑ **List some ways that modern cities in developed countries have improved sanitation conditions over the last 200 years. You may use the Internet to research your answers.**

____

____

____

____

____

____

Visual Reading Tool: Examining Patterns of Human Population Growth

Use the Human Population Growth Graph to help you answer the following questions.

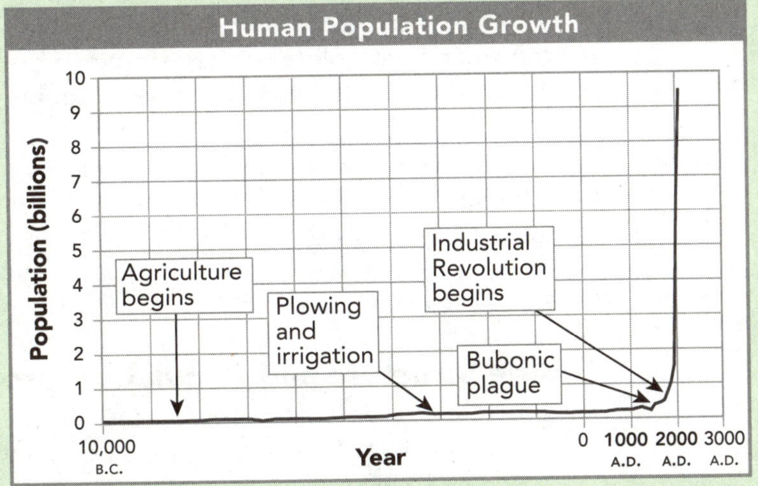

Source: U.S. Census Bureau, International Data Base, August 2016 Update.

1. When did the human population reach one billion? Round to the nearest century.

____

2. Using the graph, explain why the human population began growing rapidly during this time period.

____

____

____

BUILD Vocabulary

demography scientific study of human populations

demographic transition change in a population from high birth and death rates to low birth and death rates

Prefixes The prefix *demo-* comes from the Greek word *demos*, meaning "people." The same prefix is used in *democracy*. The demographic transition refers to a transition, or change, that is observed in human populations as countries become more developed. ☑ **What factors are measured to determine if a demographic change is occuring?**

____

____

____

____

____

Patterns of Human Population Growth

KEY QUESTION *Why do population growth rates differ among countries?*

The scientific study of human populations is called **demography**. Demography examines characteristics of human populations and predicts how they will change over time. Birthrates, death rates, and the age structure of a population help predict why some countries have high growth rates while other countries' populations increase more slowly.

The Demographic Transition Population growth has slowed dramatically over the past century in the United States, Japan, and much of Europe. Demographers hypothesize that these countries have completed the demographic transition. The **demographic transition** is a change from high birthrates and death rates to low birthrates and death rates. There are five stages to the demographic transition. In Stage 1, human birthrates and death rates are high. This describes most of human history. Next, advances in nutrition, sanitation, and medicine lead to lower death rates in Stage 2. In Stage 2, birthrates remain high and greatly exceed the death rate. The United States passed through Stage 2 between 1790 and 1910. As living standards rise, families have fewer children and the birthrate falls, which leads to Stage 3. In Stage 4, the falling birthrate leads to slower population growth. The demographic transition is complete, at Stage 5, when the birthrate is roughly equal to the death rate, and population growth stops.

Most ongoing population growth is happening in only ten countries, including India and China. Population growth is also high in parts of Africa. Emigration from those growth areas to countries whose populations have stopped growing accounts from much of the population growth recorded in those countries.

Age Structure and Population Growth The age structure of a population reveals the number of females and males of different ages. A higher percentage of young people indicates an increasing population, and a higher percentage of older people indicates a decreasing population. As shown in the age structure diagrams on page 64, the United States has nearly equal numbers of people in each age group. This indicates that our population is increasing slowly.

Demographers can predict how fast a population is growing by studying age structure diagrams and by taking into account other factors, such as the effects of deadly diseases and malnutrition. Current age structure diagrams suggest that although global population will continue to grow slowly, by 2050 the world population will reach 9 billion.

READING TOOL

Academic Words

malnutrition lack of proper nutrition, caused by not having enough food to eat or by eating food that is low in needed nutrients

Prefixes *Malnutrition* has the root word *nutrition*. The prefix *mal-* means "bad." ☑ **What does the word *maltreat* mean?**

____

____

Visual Reading Tool: Determining Age Structure Patterns

Use the Three Patterns of Population Change Graph to help you answer the following questions.

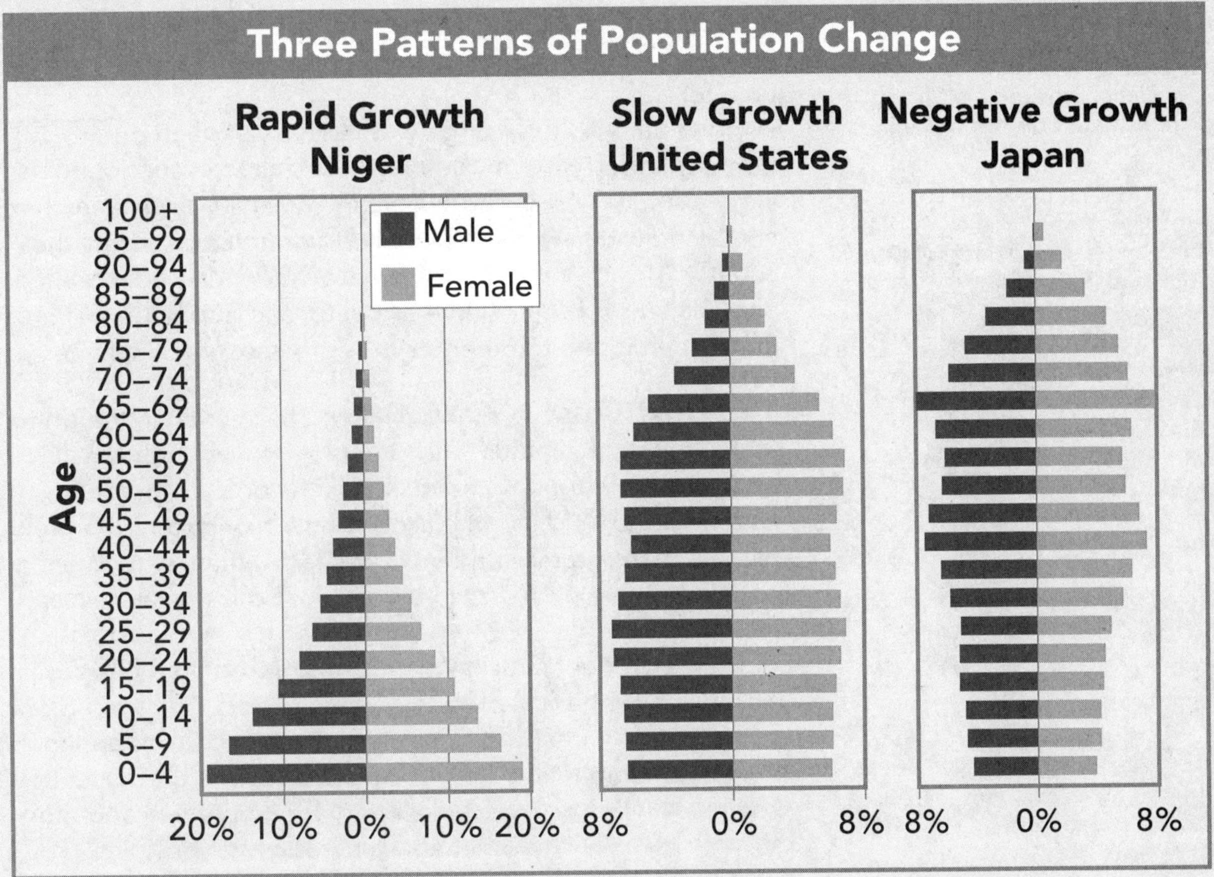

Source: United Nations, World Population Prospects

1. What percentage of Japan's population is between the ages of 0–4 years?

____

2. Using the graph, explain why Niger's population is going through rapid growth.

____

____

3. What could cause Niger's rapid population growth?

____

____

Human Populations, Environments, and Change

KEY QUESTION *How does the environment affect human population changes?*

Environmental extremes, or changes in the resource availability, have profoundly altered human death rates, driven mass migrations, or both. Most historical events were caused by natural environmental changes. Some events unfolding today have been linked to changes in the global climate system.

The Irish Potato Famine The human population of Ireland was devastated in the early 1840s by a nationwide disaster called the Irish potato famine. Because of successful potato farming, Ireland's population had increased exponentially from around 4.5 million to almost 8 million in less than 50 years.

However, Irish farmers grew only one variety of potato. Many Irish depended on this variety for both income and food. This set the stage for disaster. Two years of unusually wet weather, combined with a water mold, killed potato crops across the country. This change in resource availability caused more than one million people to starve to death, and about 1.5 million more to emigrate to other countries to escape the famine.

The Dust Bowl A similar situation happened in the United States during the 1930s. The Great Plains was a diverse grassland, with tough grasses that withstood temperature extremes and held soil in place with their long roots. Farmers plowed these grasses under and replaced them with wheat and corn. Several rainy years were good for both the farmers and their crops.

Then a drought struck. Windstorms picked up the topsoil that was no longer held in place by grasses' roots. The wind-blown dirt grew into massive dust storms that ruined crops and made the entire region, from Texas to Nebraska, into the "Dust Bowl." The result was the largest mass migration in American history, as farmers moved to other states to look for jobs.

California Droughts, Wildfires, and Floods During the winter of 2017–2018, southern California was hit first by wildfires, and then by floods. These events were driven by extreme changes in the availability of water resources, which affected plant populations in and around the coastal ranges. Human populations were also affected.

The winter of 2017–2018 was preceded by a five-year drought, followed by an usually wet winter. Plant growth was high that winter. However, the following summer saw a record heat wave that dried out much of the plant matter. These conditions led to some of the largest wildfires in state history. The wildfires were followed by massive amounts of rain in the coastal ranges over just a few hours' time. These rains caused large mudslides.

It is difficult to say that any single weather event is caused by global climate change. But many models of the global climate system predict that weather extremes will increase as climate change continues. These studies also predict that precipitation in California will decrease by as much as 15 percent over the next 20–30 years. This change in resource availability will increase the frequency and severity of wildfires, droughts, and water shortages.

READING TOOL

Sequence of Events The winter of 2017–2018 was a hard one for the state of California. ☑ **What were the events and that caused this?**

____

____

____

____

____

2 Chapter Review

Review Vocabulary

Choose the letter of the best answer.

1. the age and sex of members of a population

A. limiting factor

B. carrying capacity

C. age structure

D. demographic transition

2. the number of individuals an environment can support

A. demography

B. carrying capacity

C. limiting factor

D. emigration

Match the vocabulary term to its definition.

3. ________ the number of individuals per unit area

4. ________ movement of individuals into an area

5. ________ causes a decrease in population growth

a. limiting factor

b. population density

c. immigration

Review Key Questions

Provide evidence and details to support your answers.

6. A species is introduced into a new environment with plentiful resources and few predators. What will a graph of its population look like at first, and what is this pattern of growth called?

____

____

7. Hunters kill all of the wolves in a region. The wolves mostly ate deer. Why might there be fewer deer a few years after the wolves are killed?

____

____

8. How could a drought reduce the carrying capacity of an environment for a predator?

____

____

9. How can you tell if a human population has passed through the demographic transition?

____

____

CHAPTER 3

LESSON 1 Energy, Producers, and Consumers

READING TOOL Make Connections The concept map below shows the relationships between different organisms in this lesson. As you read, complete the concept map using vocabulary terms and other key terms from the lesson. After you have completed the concept map, use a colored pencil to shade all the producers. Then use a different colored pencil to shade all the consumers.

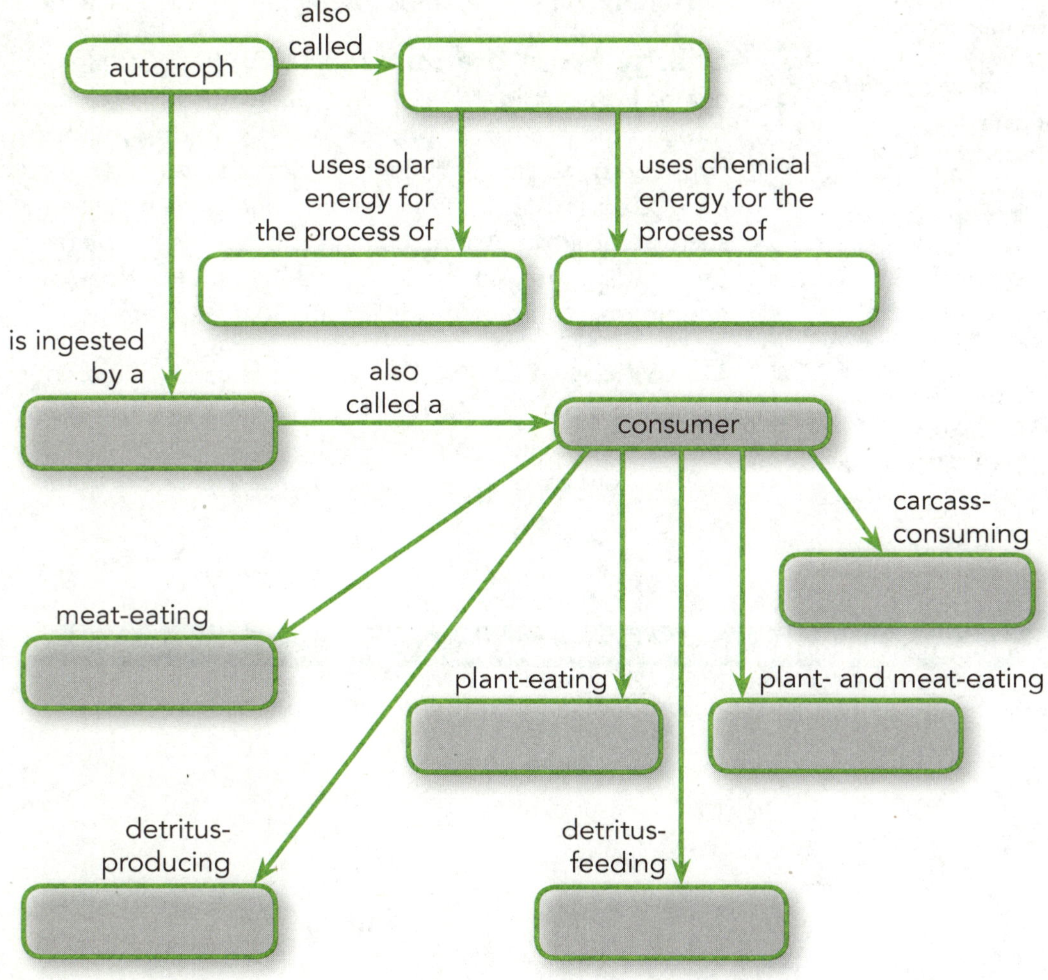

Lesson Summary

As you read, circle the answers to each Key Question. Underline any words you do not understand.

BUILD Vocabulary

autotroph an organism that is able to capture energy from sunlight or chemicals and use it to produce its own food from inorganic compounds; also called a producer

primary producer first producer of energy-rich compounds that are later used by other organisms

photosynthesis process used by plants and other autotrophs to capture light energy and use it to power chemical reactions that convert carbon dioxide and water into oxygen and energy-rich carbohydrates such as sugars and starches

chemosynthesis process in which chemical energy is used to produce carbohydrates

Primary Producers

KEY QUESTION *What are primary producers?*

All living things need energy, but no living thing can create energy. Organisms called **autotrophs** capture energy from nonliving sources. Autotrophs store this energy in forms that make it available to other organisms, which is why they are also called **primary producers**. Primary producers are the first producers of energy-rich compounds that can be used by other organisms. All life depends on primary producers.

Energy From the Sun The energy for most life on Earth comes from sunlight. Algae and plants absorb solar energy through the process of **photosynthesis**. Photosynthesis uses light energy to power chemical reactions that convert carbon dioxide and water into oxygen and energy-rich carbohydrates such as sugars and starches. This process also adds oxygen to the atmosphere and removes carbon dioxide. Algae and plants are the main primary producers in most ecosystems.

Life Without Light Some bacteria can capture energy from inorganic molecules such as hydrogen sulfide. These bacteria use a process called **chemosynthesis** (kee moh SIN thuh sis), in which chemical energy is used to produce carbohydrates.

Visual Reading Tool: Photosynthesis and Chemosynthesis

Write the names of the reactants and products of photosynthesis and chemosynthesis.

______ + ______ + Light Energy → ______ + ______

______ + ______ + ______ + Chemical Energy → ______ + ______ ______

1. Describe how photosynthesis and chemosynthesis differ in terms of how energy is converted.

______

______

______

2. What important product do both photosynthesis and chemosynthesis have in common?

______

Chemosynthetic bacteria thrive in places of total darkness and high temperature, such as Earth's crust and volcanic vents in the ocean floor. They are also found in underground streams, caves, and the mud of tidal flats.

Consumers

KEY QUESTION *How do consumers obtain energy and nutrients?*

Animals, fungi, and many bacteria cannot capture energy directly from sunlight or inorganic sources. These organisms, called **heterotrophs** (HET uh roh trohfs), acquire energy from other organisms, usually by eating them. Heterotrophs are also called **consumers**. Consumers are organisms that rely on other organisms for energy and nutrients.

Types of Consumers Consumers are classified by the way they acquire energy and nutrients.

- Carnivores eat other animals.
- Herbivores eat plant leaves, roots, seeds, and fruits.
- Omnivores, such as humans, eat both plants and animals.
- Scavengers eat carcasses of dead animals.
- Decomposers "feed" by chemically breaking down organic matter. This produces **detritus**, small pieces of dead and decaying plant and animal remains.
- Detritivores (dee TRYT uh vawrz) chew or grind detritus into smaller pieces, often digesting the decomposers that live on detritus.

Beyond Consumer Categories Many organisms do not fit neatly into one category. For example, some carnivores, such as hyenas, will scavenge. Many aquatic animals eat a mixture of algae, animal carcasses, and other organic matter.

Consumers in one category may differ from one another in subtle ways. Herbivores may eat different parts of plants. Different plant parts often contain different amounts of available energy. Fruits and seeds are easy to digest and contain a lot of energy and nutrients. Leaves are plentiful but hard to digest and poor in nutrients. No multicellular organism by itself can break down the cellulose molecules found in leaves. Animals that eat leaves have cellulose-digesting microorganisms inside their guts!

Some grazing animals, such as cattle, spend a long time chewing food into pulp. When they swallow the pulp, it goes into a part of their digestive tract that has microorganisms that can break down cellulose. Many grazers regurgitate the mixture of food and bacteria, called cud. They chew the cud and swallow it again. With all this extra work, grazers extract only a small amount of energy from the plants they eat. They spend a lot of time eating.

BUILD Vocabulary

heterotroph organism that obtains food by consuming other living things; also called a consumer

consumer organism that relies on other organisms for its energy and food supply; also called a heterotroph

detritus small pieces of dead or decaying plant or animal remains

Word Origins The word element *-troph* comes from the Greek word *trophos*, which means "feeder." The word elements *auto-* and *hetero-* are also of Greek origin. *Autos* means "self," while *heteros* means "other." ☑ **Using the word origins, explain the difference between an autotroph and an heterotroph.**

READING TOOL

Academic Words

produce create or form something as part of a physical, chemical, or biological process

acquire to gain an object or asset for oneself

☑ **Look at the photosynthesis diagram on the prior page. If there were suddenly no sunlight reaching Earth, how would this affect the ability of plants to produce carbohydrates?**

CHAPTER 3

LESSON 2

Energy Flow in Ecosystems

READING TOOL **Main Idea and Details** As you read your textbook, identify the main ideas and details or evidence that support the main ideas. Use the lesson headings to organize the main ideas and details. Record your work in the table. Two examples are entered for you.

Heading	Main Idea	Details/Evidence
Food Chains and Food Webs		
Food Chains	A food chain shows how energy transfers through feeding relationships.	
Food Webs • Food Chains Within Food Webs • Decomposers and Detritivores in Food Webs		
Food Webs and Disturbance		
Ecological Pyramids		
Pyramids of Energy		On average, about 10% of the energy is transferred from one trophic level to the next.
Pyramids of Biomass and Numbers		

Lesson Summary

Food Chains and Food Webs

KEY QUESTION *How does energy flow through ecosystems?*

When one organism eats another, energy moves from the "eaten" to the "eater." In every ecosystem, primary producers and consumers are linked through feeding relationships. These relationships vary, but energy in an ecosystem always flows in one direction: from primary producers through various consumers.

Food Chains The simplest way to think of energy moving through an ecosystem is to imagine it flowing along a food chain. A **food chain** is a series of organisms in which energy is transferred from one organism to another. Food chains vary in length, with some food chains having just one or two steps from a primary producer. For example, in a short food chain, a plant is eaten by a herbivore, which is eaten by a carnivore. Other food chains can be much longer. For example, food chains in the ocean may have four or five steps from primary producers to the largest fish. In the ocean, primary producers are usually tiny floating algae called **phytoplankton**. Phytoplankton are eaten by small animal plankton called zooplankton. The animal plankton are eaten by a series of larger consumers.

Food Webs Many animals eat more than one kind of food. This means that the movement of energy and matter is not a simple chain, but can be much more complicated. A network of feeding interactions, through which both energy and matter move, is called a **food web**.

Food Chains Within Food Webs Within a food web, there are many food chains connecting a primary producer to different consumers. A food web, therefore, is a network that includes all the food chains in an ecosystem. Food webs can be very complicated because of the large number of producers and consumers found within some ecosystems.

Decomposers and Detritivores in Food Webs
Decomposers and detritivores have vital roles in the movement of energy and matter through food webs. Many producers and consumers die without being eaten. Decomposers convert dead material to detritus, which is eaten by detritivores. Decomposition also releases matter in the form of nutrients that can be used by primary producers. Without decomposers, nutrients would remain locked within dead organisms.

As you read, circle the answers to each Key Question. Underline any words you do not understand.

BUILD Vocabulary

food chain in an ecosystem, a series of organisms in which organisms transfer energy by eating and being eaten

phytoplankton photosynthetic algae found near the surface of the ocean

food web network of complex interactions formed by the feeding relationships among the various organisms in an ecosystem

Use Prior Knowledge A chain could be made of beads on a string, or loops of paper or metal. Many chains could join together to make a model of a spider web. Food chains join together to form a food web.

☑ **Draw a model of a spider web at the top right corner of this page. Then describe how a spider web is similar to a food web.**

____

____

____

____

____

____

Visual Reading Tool: Food Webs

1. Find a food chain that connects algae to the alligator. Then find another food chain from the saltmeadow grass to the alligator. Use two pencils of different colors to highlight the two food chains.

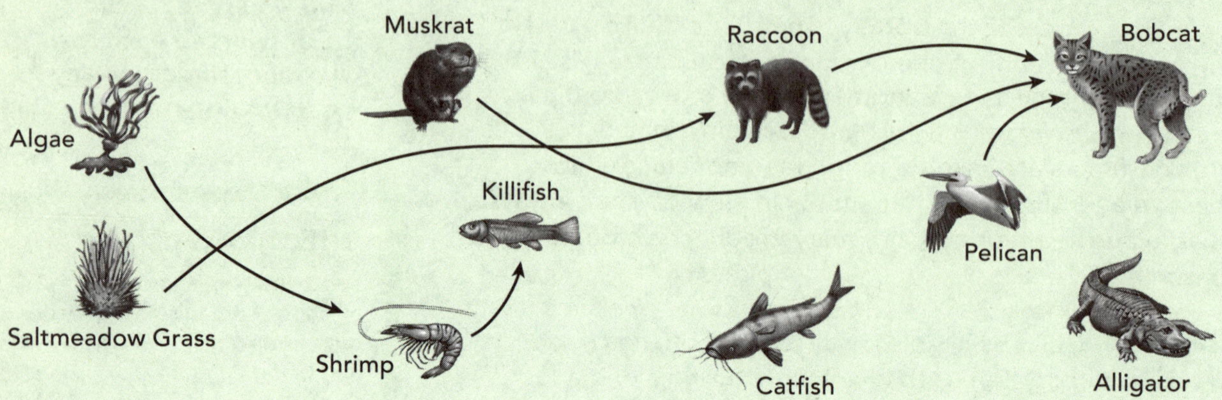

2. How are primary producers important to the alligator's energy supply?

____

____

____

3. How could decomposers be added to the diagram? Which parts of the food web do they affect?

____

____

____

Food Webs and Disturbance Changes to a food web can cause a variety of effects. These effects are hard to predict because food webs are complex. Sometimes the effects of changes are minor. Some animals can adjust well to changes in food webs, for example, if they eat a variety of foods. Other times a change can have dramatic effects throughout a food web.

READING TOOL

Academic Words

adjust To adjust is to change slightly, often to meet a need. Some animals adjust their diets when food sources change.

☑ **Look at the food web above. Suppose that the population of pelicans declined. How might bobcats have to respond to this change?**

____

____

Ecological Pyramids

KEY QUESTION *How do ecological pyramids help analyze energy flow through trophic levels?*

Each step in a food chain or food web is called a **trophic level**. Primary producers make up the first trophic level. Consumers occupy the other levels. **Ecological pyramids** are models of trophic levels in a food chain or food web. The shape of the pyramid shows the relative amount of energy or matter in each level.

Pyramids of Energy Only a small amount of the energy in any trophic level is available to organisms at the next trophic level. This is because organisms use much of the energy they consume on processes to stay alive. Energy is also released as heat. Pyramids of energy show the relative amount of energy available at each trophic level of a food chain or food web. The pyramid is widest at the bottom. The shape of the pyramid shows the efficiency of energy transfer between levels. On average, about 10 percent of the energy in one trophic level is transferred up to the next trophic level.

Pyramids of Biomass and Numbers The amount of living tissue in a trophic level is called its **biomass**. The amount of biomass in a trophic level is determined by the amount of energy in that level. A pyramid of biomass is a model that shows the relative amount of living organic matter in each trophic level of an ecosystem.

A pyramid of numbers is a model that shows the relative number of individual organisms at each trophic level in an ecosystem. The pyramid of numbers for an ecosystem is usually similar in shape to the pyramid of biomass. The number of organisms on each level decreases from the level below it. Sometimes consumers are much smaller than the organisms they feed upon. For example, thousands of insects may eat from a single tree. In such cases, the pyramid of numbers may be upside down, but the pyramid of biomass will still be smaller at the top than at the bottom.

BUILD Vocabulary

trophic (TROH fick) level each step in a food chain or food web

ecological (ee coh lah gi kal) pyramid illustration of the relative amounts of energy or matter contained within each trophic level in a food chain or food web

biomass the total mass of living tissue within a trophic level

Word Origins The word *trophic* comes from a Greek word that means "food or feeding." **☑ What other terms did you study in this chapter that contain the root word *troph*?**

____

Visual Reading Tool: Ecological Pyramids

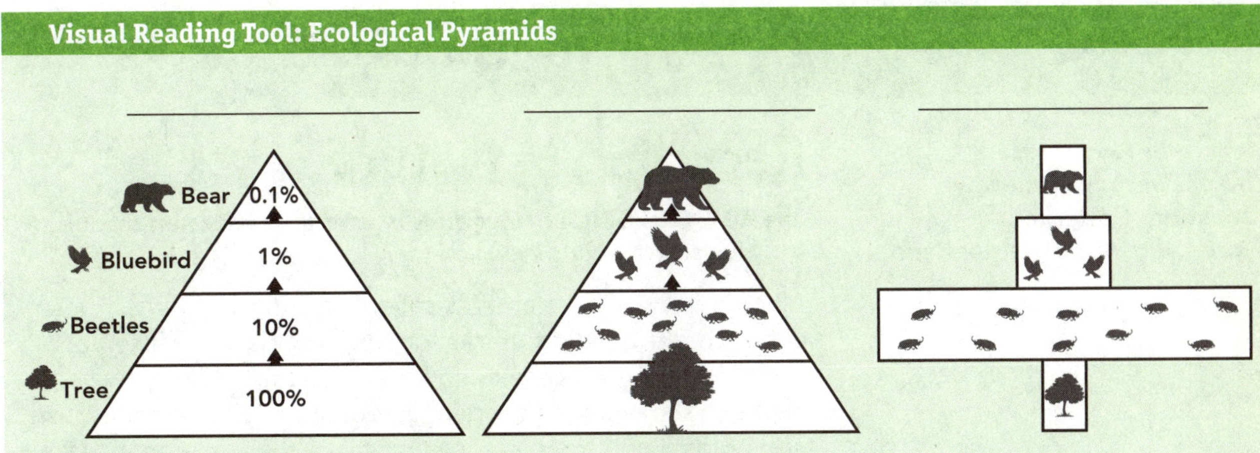

Write the name of the pyramid on the line above each pyramid. Then, below, explain the relationships among trophic levels that are shown by the pyramids.

____

____

____

CHAPTER 3

LESSON 3

Cycles of Matter

READING TOOL **Compare and Contrast** Before you read, preview the cycle diagrams in your textbook. Note the similarities and differences of the cycles in the graphic organizer.

Water Cycle	Carbon Cycle	Nitrogen Cycle

All Three Cycles

Lesson Summary

As you read, circle the answers to each Key Question. Underline any words you do not understand.

Recycling in Nature

KEY QUESTION *How does matter flow between trophic levels and among ecosystems?*

All organisms need elements called *essential nutrients*. These elements are building blocks for compounds that make up living tissue. Living cells need large amounts of six of these elements—oxygen, hydrogen, carbon, nitrogen, phosphorus, and potassium. Organisms cannot make these elements. Like all matter, these elements can never be created or destroyed. Matter flows one-way from one tropic level to the next. Some energy is lost along the way. Living things can use energy or store it, but they cannot re-use it. Elements are recycled within and among ecosystems, through cycles that may involve the biosphere, geosphere, hydrosphere, and atmosphere. These **biogeochemical cycles**, powered by the flow of energy, continue indefinitely.

Biological Processes Biological processes are any activity done by organisms, such as photosynthesis. They occur mainly in the biosphere but involve all three spheres.

Geological Processes Geological processes include volcanoes, earthquakes, and the formation of rock. They occur mainly in the geosphere but also affect the other three spheres.

Physical and Chemical Processes Physical and chemical processes include the formation of precipitation, the flow of water, and lightning. They occur mainly in the hydrosphere, atmosphere, and geosphere but also affect the biosphere.

Human Activities Human activities that affect cycles of matter on a global scale include the burning of fossil fuels and forests. They can drive changes in all the other spheres.

The Water Cycle

KEY QUESTION *How does water cycle globally?*

Water cycles among the hydrosphere, atmosphere, and geosphere—sometimes outside the biosphere and sometimes in it. Water enters the atmosphere as water vapor when it evaporates from bodies of water. Water evaporates from leaves through transpiration (tran spuh RAY shun).

Water vapor condenses into droplets that form clouds. Droplets fall as rain, snow, sleet, or hail. On land, precipitation flows along the surface as runoff. Runoff enters streams and rivers and flows into oceans or lakes. Water enters the soil as groundwater and then enters plants through their roots. Water reenters the atmosphere through evaporation and transpiration. Human activity affects the water cycle in an ecosystem.

Nutrient Cycles

KEY QUESTION *What is the importance of the main nutrient cycles?*

Nutrients are elements that an organism needs to sustain life. Every organism needs nutrients to build tissues and carry out life functions. Like water, nutrients pass through organisms and the environment through biogeochemical cycles. The carbon, nitrogen, and phosphorus cycles are important parts of the spheres and are vital for ecosystem functioning. Oxygen participates in the carbon, nitrogen, and phosphorus cycles by combining with these elements. Photosynthesis releases oxygen gas. Oxygen is also used in cellular respiration.

The Carbon Cycle Carbon is a major component of organic compounds, including carbohydrates, lipids, proteins, and nucleic acids. Fossil fuels are made of carbon. Animal skeletons and some types of rocks contain carbon as calcium carbonate. Carbon dioxide (CO_2) is an important gas in the atmosphere.

BUILD Vocabulary

biogeochemical cycle process in which elements, chemical compounds, and other forms of matter are passed from one organism to another and from one part of the biosphere to another

nutrient chemical substance that an organism needs to sustain life

Root Words The Latin word *nutrire* means "to feed or nourish."

What is an example of a nutrient discussed in this lesson? Describe how it helps to nourish an organism.

Visual Reading Tool: The Carbon Cycle

1. Use colored pencils to color the arrows in the diagram according to the processes listed in the key. Color the biological processes blue; the human processes orange; the geological processes green; and the physical and chemical processes red.

2. Why are carbon reservoirs important in the carbon cycle?

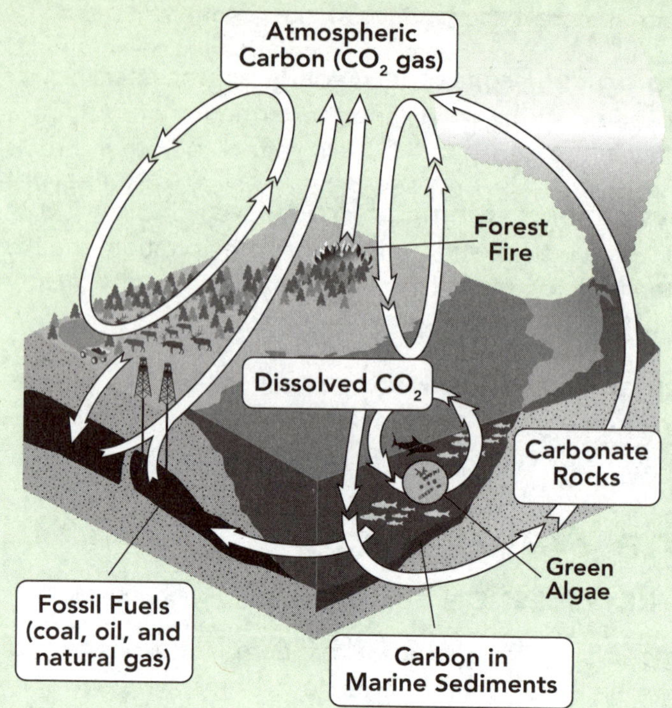

3. Describe one path that a carbon atom could follow through the carbon cycle.

4. How does the diagram show the effects of photosynthesis and cellular respiration?

BUILD Vocabulary

carbon reservoirs places where carbon is stored, such as the ocean, forests, and deposits of limestone

Places where carbon is stored are called **carbon reservoirs**. Earth's four major carbon reservoirs include the atmosphere, the oceans of the hydrosphere, and the rocks and fossil fuels of the geosphere. Carbon is also stored in the biosphere, in the form of living tissue and organic carbon in soil. Carbon moves into and out of these reservoirs as part of the carbon cycle.

Biological Processes Photosynthesis removes carbon dioxide from the atmosphere. Respiration returns carbon dioxide to the atmosphere. Producers use carbon dioxide to make carbohydrates that are consumed by heterotrophs. Decomposers break down carbohydrates, releasing carbon (and other nutrients) to the environment. Not all carbon is released by decomposition. Remains of primary producers buried millions of years ago were transformed into fossil fuels.

A Quantitative View of the Carbon Cycle Because the carbon cycle is so important, it is not enough to know where carbon is stored and through which pathways it moves. We need to know how much carbon is stored in each reservoir and how much carbon moves through each part of the cycle. Scientists are working to make a quantitative model that includes this data.

Seasonal Effects of Photosynthesis and Respiration
Although they are tiny in comparison to Earth, living organisms can affect the atmosphere's composition. Scientists have observed seasonal effects of biological processes on the carbon dioxide concentration in the atmosphere.

In the northern hemisphere, the rates of photosynthesis begin to rise in the late spring. This is when primary producers on land and in the oceans are activity photosynthesizing, removing carbon dioxide from the air. Some of the carbon dioxide is returned to the atmosphere by respiration and decomposition. Some is stored, or sequestered, in biomass of primary producers. During this time, carbon dioxide concentration in the atmosphere falls.

Starting in late fall, photosynthesis slows rapidly due to the season's low temperatures. Primary producers remove much less carbon dioxide from the air. At the same time, respiration and decomposition continue to return carbon dioxide to the atmosphere. Carbon dioxide concentration in the atmosphere rises.

These trends are shown in the Keeling curve, a graph that shows carbon dioxide concentration data. The Keeling curve also shows that the average carbon dioxide concentration in the atmosphere has been slowly but steadily rising every year.

Chemical and Physical Processes Carbon dioxide is constantly exchanged between the atmosphere and the hydrosphere through chemical and physical processes. This exchange is driven by photosynthesis and respiration. Carbon dioxide in the atmosphere can also dissolve in rainwater, forming a weak acid.

Geological Processes Dissolved carbon dioxide in the ocean can form carbonates that combine with skeletons of marine organisms to form rocks. These rocks are driven deep underground by geological activity. Heat and volcanic eruptions release this carbon dioxide into the atmosphere.

Human Activities When humans burn coal, oil, natural gas, or even forests, we change the global carbon cycle. We return carbon that was stored slowly over millions of years in carbon reservoirs to the atmosphere in a very short time. This rise in atmospheric carbon dioxide concentration is what is shown on the Keeling curve. More carbon dioxide in the atmosphere adds to the greenhouse effect. This raises average global temperature and drives climate change.

READING TOOL

Academic Words

sequester To sequester something is to isolate or separate it from other things. When carbon is sequestered in biomass, it is kept apart from Earth's atmosphere.

☑ **What would happen to the carbon in biomass if humans burned the biomass?**

____

____

____

____

____

The Nitrogen Cycle All organisms require nitrogen to make amino acids and nucleic acids. Most nitrogen is in the form of nitrogen gas in the atmosphere. Nitrogen-containing compounds, such as ammonia, nitrite, and nitrate, are in the biosphere, geosphere, and hydrosphere.

BUILD Vocabulary

nitrogen fixation process of converting nitrogen gas into nitrogen compounds that plants can absorb and use

denitrification process by which soil bacteria convert nitrates into nitrogen gas

limiting nutrient single essential nutrient that limits productivity in an ecosystem

Use Prior Knowledge To fix something is to repair it or make it useful. Nitrogen fixation changes nitrogen into a form that is useful to living things. **Which type of living things perform nitrogen fixation?**

____

____

Biological, Chemical, and Physical Nitrogen gas is abundant, but most organisms can't use it. Only certain types of bacteria can convert nitrogen gas into ammonia through a process called **nitrogen fixation**. Nitrogen-fixing bacteria live in soil and on the roots of certain plants. Other bacteria convert ammonia into nitrite and nitrate, which can be used by primary producers. When consumers eat producers, those nitrogen compounds are reused. Decomposers release nitrogen compounds from animal wastes and dead organisms. Some bacteria obtain energy by converting nitrates into nitrogen gas, which is released into the atmosphere in a process called **denitrification**.

Human Activities Human involvement in the nitrogen cycle increased greatly when chemists discovered a process to use nitrogen gas from the atmosphere to make chemicals that are used in fertilizer. Humans now use this process to fix more nitrogen than all natural processes combined.

The Phosphorus Cycle Phosphorus is necessary for molecules such as nucleic acids. Phosphorus does not cycle through the atmosphere. Phosphorus is found as phosphates in the geosphere and is dissolved in water in the hydrosphere.

Nutrient Limitation

KEY QUESTION *How does nutrient availability affect primary productivity?*

If ample sunlight and water are available, the primary productivity of an ecosystem may be limited by the availability of nutrients. Any nutrient whose supply limits productivity is called a **limiting nutrient**.

Nutrient Limitation in Soil Plant growth can be limited by the supply of one or more nutrients. Nutrient limitation is why farmers use fertilizers. Most fertilizers contain nitrogen, phosphorus, and potassium. Micronutrients such as calcium, magnesium, sulfur, iron, and manganese are sometimes included in small amounts.

Nutrient Limitation in Aquatic Ecosystems

Nitrogen is often the limiting nutrient in the ocean. In freshwater, phosphorus is often the limiting nutrient.
Runoff from rain may contain fertilizer from farms. This delivers a large amount of limiting nutrients into bodies of water. This stimulates producers such as algae to grow more than normal, causing what is called an algal bloom. Severe algal blooms can disrupt the functioning of ecosystems.

3 Chapter Review

Review Vocabulary

Choose the letter of the best answer.

1. The conversion of nitrogen gas (N_2) to ammonia is called

A. denitrification

B. nitrogen cycle

C. nitrogen fixation

D. nitrogen limitation

2. Which rely on other organisms for their energy and food supply?

A. primary producers

B. biomass

C. autotrophs

D. consumers

Match the vocabulary term to its definition.

3. ______	The total amount of living tissue	a. biomass
4. ______	Small pieces of dead or decaying plant or animal remains	b. denitrification
5. ______	A model of feeding levels in a food chain or food web	c. energy pyramid
6. ______	Changing nitrogen compounds to nitrogen gas	d. detritus

Review Key Questions

Provide evidence and details to support your answers.

7. How does energy flow through ecosystems?

____

8. Describe two ways that primary producers produce high-energy compounds.

____

____

9. How does nutrient availability relate to productivity and species survival?

____

____

____

CHAPTER 4

LESSON 1

Energy and Life

READING TOOL **Main Idea** As you read the lesson, complete the main idea table for each heading. The first one has been completed for you.

Heading	Main Idea
Chemical Energy and ATP	Chemical energy is contained in the bonds between atoms. ATP is the molecule that organisms use to temporarily store energy.
• Storing Energy	
• Releasing Energy	
• How Cells Use ATP	
Heterotrophs and Autotrophs	

Lesson Summary

Chemical Energy and ATP

As you read, circle the answers to each Key Question. Underline any words you do not understand.

KEY QUESTION *Why is ATP useful to cells?*

Cells require energy to perform work, and energy makes life possible. We humans cannot use sunlight as a source of energy, but must take in food made by other organisms, plant or animal, to acquire energy. We are heterotrophs.

Energy comes in many forms, including light, heat, and electricity. Energy can be stored in chemical compounds, too. For example, when you light a candle, the wax melts, soaks into the wick, and is burned. As the candle burns, chemical bonds between carbon and hydrogen atoms in the wax are broken. New bonds then form between these atoms and oxygen, producing CO_2 and H_2O (carbon dioxide and water). These new bonds are at a lower energy state than the original chemical bonds in the wax. The energy is released as heat and light in the glow of the candle's flame.

Storing Energy All living cells store energy in the chemical bonds of certain compounds. Of these compounds, one of the most important is adenosine triphosphate (ATP). ATP consists of adenine, a 5-carbon sugar called ribose, and three phosphate groups. The phosphate groups are the key to ATP's ability to store and release energy. Adding a phosphate group to adensosine diphosphate (ADP) adds energy to the molecule and changes it to ATP. When a cell requires this energy, it removes the third phosphate group from ATP, changing it to ADP again.

Releasing Energy ATP can release energy by breaking the bonds between its phosphate groups. This characteristic of ATP makes it exceptionally useful as a basic energy source for all cells. ATP is the most immediate source of energy for cells.

How Cells Use ATP Cells use the energy provided by ATP to carry out active transport. Many cell membranes contain sodium-potassium pumps, which are membrane proteins that pump sodium ions (Na^+) out of the cell and potassium ions (K^+) into the cell. ATP provides the energy that keeps this pump working, which involves maintaining a carefully-regulated balance of ions on both sides of the cell membrane. The energy stored in ATP also enables cells to move, providing power for motor proteins that contract muscles and generate the wavelike movement of cilia and flagella.

Energy from ATP can be transferred to other molecules in the cell to power processes such as protein synthesis. The chemical energy from ATP can even be converted to light. In fact, the blink of a firefly comes from an enzyme that is powered by ATP!

Most cells have only enough ATP to last for a few seconds of activity. ATP is not a good molecule for storing large amounts of energy over the long term. A single molecule of the sugar glucose, for example, stores more than 90 times the energy required to add a phosphate group to ADP to produce ATP. Therefore, it is more efficient for cells to keep only a small supply of ATP on hand. Cells regenerate ATP from ADP as needed by using the energy in sugars and other sources.

BUILD Vocabulary

adenosine triphosphate (ATP) compound used by cells to store and release energy

Word Origins The name photosynthesis comes from the Greek words *phós* (light) and *synthesis* (putting together).

☑ **What other words do you know that begin with the prefix *photo*-?**

____

____

BUILD Vocabulary

photosynthesis process used by plants and other autotrophs to capture light energy and store it in energy-rich carbohydrates such as sugars and starches

READING TOOL

Compare and Contrast

Heterotrophs cannot make their own energy, so they obtain it from eating other living organisms, such as autotrophs. ☑ **What are the two different types of autotrophs, and which is more common on our planet?**

____

____

____

____

____

____

____

Heterotrophs and Autotrophs

KEY QUESTION *What happens during the process of photosynthesis?*

All animals obtain the chemical energy they need from the food they consume. Animals are known as heterotrophs, which are organisms that obtain energy by consuming other organisms.

Some heterotrophs eat plants and are known as herbivores. Others, such as the heron, consume other animals and are known as carnivores. Animals that eat both plants and other animals are known as omnivores. Decomposers are heterotrophs that consume dead organisms and the wastes of living organisms. A mushroom is one example of a decomposer.

Autotrophs are organisms that make their own food using an external source of energy. Most autotrophs use sunlight as a source of energy and are known as photoautotrophs. Chemoautotrophs use chemicals as a source of energy, and are found only near vents on the ocean floor. **Photosynthesis** is the process by which photoautotrophs convert light energy into chemical energy. Photosynthetic organisms include plants, algae, and bacteria known as cyanobacteria. Nearly all life on Earth depends on autotrophs that capture sunlight energy and synthesize high-energy carbohydrates—sugars and starches—that can be used as food.

Visual Reading Tool: Adenosine Triphosphate

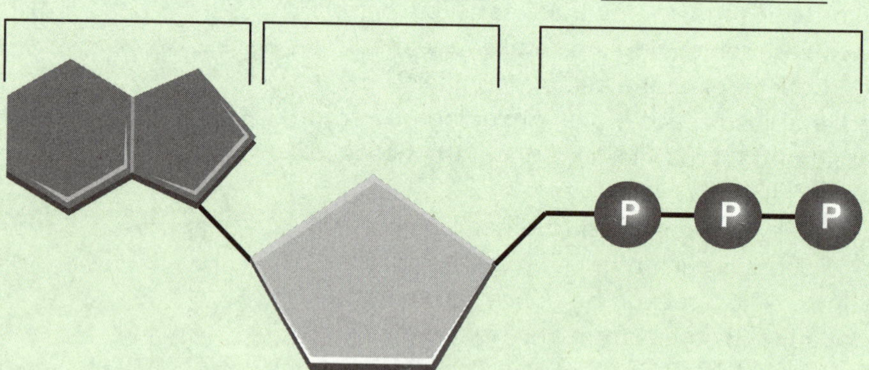

1. Label the ATP shown above.
2. Which part of the structure is a type of sugar? ______________________
3. Which part contains important bonds that store energy? ______________________
4. How does ADP get converted to ATP? ______________________

____
5. Which molecule has a higher potential energy. ADP or ATP? ______________________

CHAPTER 4

LESSON 2

Photosynthesis: An Overview

READING TOOL **Make Connections** Fill in the concept map to show the organization of a chloroplast. Then below, answer the questions to describe how the different parts are related to each other.

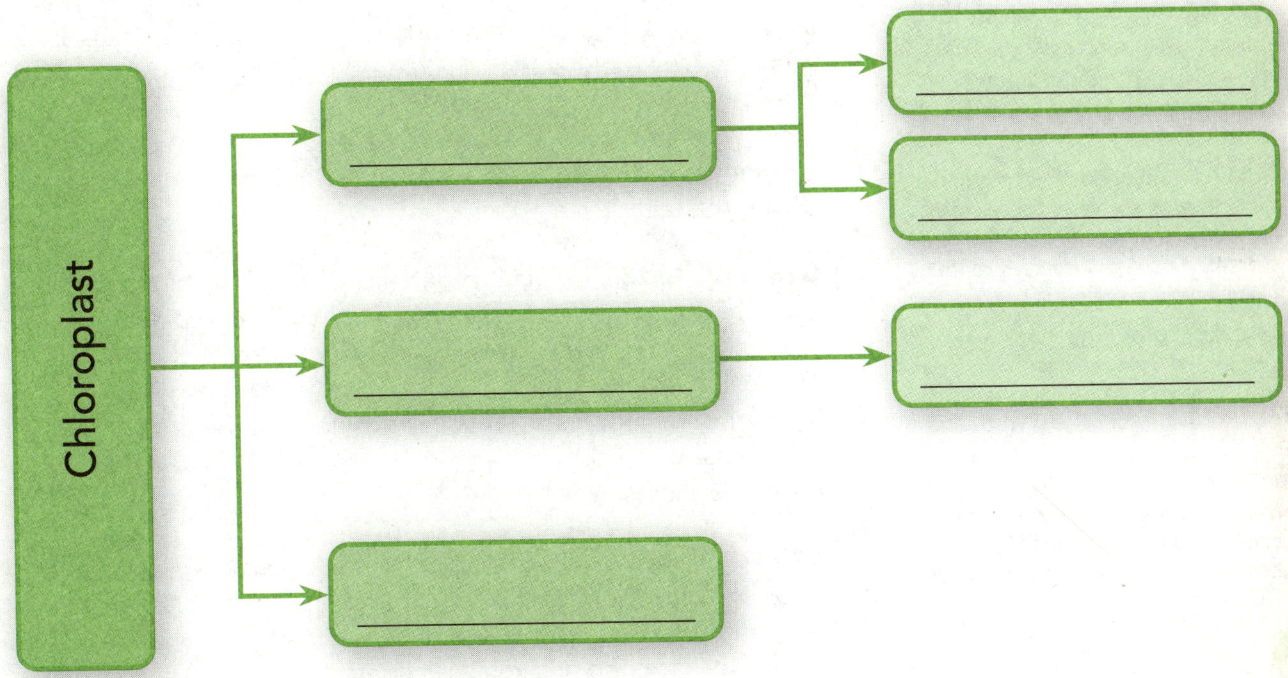

Complete each of the following sentences.

Saclike membranes that contain chlorophyll are known as __________.

__________ is a stack of thylakoids.

__________ is the fluid portion of the chloroplast outside of the thylakoids.

Two __________ surround and enclose the chloroplasts.

Lesson Summary

Chlorophyll and Chloroplasts

KEY QUESTION *What role do pigments play in the process of photosynthesis?*

Our lives, and the lives of nearly every living thing on the surface of Earth, are made possible by the sun and the process of photosynthesis. In order for photosynthesis to occur, light energy from the sun must somehow be captured.

As you read, circle the answers to each Key Question. Underline any words you do not understand.

BUILD Vocabulary

pigment light-absorbing molecules used by plants to gather the sun's energy

chlorophyll principal pigment of plants and other photosynthetic organisms

thylakoid saclike membranes found in chloroplasts, the location of the light-dependent reactions

stroma fluid portion of the chloroplasts; outside of the thylakoids, location of the light-independent reactions (Calvin cycle)

NADP⁺ (nicotinamide adenine dinucleotide phosphate) carrier molecule that transfers high-energy electrons from chlorophyll to the Calvin cycle

Word Origins The word "thylakoid" comes from the Greek word *thylakos*, meaning sac or pouch. There once was a species of marsupials called the thylacine that went extinct in the 1930's.

☑ **Based upon what you know about the Greek word *thylakos*, how do you think the thylacines carried their young?**

____

Light The sun's energy travels to Earth in the form of light. Sunlight, which our eyes perceive as "white" light, is actually a mixture of different wavelengths. Our eyes see the different wavelengths of the visible spectrum as different colors: shades of red, orange, yellow, green, blue, indigo, and violet.

Pigments Light-absorbing compounds are known as **pigments**. Photosynthetic organisms primarily use the pigment chlorophyll to capture the energy in sunlight. The principal pigment of green plants is known as **chlorophyll**. Two types of chlorophyll, *a* and *b*, are found in plants, and are available to absorb different parts of the visible light spectrum, primarily blue-violet and red. Chlorophyll does not absorb the color green. Leaves appear green because they reflect these wavelengths. Plants also have red and orange carotene pigments, which we can only see when leaves begin to die during the fall.

Chloroplasts The plant organelle known as a chloroplast is where photosynthesis takes place. Within chloroplasts are grana, which are stacks of **thylakoids** that contain chlorophyll. The rest of the fluid outside of this is called **stroma**. The number of chloroplasts per cell varies across different plants. Chloroplasts can sometimes move within plants, as well as duplicate themselves.

Energy Collection The light energy collected by a cluster of pigments, including chlorophyll, is transferred to the reaction center in the center of the cluster where a particular chlorophyll molecule is excited and releases energized electrons. These high-energy electrons are vital to later steps of photosynthesis.

High-Energy Electrons

KEY QUESTION *What are electron carrier molecules?*

Specific molecules called electron carriers are necessary to convey the highly reactive and high-energy electrons that are produced by chlorophyll. The electron carrier moves the electrons with their energy to other molecules where they are needed.

Nicotinamide adenine dinucleotide phosphate, or **$NADP^+$**, is one such electron carrier. When it accepts two high-energy electrons, $NADP^+$ also bonds a hydrogen ion, which turns it into NADPH. Now the captured energy can be moved to the location in the chloroplast where sugars are manufactured.

An Overview of Photosynthesis

KEY QUESTION *What are the reactants and products of photosynthesis?*

Photosynthesis uses the energy of sunlight to convert water and carbon dioxide (low-energy reactants) into high-energy sugars and oxygen (products).

Light-Dependent Reactions The **Light-dependent Reactions** need sunlight. The sunlight energy is captured by pigments in the thylakoid membrane. The energy is used to convert ADP into ATP and $NADP^+$ into NADPH. These sources of energy are important for other steps in photosynthesis. Also, water is split apart, which makes more electrons available, and produced oxygen (O_2) and hydrogen ions (H^+).

Light-Independent Reactions The **Light-independent Reactions** (Calvin cycle) occur in the stroma and do not use sunlight. The energy in ATP and NADPH, produced in the light-dependent reactions, is used to "fix" carbon dioxide. That is, carbon dioxide (CO_2) is combined with H^+ to produce sugars, primarily glucose ($C_6H_{12}O_6$). The plant makes these sugars as food for itself.

BUILD Vocabulary

light-dependent reactions set of reactions in photosynthesis that use energy from light to produce ATP and NADPH

light-independent reactions set of reactions in photosynthesis that do not require light; energy from ATP and NADPH is used to build high-energy compounds such as sugar

Visual Reading Tool: Inside a Chloroplast

1. Fill in the reactants and products of the light-dependent and light-independent reactions of photosynthesis.

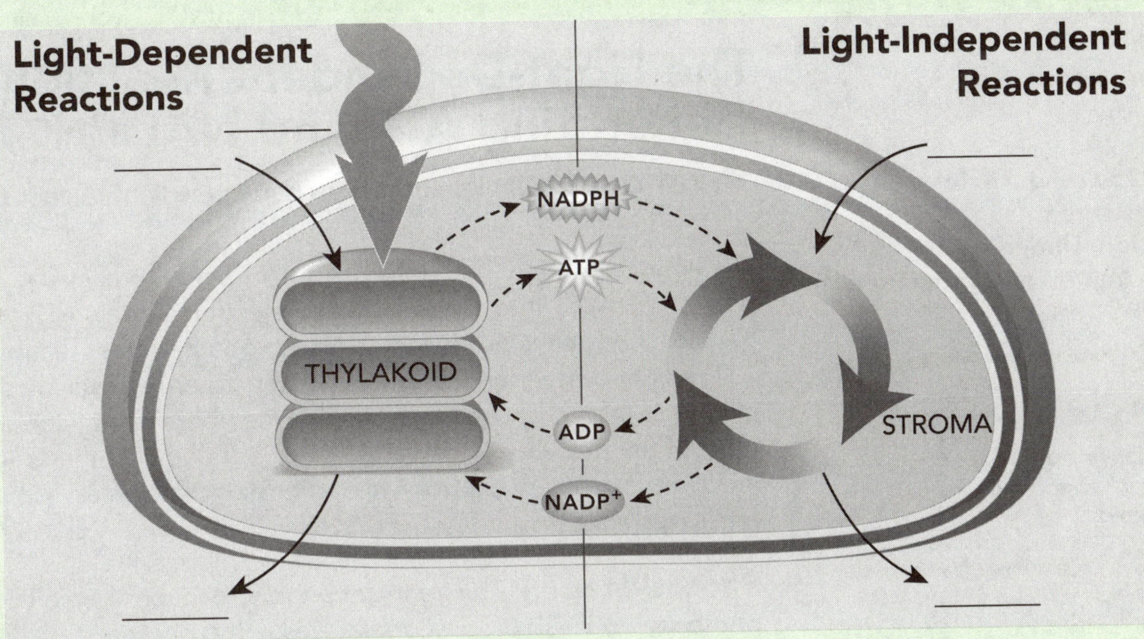

2. What is the NADPH responsible for? ____________________

____

3. Where do the "light" reactions (light-dependent) take place? ____________________

CHAPTER 4

LESSON 3

The Process of Photosynthesis

READING TOOL **Main Idea** As you read the lesson, complete the main idea table for the primary headings below.

Heading	Main Idea
The Light-Dependent Reactions: Generating ATP and NADPH	
The Light-Independent Reactions: Producing Sugars	
Factors Affecting Photosynthesis	

Lesson Summary

The Light-Dependent Reactions: Generating ATP and NADPH

As you read, circle the answers to each Key Question. Underline any words you do not understand.

BUILD Vocabulary

photosystem cluster of chlorophyll and proteins found in thylakoids

KEY QUESTION *What happens during the light-dependent reactions?*

The light-dependent reactions use solar energy to convert ADP and $NADP^+$ into the energy and electron carriers ATP and NADPH. Oxygen is produced as a by-product of this reaction.

The light-dependent reactions occur across the thylakoids of chloroplasts. Thylakoids are saclike membranes that contain most of the machinery needed to carry out photosynthesis, including clusters of chlorophyll and proteins known as **photosystems**.

Photosystem II The light-dependent reactions begin in photosystem II. Chlorophyll molecules in the photosystem absorb light. This absorption of light raises electrons in chlorophyll to a higher energy level, and these high-energy electrons (e–) are passed from chlorophyll to the electron transport chain.

Electron Transport Chain The **electron transport chain** uses energy from the electrons to pump protons (H^+) through the proteins in the chain from the stroma to the inside of the thylakoid sac. At the end of the electron transport chain, the electrons themselves pass to a second photosystem called photosystem I.

Photosystem I In Photosystem I the low-energy electrons from the electron transport chain are passed to chlorophyll molecules and re-energized using light energy. The energized electrons are passed on to an enzyme that facilitates the production of NADPH from $NADP^+$ and hydrogen ions. The NADPH can now move on to the light-independent reactions.

Hydrogen Ion Movement and ATP Formation All of the prior steps involved some increasing of H^+ concentration inside the thylakoids. Now there is a concentration gradient between the inside and outside of the thylakoid. Because molecules tend to move from a high to low concentration, the H^+ ions will move back across the thylakoid, if given the opportunity. **ATP synthase** provides a pathway for the hydrogen ions. As H^+ ions move across the thylakoid, through the ATP synthase protein, ADP is converted into ATP by the addition of a phosphate group.

Summary of Light-Dependent Reactions Light energy is used to convert ADP to ATP, and $NADPH^+$ to NADPH. Water is split apart to make electrons available to photosystem II, which produces O_2 and hydrogen ions.

The Light-Independent Reactions

KEY QUESTION *What happens during the light-independent reactions?*

During the light-independent reactions, ATP and NADPH from the light-dependent reactions are used to synthesize high-energy sugars. The light-independent reactions are commonly referred to as the **Calvin cycle**. The Calvin cycle occurs in the stroma of the chloroplast.

Carbon Dioxide Enters the Cell Carbon dioxide that has entered the leaves through the stomata is used in the Calvin cycle to produce higher energy sugars. An enzyme called RuBisCO "grabs" the CO_2 and brings it into the cycle where the energy from ATP and NADPH is used, through a series of steps, to produce a simple 3-carbon sugar for every 3 carbon dioxides that enter the cycle.

Sugar Production The two 3-carbon compounds are vital later on, helping to make other carbon-based compounds. One glucose molecule is a 6-carbon compound and would require 6 "turns" of the Calvin cycle.

BUILD Vocabulary

electron transport chain series of electron carrier proteins that shuttle high-energy electrons in preparation for ATP-generating reactions

ATP synthase enzyme that spans the thylakoid membrane and produces ATP from ADP when hydrogen ions (H^+) pass through it

Calvin Cycle the light-independent reactions of photosynthesis in which energy from ATP and NADPH is used to build high-energy compounds such as sugar

Suffixes When words end in *-ase* this usually indicates an enzymatic protein. ATP synthase is an enzymatic protein that creates ATP.

☑ **What molecules need to travel through ATP synthase to help it create ATP?**

____

READING TOOL

Apply Prior Knowledge Think about how you would care for a houseplant. It needs water, access to sunlight, and a supply of air.

☑ **Now that you know more about the specific processes of photosynthesis, explain exactly why a plant needs carbon dioxide from the air.**

____

____

____

____

____

____

Summary of the Calvin Cycle Six carbon dioxide molecules are needed to produce a 6-carbon sugar molecule, glucose. ATP and NADPH provided energy for these reactions to occur. The plant uses the sugars for growth and maintenance. Animals access the sugars when they eat the plant.

The End Results High energy sugars and O_2 gas are the end products of photosynthesis. The basic photosynthetic steps consisting of the light reactions and Calvin cycle is known as the C3 photosynthetic pathway. It is labeled as C3 because the first molecule generated during the Calvin cycle contains 3 carbon atoms.

Factors Affecting Photosynthesis

KEY QUESTION *What factors affect photosynthesis?*

Many factors affect the rate of chemical reactions, including those that occur during photosynthesis.

Temperature, Light, and Water The reactions of photosynthesis function best within a certain range of environmental conditions. The enzymes that carry out the Light-Dependent and Light-Independent reactions function best between 0°C and 35°C. Above or below that, it slows the rate of photosynthesis and can even stop it completely. Plants also need access to sunlight. High intensity light increases the rate of photosynthesis up to a certain point where plants reach their maximum photosynthetic rate. The last factor that affects photosynthesis is water availability. A shortage of water can halt photosynthesis. Some plants that live in dry conditions, such as desert plants and conifers, have waxy coatings on their leaves that reduce water loss.

Photosynthesis Under Extreme Conditions Plants have openings on the underside of their leaves that are called stomata. They allow for CO_2 to enter the leaf and excess O_2 to leave. Unfortunately these openings also allow water to leave the leaf. Under hot and dry conditions the rate of water loss can be very high and the plant can run low on water. Plants have many adaptations to conserve water, including the physiological adaptations of C4 plants and CAM photosynthesis.

C4 Plants Dry conditions force plants to close their stomata in order to conserve water. Photosynthesis in C3 plants quickly comes to a stop because there is not enough CO_2 inside the leaves. However, C4 plants are able to fix CO_2 at much lower concentrations because they have an extra enzyme that assists RuBisCO. The name "C4" comes from the fact that the first compound formed in this pathway contains four carbon atoms instead of three. C4 plants include important crop plants like corn, sugar cane, and sorghum.

CAM Plants Crassulacean acid metabolism (CAM) plants open their stomata at night to allow for gas exchange when water loss will be minimized. They store the CO_2 that they collect at night as in an organic acid. When day comes, they then release the CO_2 in order to perform photosynthesis as usual. This evolved in some plants as an adaptation to arid conditions. The jade plant is one example of the Crassulacea family.

Visual Reading Tool: The Light-Independent Reactions

1. Label the diagram with the four molecules that carry energy through photosynthesis.

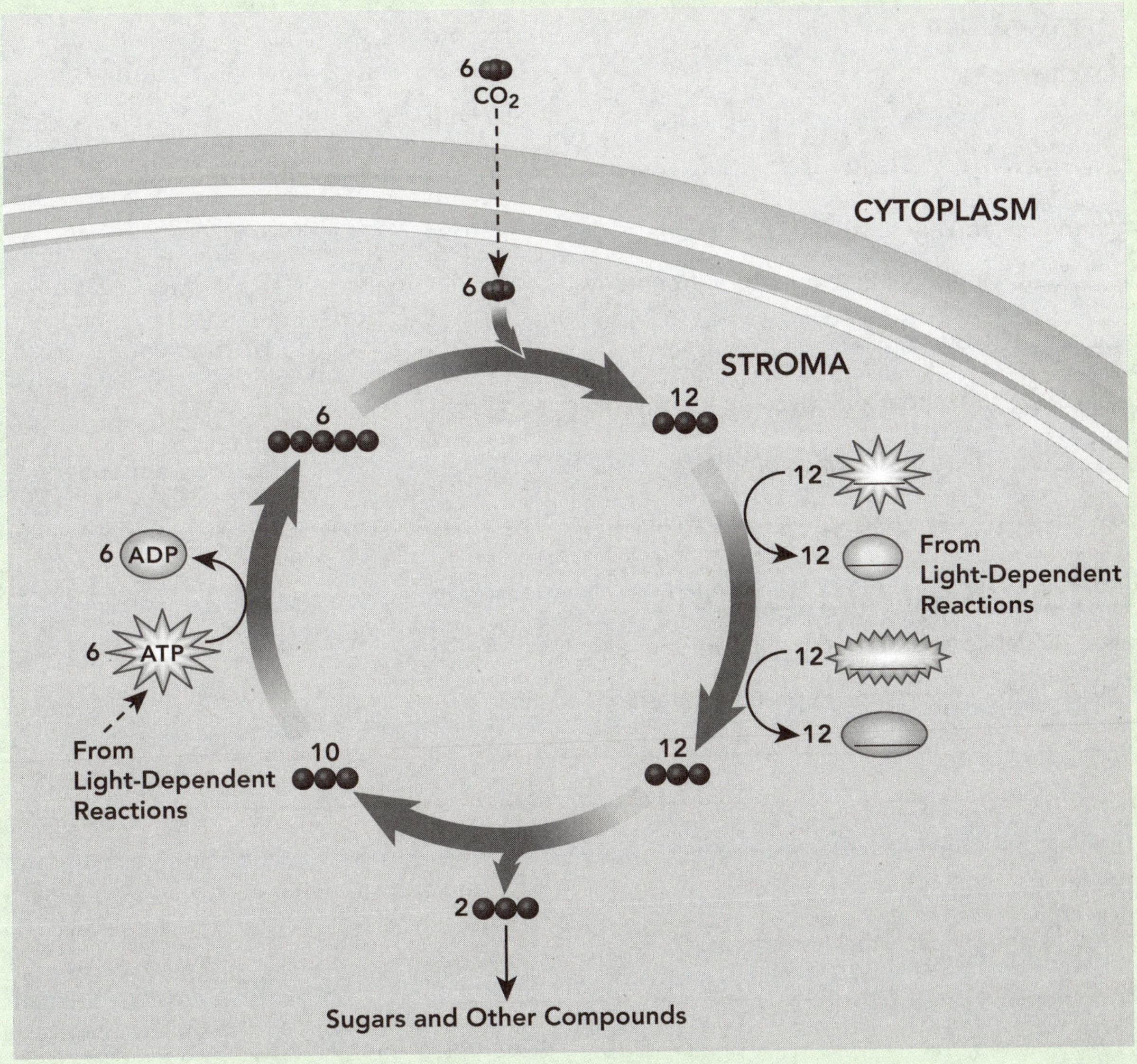

2. Where does the ATP and NADPH get created? ______________________

3. How many molecules of carbon dioxide are required to produce a 6-carbon sugar? ________

4 Chapter Review

Review Vocabulary

Choose the letter of the best answer.

1. The main pigment of green plants is:

A. thylakoid

B. carotene

C. chlorophyll

D. chloroplast

2. What concentration gradient powers ATP synthase?

A. O_2

B. CO_2

C. H^+

D. H_2O

Match the vocabulary term to its definition.

3. ________ material that absorbs light energy

4. ________ source of temporary energy

5. ________ reactions that occur in the thylakoid membrane

6. ________ fluid matrix of chloroplasts

a. stroma

b. pigment

c. ATP

d. light-dependent

Review Key Questions

Provide evidence and details to support your answers.

7. What is the importance of photosynthesis for all life?

____

____

____

8. How is energy captured from the sun?

____

____

9. In what stages are carbon dioxide and oxygen involved in photosynthesis ATP production?

____

____

CHAPTER 5

LESSON 1

Cellular Respiration: An Overview

READING TOOL **Active Reading** As you read your textbook, record key ideas on the summary table for each heading in the chapter. The first one is done for you.

Heading	Summary
Chemical Energy and Food	Heterotrophs get the energy they need from the food they eat. In food it is measured in units called Calories.
Overview of Cellular Respiration	
• Stages of Cellular Respiration	
• Oxygen and Energy	
Comparing Photosynthesis and Cellular Respiration	

Lesson Summary

Chemical Energy and Food

KEY QUESTION *Where do organisms get energy?*

Heterotrophs get the energy they need from the food they eat. Energy is stored in a variety of macromolecules in the body, including fats, proteins, and carbohydrates. The energy is measured in a unit known as a **calorie**. A calorie is the amount of energy needed to raise the temperature of 1 gram of water by 1 degree Celsius. There are 1000 of these calories in 1 food Calorie (that is seen on a food label). When measuring calories, fats tend to have 9000 calories (9 food Calories) of energy per gram, while proteins and carbohydrates have 4000 calories (4 food Calories). The cells in the body release and use this energy over time using the process of cellular respiration.

As you read, circle the answers to each Key Question. Underline any words you do not understand.

BUILD Vocabulary

calorie the amount of energy needed to raise the temperature of 1 gram of water by 1 degree Celsius

Overview of Cellular Respiration

KEY QUESTION *What is cellular respiration?*

Energy is released from food in the presence of oxygen during a complex process known as **cellular respiration**. There are many reactions in this process, but simply put, the process takes oxygen and glucose and converts it into carbon dioxide, water, and energy. This process happens over time, and energy is released gradually in the form of ATP.

In Symbols:

$$6O_2 + C_6H_{12}O_6 \rightarrow 6CO_2 + 6H_2O + \text{Energy}$$

In Words:

Oxygen + Glucose → Carbon Dioxide + Water + Energy

If cellular respiration took place in just one step, all of the energy from glucose would be released at once, and most of it would be lost in the form of heat.

Stages of Cellular Respiration There are three stages of cellular respiration. During the first stage, called glycolysis, glucose is broken down and small amounts of ATP are produced. In the next stage, the Krebs cycle, pyruvic acid that was produced during glycolysis is broken down, and energy carriers are produced. These energy carriers move into the final stage of cellular respiration, the electron transport chain. Here the electron carriers release their stored energy and produce ATP.

Oxygen and Energy Oxygen is required at the very end of the electron transport chain. Any time a cell's demand for energy increases, its use of oxygen increases, too. The double meaning of respiration points out a crucial connection between cells and organisms.

High energy–yielding pathways in cells require oxygen, and that is the reason we need to breathe, or respire. Pathways of cellular respiration that require oxygen are said to be **aerobic** ("in air"). The Krebs cycle and the electron transport chain are both aerobic processes. Glycolysis, however, does not directly require oxygen, nor does it rely on an oxygen-requiring process to run. Glycolysis is therefore said to be **anaerobic** ("without air"). Even though glycolysis is anaerobic, it is considered part of cellular respiration because its products are key reactants for the aerobic stages.

Glycolysis occurs in the cytoplasm. In contrast, the Krebs cycle and electron transport chain, which generate the majority of ATP during cellular respiration, take place inside the mitochondria. If oxygen is not present, another anaerobic pathway, known as fermentation, makes it possible for the cell to keep glycolysis running, generating ATP to power cellular activity.

BUILD Vocabulary

cellular respiration process that releases energy from food in the presence of oxygen

aerobic process that requires oxygen

anaerobic process that does not require oxygen

Prior Knowledge You have probably encountered the term *Calorie* before when reading food labels. **How does a Calorie on a food label relate to a calorie that is produced in cellular respiration?**

____

____

Comparing Photosynthesis and Cellular Respiration

KEY QUESTION *What is the relationship between photosynthesis and cellular respiration?*

Photosynthesis and cellular respiration are both important processes in the harnessing and extraction of energy. In fact, they work in opposite ways. Photosynthesis is a process that deposits energy, while cellular respiration is a way to withdraw energy. Photosynthesis removes carbon dioxide from the atmosphere, while cellular respiration adds it to the atmosphere. Photosynthesis releases oxygen, while cellular respiration uses it.

The global balance between cellular respiration and photosynthesis is essential to maintain Earth as a living planet. Another necessity is a constant input of energy into the system. This input comes from the sun. You can trace the flow of energy from the sun to organisms that perform photosynthesis and then to a series of organisms that perform cellular respiration.

As you read, circle the answers to each Key Question. Underline any words you do not understand.

READING TOOL

Compare and Contrast

Photosynthesis and cellular respiration are necessary to maintain Earth as a living, healthy planet. **How do these two processes work in tandem?**

____

____

____

____

____

____

____

____

Visual Reading Tool: Cellular Respiration: An Overview

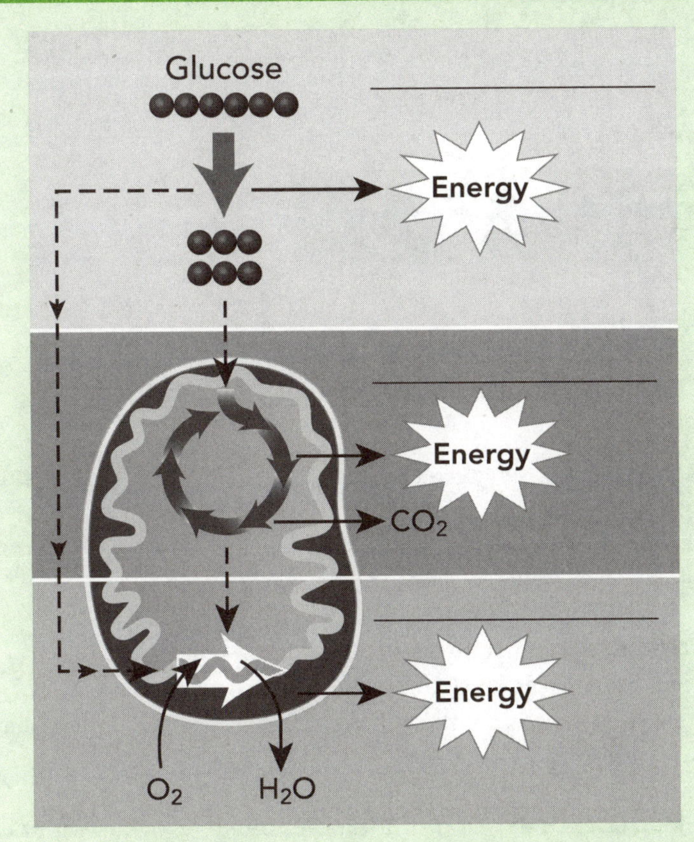

1. On the diagram, label each stage of cellular respiration: *Electron Transport Chain, Glycolysis, Krebs Cycle.*
2. What is the difference between aerobic and anaerobic processes?

   ____

   ____

3. List the two stages of cellular respiration that are aerobic.

   ____

   ____

4. In what organelle do the Krebs cycle and the electron transport chain occur in?

   ____

5. Where does glycolysis take place in the cell?

   ____

CHAPTER 5

LESSON 2

The Process of Cellular Respiration

READING TOOL **Sequence of Events** As you read your textbook, record the sequences of the three main events involved in cellular respiration. Use transition words like *first, next,* and *last* to explain these events. The first stage has an introductory sentence to get you started. Elaborate on stage one, and then fill in the rest of the flowchart, keeping in mind where each stage takes place and what is created.

STAGE ONE: GLYCOLYSIS

First, glycolysis occurs in the cytoplasm.

STAGE TWO: KREBS CYCLE

STAGE THREE: ELECRON TRANSPORT

Lesson Summary

Glycolysis

As you read, circle the answers to each Key Question. Underline any words you do not understand.

KEY QUESTION *What happens during the process of glycolysis?*

The first set of reactions in cellular respiration is known as **glycolysis**, which literally means "sugar breaking." During glycolysis, 1 molecule of glucose, a 6-carbon compound, is transformed into 2 molecules of the 3-carbon compound pyruvic acid.

ATP Production Glycolysis requires two ATP molecules to begin breaking down glucose. Throughout glycolysis a total of four ATP molecules are produced. As a result, there is a net gain of two ATP molecules.

NADH Production One of the reactions that occurs during glycolysis removes four electrons. These electrons are in a high-energy state and are transported to **NAD^+**, also known as nicotinamide adenine dinucleotide. Each NAD^+ molecule accepts a pair of high-energy electrons and a hydrogen ion.

BUILD Vocabulary

Glycolysis [gli-koli-sis] first set of reactions in cellular respiration during which one molecule of glucose (a 6-carbon compound) is transformed into 2 molecules of pyruvic acid (a 3-carbon compound)

NAD^+ (nicotinamide adenine dinucleotide) carrier molecule that transfers high-energy electrons from glucose to other molecules

This molecule, now known as NADH, holds the electrons until they can be transferred to other molecules. In the presence of oxygen, these high-energy electrons can be used to produce even more ATP molecules.

The Advantages of Glycolysis One advantage of glycolysis is that it occurs so quickly that thousands of ATP molecules are created in milliseconds. This is helpful when the energy needed by a cell increases. A second advantage is that glycolysis does not require the use of oxygen. As a result, it can provide usable energy to the cell when oxygen is not available. However, if oxygen is available, the pyruvic acid and NADH that are created from glycolysis can be used for other processes in cellular respiration to produce additional ATP molecules.

The Krebs Cycle

KEY QUESTION *What happens during the Krebs cycle?*

The **Krebs cycle** is the second stage of cellular respiration. It occurs when the pyruvic acid that is formed from glycolysis is broken down in a series of reactions. These reactions extract energy and produce the reactant that allows the cycle to start again.

Citric Acid Production At the beginning of the Krebs cycle, the three-carbon compound known as pyruvic acid created from glycolysis passes through the two membrane walls of the mitochondrion. As a result, it moves into a region located in the **matrix**. One carbon atom splits off from the pyruvic acid and forms carbon dioxide. This is eventually released into the air. The other two carbon atoms form acetic acid and combine with a compound called coenzyme A to form acetyl CoA. As the Krebs cycle unfolds, this acetyl CoA transfers the two carbon atoms to a four-carbon molecule that is already present in the cycle. This results in the formation of citric acid.

Energy Extraction Through a series of many reactions, citric acid is broken down into a 5-carbon compound, and then a 4-carbon compound (releasing 2 CO_2 molecules along the way). This 4-carbon compound can then start the cycle over again by combining with acetyl CoA. Energy released by the breaking and rearranging of carbon bonds is captured in the forms of ATP, NADH, and $FADH_2$.

BUILD Vocabulary

Krebs cycle second stage of cellular respiration in which pyruvic acid is broken down into carbon dioxide in a series of energy-extracting reactions

matrix innermost compartment of mitochondrion

Multiple Meanings The word *matrix* can be used to describe things shaped in a pattern of lines and spaces. **How does this relate to a mitochondrion?**

____

____

____

Electron Transport and ATP Synthesis

KEY QUESTION *How does the electron transport chain use high energy electrons from glycolysis and the Krebs cycle?*

The final step of cellular respiration is the electron transport stage. The electron transport chain uses the high-energy electrons from glycolysis and the Krebs cycle to synthesize ATP from ADP.

READING TOOL

Make Connections Two carrier molecules are used in cellular respiration to transport high energy electrons: NADH and $FADH_2$.

☑ In what molecule does the energy from these high-energy electrons end up?

____

Electron Transport NADH and $FADH_2$ transport electrons to the electron transport chain. The electrons travel through this chain, and the resulting energy transports hydrogen ions through the membrane and into the intermembrane space. Oxygen will accept the electrons at the end of the chain and combine with hydrogen ions to form water.

ATP Production The inner membrane of the mitochondrion contains enzymes known as ATP synthases. The hydrogen ions are forced through the enzymes, causing the base to spin. As the enzyme molecules spin, they grab an ADP molecule and it attaches to a phosphate group, forming ATP.

The Totals

KEY QUESTION *How much ATP does cellular respiration generate?*

Cellular respiration occurs in three phases. When the phases are complete, the end result is 36 ATP molecules that are created with each molecule of glucose. This represents about 36 percent of the total energy of glucose. The rest of the energy is released as heat. When it comes to a way of extracting energy, the process of cellular respiration is more efficient than an automobile engine that runs on gasoline.

Visual Reading Tool: ATP Synthase

1. What stage of cell respiration is being shown here?

____

2. Which molecule has higher energy: ADP or ATP?

____

3. What do cells use ATP for?

____

4. When four hydrogen atoms bind with oxygen and four electrons, what molecule is created?

____

5. Count the number of hydrogen ions, oxygens, and electrons on both sides of the equation shown. Are they the same?

____

____

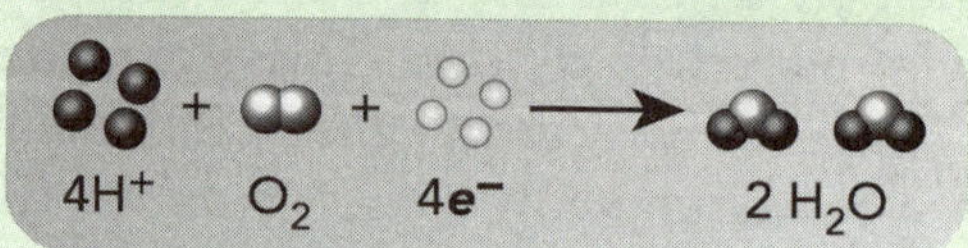

CHAPTER 5

LESSON 3

Fermentation

READING TOOL **Compare and Contrast** As you read your textbook, compare and contrast fermentation and cellular respiration using the Venn diagram. Make sure to list the similarities in the center of the diagram.

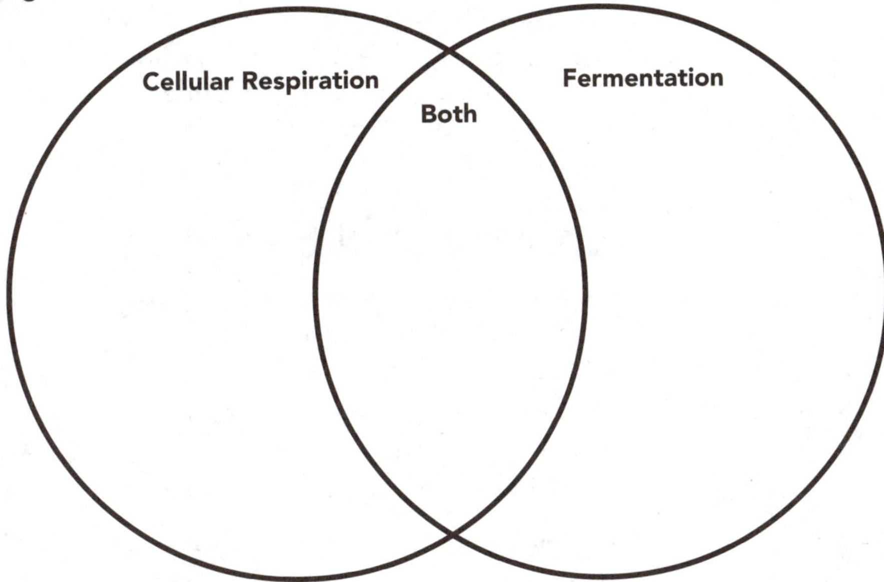

Lesson Summary

Fermentation

KEY QUESTION *How do organisms generate energy when oxygen is not available?*

When oxygen is not present, glycolysis is maintained by a pathway that makes it possible to continue to produce ATP without oxygen. The combined process of this pathway and glycolysis is called **fermentation**. In the absence of oxygen, fermentation releases energy from food molecules by producing ATP.

During fermentation, cells convert NADH to NAD^+ by passing high-energy electrons back to pyruvic acid. This allows glycolysis to keep going and to produce a steady supply of ATP. Fermentation is an anaerobic process that occurs in the cytoplasm of cells. Sometimes, glycolysis and fermentation are together referred to as anaerobic respiration. There are two slightly different forms of the process: alcoholic fermentation and lactic acid fermentation.

Alcoholic Fermentation The process of alcoholic fermentation is conducted by yeast. In this process, NADH combines with pyruvic acid to form alcohol, carbon dioxide, and NAD^+.

As you read, circle the answers to each Key Question. Underline any words you do not understand.

BUILD Vocabulary

fermentation process by which cells release energy in the absence of oxygen

Suffixes Suffixes are endings added to a word to change the meaning of a word. When the suffix *tion* is added to a word, the meaning "action" or "act of" is added to the word. So *fermentation* is the "act of fermenting." **Make a list of three other scientific words that have *-tion* as a suffix.**

____

____

The NAD^+ allows glycolysis to continue without oxygen. One common way to see this process is in the baking of bread. The yeast release carbon dioxide, which are the air pockets you see in bread. The alcohol that forms evaporates when the bread is baked.

Lactic Acid Fermentation Lactic acid fermentation is carried out by bacteria. These bacteria convert pyruvic acid and NADH into lactic acid and NAD^+. As with alcoholic fermentation, the NAD^+ allows glycolysis to continue. This process is common in food production. Yogurt, cheese, and sour cream rely on lactic acid fermentation.

Humans are also lactic acid fermenters. During brief periods without enough oxygen, many of the cells in our bodies, most often muscle cells, produce ATP by lactic acid fermentation.

Energy and Exercise

As you read, circle the answers to each Key Question. Underline any words you do not understand.

KEY QUESTION *How does the body produce ATP during different stages of exercise?*

When people exercise, their bodies use chemical energy to power their movements. Exercise uses up the available ATP quickly in the body. The body has to quickly make ATP in order to provide further energy for the body to exercise.

READING TOOL

Make Connections When sprinting, the cells in your legs need more ATP to power the rapid muscle movements. **What substance builds up in the muscles, which can cause a burning feeling?**

____

Quick Energy Under normal circumstances the body is able to take in enough oxygen to fuel cellular respiration. But sometimes, exercise involves rapid movements that occur in fast spurts. In these circumstances, the body uses the supply of ATP in the muscles quickly. While normal aerobic respiration cannot supply enough ATP to flood the muscles quickly, lactic acid fermentation can because it does not require oxygen and is a quicker process. Lactic acid fermentation can provide the muscles enough ATP for short bursts. However, the consequence is the person might need extra oxygen to help remove the excess lactic acid. This is sometimes called oxygen debt. This is why people who exercise rapidly, like sprinters, often huff and puff after exercising.

Long-Term Energy For exercise longer than about 90 seconds, cellular respiration is the only way to continue generating a supply of ATP. Cellular respiration releases energy more slowly than fermentation does, which is why even well-conditioned athletes have to pace themselves during a long race or over the course of a game. Your body stores energy in muscle cells and other tissues in the form of the carbohydrate glycogen. These stores of glycogen are usually enough to last for 15 or 20 minutes of activity. After that, your body begins to break down other stored molecules, including fats, for energy. Athletes competing in long-distance events, such as the marathon, depend on the efficiency of their respiratory and circulatory systems to provide their muscles with oxygen to support long periods of aerobic exercise.

Visual Reading Tool: Fermentation

Write labels to show where each process is occurring and the name of each process. Then answer the questions below.

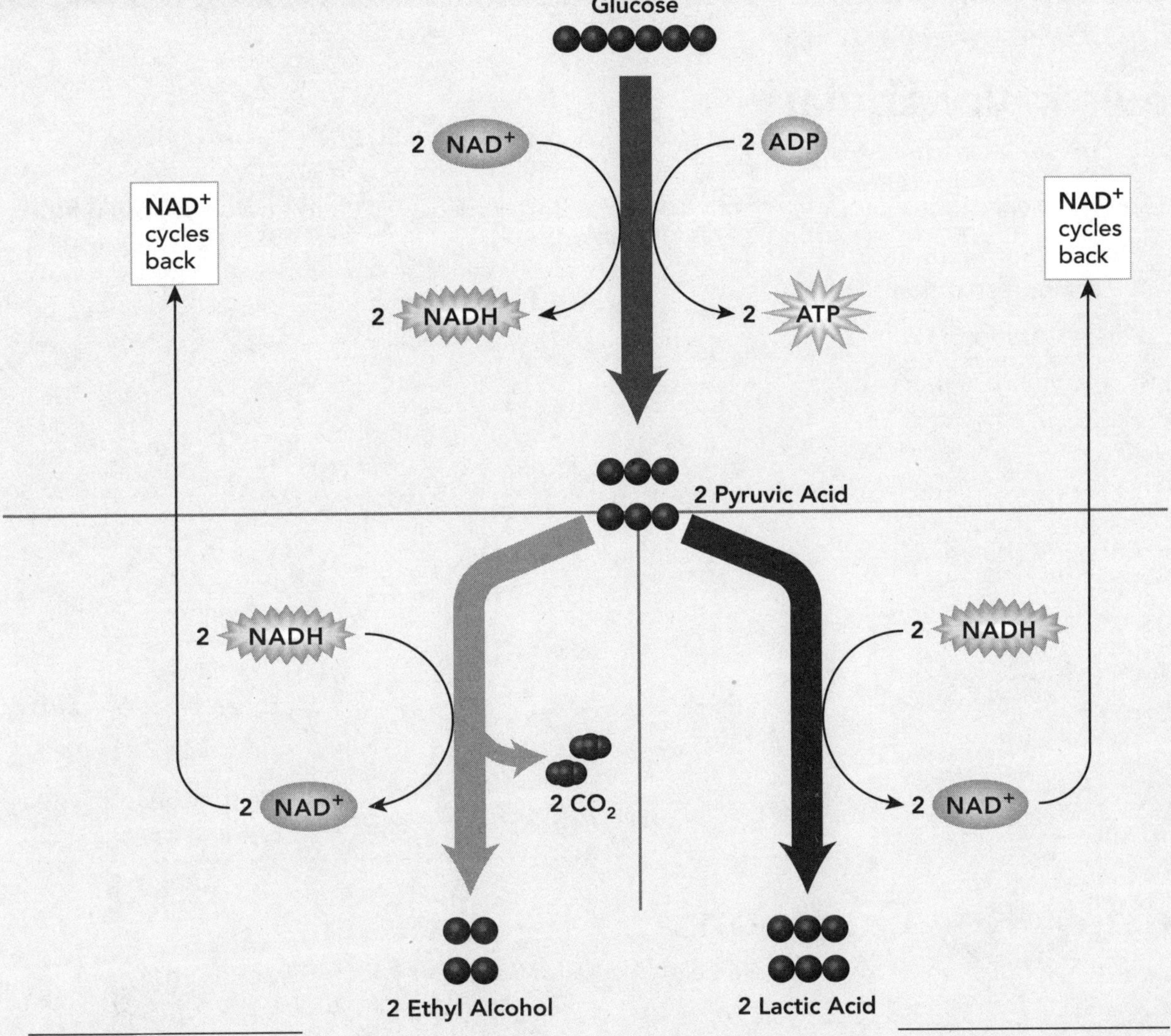

______________________ ______________________

1. In what part of the cell does glycolysis take place?

____

2. What is the importance of NAD^+ cycling back up to glycolysis?

____

____

3. What foods are created using lactic acid fermentation?

____

4. What type of organisms can carry out alcoholic fermentation?

____

5. How many ATP are created by fermentation?

____

5 Chapter Review

Review Vocabulary

Choose the letter the best answer.

1. Energy release in the presence of oxygen is called

A. cellular respiration.

B. fermentation.

C. an anaerobic reaction.

D. a matrix.

2. The name given to energy stored in food is

A. glycolysis.

B. a matrix.

C. a calorie.

D. fermentation.

Match the vocabulary term to its definition.

3. ________ aerobic

4. ________ anaerobic

5. ________ NAD^+

a. without oxygen

b. an electron carrier

c. to require oxygen

Review Key Questions

Answer these questions. Provide evidence and details to support your answer.

6. Where do heterotrophs get energy?

____

____

7. What happens during the process of glycolysis?

____

____

____

8. How do organisms generate energy when oxygen is not available?

____

____

____

____

CHAPTER 6

LESSON 1

A Voyage of Discovery

READING TOOL **Main Ideas and Details** As you read the lesson, complete the main ideas and details table. One row is completed for you.

Heading	Main Idea	Details
Darwin's Epic Journey	What did Darwin contribute to science?	Darwin developed the theory of evolution.
Observations from the Voyage		
• Species Vary Globally		
• Species Vary Locally		
• Species Vary Over Time		
• Putting the Puzzle Together		

Lesson Summary

Darwin's Epic Journey

KEY QUESTION *What did Charles Darwin contribute to science?*

Charles Darwin was born in England in 1809. In 1831, he started a five-year voyage on the ship HMS *Beagle*. The voyage of the *Beagle* took place at a time of new scientific ideas. Geologists suggested that Earth was ancient and had changed over time. Biologists suggested that life had also changed, through a process they called **evolution**. However, no scientist before Darwin had offered a scientific explanation of how evolution could occur.

Darwin developed a theory of biological evolution that offered a scientific explanation for the unity and diversity of life, by proposing how modern organisms evolved through descent from common ancestors.

As you read, circle the answers to each Key Question. Underline any words you do not understand.

BUILD Vocabulary

evolution change over time; the process by which modern organisms have descended from ancient organisms

fossil preserved remains or traces of ancient organisms

Word Origins *Evolution* comes from the Latin *volvere:* "turn, roll, revolve." With the prefix *e-*, meaning "away" or "out of," *evolution* means unfolding or unrolling. **What was Darwin's key contribution to science?**

____

____

____

Observations from the Voyage

KEY QUESTION *What three patterns of biodiversity did Darwin observe?*

Darwin saw much diversity of life during the voyage. He saw how well suited plants and animals were to their environment. Darwin wanted to explain the diversity of life in a scientific way, so he kept observing, asking questions, and formulating hypothesis. Darwin focused on three patterns of diversity: (1) species vary globally, (2) species vary locally, and (3) species vary over time.

Species Vary Globally In South America, Darwin saw flightless, ground-dwelling birds called rheas. Rheas look and act a lot like ostriches. Yet rheas only live in South America, and ostriches only live in Africa. Then, in Australia, Darwin saw another large flightless bird, the emu. Darwin also noticed that rabbits and other grassland species in Europe did not live in the grasslands of South America and Australia. In Australia, Darwin saw kangaroos and other grassland species that are found nowhere else. Darwin noticed that different, yet ecologically similar, species inhabited separate, but ecologically similar, habitats around the globe.

Species Vary Locally Darwin noticed that different, yet related, species often occupied different habitats within a local area. Darwin saw two species of rheas in South America. One lived in the grasslands while a smaller species lived in a colder scrubland. Darwin also observed local variation in the Galápagos Islands off the Pacific coast of South America. The islands are relatively close to each other but are ecologically different. People who lived there could tell which island a tortoise came from just by looking at the shape of its shell.

Visual Reading Tool: Darwin's Journey

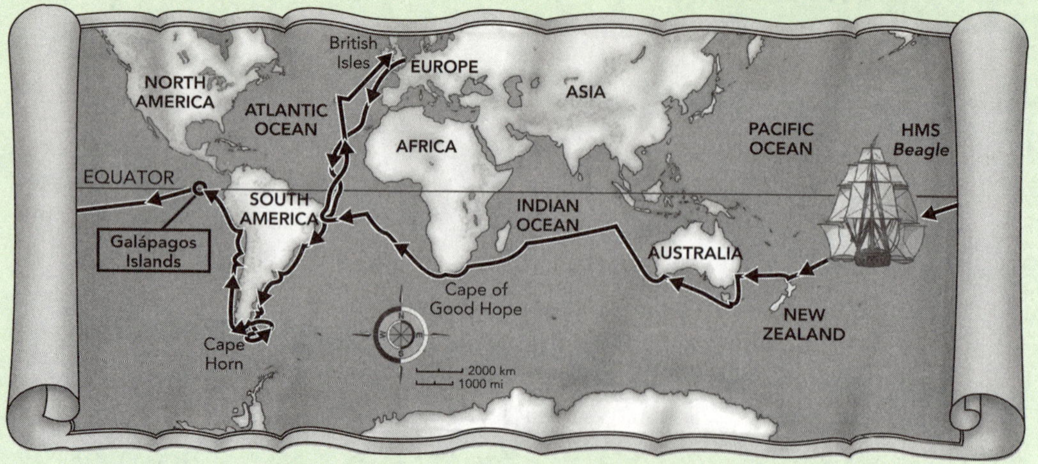

1. List the three species of flightless birds Darwin observed and draw a line to where he saw them.

____

2. List three different animals Darwin observed in the Galápagos.

____

READING TOOL

Make Connections Darwin observed many species of small finches in the Galápagos that had beaks of different shapes and sizes. ☑ **What do birds use their beaks for, and why would there be differences between species?**

____

____

____

____

Species Vary Over Time In addition to collecting specimens of living species, Darwin also collected fossils. **Fossils** are preserved remains or traces of ancient organisms. In Darwin's time, scientists knew that fossils formed a record of extinct organisms, but did not know how to interpret that record. Darwin observed that the fossil record included many extinct animals that were similar to, yet different from, living species. One fossil he collected was from an extinct animal called a glyptodont. Why had glyptodonts disappeared, and why did modern armadillos resemble them? Could glyptodonts and armadillos have had a common ancestor?

Putting the Puzzle Together When Darwin returned home, experts identified his samples. The Galápagos mockingbirds were three separate species found nowhere else. The small brown birds were species of finches that lived nowhere else, but resembled South American species. This was true of Galápagos tortoises, iguanas, and many plants. Darwin wondered if species were really fixed and unchanging as many thought. Could organisms change over time through natural processes? Could Galápagos species have evolved from South American ancestors?

CHAPTER 6

LESSON 2

Ideas That Influenced Darwin

READING TOOL **Use Structure** As you read, use the structure of the lesson to identify the science concepts and ideas that influenced Darwin. Complete the graphic organizer by writing the concepts and ideas in the box on the left side with the scientist's name, and in the boxes on the right, fill in how those ideas influenced Darwin.

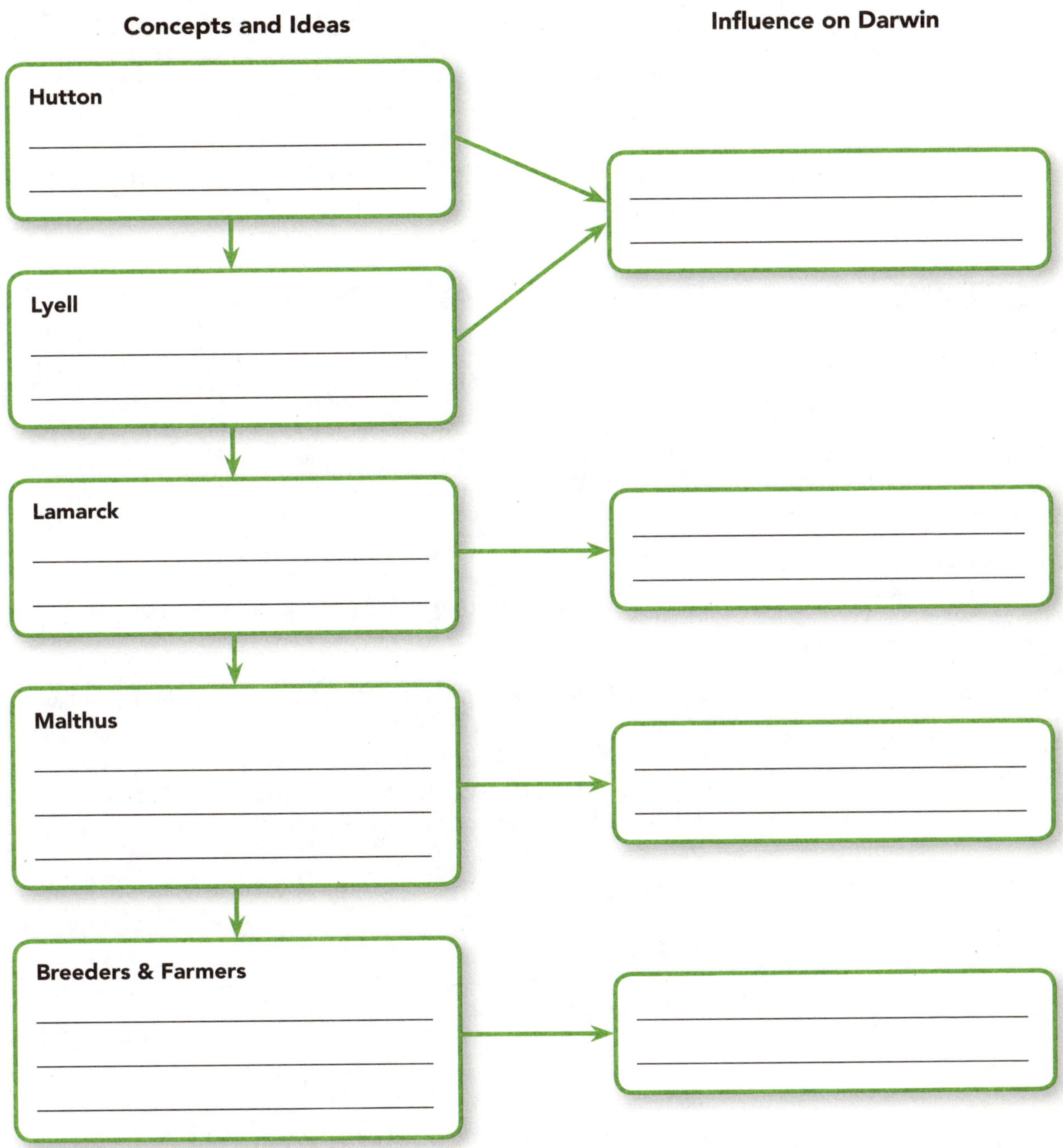

Lesson Summary

An Ancient, Changing Earth

KEY QUESTION *What did Hutton and Lyell conclude about Earth's history?*

As you read, circle the answers to each Key Question. Underline any words you do not understand.

Darwin was influenced by the work of other scientists. At the time of the *Beagle's* voyage, geologists were making new observations about forces that have shaped our planet. Naturalists were analyzing connections between organisms and their environments. These and other new ways of thinking about the natural world helped shape Darwin's thoughts. Many Europeans in Darwin's time thought that Earth was only a few thousand years old and had not changed much. Geologists James Hutton and Charles Lyell proposed hypotheses based on their own work and the work of others. Hutton and Lyell concluded that Earth is extremely old and that the processes that changed Earth in the past are the same processes that operate in the present.

READING TOOL

Academic Words Sediment is a collection of small pieces of rock that are the result of erosion. Water, wind, and ice erode, or wear down, rock into small pieces of dust, sand, and gravel. Sediment tends to end up in river valleys, along coastlines, and at the bottom of the ocean. Newer sediments are deposited on top of older sediments, forming layers. As the sediment builds up, pressure increases in the lower layers, forming sedimentary rocks. **Name three geological processes that have shaped Earth.**

____

____

Hutton and Geological Change Hutton recognized that certain kinds of rocks are formed from molten lava. He realized that other kinds of rock form slowly, from **sediment** that builds up and are squeezed into layers of rock. Hutton proposed that forces beneath Earth's surface can push layers of rock upward, tilting and twisting them in the process. These same forces can build mountain ranges. Mountains, in turn, are worn down by rain, wind, heat, and cold. These processes work very slowly. Hutton concluded that Earth must be much older than a few thousand years. Hutton introduced a concept called *deep time*—the idea that our planet's history extends back over a time so long that it is difficult for humans to imagine.

Lyell's *Principles of Geology* Lyell argued that the laws of nature are constant over time, so scientists must explain past events in terms of processes they can observe in the present. This way of thinking is called *uniformitarianism*. It states that the geological processes we can see today, such as volcanoes and erosion, are the same processes that shaped Earth millions of years ago. Like Hutton, Lyell argues that Earth is much older than a few thousand years. Darwin read Lyell's books during the *Beagle* voyage. On the voyage he experienced volcanoes and earthquakes. The earthquake lifted a stretch of rocky shorelines more than 3 meters out of the sea. When he traveled inland, he observed fossils of marine animals thousands of feet above sea level. Darwin realized that geological events repeated over many years could form mountains from rocks that had once been underneath the sea. Darwin asked himself, "If Earth can change over time, could life change too?"

Lamarck's Evolutionary Hypothesis

KEY QUESTION *How did Lamarck propose that species evolve?*

Darwin wasn't the first to suggest that species could evolve. The fossil record provided strong evidence that life had changed over time. Jean-Baptiste Lamarck proposed two of the first hypotheses about how species could change. Lamarck suggested that individual organisms could change during their lifetimes by selectively using or not using various parts of their bodies. He also suggested that individuals could pass these acquired traits on to their offspring, enabling species to change over time.

Lamarck's Ideas Lamarck proposed that all organisms have an inborn urge to become more complex and perfect. Organisms change and acquire features that help them live more successfully in their environments. According to Lamarck, water birds could have acquired long legs by wading in deeper water looking for food. Or, if a bird stopped flying, its wings would become smaller. Lamarck called traits altered by individual organisms during their lifetime *acquired characteristics*. Lamarck also suggested that acquired traits, such as longer legs, could be passed on to offspring. This principle is called *inheritance of acquired characteristics.*

Evaluating Lamarck's Hypotheses Today we know that Lamarck's hypotheses are wrong. Organisms do not have an inborn drive to become perfect. Evolution does not mean that a species becomes "better" over time. Evolution does not progress in a predetermined direction. Traits acquired by individuals during their lifetime (such as the loss of a limb) are not inherited by their offspring. However, Lamarck was one of the first naturalists to argue that species are not fixed and unchanging. Lamarck recognized that organisms' adaptations are related to their environment and the way they live. Lamarck's hypotheses were wrong, but his ideas paved the way for Darwin's ideas.

READING TOOL

Apply Prior Knowledge

Lamarck did not know what we know today about how parents pass traits or characteristics on to their offspring. Now we know that characteristics are passed on by DNA in the germ cells: sperm in the male, and eggs in the female. ☑ **If you exercise a lot and build up big muscles, will your children be born with bigger muscles? Why or why not?**

____

____

____

____

____

READING TOOL

Connect to Visuals

Thomas Malthus recognized that our planet can only support a certain amount of people before it gets overcrowded, and there are not enough resources for everyone. The graph below represents the population of Earth and the available resources over time.

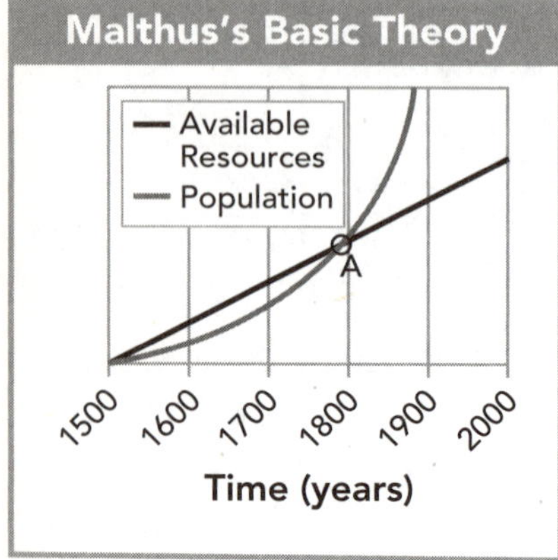

What happens after point A in regard to the population and resources available at that point in time?

____

____

____

Population Growth

KEY QUESTION *How did Malthus explain population growth?*

Before Darwin's time, the economist Thomas Malthus recognized that people were being born faster than people were dying, causing overcrowding. Malthus reasoned that if the human population grew unchecked, there wouldn't be enough living space and food for everyone. The forces that work against population growth, he suggested, include war, famine, and disease. Darwin realized that if Malthus's reasoning applied to people, it applied even more to other organisms. Many organisms can produce many more offspring than humans. Darwin realized that if all descendants of just one pair of oysters, which produce millions of eggs, were to survive, oysters would overrun Earth. However, many die and only a few survive to reproduce. This is known as differential reproductive success. This idea was important to Darwin in determining the mechanism, or natural process, that could produce evolutionary change. Darwin wanted to know which individuals survive, and why.

Artificial Selection

KEY QUESTION *How is inherited variation used in artificial selection?*

Some plants have larger or smaller fruit than average for their species. Some cows produce more or less milk than others in their herd. Farmers told Darwin that some of these differences were inherited variation—meaning they were traits that were passed from parents to offspring. Farmers would select for breeding only the plants that produced the largest fruit or cows that produced the most milk. Darwin called this selective breeding **artificial selection**. In artificial selection, nature provides the inherited variations, and humans select those variants they find useful. Darwin did not know how heredity worked, but he knew that inherited variation occurred in wild species as well as in domesticated plants and animals. Unlike earlier scientists, Darwin recognized that inherited variation was important, because it could provide the material for a natural process that could drive evolution.

BUILD Vocabulary

artificial selection selective breeding of plants and animals to promote the occurrence of desirable traits in offspring

Root Word *Artificial* has the root *artifice*, from *art*, meaning "skillful, creative," and *facere*, meaning "doing, making." *Artificial* means "made or done by humans."

Why is animal and plant breeding by farmers artificial?

____

____

____

CHAPTER 6

LESSON 3

Darwin's Theory: Natural Selection

READING TOOL **Make Connections** As you read your textbook, complete the natural selection concept map by entering an explanation for each term or concept.

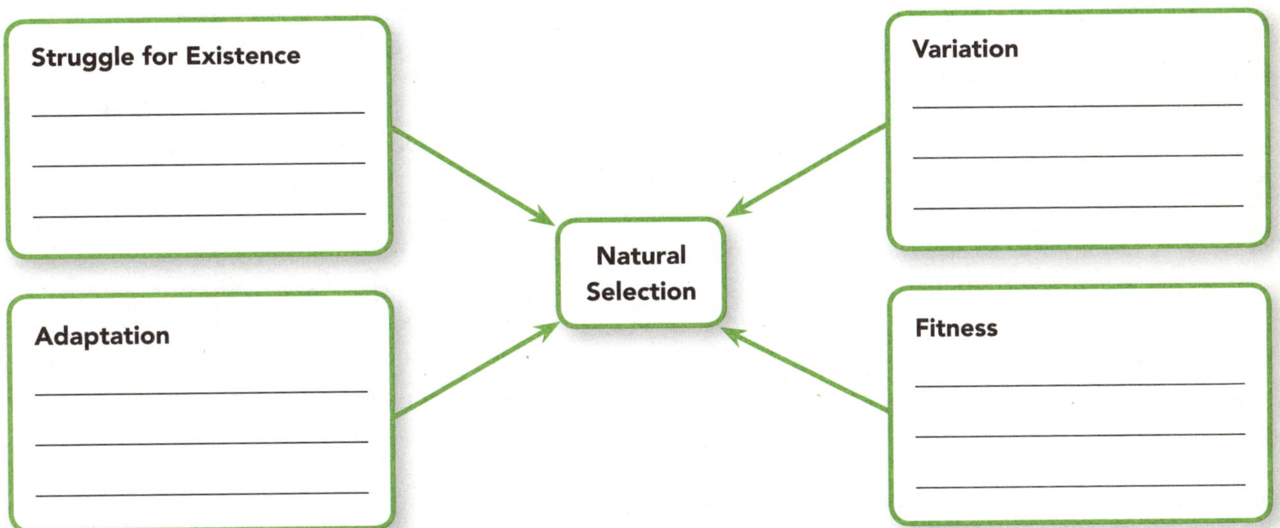

Lesson Summary

Evolution by Natural Selection

KEY QUESTION *Under what conditions does natural selection occur?*

As you read, circle the answers to each Key Question. Underline any words you do not understand.

Darwin worked out his theory of evolution by natural selection soon after reading Malthus, but did not publish his ideas for another 20 years. Darwin knew that many scientists ridiculed Lamarck's ideas, and Darwin's theory was even more radical. Darwin wanted to gather as much evidence as he could before making his ideas public.

In 1858, Alfred Russel Wallace published his ideas about evolution, which were almost identical to Darwin's. Darwin's ideas and Wallace's essay were presented together at a scientific meeting in 1858. Darwin then moved forward with his own work. He published his ideas in *On the Origin of Species* in 1859. Although both had the right idea, Darwin had more data to support his hypotheses than Wallace. Darwin's contribution was to describe a natural process that could operate like artificial selection.

The Struggle for Existence Malthus's work convinced Darwin that members of a population compete for a finite supply of resources. Darwin described this as *the struggle for existence.* Which individuals would succeed in surviving and reproducing?

BUILD Vocabulary

adaptation heritable characteristic that increases an organism's ability to survive and reproduce in an environment

fitness how well an organism can survive and reproduce in its environment

natural selection process by which organisms that are most suited to their environment survive and reproduce most successfully; also called survival of the fittest

Using Prior Knowledge You may have described someone as "fit,"or you may have taken "fitness classes." *Fit* in these cases refers to the physical condition and health of a person. ☑ **Why is survival not enough to describe biological fitness?**

____

____

Variation and Adaptation Darwin hypothesized that some individuals inherited traits that made them better suited, or better adapted, than other individuals to life in their environment. Any heritable characteristic that increases an organism's ability to survive and reproduce in its environment is called an **adaptation**. Adaptations can involve body parts or structures, physiology, or behaviors.

Survival of the Fittest Darwin, like Lamarck, recognized that there is a connection between the way an organism "makes a living" and its environment. According to Darwin, differences in adaptations affect an individual's fitness. **Fitness** describes how well an organism can survive and reproduce in its environment. Individuals with adaptations that are well suited to their environment so that they can survive and reproduce are said to have high fitness. Individuals with characteristics that are not well suited to their environment either die without reproducing, or leave few offspring, and are said to have low fitness. This differential reproductive success is called by some *survival of the fittest*. Survival means not only staying alive. In evolution, *survival* means surviving, reproducing, and passing adaptations on to the next generation.

Natural Selection Darwin named his mechanism for evolution *natural selection*. **Natural selection** is the process by which organisms in nature with variations most suited to their environment survive and leave more offspring. The different conditions of the environment influence fitness. Natural selection occurs in any situation in which:

- more individuals are born than can survive (the struggle for existence),
- natural heritable variation affects the ability to survive and reproduce (variation and adaptation), and
- fitness varies among individuals (differential reproductive success).

Well-adapted individuals survive and reproduce. Populations continue to change from generation to generation as they become better adapted or as their environment changes.

Natural selection only acts on inherited traits, because those are the only characteristics that parents can pass on to offspring. Natural selection does not make organisms "better." Adaptations only have to be good enough to enable an organism to pass on its genes. Natural selection does not move in one fixed direction. If the environment changes, this may change which traits are adaptive. This leads to a great diversity of adaptations in different environments. A species may become extinct if it cannot adapt to a changing environment fast enough. Natural selection is not the only mechanism that leads to evolutionary change.

Common Ancestry

KEY QUESTION *What does evolutionary theory suggest about the unity and diversity of life?*

Every organism is descended from parents who survived and reproduced. Those parents also descended from their parents, and so forth back through time. Just as well-adapted individuals survive, well-adapted species survive over time. Darwin proposed that living species descended with changes over time from common ancestors, an idea called *descent with modification.* Over many generations, changing environmental conditions lead to adaptations that cause a single species to split into two or more new species. Darwin supported this theory using the fossil record and Hutton and Lyell's work on deep time.

The idea that natural selection and adaptation can produce new species explains both the unity and the diversity of life. Darwin used a sketch of a branching tree to show descent from common ancestors. Look back in time and you can find common ancestors for similar species of mammals. Farther back is the common ancestor of all mammals. Farther back is the common ancestor of all animals and, farther back, of all living things. According to the principle of common descent, all species—living and extinct—are united by descent from ancient common ancestors, and they exhibit diversity due to natural selection and adaptation.

Visual Reading Tool: Finch Cladogram

The diagram below shows a tree diagram like the one Darwin used to show relationships between different species of finches on the Galápagos Islands.

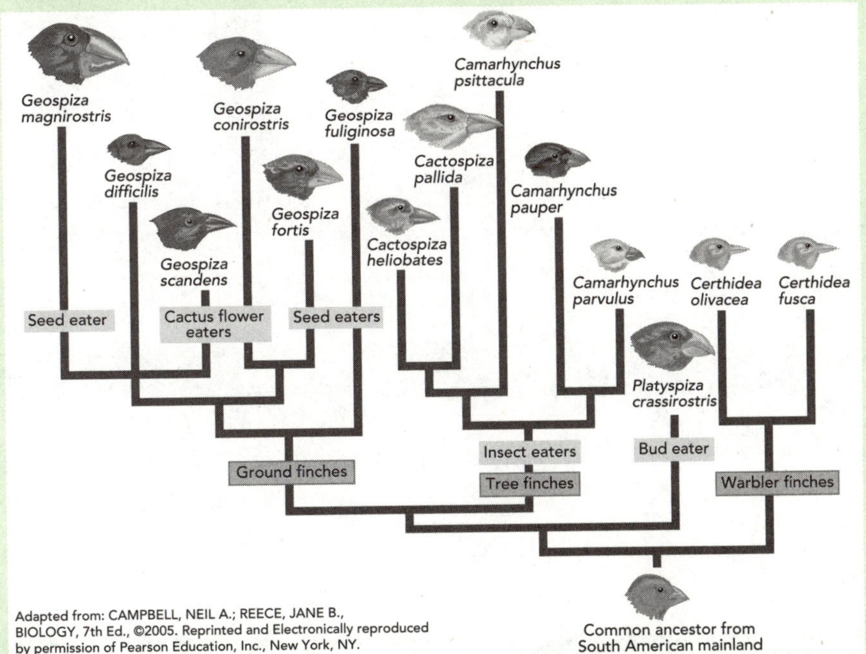

Adapted from: CAMPBELL, NEIL A.; REECE, JANE B., BIOLOGY, 7th Ed., ©2005. Reprinted and Electronically reproduced by permission of Pearson Education, Inc., New York, NY.

1. On the diagram, circle all the species that eat seeds.

2. All of these birds descended from a common ancestor. Is the common ancestor shown at the bottom or the top of the tree diagram?

____

3. What caused the different species to evolve separately of each other if they lived on the same islands?

____

____

CHAPTER 6

LESSON 4

Evidence of Evolution

READING TOOL **Active Reading** As you read, complete the chart to describe the evidence of evolution.

Concept	How Concept Supports Evolution
Biogeography	
Closely Related but Different	
Distantly Related but Similar	
The Age of Earth and Fossils	
The Age of Earth	
Recent Fossil Finds	
Comparing Anatomy and Development	
Homologous Structures	
Analogous Structures	
Development	
Genetics and Molecular Biology	
Life's Common Genetic Code	
Molecular Homology	
Testing Natural Selection	
The Grants' observations of finches on the Galápagos Islands	

Lesson Summary

Scientists in Darwin's time did not have the knowledge or technology to test his ideas. However, every scientific test since then has supported Darwin's basic ideas about evolution.

Biogeography

KEY QUESTION *How does geographic distribution of species today relate to their evolutionary history?*

Darwin recognized the importance of patterns in where organisms live. The study of where organisms live now and where they and their ancestors lived in the past is called **biogeography**. Patterns in the distribution of fossils and living species tell us how modern organisms evolved from their ancestors. Darwin made two observations involving biogeography. First, closely related species can evolve diverse adaptations in different environments. Second, distantly related species can evolve similar adaptations if they live in similar environments.

Closely Related but Different The biogeography of Galápagos bird species suggested to Darwin that different island species evolved from a mainland species. Natural selection on different islands selected individuals with different inherited variations. The populations on different islands evolved into different, but closely related, species.

Distantly Related but Similar Darwin noted that ground-dwelling birds in ecologically similar grasslands in South America, Australia, and Africa resembled one another, although they were not closely related. Natural selection in similar habitats led to similar adaptations, such as legs and feet adapted for running.

As you read, circle the answers to each Key Question. Underline any words you do not understand.

BUILD Vocabulary

biogeography study of past and present distribution of organisms

Prefixes The prefix *bio-* means "life," and the prefix *geo-* means "Earth." The study of biogeography combines Earth science and life science. **What caused the island finch species to diversify over time?**

____

____

____

____

The Age of Earth and Fossils

KEY QUESTION *How do fossils help document descent of modern species?*

The Age of Earth Darwin, along with Hutton and Lyell, knew that the Earth must be very old. The discovery of radioactivity and radioactive dating enabled geologists to determine the age of certain rocks and fossils. This data indicates that Earth is about 4.5 billion years old, old enough for evolution by natural selection to have taken place.

Recent Fossil Finds Scientists in Darwin's time had not found enough fossils to show the evolution of modern species from their ancestors. More recently discovered fossils now show clearly how modern species evolved from extinct ancestors. All records are incomplete, but many intermediate forms have been found. The fossil evidence tells an unmistakable story of evolutionary change.

READING TOOL

Connect to Visuals Examine Figure 6-14 in your textbook. This shows the evolution of whales from animals that walked on land, and highlights some of the changes that occurred in the front limbs (forelimbs) and rear limbs (hind limbs) as these animals evolved. ☑ ***Artiodactyl* has legs for walking on land. *Dorudon* has flippers for swimming. The flippers of *Dorudon* and the legs of *Artiodactyl* are what kinds of structures?**

____

BUILD Vocabulary

homologous structure structure that is similar in different species of common ancestry

vestigial structure structure that is inherited from ancestors but has lost much or all of its original function

analogous structure body part that shares a common function, but not a common structure

Word Roots *Homologous* and *analogous* share the Greek root *logos*, meaning "speech" or "reason." With the prefix *homo-*, *homologous* means "the same," and with the prefix *ana-*, *analogous* means "said to be similar." ☑ **How are homologous and analagous structures different?**

____

____

____

____

Comparing Anatomy and Development

KEY QUESTION ***What do homologous structures and similarities in development suggest about the process of evolutionary change?***

By Darwin's time, scientists knew that the bones in all vertebrate limbs resembled each other. The same basic bone structure is used for climbing, running, and flying.

Homologous Structures Similar structures, like the bones of vertebrate limbs, that are shared by species and inherited from a common ancestor are called **homologous structures**. Evolutionary theory explains the existence of homologous structures adapted to different purposes as the result of descent with modification from a common ancestor. Biologists determine that structures are homologous by studying anatomical details, the way the structures develop in embryos, and their appearance over evolutionary history.

The degree of similarity in homologous structures is related to how recently species shared a common ancestor. Many bones of reptiles and birds are more similar to one another in structure and development than they are to homologous bones in mammals. This is evidence that reptiles and birds had a common ancestor that lived more recently than the common ancestor of mammals, reptiles, and birds. The key to identifying homology is common structure and origin during development, not function. Homology occurs in plants, too. Groups of plants share homologous stems, roots, leaves, and flowers.

Some homologous structures don't serve important functions. **Vestigial structures** are inherited from ancestors but have lost much of their original size and function. An example is the hipbone of a dolphin, or remnants of limbs in legless lizards. These structures may persist because they don't affect an organism's fitness. Therefore, natural selection does not fully eliminate them.

Analogous Structures Body parts that serve similar functions, but do not share a similar structure and development, are called **analogous structures**. The wing of a bee and the wing of a bird are examples of analogous structures. Both are used for flight, but they develop from different embryonic tissues.

Development Scientists noticed long ago that early developmental stages of many vertebrates look similar. Recent studies show that the same groups of embryonic cells develop in the same order in vertebrates to produce many homologous tissues and organs. Darwin realized that similar patterns of embryological development provide evidence that organisms have descended from a common ancestor.

Genetics and Molecular Biology

KEY QUESTION *How can molecular biology be used to trace the process of evolution?*

Genetics provides strong evidence supporting evolutionary theory. At the molecular level, similarities in the genetic code of all organisms, along with homologous genes and molecules, provide evidence of common descent. Mutation and gene shuffling during sexual reproduction produce the heritable variation on which natural selection works.

Life's Common Genetic Code All living organisms use information coded in DNA and RNA to carry information from one generation to the next. This genetic code is nearly identical in all organisms, including bacteria, fungi, plants, and animals. This is evidence that all organisms evolved from common ancestors that had the same code.

Molecular Homology Homology resulting from common ancestors is seen at the molecular level too. One example of homologous genes is the set of Hox genes that determine the development of body parts. Hox genes determine which parts of an embryo become the head and which become the tail. In vertebrates, Hox genes direct the growth of the front and hind limbs. Small changes or mutations in the Hox genes can produce major changes in an organism's structure. Some homologous Hox genes are found in almost all multicellular animals, from fruit flies to humans. The Hox genes must have been inherited from ancient common ancestors.

READING TOOL

Apply Prior Knowledge Most of the enzymes and other proteins you have studied can be found in many different organisms. For example, when you studied DNA replication, you learned about the enzyme DNA polymerase. When you studied photosynthesis and cellular respiration, you learned about the enzyme ATP synthase. These two enzymes are found in nearly all living organisms. When you studied the cytoskeleton, you learned about the proteins actin and tubulin. Actin and tubulin are found in all eukaryotes. **An actin gene in humans is 92% identical to the homologous actin gene in mice. An actin gene in humans is 80% identical to the homologous gene in yeast. What does this say about how long ago these organisms had a common ancestor?**

____

____

____

____

Testing Natural Selection

KEY QUESTION *What does recent research of the Galápagos finches show about natural selection?*

Darwin did not think it was possible to observe natural selection in nature because evolutionary change happens very slowly. Recently biologists have designed experiments to study natural selection in the wild.

Back to Galápagos The longest-running study of evolution in a natural environment is the ongoing work on Darwin's finches by Peter and Rosemary Grant. The Grants have been studying the finches on the island Daphne Major in the Galápagos. For over 40 years the Grants have been capturing, identifying, and measuring every finch on the island. When new birds hatch, the Grants note the parents and tag the birds. The Grants and their assistants also count and measure all the different kinds of seeds the birds use for food. They created a device to measure the hardness of the seeds.

A Testable Hypothesis Darwin had observed that different Galápagos finch species have beaks of different sizes and shapes. He hypothesized that natural selection shaped the beaks of different populations as they adapted to eat different foods. The Grants realized this hypothesis rested on two testable assumptions. First, in order for beak size and shape to evolve, there must be heritable variation in those traits. Second, if the beak differences were involved in natural selection, birds with different beak sizes and shapes should show differential survival and reproduction.

Natural Selection The Grants found a lot of heritable variation in beak size and shape in finch populations. During their study, a severe drought occurred. Plants produced fewer seeds. As the drought continued, birds ate the smaller and softer seeds first. Over time, only the largest and hardest seeds remained. Many birds starved and the finch population decreased. The Grants showed that birds with the largest beaks were more likely to survive, which gave them higher evolutionary fitness. The drought caused the average beak size in this finch population to change greatly in a few years. If the finch population did not have enough variation for natural selection to operate, they would not have been able to adapt and change.

Evolutionary Theory Evolves Many scientific discoveries have confirmed and expanded Darwin's hypotheses. Like any scientific theory, evolutionary theory is reviewed as new data are collected. Any questions that remain are about *how* evolution works, not *whether* evolution occurs.

Visual Reading Tool: Data from the Galápagos

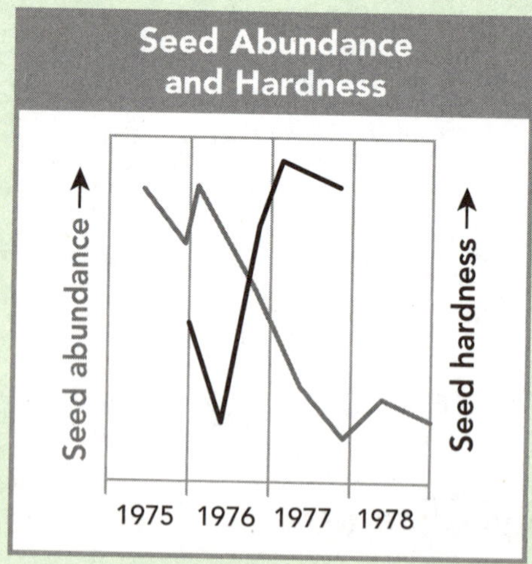

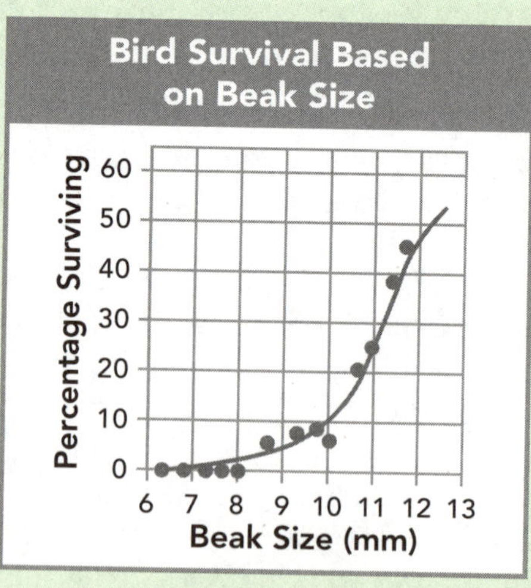

1. What caused seed abundance to decrease from 1975 to 1978? ____________________
2. What do you think the effect of the decrease in seed abundance was? ____________________
3. What is the connection between the change in seed hardness and the characteristic in the second graph? ____________________

6 Chapter Review

Review Vocabulary

Choose the letter of the best answer.

1. An inherited structure that has lost much of its original function is called a/an

A. fossil.

B. adaptation.

C. vestigial structure.

D. analogous structure.

2. The study of past and present distribution of organisms is called

A. evolution.

B. adaptation.

C. fossils.

D. biogeography.

Match the vocabulary term to its definition.

3. ________ process by which organisms survive and reproduce

4. ________ body parts similar in structure in different species

5. ________ body parts similar in function but not in structure

6. ________ heritable characteristic that increases fitness

a. analogous structures

b. homologous structures

c. adaptation

d. natural selection

Review Key Questions

Provide evidence and details to support your answers.

7. What three patterns of biodiversity did Darwin observe?

____

8. What are two ways that Lamarck's ideas paved the way for later biologists such as Darwin?

____

____

9. Why is heritable variation important for both artificial and natural selection?

____

____

10. List three forms of evidence for descent from a common ancestor.

____

____

11. How does the work of Peter and Rosemary Grant illustrate natural selection?

____

____

CHAPTER 7

LESSON 1

Finding Order in Biodiversity

READING TOOL **Sequence of Events** Determine the order of the following events, and number each event in the left column. The first one has been completed for you.

Order	Event Descriptions
1	As European scientists traveled the world, they discovered plants and animals they had never seen before. Though they wanted to communicate with each other about their discoveries, the names of organisms varied greatly from place to place, which made it hard for them to share their findings.
	The only known differences among living things were the characteristics that separated animals from plants. As a result, the two kingdoms of this time were Animalia and Plantae.
	As scientists continued to research the differences between organisms, they found that prokaryotes and eukaryotes were even more different from each other than recently thought, so they established the idea of a domain, which is larger than a kingdom.
	Carolus Linnaeus developed a naming system called binomial nomenclature. In binomial nomenclature, each species is assigned a two-part scientific name.
	Early scientists began to use Latin and Greek names to describe species, but these names often described the species in great detail, so this wasn't a useful way to classify living things.
	Researchers found that organisms were more complex than what they had thought initially, so they developed a system of classification that included the six kingdoms: Eubacteria, Archaebacteria, Protista, Fungi, Plantae, and Animalia.

Lesson Summary

Assigning Scientific Names

KEY QUESTION *What are the goals of binomial nomenclature and taxonomy?*

At first, European scientists tried to assign Latin or Greek names to each species, but the names were too long because they were described in detail, so this system did not work well. Biologists now identify and organize biodiversity through a standardized system that everyone can understand and agree upon. **Taxonomy** is a system of naming and classifying organisms based on shared characteristics and universal rules. Each scientific name must refer to only one species.

Binomial Nomenclature In the 1730s, Swedish botanist Carolus Linnaeus developed a naming system called **binomial nomenclature**, which is used today. In binomial nomenclature, each species is assigned a two-part scientific name, which is written in italics.

As you read, circle the answers to each Key Question. Underline any words you do not understand.

BUILD Vocabulary

taxonomy system of naming and classifying organisms based on shared characteristics and universal rules

binomial nomenclature classification system where each species is assigned a two-part scientific name

BUILD Vocabulary

genus group of closely related species; the first part of the scientific name in binomial nomenclature

systematics study of the diversity of life and the evolutionary relationships between organisms

taxa levels of organization into which organisms are classified

family closely related genera

order closely related families

class closely related orders

phylum closely related classes

kingdom largest, most inclusive taxonomic category

Multiple Meanings In everyday life, a *family* is a group of people who are related. In systematics, a *family* is a group of genera.

☑ **Which sentence most likely describes a family in systematics?**

1. My family will visit the farm in June.
2. Walnuts and hickory trees belong to the same family.

____

The first part of that name is the **genus** to which the species belongs. A genus is a group of similar species. The second part of a scientific name describes an important trait or the organism's habitat.

Classifying Species into Larger Groups The science of naming and grouping organisms is called **systematics**. The goal of systematics is to organize living things into groups that have biological meaning. Biologists often refer to these groups as many **taxa** or a taxon.

The Linnaean Classification System

KEY QUESTION *How did Linnaeus group species into larger taxa?*

Linnaeus developed a classification system that organized species into seven taxa based on similarities and differences: species, genus, family, order, class, phylum, and kingdom.

Species and Genus The scientific name of a camel with two humps is *Camelus bactrianus*. The genus *Camelus* also includes other species of camels that only have one hump.

Family The genera *Camelus* (camels) and *Lama* (llamas) are grouped with other genera that share many similarities into a larger taxon, the **family**, Camelidae.

Order Closely related families are grouped into an **order**. Camels and llamas are grouped with other animal families, including deer and cattle, forming the order Artiodactyla, which includes hoofed animals with an even number of toes.

Class Similar orders are grouped into a **class**. The order Artiodactyla is in the class Mammalia, which includes animals that are warm-blooded, have body hair, and produce milk for their young.

Phylum Classes are grouped into a **phylum**, which includes organisms that can look different, but share important characteristics. The class Mammalia is placed in the phylum Chordata, in which all of the animals have a nerve cord.

Kingdom The largest and most inclusive traditional taxonomic category is the **kingdom**. All multicellular animals are placed in the kingdom Animalia.

Classification Changes with New Discoveries Organisms belong to the same species if they can mate and produce fertile offspring. A species is the smallest taxon. Higher taxa, in contrast, are defined by rules created by researchers and ongoing discoveries in genetics, cell biology, development, and Darwinian theory.

Changing Ideas About Kingdoms

KEY QUESTION *What are the six kingdoms of life as they are now identified?*

During Linnaeus's time, there were two kingdoms—Animalia and Plantae—because the only known differences among organisms were those that separated animals from plants.

From Two to Six Kingdoms Because single-celled organisms were significantly different from plants and animals, researchers placed all microorganisms in kingdom Protista. Yeasts, molds, and mushrooms were placed in the kingdom Fungi. Because bacteria lack nuclei, mitochondria, and chloroplasts, all prokaryotes were placed in kingdom Monera, while single-celled eukaryotic organisms remained in kingdom Protista. By the 1990s, researchers learned that monerans were genetically and biochemically different, so they were separated into Eubacteria and Archaebacteria, forming six kingdoms.

BUILD Vocabulary

domain taxonomic category that is even larger than a kingdom

Three Domains To account for new differences among prokaryotes, biologists established a new taxon, the **domain**, which is larger than a kingdom. The three domains are Bacteria, Archaea, and Eukarya.

Visual Reading Tool: Analyzing Data

Use the classification table below to answer the questions about the 3 domains of living things.

Classification of Living Things

DOMAIN	Bacteria	Archaea	Eukarya			
KINGDOM	Eubacteria	Archaebacteria	"Protista"	Fungi	Plantae	Animalia
CELL TYPE	Prokaryote	Prokaryote	Eukaryote	Eukaryote	Eukaryote	Eukaryote
CELL STRUCTURES	Cell walls with peptidoglycan	Cell walls without peptidoglycan	Cell walls of cellulose in some; some have chloroplasts	Cell walls of chitin	Cell walls of cellulose; chloroplasts	No cell walls or chloroplasts
NUMBER OF CELLS	Unicellular	Unicellular	Most unicellular; some colonial; some multicellular	Most multicellular; some unicellular	Most multicellular; some green algae unicellular	Multicellular
MODE OF NUTRITION	Autotroph or heterotroph	Autotroph or heterotroph	Autotroph or heterotroph	Heterotroph	Autotroph	Heterotroph
EXAMPLES	*Streptococcus*, *Escherichia coli*	Methanogens, halophiles	*Amoeba*, *Paramecium*, slime molds, giant kelp	Mushrooms, yeasts	Mosses, ferns, flowering plants	Sponges, worms, insects, fishes, mammals

1. What are the key differences between the three domains? ______________________

____

2. Which kingdom or kingdoms have only heterotrophs? ______________________

CHAPTER 7

LESSON 2

Modern Evolutionary Classification

READING TOOL **Cause and Effect** As you read Chapter 7, Lesson 2, explain how derived characters can be lost by defining the terms and providing examples of each.

	Derived Character	Lost Trait
DEFINITION		
EXAMPLES		

Lesson Summary

BUILD Vocabulary

phylogeny study of the evolutionary relationships among organisms

clade evolutionary branch of a cladogram that includes a single ancestor and all its descendants

As you read, circle the answers to each Key Question. Underline any words you do not understand.

Darwin's "tree of life" suggests a way to classify organisms based on how closely related they are. When taxa are rearranged this way, some old Linnaean classifications no longer work. For example, the Linnaean class Reptilia isn't valid unless birds are included—which means birds are reptiles and are descended from dinosaurs.

Evolutionary Classification

KEY QUESTION *What is the goal of evolutionary classification?*

Darwinian theory gave birth to **phylogeny**, the study of the evolutionary history of lineages of organisms. Phylogeny, in turn, led to evolutionary classification, which groups species into larger categories that reflect lines of evolutionary descent, rather than similarities and differences. The larger a taxon is, the farther back in time all of its members shared a common ancestor.

When organisms are grouped this way, they are called clades. A **clade** is a group of species that includes a single common ancestor and all descendants of that ancestor, living and extinct.

Cladograms

KEY QUESTION *What is a cladogram?*

Modern evolutionary classification uses cladistic analysis to compare selected traits to determine the order in which organisms branched off from their common ancestors. This information is then used to build a **cladogram**.

Building Cladograms Refer to Figure 7-6. Part 1 represents how one ancestral species branches into two species, each of which could found a new lineage. In part 2, the bottom represents the common ancestor shared by all organisms in the cladogram. The branching pattern shows how closely related various lineages are. Each branch point represents the last point at which species in lineages above that point shared a common ancestor.

Derived Characters Cladistic analysis focuses on certain kinds of characters, called **derived characters**. A derived character is a trait that arose in the most recent common ancestor of a lineage and was passed to its descendants.

Losing Traits Snakes are reptiles, which are tetrapods, but they don't have four limbs! The ancestors of snakes, however, did have four limbs. Somewhere in the lineage, that trait was lost. Because distantly related groups can sometimes lose a character, systematists are cautious about using the absence of a trait as a character in their analyses.

Interpreting Cladograms Look at Figure 7-8, which shows a simplified phylogeny of the cat family. The lowest branching point represents the last common ancestor of all four-limbed animals (clade Tetrapoda). The forks in this cladogram show the order in which various groups branched off from the tetrapod lineage. The positions of various characters in the cladogram reflect the order in which those characteristics arose. Each derived character listed along the main trunk of the cladogram defines a clade. Retractable claws is a derived character shared only by the clade Felidae. Derived characters that occur "lower" on the cladogram than the branch point for a clade are not derived for that particular clade.

Clades and Traditional Groups A true clade must contain an ancestral species and *all* of its descendants, with no exceptions. It also must exclude all species that are not descendants of the original ancestor.

BUILD Vocabulary

cladogram diagram showing patterns of shared characteristics among species

derived character trait that arose in the most recent common ancestor of a lineage and was passed to its descendants

Suffixes The suffix *-gram* means "something written or drawn," and usually refers to a visual representation of a concept.

☑ **Based upon what you know about clades, explain what a cladogram is in your own words.**

____

____

____

READING TOOL

Academic Words

Anatomical describes the structural characteristics of an organism

Circle the characteristic of a bird that is anatomical.

1. Birds lay eggs.
2. Birds eat seeds.
3. Birds have wings.

DNA in Classification

KEY QUESTION *How are DNA sequences used in classification?*

The goal of modern systematics is to understand the evolutionary relationships of all life on Earth, including bacteria, plants, worms, and octopuses.

Genes and Derived Characters All organisms carry genetic information in DNA. They inherit genes from earlier generations. A wide range of organisms share genes that can be used to determine evolutionary relationships. Because all genes mutate over time, shared genes contain differences that can be treated as derived characters in cladistic analysis. For that reason, similarities and differences in DNA can be used to explain evolutionary relationships.

New Techniques Suggest New Trees DNA analysis has helped to make evolutionary trees more accurate. Often, scientists use DNA evidence when **anatomical** traits alone cannot provide clear answers.

Visual Reading Tool: Analyze Cladograms

Use the cladogram at the right to answer the following questions.

1. Circle the clade that includes both amphibians and snakes.

2. What is something that all organisms in that clade have in common?

____

3. What kingdom does this cladogram fit into?

____

4. Who are the lizards most closely related to on this cladogram?

____

5. On the cladogram, star the organism that has wings as a derived character.

Clade or Not?

The Tree of All Life

KEY QUESTION *What does the tree of life show?*

Modern evolutionary classification is changing rapidly and aims to show all life on one evolutionary tree. As discoveries are made, biologists change the way organisms are grouped. Currently, organisms are grouped in three domains.

Domain Bacteria Members of the domain Bacteria (formerly Eubacteria) are unicellular and prokaryotic. Their cells have thick, rigid walls that surround a cell membrane, and their cell walls contain peptidoglycan. These bacteria range from free-living soil organisms to deadly parasites. Some photosynthesize, some need oxygen to survive, and others are killed by oxygen.

Domain Archaea Members of the domain Archaea (formerly Archaebacteria) are also unicellular and prokaryotic, but live in some of the most extreme environments on Earth, such as volcanic hot springs. Many archaea can only survive in the absence of oxygen. Their cell walls lack peptidoglycan, and their cell membranes contain unusual lipids that aren't found in other organisms.

Domain Eukarya Eukarya consists of all organisms that have a nucleus. It includes kingdoms Protista, Fungi, Plantae, and Animalia.

"Protists": Unicellular Eukaryotes Protists differ greatly from one another and are part of several evolutionary lineages. They are divided into at least five clades, with most being unicellular (the brown algae is multicellular), some photosynthetic, and others heterotrophic.

Fungi Members of the kingdom Fungi are heterotrophs with cell walls containing chitin. Examples include mushrooms and yeast.

Plantae Members of the kingdom Plantae are autotrophs with cell walls that contain cellulose. They photosynthesize using chlorophyll.

Animalia Members of the kingdom Animalia are multicellular and heterotrophic, and lack cell walls. Most animals can move about at some point during their life cycle.

A Revised Tree of Life The tree in Figure 7-12 illustrates current hypotheses about relationships among organisms; however, it gives some incorrect impressions. To more accurately portray the living world, that kind of tree would spread organisms out to reflect their genetic diversity. However, it would be difficult to read because it would span several pages. One solution, proposed by biologist David Hillis, is shown in Figure 7-13. It provides a truer representation of the full diversity of living organisms.

READING TOOL

Apply Prior Knowledge

Earlier in the book you learned about prokarytes vs. eukaryotes. Eukaryotes contain membrane-bound organelles, and prokaryotes do not. ☑ **What is another difference between prokaryotes and eukaryotes?**

____

____

____

____

____

____

7 Chapter Review

Review Vocabulary

Choose the letter of the best answer.

1. The largest taxon is called a
   A. domain.
   B. kingdom.
   C. species.
   D. clade.

2. The study of the evolutionary history of lineages of organisms is known as
   A. a genus.
   B. binomial nomenclature.
   C. phylogeny.
   D. systematics.

Review Key Questions

Provide evidence and details to support your answers.

5. Use the cladogram below to answer the following questions.

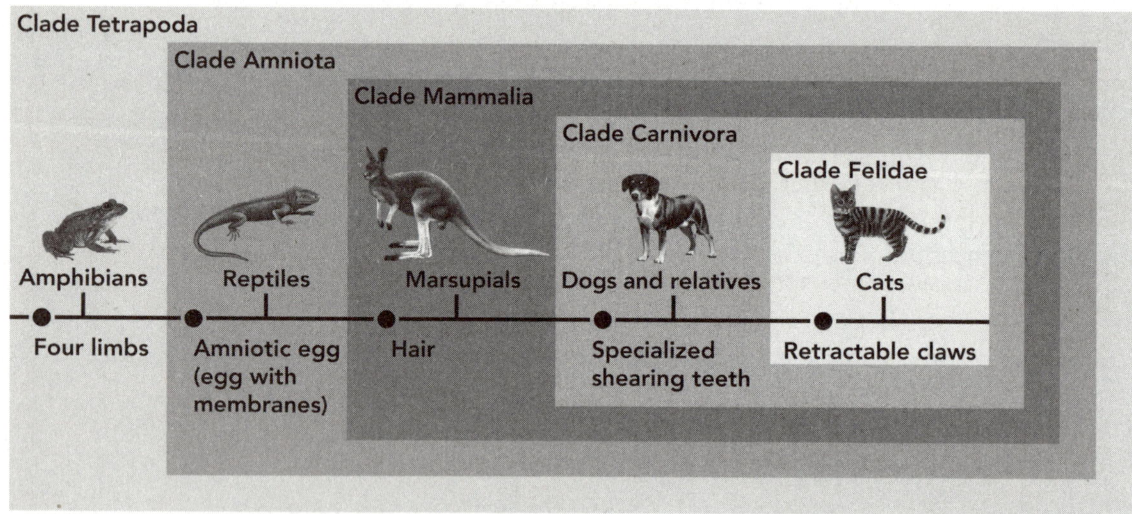

a. Which clades contain animals that have specialized shearing teeth?

____

b. Marsupials belong to which clades? ______________________________

6. What are the advantages of classifying species according to their evolutionary relationships, instead of their physical similarities?

____

____

____

____

CHAPTER 8

LESSON 1 Earth's Origin

READING TOOL **Active Reading** For each of the lesson sections listed, take notes on the processes that formed Earth.

Lesson Section	Notes
Earth's Formation and Structure	
The Dynamic Geosphere	
Weathering, Erosion, and Deposition	
Dating Earth's History	
The Geologic Time Scale	

Lesson Summary

Earth and its global systems are the environments in which life occurs. In this chapter, we will study the evolution of the interactions among Earth's geosphere, atmosphere, hydrosphere, and biosphere over Earth's history.

As you read, circle the answers to each Key Question. Underline any words you do not understand.

BUILD Vocabulary

crust Earth's thin, solid, outer skin

mantle a mostly solid shell that stretches from the crust to a depth of 2900 kilometers (1800 miles)

lithosphere a geologic unit formed by the crust and the outermost part of the mantle

core the incredibly hot layer of Earth below the mantle

Multiple Meanings The word *crust* is used in different contexts to describe the outside layer of an object. The word *core* is used in different contexts to describe the inmost part of an object. **Write a sentence that uses *crust* in a different context. Alternatively, write a sentence that uses *core* in a different context.**

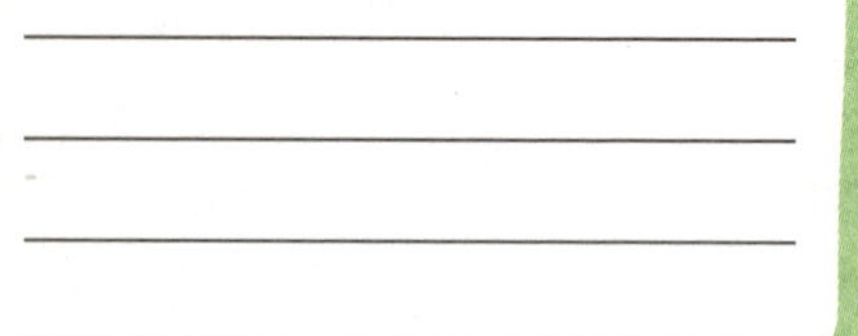

Earth's Formation and Structure

KEY QUESTION *What do scientists hypothesize about early Earth?*

Evidence suggests that Earth, our sun, and our solar system's other planets formed from a huge cloud. Those gases and particles collected into larger objects as gravity pulled them together. The gravitational energy of colliding particles was transformed into heat energy. For millions of years, Earth was a mass of liquid rock, or *magma*. Heavier elements sank toward Earth's center, and lighter elements collected near the surface.

Layers in the Geosphere As Earth began to cool, three layers formed. The **crust** is Earth's thin, solid, outer skin. The **mantle** is a mostly solid shell that makes up most of Earth's mass. Together, the crust and the outer portion of the mantle form the **lithosphere**. The incredibly hot **core** is Earth's center.

Atmosphere and Hydrosphere Earth's surface cooled, and solid rock formed. The lighter elements formed a primitive atmosphere. Earth's early atmosphere contained little or no oxygen. It was mainly composed of carbon dioxide, water vapor, and nitrogen, with smaller amounts of carbon monoxide, hydrogen sulfide, and hydrogen cyanide. Around 4 billion years ago, as Earth continued to cool, water vapor condensed and fell as rain, which gathered in liquid form in oceans on Earth's surface.

The Dynamic Geosphere

KEY QUESTION *What is the theory of plate tectonics?*

Earthquakes, volcanic eruptions, mudslides, and other events show that the geosphere is continually changing. Other dynamic events are mountain building, the movement of continents, the changing of the shape of ocean basins, and the changing of Earth's tilt and orbit.

Earth's Crust in Motion: Plate Tectonics The lithosphere is divided into huge plates. Each includes continental and oceanic crust. These plates move away from, collide with, and slide past each other at the *plate boundaries* between them. These plates move about 1–10 centimeters (0.5–4 inches) a year in relation to each other.

The theory of **plate tectonics** explains how and why Earth's lithospheric plates move relative to each other, as a result of convection currents in Earth's solid, yet slowly-flowing mantle. Plates are set in motion by convection currents in Earth's mantle. Those currents rise and create new crust in some areas, and they fall (destroying crust) in other places.

Mid-ocean Ridges: Where Plates Move Apart

Undersea mountain ranges called *mid-ocean ridges* form at some plate boundaries, where magma wells up from the mantle and forms new crust. Here at the boundaries, plates can move suddenly, causing earthquakes. The heat of the magma also creates hydrothermal vents. Organisms that get their energy from chemicals, instead of the sun, live at the vents. These vents may be where life first appeared on Earth.

Subduction Zones: Where Plates Collide At some plate boundaries, older parts of the ocean floor sink down into the mantle at subduction zones. As this crust is heated by the mantle, the rock melts and erupts from the surface of the crust, forming volcanoes.

Volcanoes at "Hotspots" In some places, a volcano is created by a plume of magma that rises at a "hotspot" in the crust. As the plates move, that volcano is carried away from the hotspot and stops erupting. A new volcano erupts over the hotspot.

Mountain Building: Where Continents Collide

Mountain ranges are formed when parts of the plates containing continental crust collide and are forced into each other.

Weathering, Erosion, and Deposition

KEY QUESTION *What processes change rock?*

Many interactions between the geosphere, atmosphere, and hydrosphere break down or chemically change rocks at or near Earth's surface. This process is called **weathering**. Wind and water wear away rock, and chemical interactions change the minerals that make up rock, weakening them.

Erosion After weathering breaks down rocks, the particles are carried away by wind, water, or glaciers in a process called erosion.

Deposition and Formation of Sedimentary Rocks Eventually, in a process called deposition, wind and water drop, or deposit, rock particles called sediment. Often, sediment is deposited on the bottom of large bodies of water. Over long periods of time, heat and pressure compress the layers of sediments, forming sedimentary rock. Fossils are often found in sedimentary rock, because sediment layers can build up fairly quickly.

BUILD Vocabulary

plate tectonics a theory that explains how and why Earth's lithospheric plates move relative to each other, as a result of convection currents in Earth's solid, yet slowly-flowing mantle

weathering interactions between the geosphere, atmosphere, and hydrosphere that break down or chemically change rocks at or near Earth's surface

Word Origins The word *weathering* is based on the Old English word *weder*, which means "air," "wind," or "storm." ☑ **There are many words that incorporate the word *weather*. What does it mean to say that an object is *unweathered*?**

____

____

____

____

READING TOOL

Cause and Effect Sedimentary rocks play an important role in the formation of fossils. Figure 8-9 in your text shows how an animal becomes fossilized. ☑ **In your own words, explain how sedimentary rocks aid in the formation of fossils.**

____

____

____

____

____

____

BUILD Vocabulary

relative dating a process in which geologists compare rock layers at different places to place rocks in chronological order

index fossils distinctive fossils used to establish and compare the relative age of rock layers and the fossils they contain

radiometric dating a technique that uses a rock sample's proportion of radioactive isotopes and stable isotopes to calculate its age

Multiple Meanings Indexes are used to organize or compare events. Index fossils are used to show when fossilized organisms were alive, based upon their location in rock layers. ☑ **Where else can you find indexes that help organize concepts?**

____

____

Dating Earth's History

KEY QUESTION *How can we date events in Earth's history?*

Earth science and paleontology try to describe and understand the history of our planet and the evolutionary history of life.

Relative Dating of Rocks **Relative dating** is a process that geologists use to place rocks in chronological order. They compare rocks layers exposed at different places to determine in what order they formed and which layers are older than others. Lower layers of rock and the fossils they contain are generally older than upper layers.

Relative Dating of Fossils To help establish the relative age of rock layers and their fossils, scientists use index fossils. **Index fossils** are distinctive fossils used to establish and compare the relative age of rock layers and the fossils they contain. A useful index fossil must be easy to recognize and occur only in a few rock layers, indicating that the species existed only for a brief span of geologic time. In addition, layers from that time period must be found in many places, indicating that the organism was widely distributed.

Directly Dating Rocks The ages of rocks can be determined using **radiometric dating**. This technique relies on radioactive isotopes, which decay, or break down, into stable isotopes at a steady rate.

Visual Reading Tool: Index Fossils

A  B  C  D  E  F 

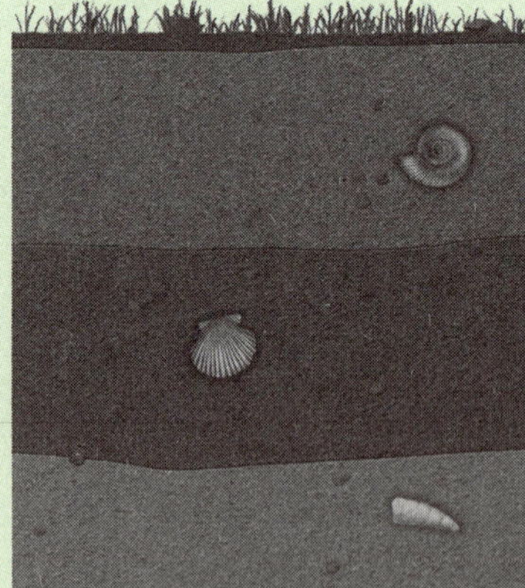

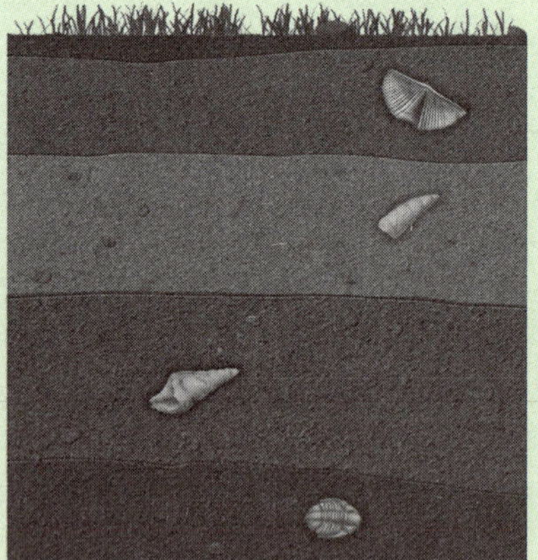

Location 1 Location 2 Location 3

1. Which fossils do Location 1 and 2 have in common? ____________

2. Which fossils do Location 2 and 3 have in common? ____________

3. What can we then say about the relatives ages of fossils A, B, C, E, and F based only on fossil D? How?

____

____

A **half-life** is the time required for half of the radioactive atoms in a sample to decay. Different radioactive isotopes decay at different rates. Radiometric dating uses the proportion of radioactive isotopes and stable isotopes to calculate the age of a sample.

Directly Dating Fossils Researchers use several techniques to put fossils in order from oldest to youngest and to figure out how old those fossils are. Recent fossils (and *only* recent fossils) can be dated directly by using an isotope known as carbon-14, which has a half-life of roughly 5730 years.

Indirectly Dating Fossils Older fossils can be dated indirectly, using isotopes with longer half-lives to date the rock layers close to those in which the fossils are found. Isotopes useful for dating include potassium-40 (half life: 1.26 billion years), uranium-238 (half life: 4.5 billion years), and rubidium-87 (half life: 48.8 billion years).

The Geologic Time Scale

KEY QUESTION *How was the geologic time scale established?*

The **geologic time scale** is a timeline of Earth's history. It is based on both relative and absolute dating. The major divisions of the geologic time scale are eons, eras, and periods.

Establishing the Geologic Time Scale Early paleontologists noticed major changes in the fossil record at boundaries between certain rock layers. Geologists used rock-layer boundaries to determine where one division of geologic time ended and the next began. The lengths of ages are not consistent. Much later, geologists began using radiometric dating to assign specific ages to the various rock layers. They are still testing, verifying, and adjusting this time scale.

Divisions of the Geologic Time Scale Geologists recognize four eons: the Hadean Eon (Earth's formation– 4 billion years ago); the Archean Eon (first life on Earth); the Proterozoic Eon (continent formation); and the Phanerozoic Eon (present).

Eons are divided into **eras**. The Phanerozoic Eon, for example, is divided into the Paleozoic, Mesozoic, and Cenozoic eras. Eras are subdivided into **periods**, which range in length from nearly 100 million years to just under 2 million years.

Naming the Divisions The divisions of the geologic time scale were named in different ways. Naming began before any rocks older than the Cambrian Period had been identified. All geologic time before the Cambrian is called Precambrian time, which covers about 90% of Earth's history.

Comparing Time The amount of time covered by the geologic time scale is so long that it is impossible for us to really understand how long ago events in Earth's history occurred, as well as what a tiny portion of time humans have been here.

BUILD Vocabulary

half-life the time required for half of the radioactive atoms in a sample to decay

geologic time scale timeline used to represent Earth's history

era major division of geologic time; usually divided into two or more periods

period division of geologic time into which eras are subdivided

Word Origins The word *period* is based on the Latin word *periodus*, meaning "a going around, a cycle" or "complete sentence." There are many words that incorporate the word *period*. Some incorporate one of the meanings of the Latin word, and some incorporate the other meaning. **What is the meaning of the word *periodical*?**

____

____

____

____

____

CHAPTER 8

LESSON 2

Life's Early History

READING TOOL **Sequence of Events** For each topic below, describe the events listed in the text in the order in which they occur.

1. Miller-Urey Experiment

2. Formation of Protocells

3. RNA World Hypothesis

4. The Biosphere as a Force in Planetary Evolution

5. Earliest Eukaryotes

6. Endosymbiotic Theory

Lesson Summary

Mysteries of Life's Origins

KEY QUESTION *What do scientists hypothesize about the origin of life?*

Researchers have made major progress in understanding the origin of life. We may not ever know all the details, but we may be able to understand what is possible. For instance, experiments have shown that complex molecules like RNA can form in the absence of life, replicate, and carry information.

The Miller-Urey Experiment In 1953, chemists Stanley Miller and Harold Urey attempted to simulate how organic compounds first formed on Earth. To simulate Earth's early atmosphere, they combined warm water with gaseous methane, ammonia, and hydrogen. Then they applied electric "lightning" sparks. Multiple amino acids, which are needed to make proteins, were produced. Miller and Urey's experiment suggests that organic compounds necessary for life could have arisen from simpler compounds on a primitive Earth.

Formation of Protocells Studies have shown that molecules similar to fatty acids—the building blocks of membrane lipids—can sometimes form spontaneously. Thus, these molecules might have been able to form membrane-like vesicles. The protocells could have formed around RNA, which then provided information for replication to occur.

RNA First? The RNA world hypothesis proposes that RNA existed before DNA. From this simple RNA-based system, several steps could have led to today's DNA-directed protein synthesis. There are many pieces of evidence to support this hypothesis. All proteins originate from RNA; even DNA nucleotides are first synthesized as RNA nucleotides.

The Biosphere as a Force in Planetary Evolution Photosynthesis evolved about 2.2 billion years ago. Early photosynthetic bacteria began to churn out oxygen, which combined with iron in the oceans. This reaction produced iron oxide that sank to the ocean floor. It is the source of most iron ore mined today.

Next, oxygen accumulated in the atmosphere, forming the ozone layer, which turned the sky blue. Over several hundred million years, oxygen concentration in the atmosphere increased. Some organisms evolved new metabolic pathways that used oxygen for respiration.

As you read, circle the answers to each Key Question. Underline any words you do not understand.

READING TOOL

Make Connections Cell membranes are made of lipids. Membranes are necessary for cells, because they separate cells from the external environment. Protocells are the first examples of membrane-like vesicles that scientists produced in a lab.

☑ **What role do cell membranes and protocells play in the RNA world hypothesis?**

____

____

____

____

BUILD Vocabulary

endosymbiotic theory theory that proposes eukaryotic cells formed from a symbiotic relationship among several different prokaryotic cells

Word Origins The word *symbiosis* comes from the Greek word *syn*, meaning "together," and the Greek word *bios*, meaning "life." The Greek word *endon* means "within."

☑ **Based on that, how does endosymbiotic theory relate to symbiosis?**

____

____

____

Origin of the Eukaryotic Cell

KEY QUESTION *What theory explains the origin of eukaryotic cells?*

The evolution of complex eukaryotic cells from much simpler prokaryotic cells set the stage for the rest of the history of life.

Earliest Eukaryotes Eukaryotes can be traced to fossils from 2.1 billion years ago. A leading theory for how eukaryotic cells evolved is biologist Lynn Margulis' **endosymbiotic theory**, which proposes that organelles in eukaryotic cells were formed when different types of cells joined in a kind of merger.

A great deal of evidence from the field of molecular biology now supports the theory that many of the complex features of eukaryotic cells evolved through endosymbiosis. Biologists think that mitochondria, which contain their own DNA, are the descendants of free-living bacteria that took up residence in the earliest eukaryotes. A similar case could be made for chloroplasts, a special organelle that is similar to ancient free-living photosynthetic cells.

Another piece of evidence supporting the endosymbiotic theory is that some cells today contain bacteria or algae that live as endosymbionts.

Visual Reading Tool: The Endosymbiotic Theory

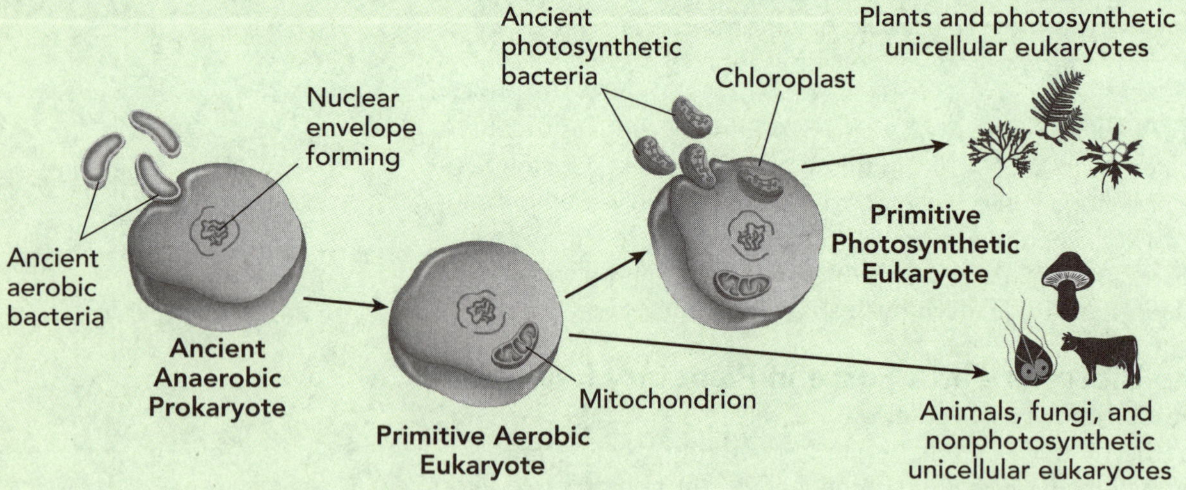

1. Which organelle developed from ancient photosynthetic bacteria within a primitive eukaryote? ______________

2. From which cell type do fungi evolve? ______________________________

3. What purpose do mitochondria serve in eukaryotic organisms, and what is the evidence to support the hypothesis that they were once free-living cells?

____

____

____

Do We Understand the Cell Completely? Not yet. Many uncertainties remain in our current understanding of the complexity of cells. Biologists today are conducting research to learn about how cells function and respond to the enviornments around them. What we do understand suggests that the complex structures and pathways found in living cells were produced by known mechanisms of evolutionary change.

The Fossil Record

KEY QUESTION *What do fossils reveal about ancient life?*

Multicellular life creates fossils much more easily than unicellular life, and scientists can learn a lot about past organisms from the evidence left behind in fossils. However, the fossil record is incomplete because while some organisms are preserved as fossils, many more die without leaving a trace. Fossils form rarely and only under certain conditions. Still, the fossil record contains an enormous amount of information that helps paleontologists understand ancient life and the changes that have occurred over the history of the Earth.

READING TOOL

Connect to Visuals

Study Figure 8-20 in your textbook. Think about the parts of the organisms that were preserved in each fossil. **Which of the fossils in the three smaller photographs would provide the most information to a scientist? Explain your reasoning.**

____

____

____

____

____

Types of Fossils Fossils vary greatly in size and completeness. Some are large and encompass entire animal skeletons, including teeth. Others are as tiny as single-celled bacteria. Some are perfectly preserved animals, complete with internal organs that may have been petrified or frozen. Some are mere fragments of an organism, such as teeth or the edge of a leaf. Sometimes, an organism leaves only trace fossils—casts of footprints, burrows, tracks, or even droppings.

Most fossils show only an organism's hard structures, such as wood, shells, bones, and teeth. Hard structures are more easily preserved. Soft body structures usually decay rapidly after death. Sometimes, soft body structures are preserved if organisms are buried in sediment so quickly that their soft tissues are protected from aerobic decay. Then fossils will show these soft structures.

Finding and Evaluating Fossils By comparing fossils to each other and to living organisms, paleontologists can propose and test evolutionary hypotheses. Fossils reveal information about the structures of ancient organisms and the sequential nature of groups in the fossil record. Fossils also reveal information about evolution from common ancestors and the ecology of ancient environments.

By examining fossils, scientists can compare body structures that can be used to test hypotheses about the appearance, evolution, and history of species. Bones and footprints can provide clues to how animals moved. Plant and pollen fossils suggest whether an area was a swamp, a lake, a forest, or a desert. When many different kinds of fossils are found together, researchers can sometimes reconstruct entire ancient ecosystems.

CHAPTER 8

LESSON 3

Earth and Life Evolve Together

READING TOOL **Use Structure** Use section headings and the graphic organizer below to fill in information about each item as it connects it to the overall lesson.

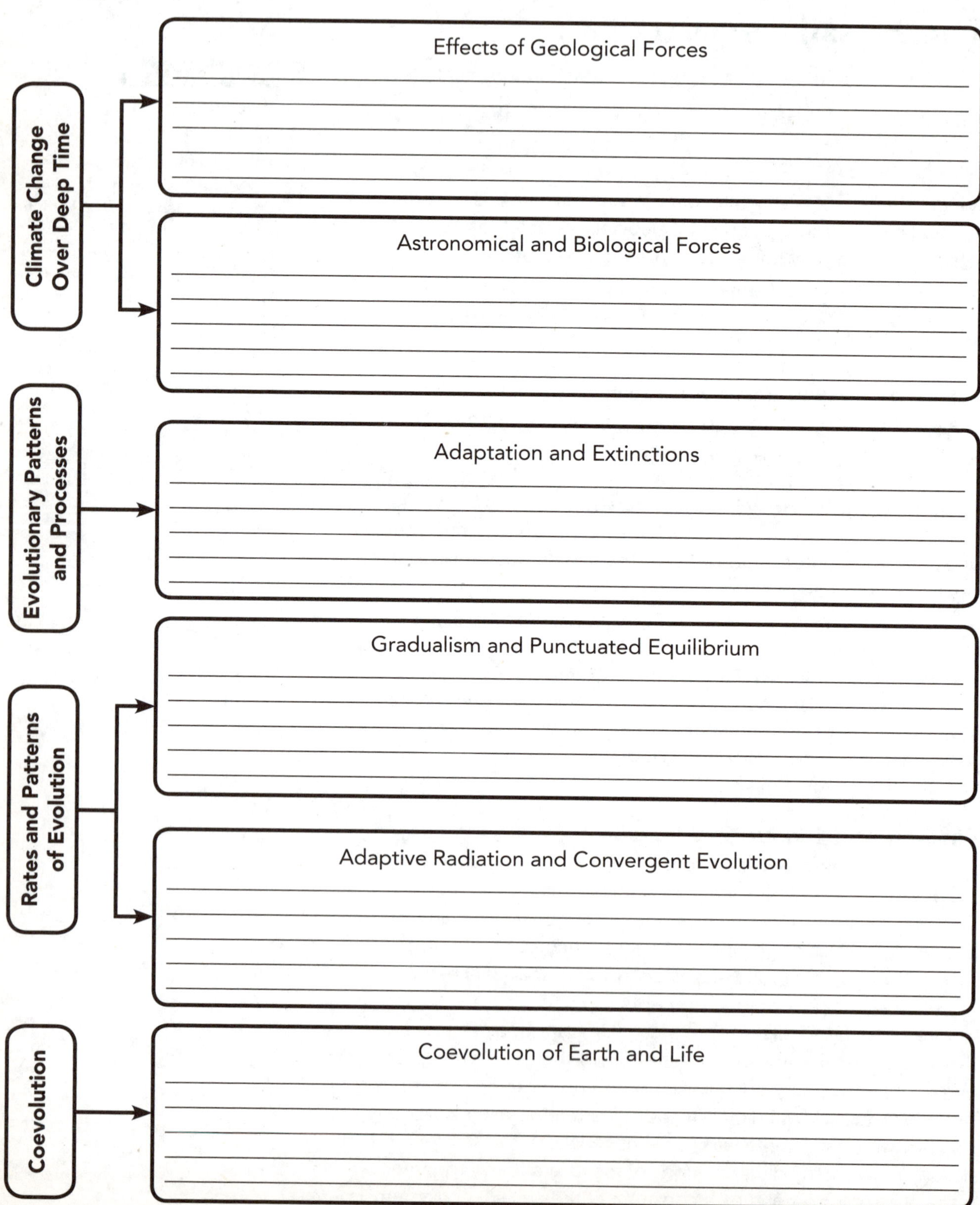

Lesson Summary

Environments around the world have been stable for about 10,000 years, since the end of the last ice age. During this period of stability, human civilization appeared and spread. But over millions of years, the geosphere and both local and global climates have changed dramatically. Now we are entering a period of rapid climate change as a result of human activity.

Climate Change Over Deep Time

KEY QUESTION *How has climate change affected the history of life?*

Earth's global and regional climates and habitats have changed repeatedly over deep time, due to small shifts in global temperature triggered by nonhuman causes, such as continental drift, mountain building, the emergence of islands, changes in levels of continents and oceans, global climate change, and meteor impacts.

Environmental changes altered interactions among and between organisms and their environments. This changed the pressures of natural selection, favoring adaptation to new conditions. New and changed habitats created new ecological niches, encouraging increased diversity among species.

Effects of Geological Forces Over millions of years, forces that shape the geosphere moved continents, built mountains, and created volcanic islands. These geological features influenced regional and global environments.

Astronomical Sources of Change Over Earth's history, comets and large meteors have periodically crashed into Earth. Some kicked enough debris into the atmosphere to cause climate change that drove major extinctions, like the one at the end of the Cretaceous Period that killed the dinosaurs.

Many changes occur to Earth's orbit. The orbit changes shape. The angle at which Earth is tilted varies. Earth wobbles on its axis like a spinning top. These variations change the amount of solar radiation that reaches different parts of the globe and contribute to the glaciers that have grown and melted at least 30 times over the last 1.8 million years.

Biological Sources of Change Over deep time, actions of living organisms have changed conditions in the atmosphere, the oceans, and the land. Plants, animals, and microorganisms are active players in global cycles of key elements, including carbon, nitrogen, and oxygen.

As you read, circle the answers to each Key Question. Underline any words you do not understand.

READING TOOL

Apply Prior Knowledge
Currently, Earth is tilted about 23.5 degrees on its axis. This tilt has dramatic effects on global cycles. **Explain the connection between the cause of glacial cycles and the cause of seasonal changes.**

____

____

____

____

____

BUILD Vocabulary

macroevolutionary pattern major changes that usually take place in larger clades

extinct having no living members

background extinction extinction caused by the slow and steady process of natural selection

mass extinction event during which many species become extinct during a relatively short period of time

Related Words Biologists use the term "extinct in the wild" to describe species that exist only in captivity.

☑ **Do you think that species that are extinct in the wild can recover?**

____

____

____

____

Evolutionary Patterns and Processes

KEY QUESTION *What patterns can be observed in the fossil record?*

Macroevolutionary patterns are major changes in anatomy, phylogeny, ecology, and behavior that usually occur in larger clades. The emergence, growth, and extinction of larger clades are examples of macroevolutionary patterns. Fossils are classified into clades, some that contain only extinct organisms, and some that include living organisms. An extinct species might be an *ancestor* of a living species, or it might just be related to the living species.

Adaptation and Extinction Species that evolve adaptations to environmental changes thrive. Species that fail to adapt become **extinct**. The "normal" rate of extinction that occurs all the time is called **background extinction**. Some clades produce many species and survive for long periods. The variety of adaptations helps the clade survive environmental changes.

Mass Extinctions When a devastating event affects species globally, a **mass extinction** can occur, in which a large proportion of species go extinct relatively rapidly. Species become extinct because their environment breaks down, and the ordinary process of natural selection cannot compensate quickly enough. Mass extinctions reduce biodiversity rapidly and dramatically. Typically, it takes 5 to 10 million years for biodiversity to recover.

Visual Reading Tool: Lineage of Modern Birds

1. Label the clades by completing the figure with the following terms: crocodiles, modern birds, *Tyrannosaurus rex*.

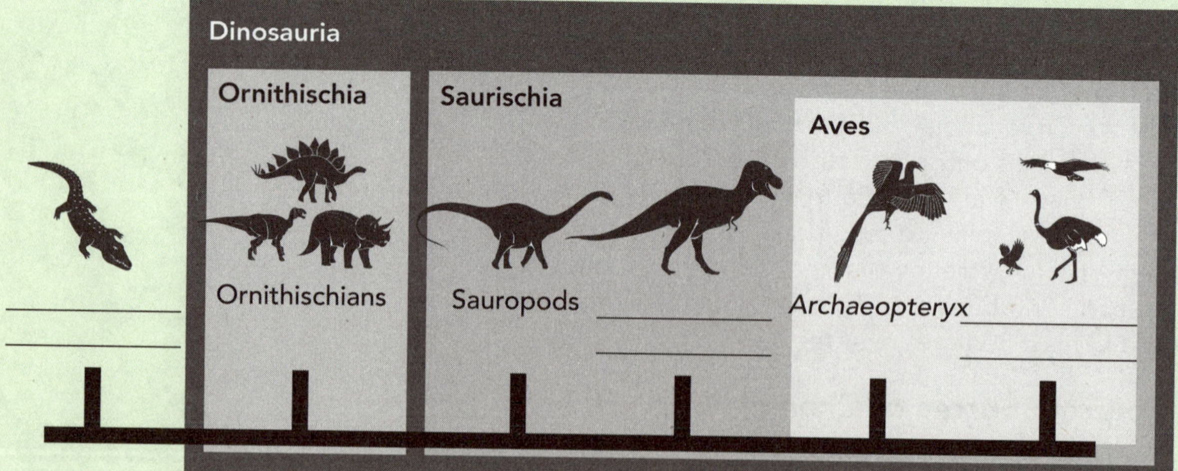

2. Which clade is not part of the Dinosauria clade? ______________________

3. Which clade contains Archaeopteryx? ______________________

Rates and Patterns of Evolution

KEY QUESTION *How fast does evolution take place?*

Fossil evidence supports the hypothesis that evolution can occur at different rates in different clades, and at different times.

Gradualism Darwin suggested that evolution proceeds slowly and steadily, an idea called **gradualism**. The fossil record shows that many species are in a state of equilibrium, or stasis. Their structures have not changed much over time, even though they continue to evolve genetically.

Punctuated Equilibrium Sometimes the fossil record shows that equilibrium can be interrupted by brief periods of change that are geologically rapid. This pattern is called **punctuated equilibrium**. Over thousands or millions of years, rapid bursts of speciation can occur.

Rapid Evolution After Equilibrium Two ways evolution can rapidly occur are through genetic drift and mass extinction.

Adaptive Radiation Descendants of an ancestral species may diversify over time into related species adapted to different niches. This process, where a single species evolves into several or many, distinct species, is called **adaptive radiation**.

Convergent Evolution The evolution of similar characteristics in unrelated organisms that live in similar environments is known as **convergent evolution**.

Coevolution

KEY QUESTION *What evolutionary characteristics are typical of coevolving species?*

The process by which two species evolve in response to changes in each other over time is called **coevolution**. The relationship between coevolving organisms often becomes so specific that evolutionary change in one organism is usually followed by a change in the other organism.

Flowers and Pollinators, Plants and Herbivorous Insects Flowers and their pollinators sometimes evolve structures that make them suitable for each other. Some plants are pollinated by only one insect species. Some herbivores can tolerate toxins a specific plant species produces to protect itself.

Coevolution of Earth and Life Massive changes to Earth, such as climate changes and the movement of continents, have led to events such as mass extinctions and adaptive radiation. Likewise, life has had significant effects on Earth, such as the development of photosynthesis.

BUILD Vocabulary

gradualism evolution of a species by gradual accumulation of small genetic changes over long periods of time

punctuated equilibrium pattern of evolution in which long, stable periods are interrupted by brief periods of more rapid change

adaptive radiation process by which a single species or a small group of species evolves into several different forms

convergent evolution process by which unrelated organisms independently evolve similarities when adapting to similar environments

coevolution process by which two species evolve in response to changes in each other over time

Word Origins The word *equilibrium* is based on two Latin words, *aequi*, which means "equal," and *libra*, which means "balance." Equilibrium is a common concept in biology and can be used in many different contexts.

☑ **When else have you used the word *equilibrium* to describe a biological concept?**

____

____

____

____

8 Chapter Review

Review Vocabulary

Choose the letter of the best answer.

1. Two species evolve in response to each other over time in

A. convergent evolution.

B. coevolution.

C. adaptive radiation.

2. Determining a fossil's age by its placement with other fossils within rock layers is called

A. the geologic time scale.

B. radiometric dating.

C. relative dating.

Match the vocabulary term to its definition.

3. ________ time for half of radioactive atoms to decay

4. ________ species that has died out and has no living members

5. ________ division of geologic time into which eras are subdivided

a. half-life

b. period

c. extinct

Review Key Questions

Provide evidence and details to support your answers.

6. Have changes in climate occurred in the past? Give examples.

7. What defines a mass extinction? What are the immediate biodiversity effects?

8. What pieces of evidence support the RNA world hypothesis?

CHAPTER 9

LESSON 1 Introduction to Animals

READING TOOL **Active Reading** As you read, keep track of the 5 things animals do to survive. Describe each of these processes in the graphic organizer below.

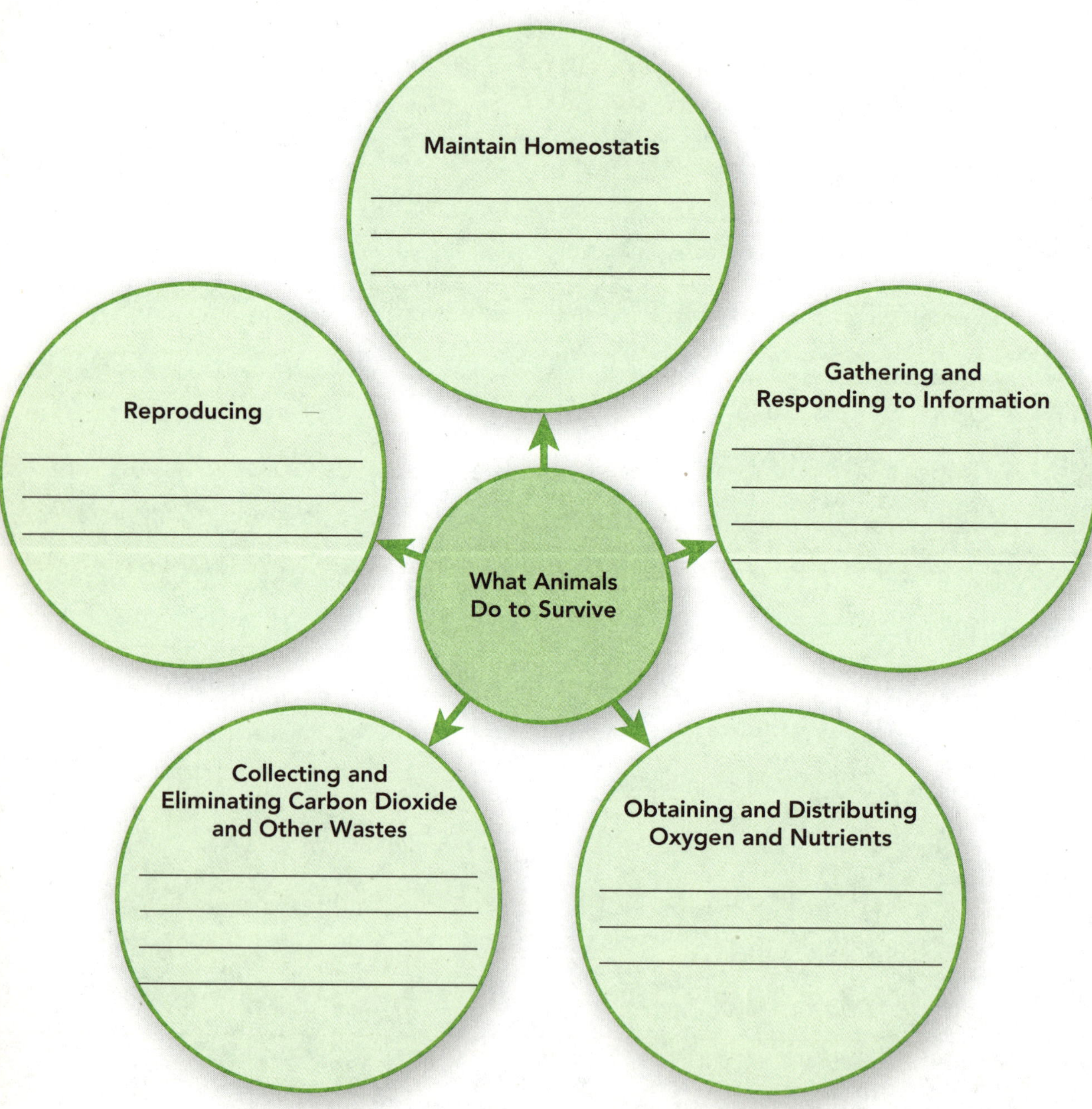

Lesson Summary

What Is an Animal?

KEY QUESTION *What characteristics do all animals share?*

Animals are multicellular, heterotrophic, eukaryotic organisms with cells that lack cell walls. Although diverse, they share some characteristics. Animals are classified into two broad categories: invertebrates and chordates.

Invertebrates Over 95 percent of animal species are informally called invertebrates. **Invertebrates** include all animals that lack a vertebral column. Because the category lumps together organisms that lack a characteristic rather than share one, they do not form a clade.

Chordates All members of the phylum Chordata are called **chordates**, and exhibit certain characteristics during at least one stage of life: a dorsal hollow nerve cord, a tail that extends beyond the anus, and pharyngeal pouches. Most chordates are **vertebrates** that develop a backbone (vertebral column), made of vertebrae (spinal bones). Nonvertebrate chordates do not have backbones.

What Animals Do to Survive

KEY QUESTION *What essential functions must animals perform to survive?*

Animals keep their internal environments stable, or maintain homeostasis. Animals maintain homeostasis by gathering and responding to information, obtaining and distributing oxygen and nutrients, and collecting and eliminating carbon dioxide and other wastes. They must also reproduce.

Maintaining Homeostasis Homeostasis in the body often works by using **feedback inhibition**, which is when a stimulus produces a response that opposes the original stimulus.

Gathering and Responding to Information The nervous system gathers information using receptors that respond to stimuli. Other nerve cells collect, process, and respond to that information.

Obtaining and Distributing Oxygen and Nutrients All animals must obtain oxygen to perform cellular respiration. Oxygen diffuses across the skin of small water animals, while larger animals have respiratory systems. Most animals eat to obtain nutrients and have digestive systems that break food down for use by the body. Acquired oxygen and nutrients must be transported throughout the body, often requiring interactions between circulatory systems and respiratory systems or digestive systems.

As you read, circle the answers to each Key Question. Underline any words you do not understand.

BUILD Vocabulary

invertebrate type of animal that lacks a backbone, or vertebral column

chordate type of animal that, at some point in its life, shows a dorsal nerve cord, a tail, and a pharyngeal pouch

vertebrate type of animal that has a backbone

feedback inhibition process in which a stimulus produces a response that opposes the original stimulus; also called negative feedback

Prefixes The prefix *in-* can mean "in, on, or not." **In the term *invertebrate*, which definition do you think fits the prefix *in-* and why?**

____

____

____

____

Collecting and Eliminating Carbon Dioxide and Other Wastes Animals' metabolic processes generate wastes needing to be eliminated. Many animals use respiratory systems to get rid of carbon dioxide. Most complex animals have excretory systems to process wastes and then expel them, or to store and expel them.

Reproducing Most animals reproduce sexually, which helps maintain genetic diversity. Many invertebrates and some vertebrates can also reproduce asexually.

Visual Reading Tool: Body Plan Trait Evolution

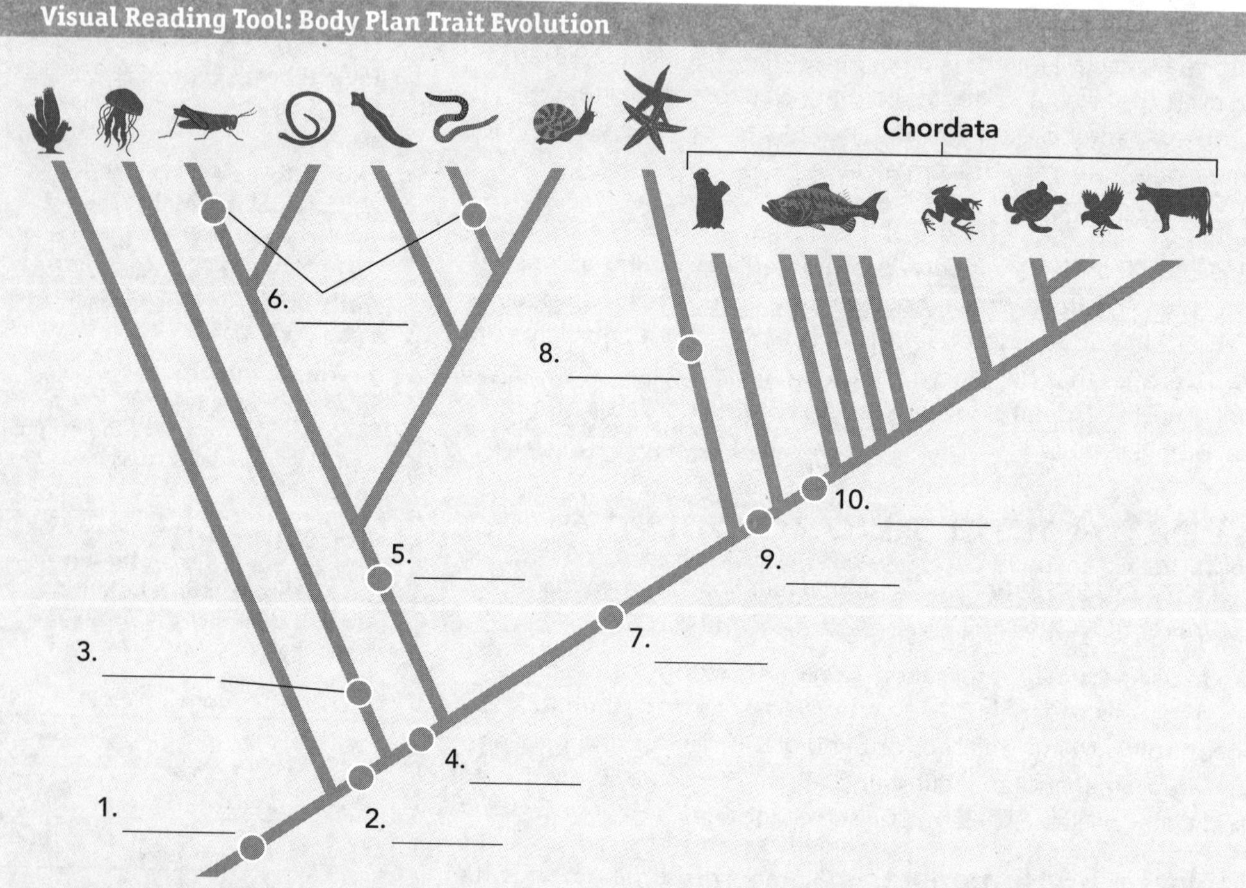

Single-celled animal ancestor

Using the figure as your guide, put each item listed below in the order in which animals developed body plan traits—from the single-celled animal ancestor to the chordates.

A. Radial symmetry

B. As adults, radial symmetry and no cephalization

C. Mouth-first development

D. Multicellularity

E. Initial segmentation

F. Chordate segmentation

G. Tissues: 2 germ layers

H. Backbone development

I. Anus first development

J. Organs: 3 germ layers; bilateral symmetry; cephalization

Animal Body Plans

KEY QUESTION *What are some features of animal body plans?*

Each animal clade has a unique organization of particular body structures, often called a body plan, which are part of biological classification. Features of animal body plans include levels of organization, body symmetry, formation of body cavities, patterns of embryonic development, segmentation, cephalization, and limb formation.

Levels of Organization The cells of most animals develop into specialized cells organized into tissues. Animals typically have several types of tissues, like epithelial, nervous, muscle, and connective tissues. During development, tissues combine to form organs. Organ systems work together to maintain homeostasis.

Body Symmetry Most animals exhibit body symmetry: radial or bilateral. **Radial symmetry** is a body plan in which any number of imaginary planes drawn through the center of the body could divide it into equal halves. **Bilateral symmetry** is a body plan in which a single imaginary plane can divide the body into left and right sides that are mirror images of each other.

Patterns of Embryological Development Animals reproducing sexually begin life as **zygotes**, or fertilized eggs. Through development, the zygote forms a hollow ball of cells, and then folds in on itself, elongating into a tube, which becomes the digestive tract. In some clades the mouth develops first; in some, the anus. Embryonic animal cells differentiate into three germ layers—endoderm, mesoderm, and ectoderm—each developing into different organs and systems. Animals with radial symmetry only have the endoderm and ectoderm. Most complex animals have a body cavity, or **coelom**.

Segmentation Many bilaterally symmetrical animals develop repeated parts, or segments. Segmented animals typically have some internal and external body parts repeated on each side of the body. Bilateral symmetry and segmentation are often found together.

Cephalization Animals with bilateral symmetry typically exhibit **cephalization**, or a concentration of sense organs and nerve cells in their heads.

Limb Formation Segmented, bilaterally symmetrical animals typically have external appendages on both sides of the body.

BUILD Vocabulary

radial symmetry body plan in which any number of imaginary planes drawn through the center of the body could divide it into equal portions

bilateral symmetry body plan in which a single imaginary plane can divide the body into left and right sides that are mirror images of each other

zygote a fertilized egg

coelom (see lum) body cavity lined with mesoderm

cephalization concentration of sense organs and nerve cells at the anterior end of an animal

Using Prior Knowledge You may have heard the word *radius* in math class, which refers to the line segment from the center of a circle to its perimeter. ☑ **Look around the room. Do you see any objects that have radial symmetry? List them.**

____

____

____

CHAPTER 9

LESSON 2

Animal Evolution and Diversity

READING TOOL **Compare and Contrast** Provide one similarity and one difference in the ways the identified animals evolved over time.

Animals	Similarities	Differences
Invertebrates		
Vertebrates		
Nonvertebrate Chordates		
Vertebrate Chordates		

Lesson Summary

The Cladogram of Animals

As you read, circle the answers to each Key Question. Underline any words you do not understand.

KEY QUESTION *How are animal clades defined?*

The features of animal body plans provide information for building the Animal Cladogram, which shows current hypotheses of relationships among clades. Animal clades are typically defined according to adult body plans and patterns of embryonic development.

Differences Between Clades Every animal clade has a unique combination of traits inherited from ancestors and new traits found only in that clade. Complex body systems are not an improvement over simpler systems. Any body system in a living animal functions well enough to enable that animal to survive and reproduce.

Evolutionary Experiments Each clade's body plan is an evolutionary experiment in which a set of body structures performs essential functions. The original versions of most major animal body plans were established hundreds of millions of years ago. As species have adapted to changing conditions, new clades are created.

Origins of the Invertebrates

KEY QUESTION *What does the cladogram of invertebrates illustrate?*

The Cambrian Explosion started about 542 million years ago and lasted 15 million years, and was when many modern phyla began appearing in the fossil record.

The Earliest Animals After the first prokaryotic cells evolved, all life remained single-celled for about 3 billion years. Research shows the first animals evolved from ancestors shared with living choanoflagellates, with the oldest evidence of multicellular life coming from 600-million-year-old microscopic fossils.

The Ediacaran Fauna Fossils from Australia's Ediacara Hills date from roughly 565 to 544 million years ago. These showed body plans different from any animals alive today, although some seem to be related to worms and jellyfishes.

The Cambrian Explosion During the Cambrian Period, animals evolved complex body plans; specialized cells, tissues, and organs; body symmetry; segmentation; front and back ends; and appendages. Some also evolved shells, skeletons, or other hard body parts.

Cladogram of Invertebrates The Invertebrate Cladogram shows current hypotheses about evolutionary relationships among major living invertebrate groups, and indicates the order in which important features evolved.

BUILD Vocabulary

cartilage type of connective tissue that supports the body and is softer and more flexible than bone

Apply Prior Knowledge Humans have cartilage at the tip of their noses. Feel the tip of your nose and move it back and forth. Now, try to do the same with the tip of your thumb. ☑ **Why is it easier to move the tip of your nose than it is to move the tip of a finger?**

____

____

____

____

Origins of the Chordates

KEY QUESTION *What can we learn by studying the chordate cladogram?*

The most ancient chordates were related to ancestors of echinoderms. One chordate fossil of a worm from the Cambrian Period included paired muscles arranged in a series, similar to those of modern chordates. Fossil beds from the later Cambria held fossils of the earliest known vertebrate, showing muscles arranged in a series; traces of fins; sets of feathery gills; heads with paired sense organs; and skeletal structure, including a skull. These last features were likely made of **cartilage**, a strong connective tissue softer and more flexible than bone. These characteristics are shared—during some part of the life cycle—by all chordates.

READING TOOL

Active Reading

There are ample fossils from the Cambrian explosion that have given scientists a good understanding of evolution during that time. ☑ **Why were these organisms able to be fossilized so well?**

____

____

____

____

Visual Reading Tool: Identifying Invertebrates

On the chart below, fill in the type of invertebrate that the row describes. Use the small icons to help you.

1.		Simplest organism in clade Metazoa; they have tiny pores all over their bodies.
2.		Aquatic, mostly soft-bodied, carnivorous, racially symmetrical with stinging tentacles around their mouths.
3.		Segmented bodies, tough external skeleton, cephalization, jointed appendages.
4.		Unsegmented bodies with specialized tissues and organ system, digestive tracts with mouth and anus openings.
5.		Soft, flattened, unsegmented bodies that lack a coelom and anus.
6.		Segmented bodies with a ring-like appearance.
7.		Soft-bodied animals that typically have internal or external shells and complex organ systems.
8.		Spiny skin, five-part radial symmetry, internal plate skeleton, water vascular system.

Cladogram of Chordates Modern chordates consist of six groups: nonvertebrate chordates and five vertebrate groups—fishes, amphibians, reptiles, birds, and mammals. Almost all living chordates are vertebrates; most of those are fishes. The Chordate Cladogram presents current hypotheses about evolutionary relationships among chordate groups. Within it are markers noting the evolutionary appearance of various characteristics that jump-started major adaptive radiations.

Nonvertebrate Chordates Tunicates and lancelets are chordates lacking backbones. Fossil evidence shows that their ancestors diverged from vertebrate ancestors over 550 million years ago.

Jawless Fishes The earliest fishes appeared about 510 million years ago. Fossils show they had no jaw or teeth, their skeletons were made of cartilage, and many had bony shields on their heads or other armor. Two other clades gave rise to modern lampreys and hagfishes.

Sharks and Their Relatives Other ancient fishes evolved jaws, allowing them to bite and chew. Early fishes also evolved paired pectoral and pelvic fins attached to limb girdles. These offer greater body movement control, while tail fins and muscles allow for greater thrust. These adaptions launched the adaptive radiation of the Chondrichthyes: sharks, rays, and skates.

Bony Fishes Another group of ancient fishes evolved skeletons of true bone, launching the radiation of bony fishes, the Osteichthyes.

Ray-Finned Fishes Most modern bony fishes belong to the huge group called ray-finned fishes, referring to fins formed from bony rays connected by a layer of skin.

Lobe-Finned Fishes Lobe-finned fishes evolved fleshy fins supported by larger bones. One group of ancient lobe-finned fishes evolved into the ancestors of four-limbed vertebrates, or **tetrapods**.

The "Fishapod" Fossils show how lines of lobe-finned fishes evolved sturdier appendages. One of these has a mix of fish and tetrapod features and could be called a "fishapod"—part fish, part tetrapod.

Amphibians The word *amphibian* means "double life," since most amphibians live in water as larvae and on land as adults. Most require water for reproduction, breathe with lungs as adults, have moist skin with mucous glands, and lack scales and claws. Early amphibians were ancestors of reptiles, birds, and mammals. Their adaptations to breathe air and protect themselves from drying out fueled another adaptive radiation. Only three orders of amphibians survive today.

BUILD Vocabulary

tetrapod vertebrate with four limbs

Suffixes The suffix *-pod* means "foot." It is often used in biology to describe how many limbs an animal has, but also has uses in other fields of study. In photography, a camera can sit on a tripod to be held steady. ☑ **Why do photographers refer to that piece of equipment as a tripod?**

____

____

____

____

READING TOOL

Make Connections

Now that you know what the suffix *-pod* means, let's apply other prefixes to it. ☑ **If a tetrapod has four limbs, how many limbs would a quintapod have? What about a decapod? What about a dodecapod?**

____

____

____

____

READING TOOL

Applying Prior Knowledge

Modern birds evolved from feathered dinosaurs and are considered reptiles. In earlier chapters, you learned how climate change is affecting some birds.

☑ **Describe one way modern birds 100 years from now might evolve to combat rising global temperatures.**

____

____

____

____

Reptiles

Reptiles evolved from ancient amphibians with dry, scaly skin, well-developed lungs, strong limbs, and land-developing shelled eggs. Five living reptile groups include lizards and snakes, crocodilians, turtles and tortoises, the tuatara, and birds.

Enter the Dinosaurs A great reptile adaptive radiation continued through the Triassic and Jurassic Periods. Some dinosaurs ate plants; others were carnivorous. Some lived in family groups and cared for eggs or young. Some had feathers, possibly first serving to regulate body temperature. Evolutionary lineage from feathered dinosaurs led to modern birds.

Exit the Dinosaurs The Cretaceous Period ended with a mass extinction, which included most of the dinosaurs, and many plant and animal groups. This may have been caused by a combination of natural disasters precipitated by an asteroid hitting Earth.

Birds A series of well-preserved ancient birds and feathered dinosaurs showed that modern birds had dinosaur ancestors, and so they are included in a clade containing dinosaurs. Because dinosaurs are part of a larger clade of reptiles, modern birds are also reptiles. Archaeopteryx was the first bird-like fossil discovered. From the late Jurassic Period, it was a small, running dinosaur with highly evolved feathers. Characteristics of birds include feathers; strong, lightweight bones; two scale-covered legs; and front-limb wings. Birds are endoderms; most reptiles are ectotherms.

Mammals

The clade Mammalia includes about 5000 endothermic member-species sharing characteristics, including mammary glands, hair, and a four-chambered heart.

The First Mammals True mammals appeared during the late Triassic Period, and were small, resembling modern tree shrews. While dinosaurs ruled, mammals remained small and were probably more nocturnal. New evidence shows that the first members of modern mammalian groups evolved during this period. After dinosaurs became extinct, mammals underwent a long adaptive radiation. The Cenozoic Era is often called the Age of Mammals.

Modern Mammals By the beginning of the Cenozoic, three major mammal groups had evolved—monotremes, marsupials, and placentals. They differ in their means of reproduction and development.

CHAPTER 9

LESSON 3

Primate Evolution

READING TOOL **Sequence of Events** Use the following graphic organizer to identify in which order the different species of primates developed.

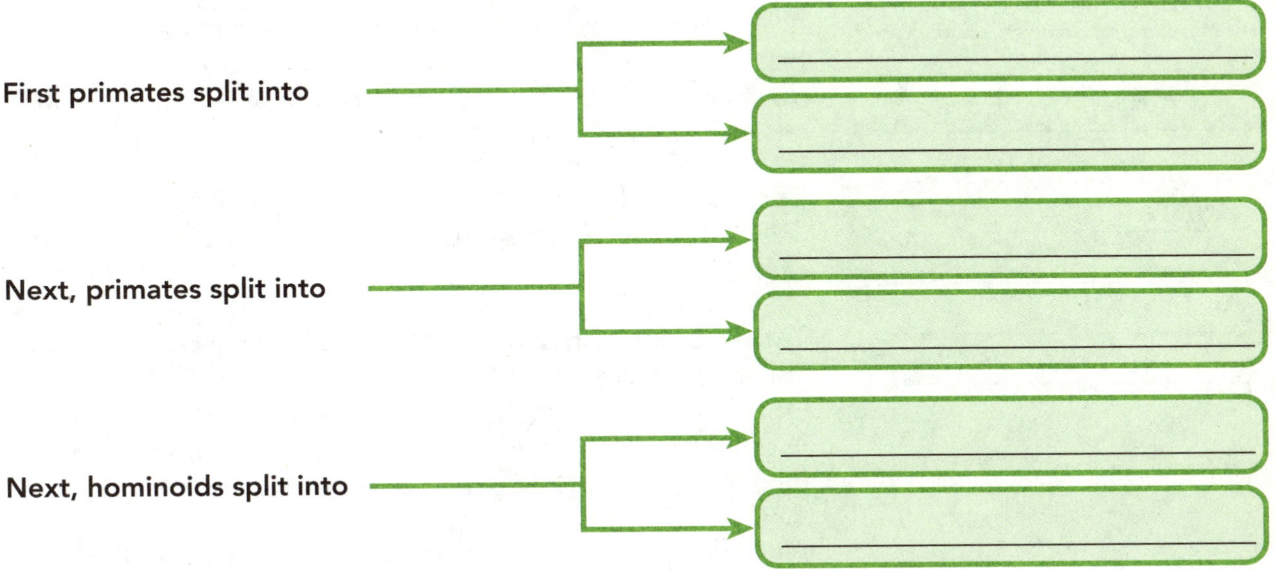

Lesson Summary

What Is a Primate?

KEY QUESTION *What characteristics do all primates share?*

Primates are intelligent and social creatures exhibiting complex behaviors. In general, a primate is a mammal with relatively long fingers, toes with nails instead of claws, arms that can rotate around shoulder joints, a strong clavicle, binocular vision, and a well-developed cerebrum.

Fingers, Toes, and Shoulders Primates typically have five flexible fingers and toes on each hand or foot to curl and grip objects. Most primates have thumbs and big toes, and arms well suited to climbing.

Binocular Vision Both eyes of many primates face forward, with overlapping fields of vision, depth perception, and a three-dimensional view of the world.

As you read, circle the answers to each Key Question. Underline any words you do not understand.

READING TOOL

Applying Prior Knowledge

The climates in Central and South America vary greatly from the climate and habitats of Africa. ☑ **Why does it make sense that monkeys in the former areas evolved long tails, while those in the latter areas did not?**

Well-Developed Cerebrum In primates, the cerebrum (or "thinking" part of the brain) is large and intricate, enabling complex behaviors. Many primate species create elaborate social systems that include extended families, adoption of orphans, and even warfare between rival troops.

Evolution of Primates

KEY QUESTION *What are the major groups of primates?*

Humans and other primates share a common ancestor that lived over 65 million years ago, though the two groups split early. Primates in one groups, which contains lemurs and lorises, don't look much like typical monkeys. The other group includes tarsiers and the anthropoids, or humanlike primates.

Lemurs and Lorises Most lemurs and lorises are small and nocturnal, have large eyes that see in the dark, and have long snouts.

Tarsiers and Anthropoids Primates more closely related to humans than lemurs belong to a different group having broader faces and widely separated nostrils. The group includes Asian tarsiers and anthropoids, the latter of which split into two groups about 45 million years ago.

New World Monkeys One anthropoid branch, the New World monkeys, is found in Central and South America. They mainly live in trees, have long flexible arms, and have long prehensile tails.

Old World Monkeys and Great Apes The other anthropoid branch includes the Old World monkeys and great apes and evolved from Africa and Asia. Old World monkeys spend time in trees, but lack prehensile tails. Great apes, or **hominoids**, include gibbons, orangutans, chimpanzees, and humans.

BUILD Vocabulary

hominoids group of anthropoids that includes gibbons, orangutans, gorillas, chimpanzees, and humans

opposable thumb thumb that enables grasping objects and using tools

Using Prior Knowledge Very few species on our planet have opposable thumbs. ☑ **What advantages do opposable thumbs give to animals?**

Hominin Evolution

KEY QUESTION *What adaptations enable later hominin species to walk upright?*

Between 6 and 7 million years ago, hominins, the lineage that includes modern humans and closely related species, split from the lineage that led to chimpanzees. Hominins evolved **opposable thumbs** and large brains. The skull, neck, spinal column, hip bones, and leg bones of early hominin species changed shape in ways that enabled later species to walk upright. Hominins, brains are much larger than those of chimpanzees with the biggest difference being the size of the cerebrum.

Hominin Relationships The hominin fossil record includes seven species and a few subspecies. All of these are relatives of modern humans, but not all are human ancestors.

Visual Reading Tool: Comparing Primates

Lemurs | Lorises and bush babies | Tarsiers | New World monkeys | Old World monkeys | Gibbons | Orangutans | Gorillas | Chimpanzees | Humans

Lemurs and lorises
Tarsiers
Anthropoids

Compare and contrast physical characteristics and locations of various primates. Enter your answers into the chart.

	Lemurs & Lorises	Tarsiers & New World Monkeys	Old World Monkeys & Hominoids
Physical characteristics			
Locations			

New Findings and New Questions The study of human ancestors, which includes studying fossils and DNA, is constantly changing. Since the 1990s, fossil discoveries have more than doubled the number of known hominin species. The oldest known hominin is the *Sahelanthropus*, which is about 7 million years old, though scientists are still debating whether the creature was a true hominin, as well as how it relates to other fossil hominins and to humans.

Australopithecus The genus *Australopithecus* lived from about 4 million to about 1.5 million years ago. They walked on two feet, or were **bipedal**. Their skeletons suggest they spent time in trees, while their tooth structure suggests they ate a lot of fruit. The best-known species is *Australopithecus afarensis*, of which the best-known specimen, called "Lucy," was discovered in 1974. In 2006, "the Dikka Baby" fossil, another *A. afarensis* specimen, was found in Africa. Leg bones confirmed that it was bipedal, and arm and shoulder bones suggest that it was a stronger climber than modern humans.

BUILD Vocabulary

bipedal having two-foot locomotion

Related Words Humans are the only purely bipedal animals on our planet. Most other animals are quadrupedal. ☑ **Based upon what you know about the word *bipedal*, and what you know about numerical prefixes, how many legs does a quadruped walk on?**

____

READING TOOL

Sequence of Events

Between 6 and 7 million years ago, hominins split from the lineage that would become chimpanzees.

☑ **Considering all of hominin development, what were the last two major developments of note?**

____

____

____

____

The Road to Modern Humans

KEY QUESTION *What is the current scientific thinking about the genus Homo?*

Many species in our genus existed before *Homo sapiens*, with at least three other *Homo* species existing alongside early humans.

The Genus Homo A new group of hominin species appeared in the fossil record about 2 million years ago. Several resembled modern humans enough to be classified in the genus *Homo*. The earliest species assigned to *Homo* is *Homo ergaster*.

Homo naledi A collection of hominin remains, referred to as *Homo naledi*, was discovered in 2015 in South Africa. The fossils included nearly complete skeletons from several small-brained hominins with a mix of ape-like and human-like species.

Homo neanderthalensis (or H. sapiens neanderthalensis) Neanderthals flourished in Europe and Western Asia about 200,000 years ago. They made stone tools, lived in complex social groups, had controlled use of fire, were expert hunters, and buried their dead with simple rituals. Fossils showed that they survived in parts of Europe until 28,000 to 24,000 years ago.

Out of Africa—But When and Who? Researchers agree that our genus originated in Africa and migrated all over the world. Questions remain about the evolution and migration of species within our genus. Evidence suggests that some hominins left Africa long before *Homo sapiens* evolved, and scientists believe that several species migrated in waves.

Homo erectus in Asia Some researchers suggest that groups of *Homo erectus* left Africa and traveled to Southeast Asia, indicating that they may have wandered far from Africa.

The First Homo sapiens Paleontologists debate where and when *Home sapiens* arose. The multiregional hypothesis suggests that modern humans evolved independently in several places, while other genetic evidence suggests that modern humans can be traced back to interbreeding ancient hominin species. The "out of Africa" theory suggests that modern humans evolved in Africa 200,000 years ago, migrated through the Middle East, and replaced earlier hominin species.

Modern Humans *Homo sapiens* with modern skeletons arrived in the Middle East about 100,000 years ago. By about 50,000 years ago, *Homo sapiens* were using tools made out of stone, bones, and antlers. They were also performing rituals when they buried the dead. In short, *Homo sapiens started* behaving like modern humans of today. During this time, too, Neanderthals and *Homo sapiens* lived in the same environment for thousands of years.

CHAPTER 9

LESSON 4

Social Interactions and Group Behavior

READING TOOL **Compare and Contrast** Compare and contrast the similarities and differences among each of the identified items. List two similarities and one difference in each row.

Items	Similarities	Differences
Habituation & Insight Learning		
Classical & Operant Conditioning		
Courtship & Territoriality		
Visual, Chemical, and Sound Signals		

1. What type of conditioning, or learning, are you demonstrating by studying for a test, and why?

____

____

____

____

____

2. Explain one similarity and one difference between human societies and bee societies.

Similarity: ______________________________

____

Difference: ______________________________

____

____

Lesson Summary

Behavior and Evolution

As you read, circle the answers to each Key Question. Underline any words you do not understand.

KEY QUESTION *How can behavior serve as an adaptation that affects reproductive success?*

Behavior is a response to a stimulus within an organism's environment. Although many behaviors are triggered by external stimuli, an individual's response to that stimulus often depends on its internal condition. Some behaviors are also influenced by inherited genes, and can therefore evolve in response to natural selection.

BUILD Vocabulary

behavior way an organism reacts to changes in its internal condition or external environment

Related Words To understand behavior, it is important to know the difference between internal and external conditions and stimuli. Internal stimuli are based on something an individual feels, like hunger, pain, or love. External stimuli are those that exist outside of the body. **What are some external stimuli that can change the behavior of an organism?**

____

____

Learned Behavior

KEY QUESTION *What are the major types of learning?*

Many complex animals live in unpredictable environments where fitness depends on changing behaviors as a result of learning. Scientists have identified four major types of learning, discussed below.

Habituation The simplest type of learning is habituation, a process by which an animal decreases or stops responding to stimuli that neither reward nor harm it.

Insight Learning The most complicated form of learning is insight learning, which occurs when an animal applies something it has already learned to a new situation.

Classical Conditioning Classical conditioning is a form of learning in which a certain stimulus comes to produce a particular response, usually through association with a positive or negative experience.

Operant Conditioning Operant conditioning occurs when an animal learns to behave in a certain way to receive a reward or to avoid punishment. It was first described by B.F. Skinner, who performed tests on animals using a "Skinner Box," which had a button or lever that delivered a food reward when pressed. The animal learned through operant conditioning that pressing the lever meant it would be given food.

READING TOOL

Cause and Effect

Domesticated animals rely on humans to take care of them. **If a cat learns that when he wakes his human up in the morning, the human provides him with food, what effects might this have on the cat's behavior? Name two.**

____

____

____

____

____

____

____

Behavioral Cycles

KEY QUESTION *How do periodic environmental changes affect behavior?*

Animals are affected by the environment, and do not behave in the same way all the time or in all places. Many animals respond to periodic environmental changes with daily behavioral cycles, called circadian rhythms, or seasonal behavioral cycles.

Social Behavior

KEY QUESTION *How can social behaviors increase evolutionary fitness?*

Social behaviors, such as choosing mates, defending territories or resources, and forming social groups, can increase evolutionary fitness.

Courtship Members of sexually reproducing animal species must locate and mate with other members of the same species to reproduce. Courtship is behavior during which members of one sex advertise their willingness to mate, and members of the opposite sex choose which mate they will accept.

Territoriality and Aggression Many animals occupy and defend a specific area, or territory, that contains resources, like food, water, nesting sites, shelter, and potential mates. If a rival enters a territory, the "owner" attacks in an effort to drive the rival away.

Animal Societies A **society** is a group of animals of the same species that interact closely and often cooperate. Societies offer a range of advantages that can produce differential reproductive success between group members and individuals. Members of a society are often related to one another. The theory of **kin selection** holds that helping relatives can improve an individual's evolutionary fitness because related individuals share a large proportion of their genes. Helping relatives survive increases the chances that the shared genes will be passed to offspring.

Communication

KEY QUESTION *How do animals communicate?*

Social behavior involves more than one individual and requires **communication**—the passing of information from one individual to another. Animals may use a variety of signals to communicate, explained below.

Visual Signals Many animals use visual signals, and have eyes able to sense shapes and colors.

Chemical Signals Many animals have well-developed senses of smell, and they communicate with chemical signals, like pheromones.

Sound Signals Many species make and detect sounds, with some evolving elaborate sound-based communication systems.

Language The most complicated form of communication is **language**—a system that combines sounds, symbols, and gestures according to rules about sequence and meaning, such as grammar and syntax.

BUILD Vocabulary

society group of closely related animals of the same species that interact for the benefit of the group

kin selection theory that states that helping relatives can improve an individual's evolutionary fitness because related individuals share a large proportion of their genes

communication passing of information from organism to another

language system of communication that combines sounds, symbols, and gestures according to a set of rules about sequence and meaning, such as grammar and syntax

Multiple Meanings The word *society* is not only used to describe a group of same-species animals working together for the benefit of all. It is also used to describe people living in a more or less ordered community, as well as an organization or club formed for a particular activity or purpose.

☑ **Explain a way that being in a society benefits animals.**

____

____

____

____

9 Chapter Review

Review Vocabulary

Match the vocabulary term to its definition.

1. ________ tetrapod
2. ________ bipedal
3. ________ hominoids

a. refers to two-foot locomotion

b. refers to a vertebrate with four limbs

c. group of anthropoids that includes gibbons, orangutans, chimpanzees, and humans

Fill in the blanks with the correct terms.

4. ____________________ is a body plan in which a single imaginary line can divide the left and right sides into mirror images of each other, while ____________________ is a body plan in which any number of imaginary planes drawn through the center could divide it into equal halves.

Review Key Questions

Provide evidence and details to support your answers.

5. In your own words, describe three things organisms do to maintain a state of homeostasis.

6. Why are the cladograms continually changing?

7. Where did *Homo sapiens* evolve, and how did they move around Earth?

8. Explain how visual, chemical, and sound signals coming from humans are different if they are trying to attract mates or repel rivals.

CHAPTER 10

LESSON 1

The Work of Gregor Mendel

READING TOOL **Sequence of Events** As you read your textbook, identify the sequence of events that influenced Mendel's conclusions about genetics. Pay attention to his experiments with the F_1 and F_2 generations. The first event is filled in for you.

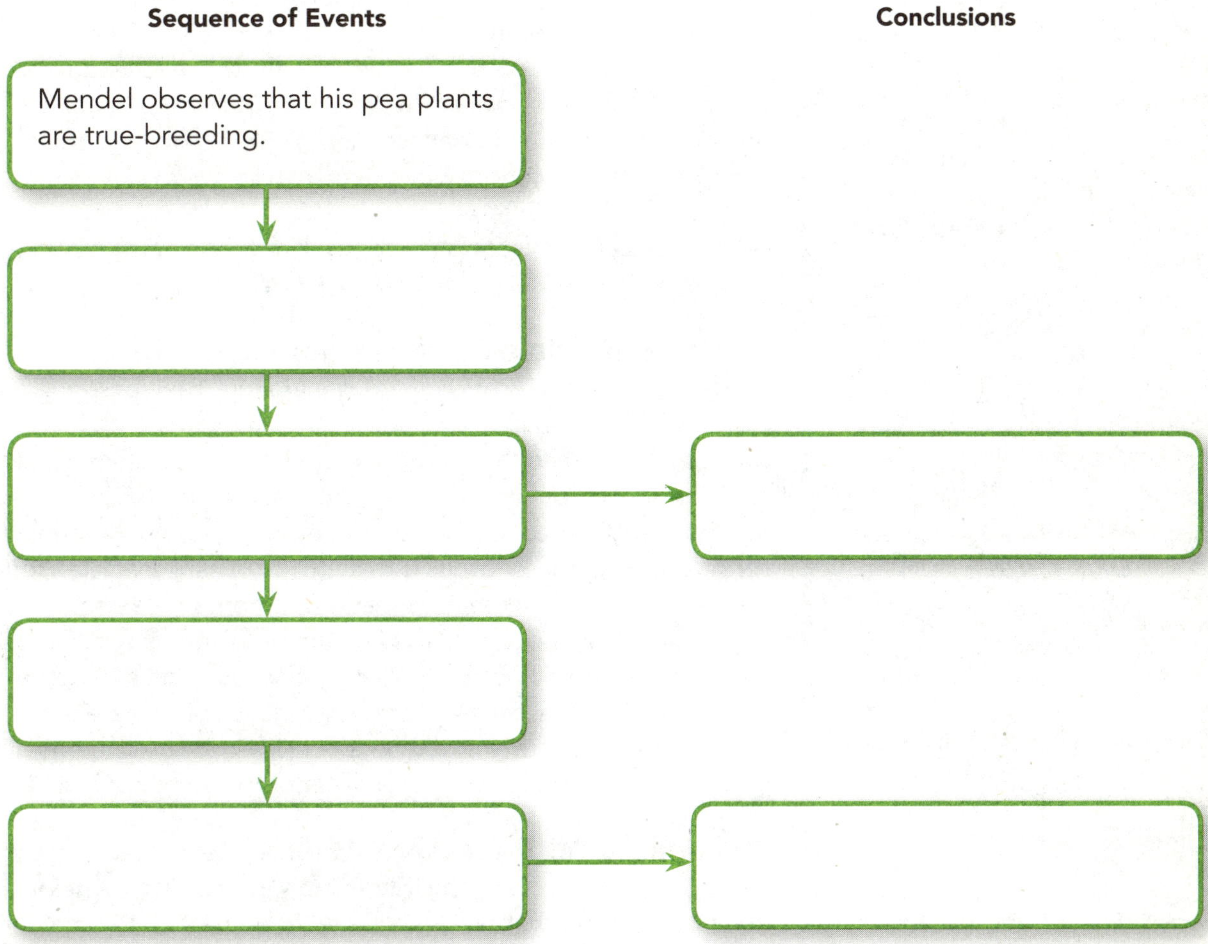

Lesson Summary

Mendel's Experiments

KEY QUESTION *Where does an organism get its unique characteristics?*

All living organisms have characteristics that are inherited from their parent or parents. The scientific study of biological inheritance is called **genetics**. Modern genetics began with the work of Gregor Mendel in the 1800s. Mendel studied inheritance in peas, which produce hundreds of offspring.

As you read, circle the answers to each Key Question. Underline any words you do not understand.

Build Vocabulary

genetics scientific study of heredity

fertilization process of sexual reproduction in which male and female reproductive cells join to form a new cell

trait specific characteristic of an individual

hybrid offspring of crosses between parents with different traits

gene sequence of DNA that codes for a protein and thus determines a trait; factor that is passed from parent to offspring

allele one of a number of different forms of a gene

principle of dominance Mendel's second conclusion, which states that some alleles are dominant and others are recessive

segregation separation of alleles during gamete formation

gamete sex cell

Using Prior Knowledge Some cars are hybrid automobiles. Most automobiles are powered only by gasoline engines, and a few are powered by electric motors. In a hybrid automobile, there are two sources of power: a gasoline engine and an electric motor. ☑ **Give an example of a trait that Mendel studied in hybrids.**

____

____

The Role of Fertilization During sexual reproduction, male and female reproductive cells join in a process called **fertilization** to produce a new cell. In peas, this cell develops into an embryo encased in a seed. Peas are normally self-pollinating, which means that the male and female reproductive cells come from within the same flower. Plants like this inherit all of its characteristics from its single parent. Mendel had stocks of pea plants with different specific characteristics, or **traits**. The stocks were true-breeding, meaning that when self-pollinated, the offspring had the same traits as the parents. One stock produced tall plants and another produced short plants. One produced green seeds and another produced yellow seeds. Mendel crossed his stocks of plants, causing one plant to reproduce with a plant from another stock. He did this by placing pollen from one plant on the female part of another. This process is called cross-pollination. Mendel examined seven traits of pea plants. Each trait had two different characteristics, such as green or yellow pods. The offspring of crosses between parent plants with different characteristics are called **hybrids**.

Genes and Alleles In genetic crosses, the original pair of plants are called the P, or parental, generation. Their offspring are called the F_1, or first filial, generation. In one experiment, Mendel was surprised to find that his F_1 plants had the characteristics of only one of their parents. For each cross, the characteristics of the other parent seemed to disappear from the offspring. Mendel's first conclusion from these results is that an individual's characteristics are determined by factors that are passed from one parental generation to the next. Today we call these factors **genes**. Each trait that Mendel studied was controlled by a single gene that occurred in two varieties. The different forms or varieties of a single gene are called **alleles** (uh LEELZ). For the gene for pea plant height, one allele produced tall plants and another allele produced short plants.

Dominant and Recessive Alleles Mendel's second conclusion is called the **principle of dominance**. The principle of dominance states that some alleles are dominant and some alleles are recessive. An organism that has both a dominant allele and a recessive allele for a trait will show the dominant characteristic. Mendel found that the allele for tall plants was dominant over the recessive allele for short plants, and the allele for yellow pods was dominant over the recessive allele for green pods.

Segregation

KEY QUESTION *How are different forms of a gene distributed to offspring?*

Mendel had another question: Had the recessive alleles disappeared, or were they still present in the new plants? To find out, he allowed all seven kinds of F_1 hybrids to self-pollinate. This cross of the F_1 generation produced the F_2 (second filial) generation.

The F_1 Cross When Mendel examined the F_2 plants, he found that traits produced by the recessive alleles reappeared in this generation. About one fourth of the F_2 plants showed the trait controlled by the recessive allele. Why did these traits appear to disappear in the F_1 generation and then reappear in the F_2 generation?

Explaining the F_1 Cross Mendel assumed that a dominant allele had masked the corresponding recessive allele in the F_1 generation. However, the recessive trait did appear in the F_2 generation. This indicates that at some point the allele for yellow pods had separated, or segregated, from the allele for green pods. Mendel suggested that the **segregation** of the alleles for yellow and green pods occurred during the formation of the reproductive cells, or **gametes** (GAM eetz).

The Formation of Gametes All of the F_1 plants inherited an allele (*G*) for green pods from the green parent and an allele (*g*) for yellow pods from the yellow parent. (For each trait, we use a capital letter to represent the dominant allele, and the same letter in lowercase to represent the recessive allele). Because the allele for green pods is dominant, all of the F_1 plants (*Gg*) have green pods. During gamete formation, the alleles for each gene segregate from each other, so that each gamete carries only one allele for each gene. Each F_1 plant produces two kinds of gametes, those with the green pod allele (*G*) and those with the yellow pod allele (*g*). When a gamete with the allele for yellow pods pairs with another gamete with the allele for yellow pods, the resulting F_2 plant (*gg*) has yellow pods. If one or both gametes that pair have the allele for green pods (*GG* or *Gg*), an F_2 plant with green pods is produced.

READING TOOL

Cause and Effect What happened to the yellow-pod characteristic in the F_1 cross?

☑ **Write the effect of the F_1 cross on the yellow-pod characteristic, and then write the cause.**

Effect: ______________________

____

____

Cause: ______________________

____

Visual Reading Tool: Segregation

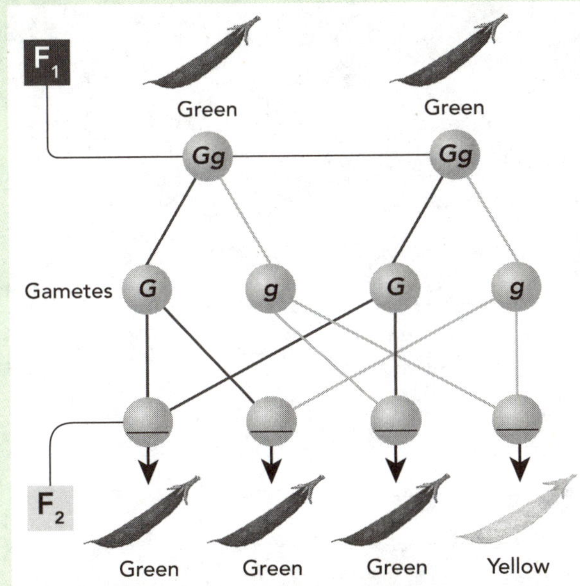

A cross between yellow-pod and green-pod pea plants results in only green-pod plants in the F_1 offspring. When the F_1 offspring are crossed with themselves, the yellow pods reappear in the F_2 generation. Use the figure to answer the questions.

1. In the figure, label each individual in the F_2 generation with the alleles it inherited from the F_1 generation.
2. What color is a pod with the *gg* alleles? ____________
3. What color is a pod with the *GG* or *Gg* alleles? ____________
4. Describe in your own words how a plant with a yellow pod can have two green-pod parents.

____

____

LESSON 2 Applying Mendel's Principles

READING TOOL Connect to Visuals Before you read, preview **Figure 10-7**. Try to infer the purpose of this diagram. As you read, compare your inference to the text. After you read, revise your statement if needed or write a new one about the diagram's purpose. Take notes on the lines provided. Then view the Punnett square and answer the questions below regarding the genotypes and phenotypes.

Inference:

____

____

Revision:

____

____

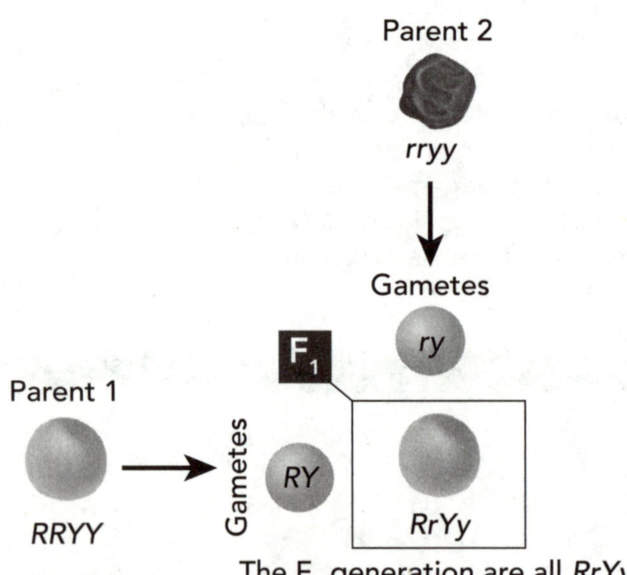

The F_1 generation are all *RrYy*.

1. What is the phenotype of parent 1? ____________________
2. What is the genotype of parent 1? ____________________
3. What is the phenotype of parent 2? ____________________
4. What is the genotype of parent 2? ____________________
5. What is the phenotype of the F_1 offspring? ____________________
6. What is the genotype of the F_1 offspring? ____________________
7. What kind of cross does this figure describe? ____________________

Lesson Summary

Probability and Heredity

KEY QUESTION *How can we use probability to predict traits?*

By analyzing his data, Mendel realized that the principles of probability could explain the results of his crosses. **Probability** is the likelihood that a particular event will occur.

Using Segregation to Predict Outcomes During gamete formation, alleles segregate randomly. Therefore, the principles of probability can predict the outcomes of genetic crosses, similar to the way probability is used to predict the outcomes of coin tosses. In Mendel's F_1 cross, each F_1 plant (*Gg*) has one green pod allele and one yellow pod allele, so $\frac{1}{2}$ of the gametes produced by the F_1 plants have yellow alleles (*g*). Because the yellow pod (*g*) allele is recessive, the only way to produce a plant with yellow pods (*gg*) is for two gametes, each carrying the *g* allele, to combine. Each gamete produced by the F_1 plants has a one in two, or $\frac{1}{2}$, chance of carrying the *g* allele. Since each plant is formed from two gametes, the probability of both gametes carrying the *g* allele is $\frac{1}{2} \times \frac{1}{2} = \frac{1}{4}$. Therefore, roughly one fourth of the F_2 offspring should have yellow pods, and the remaining three fourths should have green pods. Both the *GG* and *Gg* allele combinations result in green pea pods. Organisms that have two identical alleles for a particular gene, such as *GG* or *gg*, are said to be **homozygous**. Organisms that have two different alleles for the same gene, such as *Gg*, are said to be **heterozygous**.

Probabilities Predict Averages Probabilities predict the average outcome of a large number of events. In genetics, the predicted ratios may only occur when observing a large number of offspring. An F_2 generation with only a few offspring may not match Mendel's predicted ratios, but if there are hundreds or thousands of offspring, the results should come close to the predicted ratios.

Genotype and Phenotype One of Mendel's most important insights is that every organism has a genetic makeup as well as observable physical characteristics. The physical traits are called the **phenotype**, and the genetic makeup is called the **genotype**. Mendel's F_2 plants had three different genotypes—*GG*, *Gg*, and *gg*—but only two phenotypes: green or yellow pods. The *GG* and *Gg* genotypes have the same phenotype, green pods.

As you read, circle the answers to each Key Question. Underline any words you do not understand.

BUILD Vocabulary

probability likelihood that a particular event will occur

homozygous having two identical alleles for a particular gene

heterozygous having two different alleles for a particular gene

phenotype physical characteristics of an organism

genotype genetic makeup of an organism

Using Prior Knowledge In math class, you have studied probability using coin tosses. Flipping a coin is like studying the genetics of a gene with two different alleles. Each coin flip has a probability of $\frac{1}{2}$ of landing heads up. The probability of flipping two coins and getting heads on both tosses is $\frac{1}{2} \times \frac{1}{2} = \frac{1}{4}$. ☑ **If you flip a coin 50 times, about how many times would you expect to get heads?**

____

Using Punnett Squares Punnett squares are one good way to predict the outcome of genetic crosses. **Punnett squares** use mathematical probability to help predict the genotype and phenotype combinations in genetic crosses. The number of possible alleles from each parent determines the number of rows and columns in the Punnett square.

Independent Assortment

KEY QUESTION *How do alleles segregate when more than one gene is involved?*

Mendel wondered if the segregation of one pair of alleles affects another pair. For example, does the gene that determines the shape of a seed affect the gene for seed color? This type of experiment is known as a two-factor, or dihybrid, cross because it involves two different genes. Single-gene crosses are monohybrid crosses.

Visual Reading Tool: Two-Factor Cross: F_2

The Punnett square shows the results of self-crossing the F_1 generation of a cross between round yellow peas and wrinkled green peas.

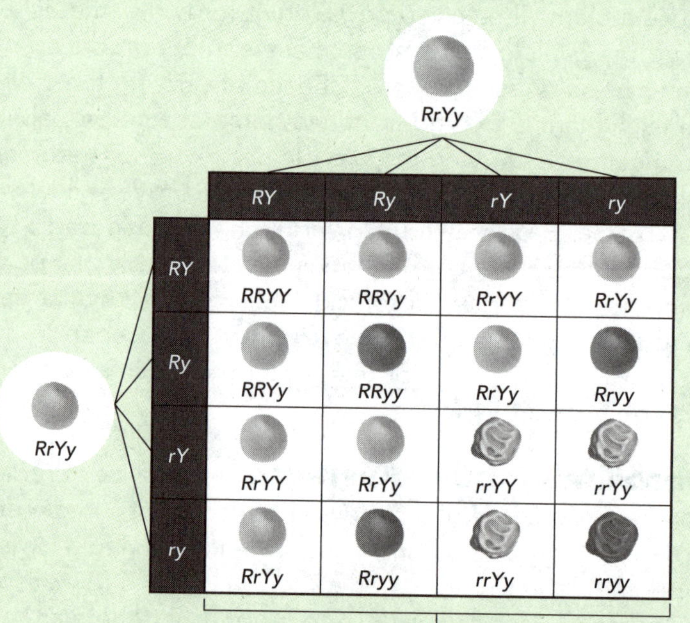

F_2 Generation

1. List the different genotypes in the F_2 generation. What is the frequency of each genotype? One is filled out for you.

Genotype	Frequency
RRYY	$\frac{1}{16}$
rryy	$\frac{1}{16}$

2. List the different phenotypes in the F_2 generation. What is the frequency of each phenotype? One is filled out for you.

Phenotype	Frequency
wrinkled, green	$\frac{1}{16}$

The Two-Factor Cross: F_1 First, Mendel crossed true-breeding plants that produced only round, yellow peas with plants that produced only wrinkled, green peas.

The genotype is *RRYY* for the round, yellow peas and *rryy* for the wrinkled, green peas. All of the F_1 offspring produced round yellow peas. This shows that the alleles for yellow and round peas are dominant and the alleles for green and wrinkled peas are recessive. The genotype of the F_1 plants is *RrYy*. The F_1 plants are all heterozygous for seed shape and color.

The Two-Factor Cross: F_2 Mendel then crossed the F_1 plants to produce F_2 offspring. Each F_1 plant was formed from the fusion of a gamete with the dominant *RY* alleles with a gamete carrying the recessive *ry* alleles. Would the two dominant alleles always stay together or would they segregate independently, forming new combinations? If they segregated independently, a Punnett square shows that there will be a 9:3:3:1 ratio of round, yellow seeds to round, green seeds to wrinkled, yellow seeds to wrinkled, green seeds. In Mendel's experiment, the F_2 plants produced 556 seeds in a roughly 9:3:3:1 ratio. There were 315 round, yellow seeds, and 32 wrinkled, green seeds. However there were 209 seeds that had round, green seeds or wrinkled, yellow seeds. These were phenotypes that were not found in either parent. Therefore, the alleles for seed shape segregate independently from the alleles for seed color. Genes that segregate independently do not influence each other's inheritance. The principle of **independent assortment** states that genes for different traits can segregate independently during the formation of gametes. Independent assortment explains much of the variation observed in organisms that have the same parents.

BUILD Vocabulary

Punnett square diagram that can be used to predict the genotype and phenotype combinations of a genetic cross

independent assortment one of Mendel's principles that states that genes for different traits can segregate independently during the formation of gametes

Word Origins The Punnett square is named after Reginald Punnett, a British geneticist from the early 1900s. ☑ **How many squares are in a Punnett square for a one-factor cross?**

____

How many for a two-factor cross?

____

READING TOOL

Use Structure Mendel's principles of heredity are listed on this page in a bulleted list. Read the list carefully and answer the question below. ☑ **Two offspring from the same parents can have different phenotypes. How is this possible?**

____

____

____

____

____

____

____

A Summary of Mendel's Principles

KEY QUESTION *What did Mendel contribute to our understanding of genetics?*

Mendel's principles of heredity, observed through patterns of inheritance, form the basis of modern genetics. The following principles of heredity apply to many organisms, not just pea plants.

- The inheritance of biological characteristics is determined by individual units called genes.
- Where two or more forms (alleles) of the gene for a single trait exist, some alleles may be dominant and others may be recessive.
- In most sexually reproducing organisms, each adult has two copies for each gene—one from each parent. These genes segregate from each other when gametes are formed.
- Alleles for different genes usually segregate independently of each other.

CHAPTER 10

LESSON 3

Other Patterns of Inheritance

READING TOOL **Main Idea and Details** As you read your textbook, identify the five different types of nontraditional inheritance. In each box in the graphic organizer below, give an example of that main idea from the text.

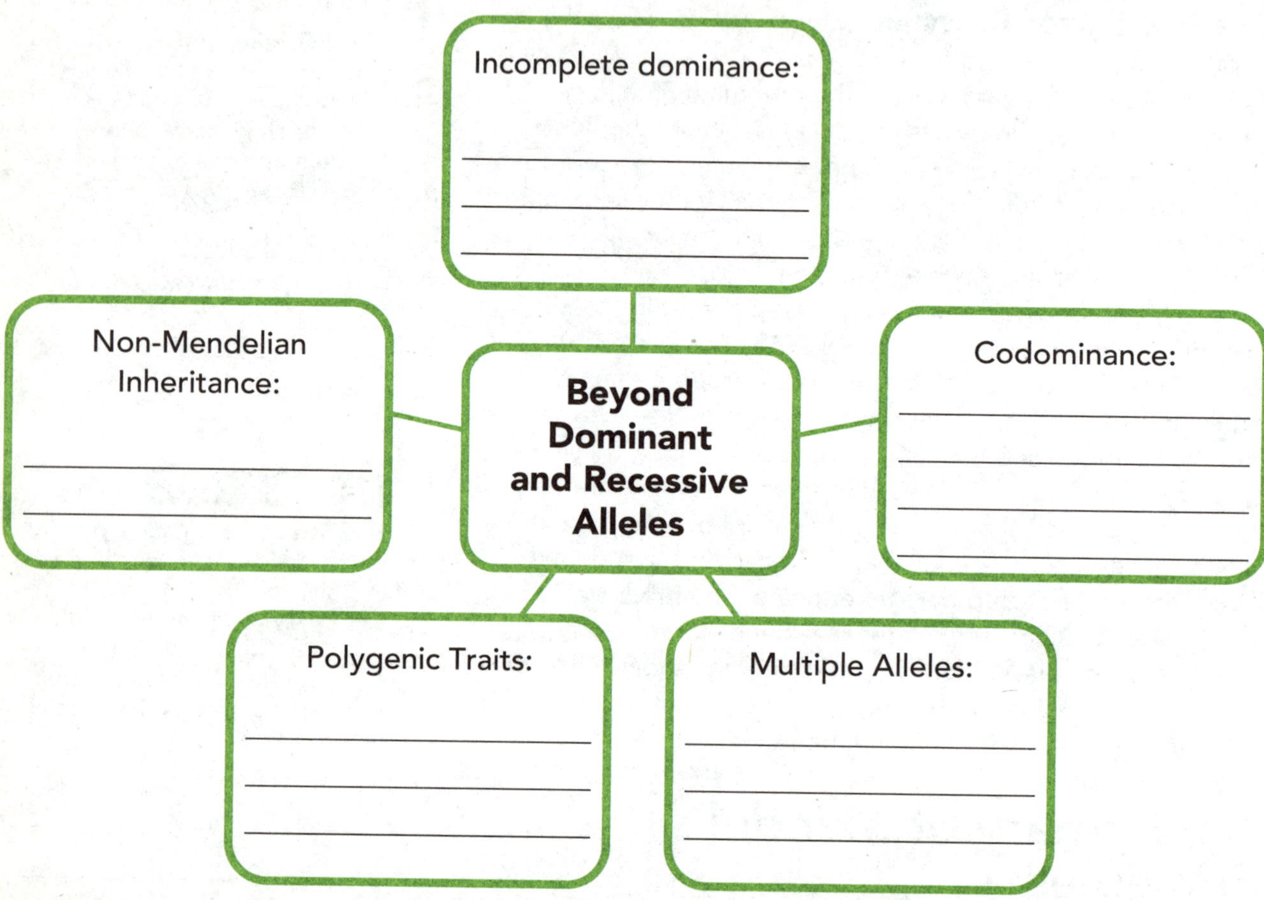

Lesson Summary

Beyond Dominant and Recessive Alleles

As you read, circle the answers to each Key Question. Underline any words you do not understand.

KEY QUESTION *What are some exceptions to Mendel's principles?*

Incomplete Dominance Some alleles are neither completely dominant nor recessive. In the four o'clock plant (*Mirabilis jalapa*), a cross between a red-flowered (*RR*) plant and a white-flowered (*rr*) plant produces F_1 plants with pink flowers (*Rr*). This situation is called incomplete dominance. In **incomplete dominance**, the heterozygous phenotype lies somewhere between the two homozygous phenotypes.

Codominance **Codominance** is when the phenotypes produced by both alleles are clearly expressed. In some chickens, the allele for black feathers is codominant with the allele for white feathers. Heterozygous chickens have a mixture of black and white feathers. Unlike the blending of red and white colors in heterozygous four o'clock flowers, the black and white colors remain separate in chickens.

Multiple Alleles In nature, many genes have more than two alleles. Many genes exist in several different forms and are therefore said to have **multiple alleles**. A gene with more than two alleles has multiple alleles. An individual usually has two copies of each gene, but in a population there are many different alleles. A rabbit's coat color is determined by a single gene with at least four different alleles, and the four alleles display a pattern of dominance that can produce four different coat colors.

Polygenic Traits Many traits are produced by the interaction of several genes. Traits controlled by two or more genes are said to be **polygenic traits**. Polygenic means "many genes." There may be as many as a dozen genes that are responsible for the many different shades of human eye colors.

Non-Mendelian Inheritance Some traits follow non-Mendelian patterns of inheritance. Leaf color in *Mirabilis jalapa* is determined by the leaf color in the maternal parent. This pattern, known as maternal inheritance, would not be predicted from Mendel's principles. Maternal inheritance occurs because chloroplasts and mitochondria are inherited from the maternal gamete, or egg cell. Chloroplasts and mitochondria contain genes on small DNA molecules. Genes in the chloroplast determine leaf color in *Mirabilis*. Therefore, this trait shows maternal inheritance. Another source of non-Mendelian inheritance is genetic imprinting. In genetic imprinting, certain genes have been chemically modified in one parent in a way that prevents their expression in the next generation.

Genes and the Environment

KEY QUESTION *Does the environment have a role in how genes determine traits?*

An organism's characteristics are not only determined by the genes it inherits. Environmental conditions can affect gene expression and influence genetically determined traits. In some butterflies, the amount of pigmentation in the wing is influenced by the length of daylight during the time of year the larva hatches. Butterflies hatched when there is less daylight have more pigmentation, and therefore darker markings, than butterflies hatched when there is more daylight.

BUILD Vocabulary

incomplete dominance situation in which one allele is not completely dominant over another allele

codominance situation in which the phenotypes produced by both alleles are completely expressed

multiple alleles a gene with more than two alleles

polygenic trait trait controlled by two or more genes

Prefixes *Poly-* is a prefix that means "many." Many roots that can use the prefix *poly-* can also use the prefix *mono-*, which means "one." **What would be a word for a trait controlled by a single gene?**

___

READING TOOL

Connect to Visuals In four o'clock plants, the gene for flower color is inherited by incomplete dominance. View the Punnett square below that shows the cross of a pink plant with a white plant.

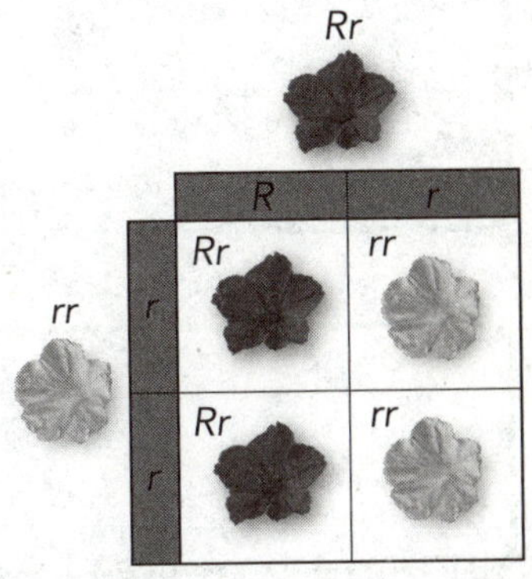

What is the probability that the offspring of this cross has white flowers?

___

CHAPTER 10

LESSON 4

Meiosis

READING TOOL **Sequence of Events** Identify the sequence of events in the process of meiosis. Take notes in the chart.

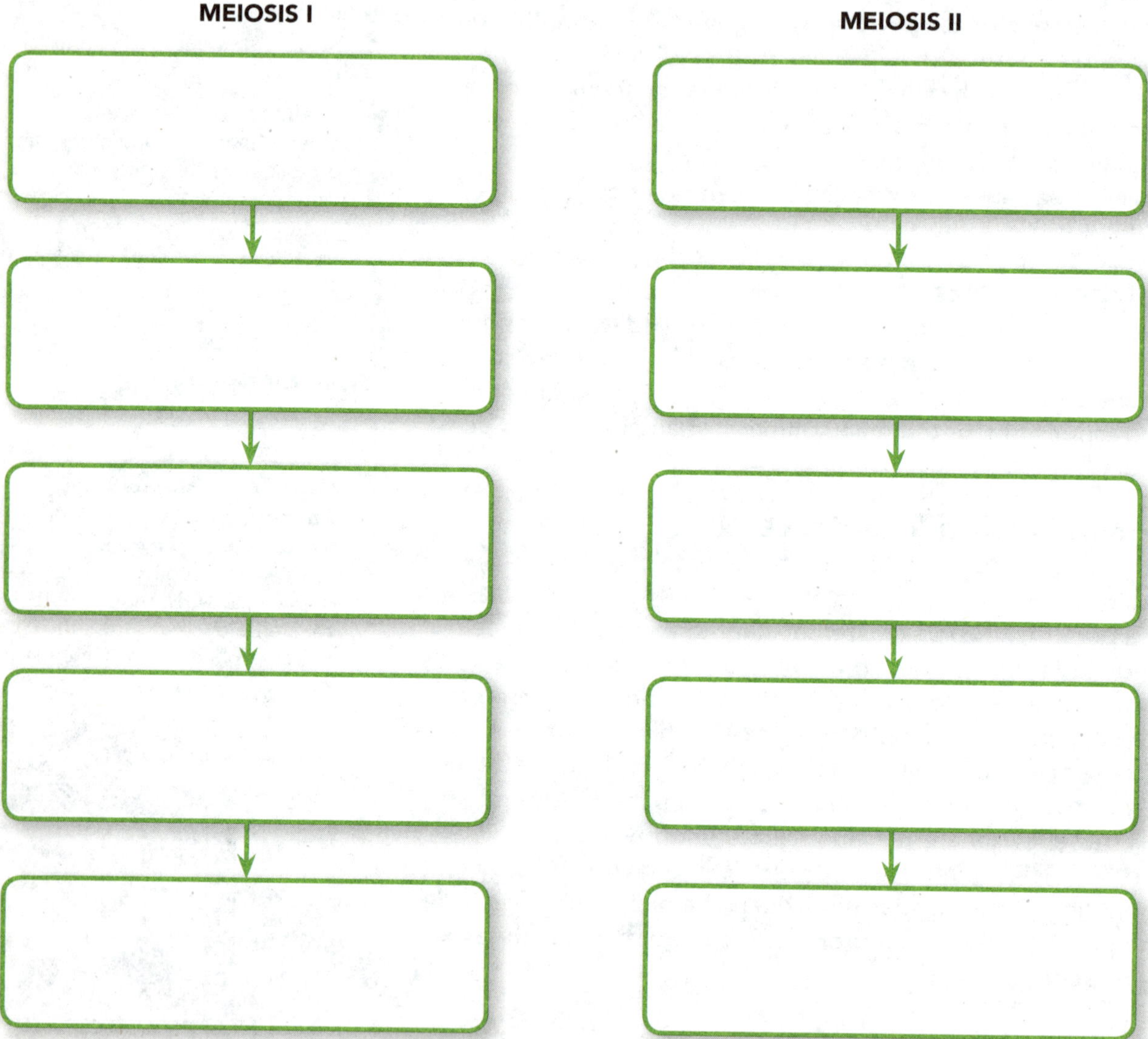

Lesson Summary

Chromosome Number

KEY QUESTION *How many sets of genes are found in most adult organisms?*

Mendel's principles require at least two events to occur. First, an organism with two parents must inherit one copy of every gene from each parent. Then, when the organism reproduces, its two sets of genes must be separated so that each gamete contains just one set of genes. Genes are located on chromosomes, strands of DNA and proteins in the cell.

Diploid Cells Each cell of the fruit fly *Drosophila melanogaster* has eight chromosomes. Four of these chromosomes come from the male parent and four from the female parent. The two sets of chromosomes are **homologous**, meaning that each chromosome from the male parent has a corresponding chromosome from the female parent. A cell with two sets of homologous chromosomes is **diploid**, meaning "double." The diploid cells of most adult organisms contain two complete sets of inherited chromosomes and two complete sets of genes. The diploid number of chromosomes can be represented by the symbol 2N. For *Drosophila*, the diploid number is 8, or 2N = 8.

Haploid Cells Some cells, such as gametes, have a single set of chromosomes and therefore a single set of genes. Such cells are **haploid**, meaning "single." The haploid number of chromosomes is represented by N.

Phases of Meiosis

KEY QUESTION *What events occur during each phase of meiosis?*

Sexually reproducing organisms produce haploid (N) gamete cells from diploid (2N) cells in meiosis (my OH sis). **Meiosis** is a process in which the homologous chromosomes of a diploid cell are separated from each other. Meiosis involves two distinct cell divisions called meiosis I and meiosis II. Through meiosis, a single diploid cell produces four haploid cells.

Meiosis I Prior to meiosis I, the cell replicates its chromosomes during interphase. Each replicated chromosome consists of two identical chromatids joined at the center.

As you read, circle the answers to each Key Question. Underline any words you do not understand.

BUILD Vocabulary

homologous type of chromosomes in which one set comes from the male parent and one set comes from the female parent

diploid a cell that contains two sets of homologous chromosomes

haploid a cell that contains only a single set of genes

meiosis process in which the number of chromosomes per cell is cut in half through the separation of homologous chromosomes in a diploid cell

Prefixes The prefix *homo-* means "same," and, in general usage, means "same position," or "same structure." *Homologous* chromosomes are two chromosomes from different parents that have the same genes and structure. **What other word from this unit has the prefix *homo-* and means to have two copies of the same allele?**

____

BUILD Vocabulary

tetrad structure containing four chromatids that forms during meiosis

crossing-over process in which homologous chromosomes exchange portions of their chromatids during meiosis

Word Origins *Tetrad* means "four" and comes from a Greek root. You may be familiar with other words or prefixes that mean "four," such as *quartet* or *quad-*, both of which come from Latin roots. Tetrapod and quadruped mean the same thing in regards to the number of legs that an animal has.

☑ **How many feet do tetrapod/quadrupeds have?**

____

Prophase I After interphase I, the chromosomes pair up. In prophase I of meiosis, each replicated chromosome pairs with its corresponding homologous chromosome. This pairing forms a structure with four chromatids called a **tetrad**. As the chromosomes pair, they sometimes exchange pieces of the homologous chromosomes in a process called **crossing-over**. Crossing-over produces new combinations of alleles on each chromosome.

Metaphase I and Anaphase I As prophase I ends, a spindle forms and attaches to each tetrad. During metaphase I of meiosis, paired homologous chromosomes line up across the center of the cell. Then the homologous pairs of chromosomes separate. During anaphase I, spindle fibers pull each homologous chromosome pair toward opposite ends of the cell.

Telophase I and Cytokinesis When anaphase I is complete, the separated chromosomes cluster at opposite ends of the cell. The next phase is telophase I, in which a nuclear membrane forms around each cluster of chromosomes. Cytokinesis follows, forming two new cells. Meiosis I produces two daughter cells. Since each pair of homologous chromosomes are separated, neither cell has the two complete sets of chromosomes found in a diploid cell. The two sets of chromosomes have been shuffled, so that the sets of chromosomes and alleles differ from those in the diploid cell that started meiosis I.

Meiosis II The two cells now enter a second meiotic division called meiosis II. Neither cell replicates its chromosomes before entering meiosis II.

Prophase II As cells enter prophase II, their chromosomes—each consisting of two chromatids—become visible. The chromosomes do not pair, because the homologous pairs were already separated during meiosis I.

Metaphase II, Anaphase II, Telophase II, and Cytokinesis During metaphase of meiosis II, the chromosomes line up in the center of each cell. As the cells enter anaphase, the paired chromatids separate. The final four phases of meiosis II are similar to those in meiosis I. However, the result is four haploid cells that contain the haploid number (N) of chromosomes. The haploid cells produced by meiosis develop into the gametes for sexual reproduction. The male gametes are usually called sperm, and the female gametes are called egg cells.

Comparing Meiosis and Mitosis

KEY QUESTION *How is meiosis different from mitosis?*

Meiosis and mitosis are very different. Mitosis can be a form of asexual reproduction. Meiosis is an early step in sexual reproduction. Mitosis and meiosis also differ in the way chromosomes are divided between daughter cells and in their number of cell divisions.

Replication and Separation of Genetic Material

A cell replicates, or copies, all of its chromosomes before entering either mitosis or meiosis. In mitosis, each daughter cell receives a complete diploid set of chromosomes. In meiosis, homologous chromosomes are separated, and each daughter cell receives only a haploid set of chromosomes. In meiosis, the two alleles for each gene are segregated and end up in different gamete cells. The sorting and recombination of genes in meiosis increases genetic variation.

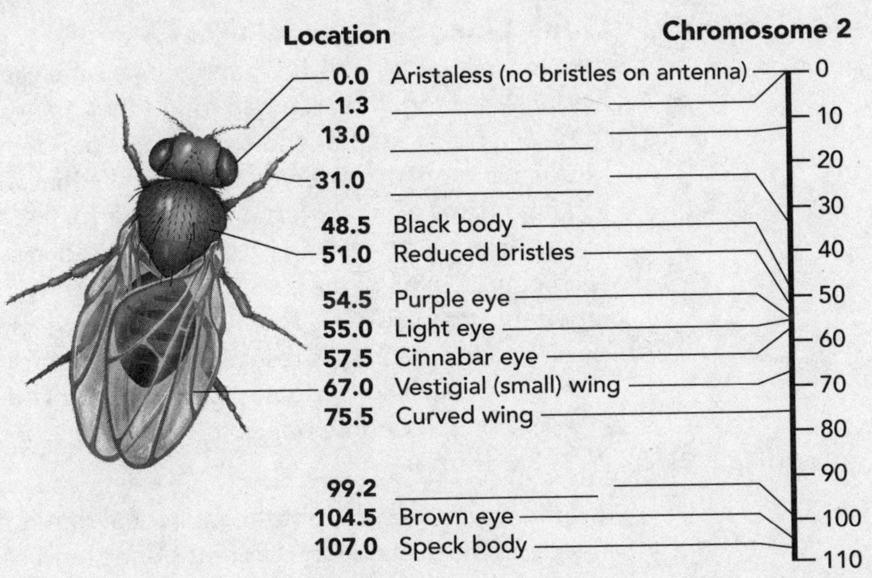

This gene map shows the locations of genes on chromosome 2 of the fruit fly *Drosophila melanogaster.*

1. Write in the following genes at their listed location on the gene map.
   Arc (bent wings): 99.2 Dumpy wing: 13.0
   Dachs (short legs): 31.0 Star eye: 1.3
2. Which pair of genes are closer together on the chromosome—*dachs* and *dumpy wing*, or *arc* and *star eye*? ______________________
3. Which pair of genes are more likely to assort independently—*dachs* and *dumpy wing*, or *arc* and *star eye*? ______________________
4. What process can lead to genes on the same chromosome assorting independently?
   ____
5. When does the process from question 4 occur during meiosis? ______________________

READING TOOL

Compare and Contrast

Mitosis and *meiosis* are two similar biological processes with important differences. They both start with a diploid cell, but end up with very different products. **☑ What is the final product for each process?**

____

____

____

____

____

____

Changes in Chromosome Number Mitosis does not change the chromosome number of the original cell. This is not the case for meiosis, which reduces the chromosome number by half. A diploid cell that enters mitosis with eight chromosomes will produce two diploid daughter cells, each with eight chromosomes. A diploid cell that enters meiosis with eight chromosomes will pass through two meiotic divisions to produce four haploid daughter cells, each with four chromosomes.

Number of Cell Divisions Mitosis is a single cell division. Meiosis requires two rounds of division. Mitosis results in the production of two genetically identical diploid cells, whereas meiosis produces four genetically different haploid cells.

Gene Linkage and Gene Maps

KEY QUESTION *How can two alleles from different genes be inherited together?*

Genes located on different chromosomes assort independently. What about genes on the same chromosome?

Gene Linkage Thomas Hunt Morgan's research on the *Drosophila* fruit fly showed that genes on the same chromosome are inherited together. Morgan found that many genes appeared to be "linked" together and are not independently assorted. Morgan and others observed many genes that were inherited together. They were able to group all of the fly's genes into four linkage groups. The linkage groups assorted independently from each other, but all of the genes in one group were inherited together. *Drosophila* has four linkage groups, and four pairs of chromosomes. Morgan's results led to two conclusions.

- First, each chromosome is a group of linked genes.
- Second, Mendel's principle of independent assortment holds true.

It is the chromosomes, not the individual genes, that assort independently. Alleles of different genes tend to be inherited together from one generation to the next when those genes are located on the same chromosome. Mendel missed gene linkage, because several of the genes he studied are on different chromosomes. Others are on the same chromosome, but are so far apart that they also assort independently.

Gene Mapping One of Morgan's students, Alfred Sturtevant, reasoned that the farther apart two genes were on a chromosome, the more likely it was that crossing-over would occur between them. If genes are far apart and more likely to cross-over, then they are more likely to assort independently. Sturtevant used the frequency of crossing-over between genes to determine their distances from each other. Sturtevant produced in one night a gene map showing the relative locations of each known gene on one of the *Drosophila* chromosomes.

10 Chapter Review

Review Vocabulary

Choose the letter of the best answer.

1. A diagram to predict the outcome of a genetic cross is a/an

A. independent assortment.

B. Punnett square.

C. polygenic trait.

2. The exchange of genetic information between homologous chromosomes during meiosis is called

A. segregation.

B. a polygenic trait.

C. crossing-over.

Match the vocabulary term to its definition.

3. ______ the offspring of parents with contrasting characteristics

4. ______ structure formed by paired homologous chromosomes

5. ______ the genetic makeup of an organism

a. hybrid

b. genotype

c. tetrad

Review Key Questions

Provide evidence and details to support your answers.

6. How are alleles segregated in sexually reproducing organisms?

____

____

7. In a Punnett square for a two-factor cross, is it possible for all of the offspring to be identical? Explain why or why not.

____

____

8. A parent with blood type A (genotype AO) and a parent with blood type B (genotype BO) have children with blood types A, B, and AB. What type of inheritance pattern is shown by the child with type AB blood and why?

____

9. How does meiosis increase genetic variation?

____

____

CHAPTER 11

LESSON 1

Identifying the Substance of the Gene

READING TOOL **Sequence of Events** As you read, pay attention to the experiments that were carried out to help scientists understand genes and how DNA affects living things. Take notes on the importance of each experiment in the graphic organizer below.

Griffith	Avery	Hershey-Chase

Lesson Summary

Bacterial Transformation

As you read, circle the answers to each Key Question. Underline any words you do not understand.

KEY QUESTION *What clues did bacterial transformation yield about the gene?*

Through experimentation and watching the process of transformation in bacteria, scientists learned that DNA stores and transmits genetic information from one generation to the next.

About a century ago, scientists who wanted to understand genetics better began experimenting to learn the chemical nature of genes. In 1928, the British scientist Frederick Griffith was investigating how certain types of bacteria produce pneumonia, a serious lung disease. Griffith had isolated two very similar types of bacteria from mice. Both types grew very well in culture plates in Griffith's lab, but only one of them caused pneumonia. The disease-causing bacteria (the "S" type) grew into smooth-edged colonies on culture plates, whereas the harmless bacteria (the "R" type) produced colonies with rough edges. The difference in appearance made the two types easy to tell apart.

Griffith's Experiments When Griffith injected mice with disease-causing bacteria, they developed pneumonia, while those injected with harmless bacteria remained healthy. An injection combining heat-killed, disease-causing bacteria and harmless bacteria still made the test mice sick.

Transformation Griffith identified that a chemical factor turned dead and harmless bacteria into disease-causing bacteria through a process called **transformation**. He determined that the disease-causing ability was transferred to the bacteria's offspring; thus transformation was caused by a gene.

The Molecular Cause of Transformation In 1944, Oswald Avery and a team of scientists tried to repeat Griffith's experiments to identify the molecule in the heat-killed bacteria that caused the transformation. They first removed molecules from heat-killed bacteria and used enzymes that destroyed their proteins, lipids, carbohydrates, and RNA. Despite this, transformation still occurred. A second experiment, where enzymes were used to destroy DNA, proved that when this happened, transformation did not occur. Their experiment proved that DNA must be responsible for the process of transformation.

Bacterial Viruses

KEY QUESTION *What role did bacterial viruses play in identifying genetic material?*

Experiments with bacterial viruses demonstrated that DNA and not the cell's protein coat carried genetic material.

Bacteriophages A **bacteriophage** is a virus that infects bacteria. One way bacteriophages infect bacteria is by inserting genetic information into a cell and reproducing until the bacteria bursts.

The Hershey-Chase Experiment To determine which part of the virus entered the bacterium, Hershey and Chase grew viruses with radioactive isotopes. These identified which molecules entered the bacteria—showing that DNA, not the protein coat, held the genetic material.

READING TOOL

Active Reading

During his experiments, Griffith figured out that the "S" type bacteria caused pneumonia in mice, and the "R" type did not. ☑ **Why was Griffith surprised when the mice injected with both harmless and heat-killed bacteria developed pneumonia and died?**

____

____

____

____

____

____

BUILD Vocabulary

transformation process in which one strain of bacteria is changed by a gene or genes from another strain of bacteria

bacteriophage (bak-tir-ē-ə-fāj) type of virus that infects bacteria

ROOT WORDS If you break the term *bacteriophage* down into two parts—*bacterio* and *phage*—it may help you understand it better. From the definition, you can see that *phage* is a type of virus. With *bacterio* at the beginning of it, you can see the relation between the two parts of the word. ☑ **What does a bacteriophage inject into a bacterial cell?**

____

The Role of DNA

KEY QUESTION *What is the role of DNA in heredity?*

DNA stores and copies genetic information, and then transmits it to offspring. Through DNA, genes are expressed and cells develop with specific characteristics.

Storing Information DNA's primary job is to store genetic information. It is the heredity molecule, and it controls cell development. All information for a single cell to develop into a complex organism is stored in DNA.

Copying Information DNA's second job is to copy all of its genetic information exactly.

Gene Expression DNA's third job is to express the genetic information into other cells so they develop into exactly what they are coded to be.

Visual Reading Tool: Bacteriophages and the Hershey-Chase Experiment

T4 Bacteriophage

1. Label the parts of a bacteriophage.
2. What part of the bacteriophage gets injected into a bacterial cell?

___

3. What part of the bacteriophage attaches and anchors itself to the bacteria?

___

4. What type of organism is a bacteriophage? Circle your answer.
   bacteria, virus, eukaryote

CHAPTER 11

LESSON 2

The Structure of DNA

READING TOOL **Connect to Visuals** Refer to the given scientists and the associated textbook figure numbers to help you understand the events that led to solving the structure of DNA. In the boxes, write the names of the scientists and a short description of the experiment or discovery.

Scientist	Summary of Experiment
Chargaff (Figure 11-10)	
Franklin (Figure 11-7)	
Watson and Crick (Figure 11-8)	

Lesson Summary

The Components of DNA

KEY QUESTION *What are the chemical components of DNA?*

DNA is a nucleic acid made of nucleotides joined into long strands or chains by covalent bonds.

Nucleic Acids and Nucleotides The monomer of nucleic acids is a nucleotide. They are long chains that are somewhat acidic. Nucleotides include three basic components: a 5-carbon sugar molecule, a phosphate group, and a nitrogenous base. Nucleotides join together to form strands of DNA.

Nitrogenous Bases The nucleotides that make up DNA have four types of nitrogenous bases: adenine, guanine, cytosine, and thymine. Each of these is often referred to by its first initial: A, G, C, or T. Covalent bonds connect the sugar of one nucleotide with the phosphate group of another nucleotide—and these can join in any sequence.

As you read, circle the answers to each Key Question. Underline any words you do not understand.

READING TOOL

Cause and Effect Let's explore cause and effect for a moment.

☑ **If Franklin had never used X-ray technology to take pictures of DNA, how might Watson and Crick's work have been different?**

____

____

____

____

Solving the Structure of DNA

KEY QUESTION *What clues helped scientists to determine the structure of DNA?*

The data in Franklin's X-ray pattern enabled Watson and Crick to build a model that explained the specific structure and properties of DNA.

Chargaff's Rule Biochemist Erwin Chargaff discovered similarities in the percentages of bases in DNA. He identified that each sample of DNA included an equal percentage of adenine (A) and thymine (T), as well as an equal percentage of guanine (G) and cytosine (C). This realization created what's known as Chargaff's rule: [A] = [T], and [G] = [C].

Franklin's X-Rays Scientist Rosalind Franklin used X-ray diffraction to study the structure of DNA molecules. After stretching the DNA fibers to make the strands as parallel as possible, she X-rayed the samples and recorded the patterns they created. Although she was not able to fully determine the structure of the molecule, her work provided insight into the helix shape of DNA strands.

The Work of Watson and Crick James Watson and Francis Crick were studying the structure of DNA at the same time as Franklin. Although they were able to build three-dimensional models of DNA, they still could not explain its properties. After seeing Franklin's X-ray of DNA, they determined that its structure was that of a double helix.

The Double-Helix Model

KEY QUESTION *What does the double-helix model show about DNA?*

The double-helix model explains Chargaff's rule of base pairing and how two strands of DNA are held together.

Antiparallel Strands The two strands of DNA's double helix run antiparallel, or in opposite directions. This structure connects the nitrogenous bases on each strand, and allows DNA to carry nucleotides in a specific sequence.

Hydrogen Bonds DNA strands are held together by hydrogen bonds formed between nucleotides. Nitrogenous bases bond with certain other bases in a process called **base pairing**. For DNA, adenine (A) bonds with thymine (T), and guanine (G) bonds with cytosine (C).

Base Pairing Base pairing clarified how Chargaff's rule applied to DNA, and why (A) = (T) and (G) = (C). This led to a Nobel Prize for Watson, Crick, and Franklin. Although base pairing explained DNA structure and sequences, it did not explain how DNA carried or used the genetic information.

BUILD Vocabulary

base pairing principle that bonds in DNA can form only between adenine and thymine and between guanine and cytosine

Related Words In genetics, the word *base* is shorthand for *nitrogenous base* and generally refers to A's, T's, C's, and G's.

What are the three main parts of a nucleotide?

____

____

Visual Reading Tool: Identifying Base Pairs

1. Fill in the missing nucleotides in the diagram.

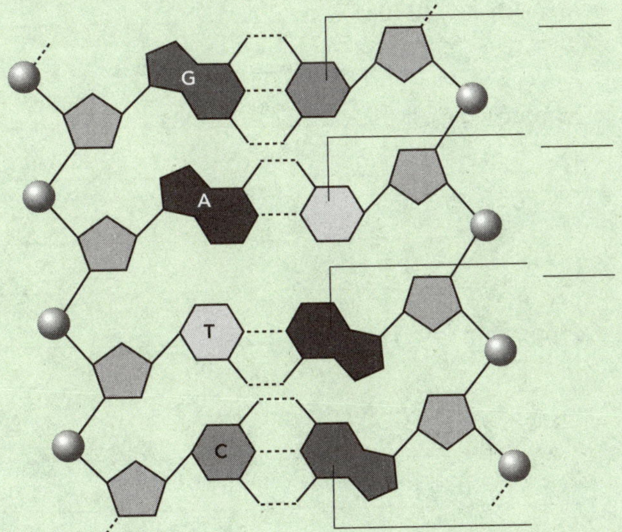

2. What do you notice about the number of hydrogen bonds that exist between the nucleotides?

____

3. Who was the scientist who discovered the rule of base pairing? ______________

4. On the diagram, what do the pentagons and spheres represent?

____

____

CHAPTER 11

LESSON 3

DNA Replication

READING TOOL **Main Idea and Details** As you read through this lesson, write the main ideas and supporting details in the chart below.

Copying the Code	• Main Idea: ________ ________ • Supporting Detail: ________ ________
The Replication Process	• Main Idea: ________ • Supporting Detail: ________ ________ ________
The Role of Enzymes	• Main Idea: ________ • Supporting Detail: ________ ________
Telomeres	• Main Idea: ________ ________ • Supporting Detail: ________ ________
Replication of Living Cells	• Main Idea: ________ ________ • Supporting Detail: ________ ________
Prokaryotic DNA Replication	• Main Idea: ________ ________ • Supporting Detail: ________ ________
Eukaryotic DNA Replication	• Main Idea: ________ ________ • Supporting Detail: ________ ________ ________

Lesson Summary

Copying the Code

KEY QUESTION *What is the role of DNA polymerase in copying DNA?*

DNA polymerase, or the main enzyme involved in DNA replication, joins nucleotides to synthesize a new complementary strand of DNA.

The Replication Process The DNA duplication process is called **replication**. During replication, DNA strands separate, and two complementary strands are created—one from each matching the opposite. Each new DNA molecule has one original and one new strand, making it identical to the original.

The Role of Enzymes An enzyme disconnects bonds between base pairs and unwinds the strands. Each strand becomes the model for the complementary strand. Then an enzyme called **DNA polymerase** creates the bonds connecting nucleotides, and ensures that each new strand is an exact copy of its original.

Telomeres The tips of eukaryotic chromosomes are called **telomeres**. These are hard to replicate, so the telomerase enzyme makes this happen. Telomerase adds short, repeated DNA sequences to telomeres during replication, and helps prevent the genes near the ends of chromosomes from getting lost or damaged during replication.

As you read, circle the answers to each Key Question. Underline any words you do not understand.

BUILD Vocabulary

replication process of copying DNA prior to cell division

DNA polymerase principal enzyme involved in DNA replication

telomere repetitive DNA at the end of a eukaryotic chromosome

Using Prior Knowledge There are three main differences between prokaryotes and eukaryotes. One difference is that one does not have a nucleus while the other does. Another difference is that the prokaryote is unicellular, while the eukaryote can be either unicellular or multicellular. **What is the third difference that you have learned about in this lesson?**

____

____

Visual Reading Tool: Structure Identification

1. Identify the following structures on the diagram: *DNA polymerase, new strand, nitrogenous bases, old strand, replication fork.*
2. On each side of the diagram, draw arrows to show the direction in which DNA replication is moving.
3. What is the job of DNA polymerase?

____

____

____

____

READING TOOL

Apply Prior Knowledge A normal human cell will have 46 chromatids before the S phase of the cell cycle: 23 from the mother and 23 from the father. ☑ **How many chromatids will a cell contain after DNA replication?**

____

Replication in Living Cells

KEY QUESTION *How does DNA replication differ in prokaryotic cells and eukaryotic cells?*

DNA replication in prokaryotic cells starts from one point and continues in two directions until replication is complete. In eukaryotic cells, it begins at multiple points and continues outward until complete.

Prokaryotic DNA Replication Replication in most prokaryotes begins at a single point and moves in two directions until the entire chromosome is copied. Regulatory proteins bind at a single point on a chromosome, sparking the S phase and DNA replication. The two chromosomes produced in this process are connected to separate points within a cell's membrane and get separated during cell division.

Eukaryotic DNA Replication Replication in eukaryotes is more complex and begins at multiple places on the DNA molecule, fanning out in two directions. Proteins ensure that base pairs are matched correctly and no damage occurs. Sometimes these proteins fail, and damaged sections of DNA are replicated. This causes changes to DNA base sequences and may have serious consequences for cell development.

Visual Reading Tool: Compare and Contrast

On each diagram below, label the following structures: *New DNA, Origin of replication, Replication fork, Unreplicated DNA.*

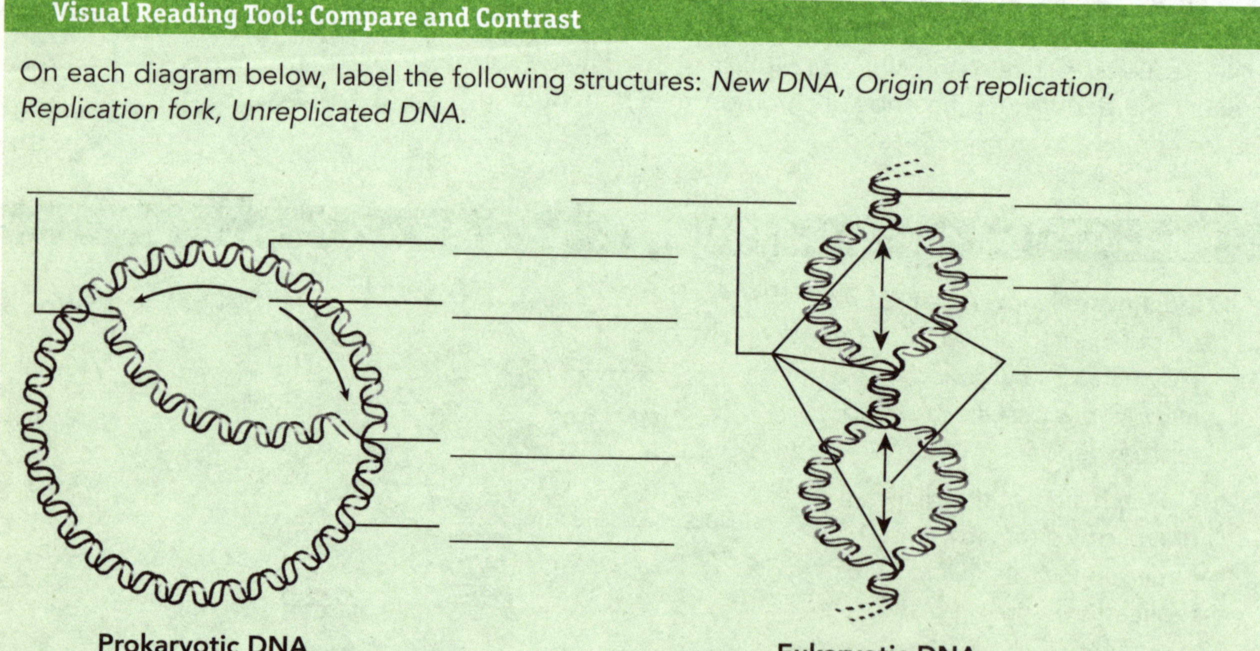

11 Chapter Review

Review Vocabulary

Match the vocabulary term to its definition.

1. ______	a kind of virus that infects bacteria	a. transformation
2. ______	the process in which bacteria is changed by a gene	b. bacteriophage
3. ______	principle that explains how bonds in DNA will form between specific nucleotides	c. base pairing
4. ______	process of copying DNA prior to cell division	d. replication

Fill in the blanks with the correct terms to complete the sentence.

5. __________ are unicellular organisms that have circular DNA, while __________ have linear DNA and can be unicellular or multicellular.

Review Key Questions

Provide evidence and details to support your answers.

6. Explain how studying viruses led to the discovery that DNA contains genetic material.

7. If DNA is charged with storing, copying, and expressing genetic traits, what might happen if DNA got damaged?

8. Explain how the sugars, phosphate groups, and nitrogenous bases in one strand of DNA connect to a complementary strand during replication.

9. Enzymes serve several functions during DNA replication. Name two of these functions.

CHAPTER 12

LESSON 1

RNA

READING TOOL **Compare and Contrast** As you read your textbook, identify the similarities and differences between RNA and DNA. Complete the Venn diagram to compare and contrast these molecules. A sample difference has been entered for you.

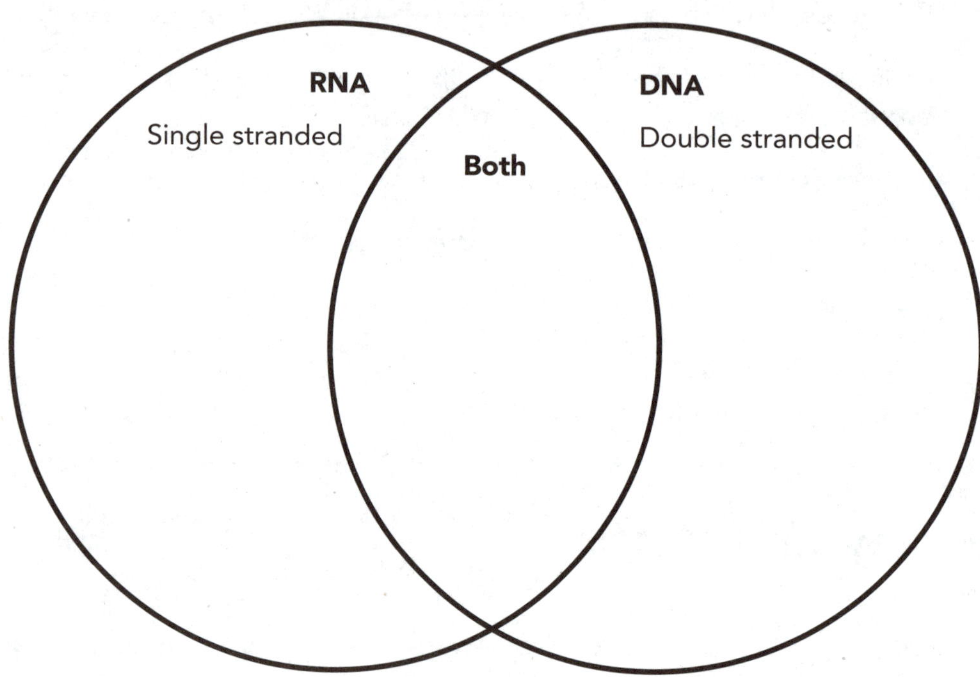

Lesson Summary

The Role of RNA

KEY QUESTION *How does RNA differ from DNA?*

As you read, circle the answers to each Key Question. Underline any words you do not understand.

BUILD Vocabulary

ribonucleic acid (RNA) single-stranded nucleic acid that contains the sugar ribose

DNA contains a genetic code that living cells can read, understand, and express. DNA is made of just four nucleotides joined together in double-stranded molecules that can be millions of bases in length. What exactly do those bases code for, and how does the cell "read" that code? That's where RNA comes in. RNA helps to put the genetic code into action. **RNA**, like DNA, is a nucleic acid that consists of a long chain of nucleotides.

Genes contain coded DNA instructions that tell cells how to build proteins. The first step in decoding these genetic instructions is to copy part of the base sequence from DNA into RNA. RNA then uses these instructions to direct the production of proteins, which help to determine an organism's characteristics.

Comparing RNA and DNA Like DNA, RNA is made up of nucleotides. Each nucleotide consists of a 5-carbon sugar, a phosphate group, and a nitrogenous base. However, DNA and RNA differ in three important ways. RNA uses the sugar ribose instead of deoxyribose, RNA generally is single stranded, and RNA contains uracil in place of thymine. These chemical differences make it easy for enzymes in the cell to tell DNA and RNA apart.

The differences between DNA and RNA allow them to perform separate functions in the cell. The information in DNA is always around, stored safely in the cell's nucleus, where it serves as a template to make multiple RNA copies. In contrast, RNA is synthesized when the products of a particular gene are needed. RNA copies travel to the ribosomes, which then put the coded instructions into action by assembling proteins in the cytoplasm.

Three Main Types of RNA RNA has many roles, one of which is protein synthesis. RNA controls the assembly of amino acids into proteins. There are three main types of RNA involved in protein synthesis: messenger RNA, ribosomal RNA, and transfer RNA. Each type of RNA molecule specializes in a different aspect of the job.

Messenger RNA (mRNA) Most genes encode instructions for assembling amino acids into proteins. The molecules of RNA that carry copies of these instructions from the nucleus to ribosomes in the cytoplasm are known as **messenger RNA** (mRNA).

Ribosomal RNA (rRNA) Proteins are assembled on ribosomes, which are small organelles composed of two subunits. The subunits are made of several **ribosomal RNA** (rRNA) molecules and as many as 80 different proteins.

Transfer RNA (tRNA) During the assembly of a protein, a third type of RNA molecule known as **transfer RNA** (tRNA) carries amino acids to the ribosome and matches them to the coded mRNA message.

BUILD Vocabulary

messenger RNA (mRNA) type of RNA that carries copies of instructions for the assembly of amino acids into proteins from DNA to the rest of the cell

ribosomal RNA (rRNA) type of RNA that combines with proteins to form ribosomes

transfer RNA (tRNA) type of RNA that carries each amino acid to a ribosome during protein synthesis

transcription synthesis of an RNA molecule from a DNA template

RNA polymerase enzyme that links together the growing chain of RNA nucleotides during transcription, using a DNA strand as a template

promoter specific region of a gene where RNA polymerase can bind and begin transcription

intron sequence of DNA that is not involved in coding for a protein

exon expressed sequence of DNA; codes for a protein

Prefixes *In-* is a prefix of Latin origin that can mean "in, on, or not."
☑ **Which meaning does *in-* have in the word *intron*? Explain your answer.**

____

____

____

____

____

RNA Synthesis

KEY QUESTION *How does the cell make RNA?*

A single DNA molecule may contain hundreds or even thousands of genes. However, only those genes being expressed are copied into RNA at any given time.

Transcription The process of copying a base sequence from DNA to RNA is known as **transcription**. In transcription, segments of DNA serve as templates to produce complementary RNA molecules.

READING TOOL

Academic Words

splice to join together

☑ **Why do exons have to be spliced together?**

____

____

____

____

____

Transcription is carried out by an enzyme called **RNA polymerase**. RNA polymerase first binds to DNA and separates the DNA strands. It then uses one strand of DNA as a template to assemble nucleotides into a complementary strand of RNA. A single gene can produce hundreds, or even thousands, of RNA molecules.

Promoters RNA polymerase does not bind to DNA just anywhere. The enzyme binds only to **promoters**, which are regions of DNA with specific base sequences that can bind to RNA polymerase. Other regions of DNA cause transcription to stop when an RNA molecule is completed.

RNA Editing New RNA molecules sometimes require editing before they are ready to be read. These pre-mRNA molecules have pieces cut out of them before they can go into action. The portions that are cut out and discarded are called **introns**. The remaining pieces, known as **exons**, are then spliced back together to form the final mRNA.

Visual Reading Tool: Introns and Exons

1. Use colored pencils to color the parts of pre-mRNA as it goes through the editing process to become RNA. Color the cap green, the introns blue, the exons purple, and the tail red.

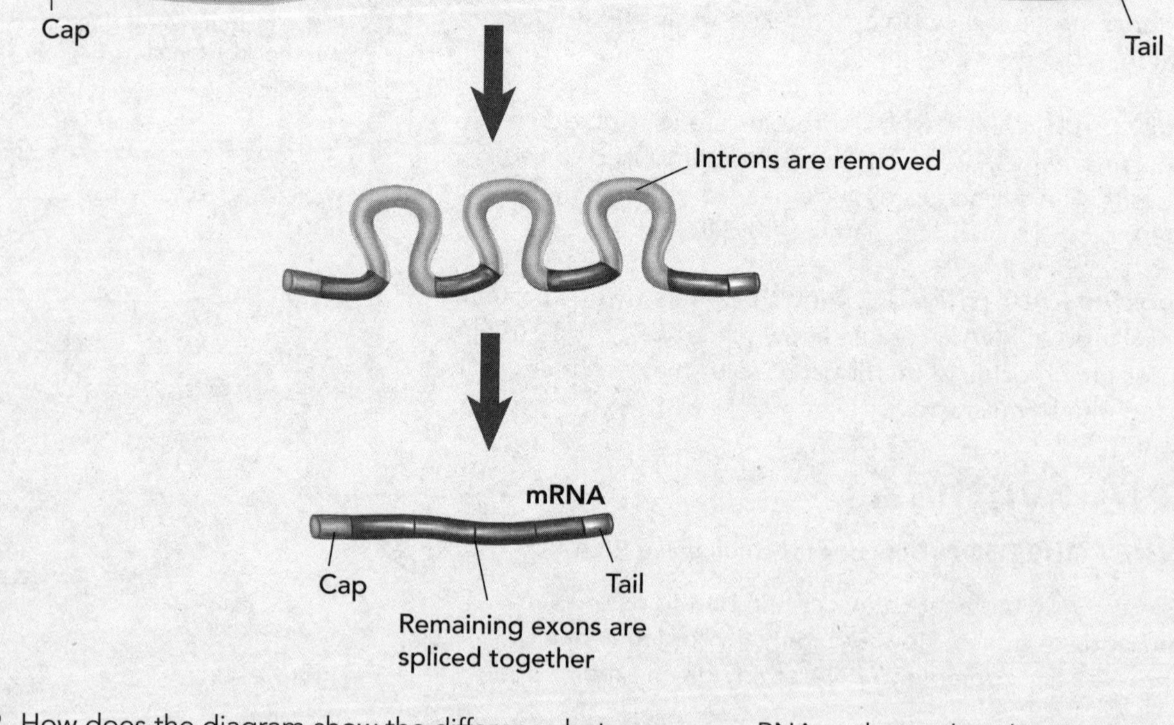

2. How does the diagram show the difference between pre-mRNA and completed mRNA?

____

____

CHAPTER 12

LESSON 2

Ribosomes and Protein Synthesis

READING TOOL **Sequence of Events** As you read your textbook, identify the steps of translation and protein synthesis. Complete the flowchart by writing the steps in the correct order. Use sequence words such as *first*, *then*, *next*, *after*, and *finally* to show the relationship between the steps. The first step has been entered for you.

First, a ribosome attaches to the mRNA molecule in the cytoplasm.

↓

↓

↓

↓

↓

Lesson Summary

As you read, circle the answers to each Key Question. Underline any words you do not understand.

BUILD Vocabulary

polypeptide long chain of amino acids that makes proteins

genetic code collection of codons of mRNA, each of which directs the incorporation of a particular amino acid into a protein during protein synthesis

codon group of three nucleotide bases in mRNA that specify a particular amino acid to be incorporated onto a protein

Root Words The root word of the word *codon* is the word *code*.

Why does this root word make sense?

____

____

____

The Genetic Code

KEY QUESTION *How does the genetic code work?*

Cells use the code in mRNA to build proteins, one amino acid after another. The first step in the process of decoding genetic messages is transcription, which is the copying of a nucleotide base sequence from DNA to mRNA. The next steps lead to the assembly of a protein. Proteins are made by joining amino acids together into chains called **polypeptides**. The specific order in which amino acids are joined together in a polypeptide chain determines the shape, chemical properties, and, ultimately, function of a protein.

The four bases of RNA form a kind of language with just four letters: A, C, G, and U. We call this language the genetic code. The **genetic code** is read three bases at a time. Each "word" of the code is three bases long and corresponds to a single amino acid. This three-base "word" is known as a codon. A **codon** consists of three consecutive bases that specify a single amino acid to be added to the polypeptide chain.

Visual Reading Tool: Reading Codons

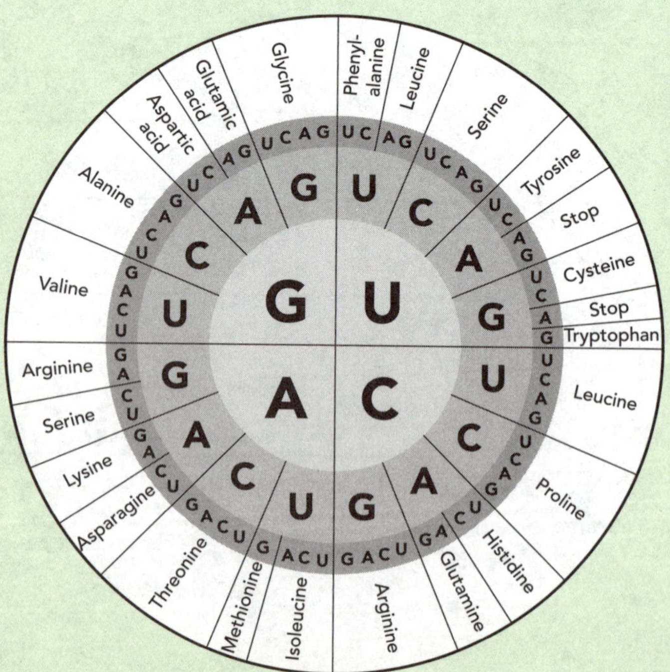

To interpret this diagram, read each codon starting at the inner circle and going toward the outer circle. For example, the codon CAC codes for the amino acid called histidine.

1. What amino acid does the codon AAU code for? ______________
2. What three codons signal that translation should stop? ______________
3. Is it possible for a codon to code for more than one amino acid? ______________
4. In RNA, uracil replaced what nitrogenous base that is found in DNA? ______________

How to Read Codons Because there are four different bases in RNA, there are 64 possible three-base codons ($4 \times 4 \times 4 = 64$) in the genetic code. Most amino acids can be specified by more than one codon. For example, UUA, UUG, CUU, CUC, CUA, and CUG all code for leucine.

Start and Stop Codons The methionine codon AUG serves as the "start" codon for protein synthesis. Following the start codon, mRNA is read three bases at a time, until it reaches one of three different "stop" codons, which end translation.

Translation

KEY QUESTION *What role does the ribosome play in assembling proteins?*

The sequence of bases in an mRNA molecule gives the order in which amino acids should be joined to produce a polypeptide. Once the polypeptide is complete, it then folds into its final shape or joins with other polypeptides to become a functional protein.

Ribosomes carry out the protein assembly tasks. Ribosomes use the sequence of codons in mRNA to assemble amino acids into polypeptide chains. The decoding of an mRNA message into a protein is a process known as **translation**.

Steps in Translation Translation begins when a ribosome attaches to an mRNA molecule in the cytoplasm. As each codon passes through the ribosome, several molecules of tRNA bring the proper amino acids into the ribosome. One at a time, the ribosome attaches these amino acids to a growing chain. Each tRNA molecule carries just one kind of amino acid. In addition, each tRNA molecule has a group of three unpaired bases that is called an **anticodon**. Each anticodon is complementary to a codon on mRNA. The polypeptide chain grows until the ribosome reaches a "stop" codon on the mRNA molecule. Then the ribosome releases both the newly synthesized polypeptide and the mRNA molecule.

The Roles of tRNA and rRNA in Translation The three major forms of RNA are all involved in the process of translation. The mRNA molecule carries the coded message that directs the process. tRNA molecules deliver the amino acids, enabling the ribosome to "read" the mRNA's message. Ribosomes themselves are composed of roughly 80 proteins and three or four different rRNA molecules. These rRNA molecules hold ribosomal proteins in place and carry out the chemical reactions that join amino acids together.

READING TOOL

Academic Words

specify To *specify* is to "identify precisely." Because each codon identifies only one amino acid, the genetic code can be accurately translated. ☑ **What is the "start" codon, and which amino acid does it specify?**

BUILD Vocabulary

translation process by which the sequence of bases of an mRNA is converted into the sequence of amino acids of a protein

anticodon group of three bases on a tRNA molecule that are complementary to the three bases of a codon of mRNA

Multiple Meanings The word *translation* is also used to describe the process of changing speech or text from one language to another. ☑ **How is the translation of mRNA like the translation of a language?**

Visual Reading Tool: Transcription and Translation

Fill in the missing labels on the diagram of protein synthesis.

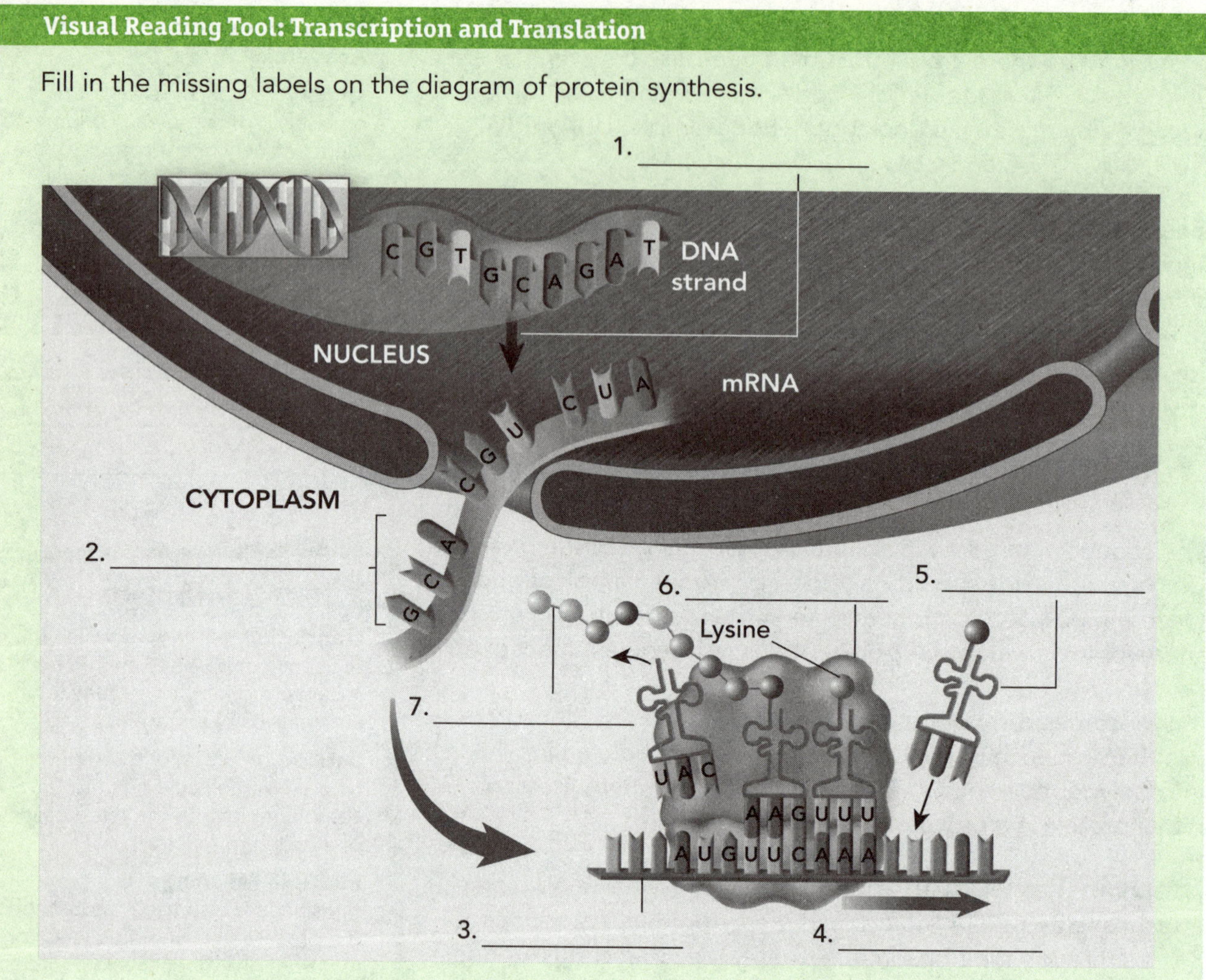

Molecular Genetics

KEY QUESTION *How does molecular biology relate to genetics?*

Most genes contain nothing more than instructions for assembling proteins. Many proteins are enzymes, which catalyze and regulate chemical reactions, thereby affecting the expression of genetic traits. In short, proteins are microscopic tools, each specifically designed to build or operate a component of a living cell.

Once scientists explained the genetic code, a new scientific field called molecular biology was established. Molecular biologists seek to understand living organisms by studying them at the molecular level, using molecules like DNA and RNA. Molecular biology provides a way to understand the links between genes and the characteristics they influence.

One of the most interesting discoveries of molecular biology is the near-universal nature of the genetic code. Although some organisms show slight variations in the amino acids assigned to particular codons, the code is always read three bases at a time, is always read in the same direction, and is always translated on ribosomes composed of RNA and protein.

READING TOOL

Make Connections In this lesson and the previous one, you learned about the related processes of RNA transcription and translation.

How is transcription related to protein translation?

____

____

____

____

____

CHAPTER 12

LESSON 3

Gene Regulation and Expression

READING TOOL **Main Ideas and Details** As you read your textbook, identify the main ideas and details or evidence that support the main ideas. Use the lesson headings to organize the main ideas and details. Record your work in the table. Two examples are entered for you.

Heading	Main Idea	Details/Evidence
Prokaryotic Gene Regulation		
The *Lac* Operon	The *lac* operon controls the production of proteins needed for *E. coli* to use lactose for food.	
Promoters and Operators • The *lac* repressor blocks transcription • Lactose turns the operon "on"		
Eukaryotic Gene Regulation		
Transcription Factors		Some transcription factors block access to genes so they are not expressed.
Cell Specialization		
Genetic Control of Development		
Homeotic Genes		
Epigenetics		
Environmental Influences		

Lesson Summary

Prokaryotic Gene Regulation

KEY QUESTION *How are prokaryotic genes regulated?*

By regulating gene expression, bacteria can respond to changes in their environment. DNA-binding proteins in prokaryotes regulate genes by controlling transcription. Some of these regulatory proteins switch genes on, while others turn genes off.

How does an organism know when to turn a gene on or off? *E. coli* provides us with an example. Three genes must be turned on together before the bacterium can break apart lactose, a type of sugar, for food. Because the three genes are "operated" together, they are called the *lac* operon. An **operon** is a group of genes that are regulated together.

The *Lac* Operon To use lactose for food, the bacterium must have the proteins coded for by the genes of the *lac* operon. The bacterium seems to "know" when the products of the *lac* operon genes are needed and when they're not needed. For example, if the bacterium grows in a medium where lactose is the only food source, the genes are transcribed to produce the proteins. If the environment changes to another food source, then the genes are not transcribed.

Promoters and Operators On one side of the operon's three genes, there are two regulatory regions. The first is a promoter (P), which is a site where RNA polymerase can bind to begin transcription. The other region is called the **operator** (O). The O site is where a DNA-binding protein known as the *lac* repressor can bind to DNA.

The Lac Repressor Blocks Transcription When lactose is not present, the *lac* repressor binds to the O region and RNA polymerase cannot reach the *lac* genes to begin transcription. The binding of the repressor protein switches the operon "off" by preventing the transcription of its genes.

Lactose Turns the Operon "On" When lactose is present, some of it attaches to the *lac* repressor and causes it to fall off the operator. RNA polymerase can bind to the promoter and transcribe the genes of the operon. As a result, in the presence of lactose, the operon is automatically switched on. Many other prokaryotic genes are switched on or off by similar mechanisms.

As you read, circle the answers to each Key Question. Underline any words you do not understand.

BUILD Vocabulary

operon in prokaryotes, a group of adjacent genes that share a common operator and promoter and are transcribed into a single mRNA

operator short DNA region, adjacent to the promoter of a prokaryotic operon, that binds repressor proteins responsible for controlling the rate of transcription of the operon

Root Words The Latin root word *oper* means "work." Similar words include *operate* or *operator*.

How does the operator region of DNA work to regulate gene expression?

____

____

____

____

____

____

____

____

____

Eukaryotic Gene Regulation

KEY QUESTION *How are genes regulated in eukaryotic cells?*

The general principles of gene expression in prokaryotes also apply to eukaryotes, but the regulation of many eukaryotic genes is much more complex.

Transcription Factors DNA-binding proteins known as transcription factors play an important part in regulating gene expression. By binding DNA sequences in the regulatory regions of eukaryotic genes, transcription factors control gene expression. A transcription factor can activate scores of genes at once, thereby dramatically affecting patterns of gene expression. Eukaryotic gene expression can also be regulated by many other factors.

Cell Specialization Gene regulation in eukaryotes is more complex than in prokaryotes because of the way in which genes are expressed in a multicellular organism. Cell differentiation requires genetic specialization, yet most of the cells in a multicellular organism carry the same DNA in their nucleus. Complex gene regulation in eukaryotes makes it possible for cells to be differentiated and specialized. Gene regulation also allows multicellular organisms to reproduce. Complex changes in gene expression allow the single cell of a new organism to develop into a functioning multicelluar organism.

Genetic Control of Development

KEY QUESTION *What controls the development of cells and tissues in multicellular organisms?*

The activation of genes in different parts of an embryo cause cells to differentiate. The process of **differentiation** gives rise to specialized tissues and organs.

Homeotic Genes A set of master control genes, known as **homeotic genes**, regulates organs that develop in specific parts of the body. Homeotic genes share a very similar 180-base DNA sequence, the *homeobox*. **Homeobox genes** code for transcription factors that activate other genes that are important in cell development and differentiation. In flies, homeobox genes known as **Hox genes** are located side by side in a single cluster. Hox genes determine the identities of each segment of a fly's body. They are arranged in the order in which they are expressed, from anterior to posterior. Hox genes exist in the DNA of other animals, including humans. These genes are also arranged from head to tail, and they tell the cells of the body how to differentiate as the body grows. This means that nearly all animals share the same basic tools for building the different parts of the body.

BUILD Vocabulary

differentiation process in which cells become specialized in structure and function

homeotic gene class of regulatory genes that determine the identity of body parts and regions in an animal embryo. Mutations in these genes can transform one body part into another.

homeobox genes genes that code for transcription factors that activate other genes that are important in cell development and differentiation

Hox gene group of homeotic genes clustered together that determine the head-to-tail identity of body parts in animals. All Hox genes contain the homeobox DNA sequence.

Word Origins The word part *homeo* comes from the Latin and Greek part *homio*, meaning "similar to" or "the same kind." Homeobox genes are a group of similar genes that regulate specific structures.

☑ **How are Hox genes, a type of homeotic gene, similar across species?**

____

____

____

____

READING TOOL

Make Connections The prefix *epi-* means "over." Epigenetic changes, such as the addition of markers, occur *above*, or *over*, the level of the genome. **If epigenetic changes take place above the level of the genome, what would be an example of a change at the level of the genome?**

____

____

____

Common patterns of genetic control exist because all these genes have descended from the genes of common ancestors. Master control genes are like switches that trigger particular patterns of development and differentiation in cells and tissues. The details can vary from one organism to another, but the switches are nearly identical.

Epigenetics In places where chromatin is tightly packed, gene expression is blocked. In regions where chromatin is opened up, gene expression is enhanced. Cells can regulate the state of chromatin by enzymes that attach chemical groups to DNA and to histone proteins.

These chemical marks on chromatin are epigenetic, or above the level of the genome. Epigenetic marks do not change DNA base sequences. Instead, they influence patterns of gene expression over long periods of time.

Environmental Influences In prokaryotes and eukaryotes, environmental factors can regulate gene expression. The environment can often influence how and when epigenetic marks are attached to chromatin. Environmental factors can also directly affect the expression of other genes.

Visual Reading Tool: Effect of Chemical Marks on Gene Expression

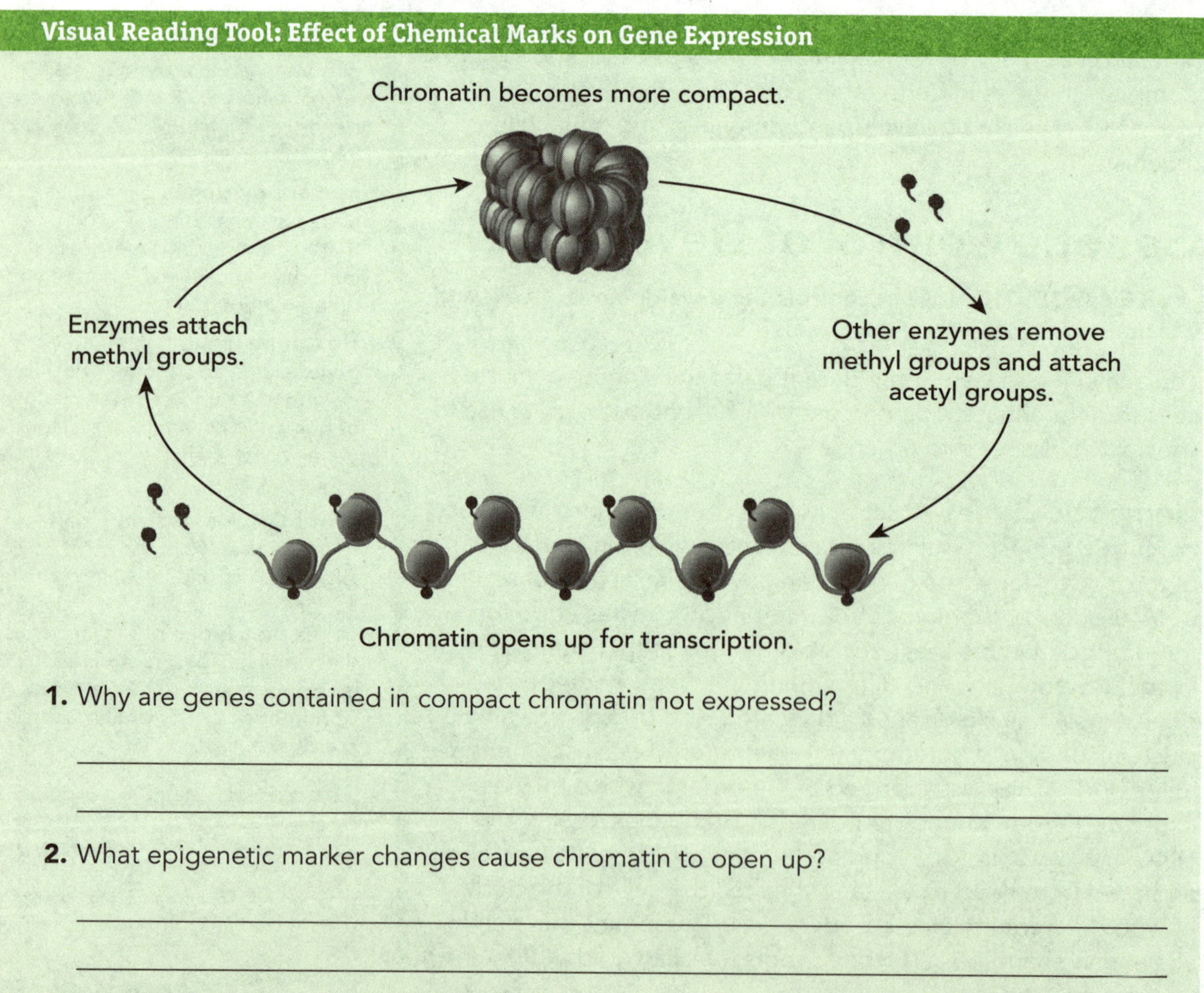

1. Why are genes contained in compact chromatin not expressed?

____

____

2. What epigenetic marker changes cause chromatin to open up?

____

____

CHAPTER 12

LESSON 4

Mutations

READING TOOL **Cause and Effect** As you read your textbook, find a brief description of each cause, or mutation, provided. Then identify its possible effect(s). Record your work in the table. An example is entered for you.

Mutation (Cause)	Description	Effect(s)
Silent Mutation	A changed codon of mRNA results in the same amino acid.	None; the amino acid sequence is unchanged and the protein is normal.
Missense Mutation		
Nonsense Mutation		
Frameshift Mutation		

Lesson Summary

Types of Mutations

As you read, circle the answers to each Key Question. Underline any words you do not understand.

BUILD Vocabulary

mutation change in the genetic material of a cell

point mutation gene mutation in which a single base pair in DNA has been changed

frameshift mutation mutation that shifts the "reading frame" of the genetic message by inserting or deleting a nucleotide

Word Origins The word *mutation* comes from the Latin word *mutare*, meaning "to change." ☑ **Which types of point mutations typically cause the most significant changes?**

____

____

____

____

KEY QUESTION *In what ways do mutations change genetic information?*

When cells make mistakes in copying their own DNA, the resulting variations are called **mutations**. Mutations are heritable changes in genetic information. Mutations can involve changes in the sequence of nucleotides in DNA or changes in the number or structure of chromosomes.

Point Mutations Mutations that change a single base pair are **point mutations**. Point mutations usually involve a substitution, in which one base is changed to a different base. Substitutions usually affect no more than a single amino acid, and sometimes have no effect at all. Mutations that don't affect amino acid sequence are known as *silent mutations*. Mutations that change the amino acid specified by a codon can be more significant and are called *missense mutations*.

If a mutation changes an mRNA codon to result in a stop codon, it is known as a *nonsense mutation* because it causes translation to stop before the protein is finished. This can result in the production of a defective protein.

Insertions and Deletions Mutations in which one base or many bases are inserted or removed from the DNA sequence are called insertions and deletions. Insertions and deletions are also called **frameshift mutations** because they shift the "reading frame" of the genetic message. Frameshift mutations can change every amino acid that follows the point of the mutation. They can alter a protein so much that it is unable to perform its normal functions.

Chromosomal Mutations Chromosomal mutations involve changes in the number or structure of chromosomes. These mutations can change the location of genes on chromosomes and can even change the number of copies of some genes. There are four types of chromosomal mutations: deletion, duplication, inversion, and translocation. Deletion involves the loss of all or part of a chromosome, duplication produces an extra copy of all or part of a chromosome, and inversion reverses the direction of parts of a chromosome. Translocation occurs when part of one chromosome breaks off and attaches to another.

Visual Reading Tool: Mutations

On the diagrams below, label each type of mutation.

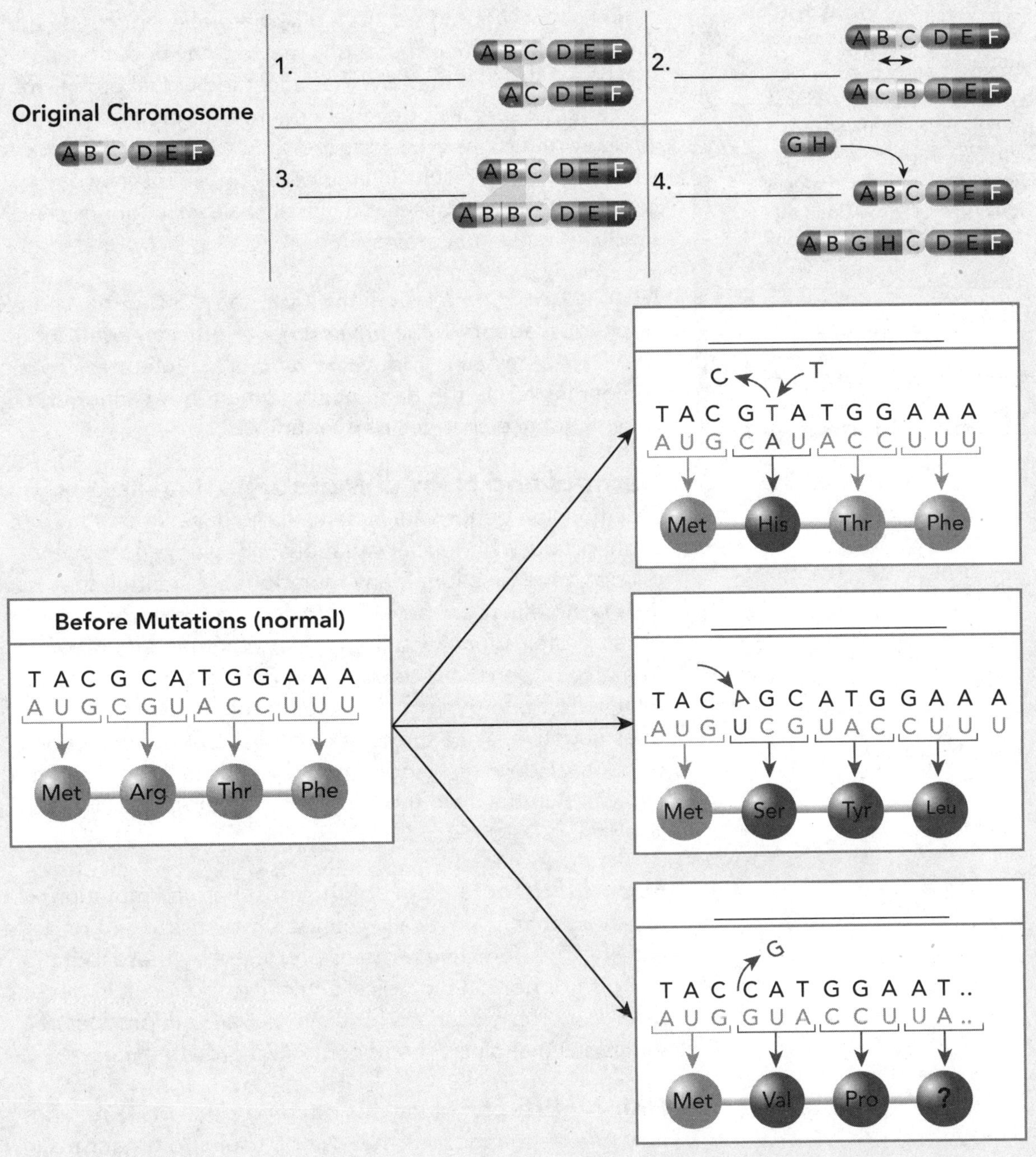

5. Numbers 1–4 are known as what type of mutation? Circle your answer.

chromosomal point missense

6. The bottom figure is known as what type of mutation? Circle your answer.

chromosomal nonsense point

7. What is the difference between point mutations and chromosomal mutations?

____

____

____

BUILD Vocabulary

mutagen chemical or physical agent in the environment that interacts with DNA and may cause a mutation

polyploidy condition in which an organism has extra sets of chromosomes

Suffixes The suffix *-gen* means "producing." ☑ **How does a mutagen produce a mutation?**

____

____

____

Effects of Mutations

KEY QUESTION *How do mutations affect genes?*

Genetic material can be altered by natural events or by artificial means. The resulting mutations may or may not affect an organism. Some mutations that affect individual organisms can also affect a species or even an entire ecosystem.

Many mutations are produced by errors in genetic processes. DNA replication results in an incorrect base roughly once in every 10 million bases. But small changes in genes can gradually accumulate over time.

Mutagens Some mutations arise from **mutagens**, chemical or physical agents in the environment. If these agents interact with DNA, they can produce mutations at high rates. Cells can sometimes repair the damage, but when they cannot, the DNA base sequence changes permanently.

Harmful and Helpful Mutations The effects of mutations on genes vary widely. Some have little or no effect, some produce beneficial variations, and some negatively disrupt gene function. Many mutations are neutral; they have little or no effect on the expression of genes or the function of the proteins for which they code. Whether a mutation is negative or beneficial depends on how its DNA changes relative to the organism's situation. Mutations are often thought of as negative, since they can disrupt the normal function of genes. However, without mutations, organisms could not evolve. Mutations are the source of genetic variability in a species.

Harmful Effects Some of the most harmful mutations are those that dramatically change protein structure or gene activity. The defective proteins produced by these mutations can disrupt normal biological activities, and result in genetic disorders. Some cancers, for example, are the product of mutations that cause the uncontrolled growth of cells.

Helpful Effects Mutations often produce proteins with new or altered functions that can be useful to organisms in different or changing environments. Plant and animal breeders often make use of "good" mutations. For example, when a complete set of chromosomes fails to separate during meiosis, the gametes that result may produce organisms with extra sets of chromosomes. The condition in which an organism has extra sets of chromosomes is called **polyploidy**. Polyploid plants are often larger and stronger than diploid plants. Important crops have been produced this way.

12 Chapter Review

Review Vocabulary

Choose the letter of the best answer.

1. The molecule that carries amino acids to the ribosome is called

A. transfer RNA.

B. ribosomal RNA.

C. messenger RNA.

2. Insertions and deletions are also known as

A. silent mutations.

B. nonsense mutations.

C. frameshift mutations.

Match the vocabulary term to its definition.

3. ________ the process of decoding an mRNA message into a protein

4. ________ the process of copying a base sequence from DNA to RNA

5. ________ the process by which variations are introduced into DNA

a. transcription

b. mutation

c. translation

Review Key Questions

Provide evidence and details to support your answers.

6. How are both DNA and RNA involved in the process of protein synthesis?

____

____

____

7. Describe gene regulation in prokaryotes.

____

____

____

____

8. How can mutations affect organisms?

____

____

____

CHAPTER 13

LESSON 1

Genes and Variation

READING TOOL **Use Structure** Use the section headings and bulleted lists below to help understand the information. What distinguishes and defines each of the list items from each other?

Genetics Joins Evolutionary Theory

- Species: ______
- Population: ______
- Gene Pool: ______
  - Allele frequency: ______
- Genotype vs. Phenotype: ______

Sources of Genetic Variation

- Mutations: ______
- Genetic Recombination during Sex: ______
- Lateral Gene Transfer: ______

Genes and Traits

- Single-gene Traits: ______
- Polygenic Traits: ______

Lesson Summary

Genetics Joins Evolutionary Theory

As you read, circle the answers to each Key Question. Underline any words you do not understand.

KEY QUESTION *How is evolution defined in genetic terms?*

Heritable traits are controlled by genes carried on chromosomes. Changes in genes and chromosomes generate variation within populations. Molecular genetic techniques can now test hypotheses about variation and selection, and help us understand evolutionary change better than Darwin ever could. Studies in population genetics reinforce Darwin's understanding that populations—not individual organisms—evolve over time. All these discoveries give biologists a deeper understanding of how evolution works.

Genes, Populations, and Species The genetic definition of a species is a group of organisms that are physically similar and able to interbreed, but that do not interbreed with other groups. The genetic definition of a population is a group of individuals of the same species that mate and produce offspring.

Populations and Gene Pools The **gene pool** of a population is made up of all genes within that group's members. This includes all alleles for each gene. The **allele frequency** is how often a specific allele occurs within the gene pool. This number is expressed as a percentage of all the alleles for that gene in the population. Allele frequency has nothing to do with whether the allele is dominant or recessive. Sometimes, the recessive allele occurs more frequently than the dominant allele. Evolution involves any change in the frequency of alleles in a population over time. Remember, populations evolve, not individuals!

Genotype, Phenotype, and Evolution The combination of all the alleles in an individual organism is called its genotype. The phenotype encompasses all of the physical aspects of the organism. Evolution only acts on the phenotype, not the genotype. Individuals with genes that produce phenotypes that increase their survival and the number of their offspring in a particular environment will pass the genes for those traits on to their more numerous offspring. This change in the frequency of a trait in a population is known as evolution.

BUILD Vocabulary

gene pool all the genes, including all the different alleles for each gene, that are present in a population at any one time

allele frequency the number of times that an allele occurs in a gene pool compared with the number of alleles in that pool for the same gene

single-gene trait trait controlled by one gene that may have one or more alleles

polygenic trait trait controlled by two or more genes, each with one or more alleles

Word Origins The word allele is a shortened version of *allelomorph*, which can be broken down into two different parts. *Allel* means "one another," and *morphe* means "form." ☑ **What do alleles show different forms of?**

____

Sources of Genetic Variation

KEY QUESTION *What are the sources of genetic variation?*

Genetic variation is produced in three main ways: mutation, genetic recombination during sexual reproduction, and lateral gene transfer. Genetic variation must be present in a population for evolution to take place.

Mutations Occasionally an error occurs in gene replication. When this happens, the gene is considered mutated. Mutations in the germ line can be inherited by an individual's offspring. Sometimes an inherited mutation can be fatal to the individual. Other times, this can have neutral or even positive effects on the individual's fitness. Mutations are important because they provide a regular source of variation for natural selection to operate on the population.

Genetic Recombination During Sexual Reproduction The special aspect of sexual reproduction is the random association of individual chromosomes of homologous pairs during meiosis and the combination of different alleles coming from two parents. This is why you appear different from your siblings, and parents. You are a combination of alleles from both parents, half from each.

READING TOOL

Connect to Visuals Figure 13-4 shows a normal distribution of a polygenic trait in humans: height. ☑ **What other polygenic trait in humans might also be represented by a bell-shaped curve?**

____

Lateral Gene Transfer The gene flow that occurs between individuals who may or may not be the same species is termed lateral gene flow. It is important for generating diversity among species. Many bacteria swap their genes on plasmids. This is how antibiotic resistance spreads.

Single-Gene and Polygenic Traits

KEY QUESTION *What determines the number of phenotypes for a given trait?*

The number of phenotypes produced for a trait depends on how many genes control the trait.

Single-Gene Traits Genes control traits in different ways. When only one gene controls one trait, this is called a **single-gene trait**. The trait may express itself as one or more phenotypes depending on how many alleles are present for the gene and whether alleles are dominant and recessive, incomplete, or codominant.

Polygenic Traits When multiple genes control a trait, it is referred to as a **polygenic trait**. The influence of the environment is often important in polygenic traits. Examples of polygenic traits in humans include hair, eye, or skin color.

Visual Reading Tool: Allele Frequencies

1. Calculate the allele frequency for black fur (B) and brown fur (b) in the mice population based on the number of each type of allele. Answer the questions below.

Sample Population

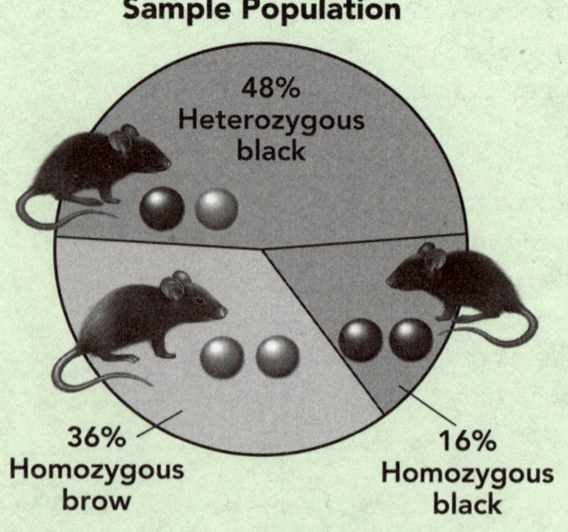

Frequency of Alleles

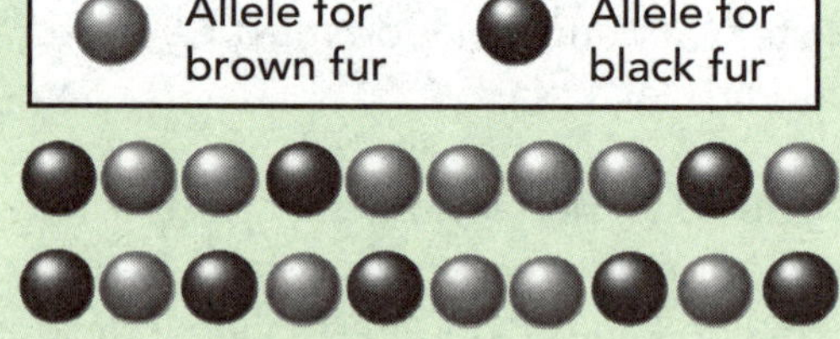

Brown allele frequency: ________

Black allele frequency: ________

2. Which allele frequency is higher? ________________

3. What is the genotype of a homozygous brown mouse? ________

4. In a population of 200 mice, how many would be homozygous black? ________

CHAPTER 13

LESSON 2

Evolution as Genetic Change

READING TOOL **Compare and Contrast** Focus on the similarities and differences of the subjects in this section. Use the titles and subtitles in the chart below to take notes differentiating the concepts for each section.

Natural Selection		
Directional	Stabilizing	Disruptive

Genetic Drift	
Bottleneck Effect	Founder Effect

Hardy-Weinberg Principle				
Nonrandom Mating	Small Populations	Gene Flow	Mutations	Natural Selection

Lesson Summary

How Natural Selection Works

KEY QUESTION *How does natural selection affect single-gene and polygenic traits?*

Individuals have inherited differences. Some better suited individuals will reproduce more successfully than others and pass those genes on to their more plentiful offspring.

Natural Selection on Single-Gene Traits Natural selection on single-gene traits can produce changes in allele frequencies that may be reflected by simple changes in phenotype frequencies.

As you read, circle the answers to each Key Question. Underline any words you do not understand.

BUILD Vocabulary

directional selection form of natural selection when individuals at one end of a distribution curve have higher fitness than individuals in the middle or at the other end of the curve

stabilizing selection form of natural selection in which individuals near the center of a distribution curve have higher fitness than individuals at either end of the curve

disruptive selection natural selection in which individuals at the upper and lower ends of the curve have higher fitness than individuals near the middle of the curve

genetic drift random change in allele frequency caused by a series of chance occurrences that cause an allele to become more or less common in a population

bottleneck effect a change in allele frequency following a dramatic reduction in the size of a population

founder effect change in allele frequencies as a result of the migration of a small subgroup of a population

genetic equilibrium situation in which allele frequencies in a population remain the same from one generation to the next

Using Prior Knowledge The bottleneck effect occurs when a significant portion of a population is killed off. ☑ **List 3 events that could cause a dramatic decrease in a population size.**

____

____

____

Natural Selection on Polygenic Traits Natural selection on polygenic traits can affect the relative fitness of phenotypes in directional selection, stabilizing selection, or disruptive selection.

Directional Selection When a preferred phenotype at one end of the distribution curve of phenotypes is favored, this type of selection is **directional selection**. The overall curve will shift toward that direction.

Stabilizing Selection If an intermediate phenotype comes under selection, then a **stabilizing selection** will take place. Extreme variations in the specific trait at both ends of the population will have less success, and so the bell curve becomes taller and narrower.

Disruptive Selection If the opposite scenario to stabilizing selection occurs, where extremes of the trait are selected for, then **disruptive selection** occurs. Thus the phenotype at both extremes become more successful, increasing the population diversity.

Genetic Drift

KEY QUESTION *What is genetic drift?*

In small populations, individuals that carry a particular allele may leave more descendants over time than other individuals by chance. These random changes in allele frequency are called **genetic drift**.

Genetic Bottlenecks When a large proportion of a given population is killed off, this can cause a restriction in the gene pool, which is called the **bottleneck effect**. A severe population bottleneck can result in decreased diversity.

The Founder Effect Sometimes a fraction of a population breaks away and colonizes a new habitat. Because the individuals in this group can contain a very different frequency of the alleles compared to the original population, it causes a **founder effect**.

Evolution Versus Genetic Equilibrium

KEY QUESTION *What conditions are required to maintain genetic equilibrium?*

Genetic equilibrium is a theoretical condition in which evolution is not occurring and the gene pool does not change. No population is ever in perfect genetic equilibrium.

Sexual Reproduction and Allele Frequency Because meiosis and fertilization do not change the proportions of allele occurrences, sexual reproduction alone does not lead to evolution.

The Hardy-Weinberg Principle

The **Hardy-Weinberg principle** predicts that five conditions can disturb genetic equilibrium and cause evolution to occur.

Nonrandom Mating **Sexual selection** is a common occurrence in sexually reproducing species, as individuals will seek out mates with the highest fitness. Phenotypic traits such as size or color will often play a role.

Small Population Size Large populations are less likely to be affected by genetic drift than small populations, because their size buffers them against random changes in allele frequencies.

Gene Flow from Immigration or Emigration The movement of genes into or out of a population is called **gene flow**. If animals come and go, this will change what alleles are available in the gene pool of the population of interest.

Mutations Just as it is a source of genetic variation, the existence of mutations means that allele frequencies will change.

Natural Selection Varying fitness levels mean that some individuals will survive better than others, leading to changing allele frequencies.

BUILD Vocabulary

Hardy-Weinberg principle principle that states that allele frequencies in a population remain constant unless one or more factors cause those frequencies to change

sexual selection when individuals select mates based on heritable traits and fitness

gene flow movement of genes into or out of a population

Visual Reading Tool: Polygenic Trait Selection

Label the different patterns of selection appropriately. Answer the questions below.

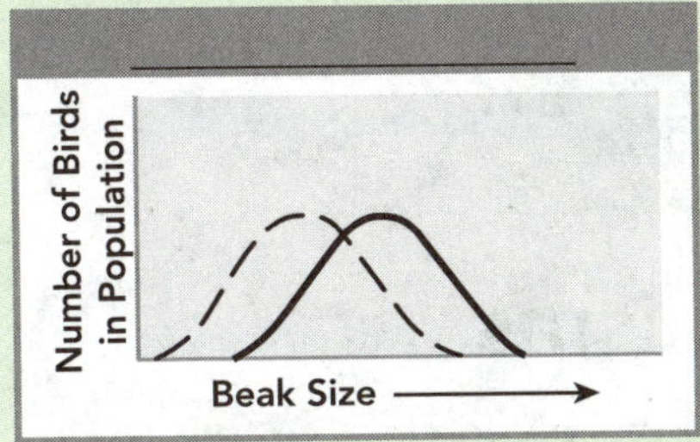

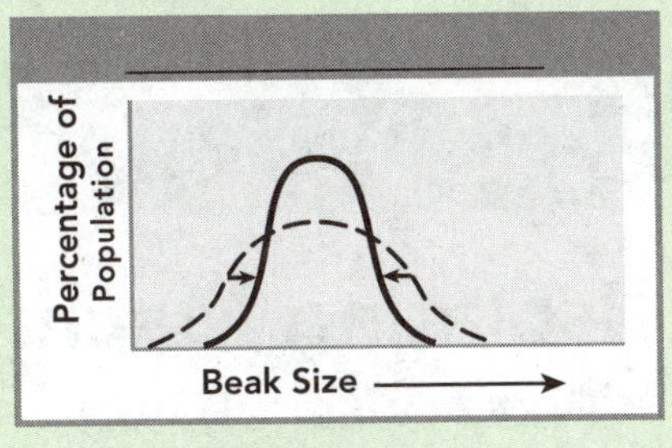

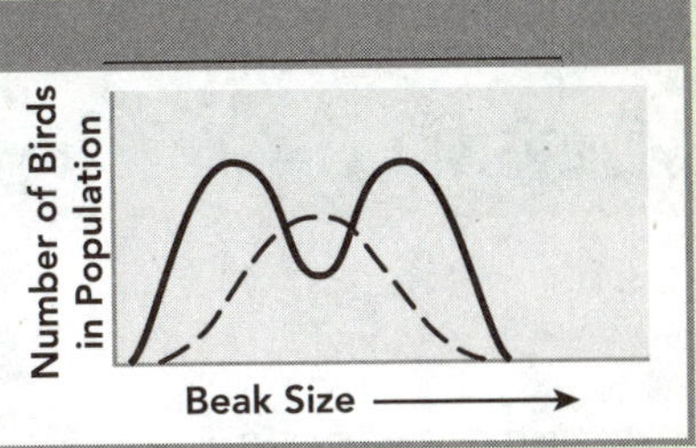

– – Original distribution
—— New distribution as a result of selection

1. Darwin's finches vary in size from 10–20 cm and 8–38 g. Warbler-finches are the smallest species of them all. At some time in history, which selection led to their evolution?

____

2. In the large cactus finch, some males have shorter beaks and other males have longer beaks. Which type of selection probably operated on this species?

____

CHAPTER 13

LESSON 3

The Process of Speciation

READING TOOL **Cause and Effect** As you read, think about the three types of reproductive isolation and what causes them. Fill in the flow chart below.

Effect: Behavioral Isolation

Cause:

Effect: Geographic Isolation

Cause:

Effect: Temporal Isolation

Cause:

Lesson Summary

Isolating Mechanisms

KEY QUESTION *What types of isolation lead to the formation of new species?*

Speciation is the process by which new species evolve. Sexual reproduction allows for genes to be passed along in a population. If some individuals stop breeding with other individuals, eventually this can lead to a split in the population. As evolution continues, if two groups stop reproducing together, the gene pool will not be shared, resulting in **reproductive isolation**. Reproductive isolation can develop in several ways, including behavioral isolation, geographic isolation, and temporal isolation.

As you read, circle the answers to each Key Question. Underline any words you do not understand.

BUILD Vocabulary

speciation formation of a new species

reproductive isolation separation of a species or population so that they no longer interbreed

Behavioral Isolation If an important behavior, such as a mating ritual, evolves differently in two groups, then this type of reproductive isolation is termed **behavioral isolation**.

Geographic Isolation Geography can be a barrier that leads to reproductive isolation. If individuals cannot physically reach each other, this is known as **geographic isolation**. Any type of isolated habitat can result in this, whether they be mountaintops or actual islands. Natural disasters can also play a part as barriers or connectors.

Temporal Isolation When two or more species experience mating seasons that do not match up, then time is the divisive factor here, and it is known as **temporal isolation**.

Speciation in Darwin's Finches

KEY QUESTION *What is a current hypothesis about Galápagos finch speciation?*

Using research-based understanding of the finch populations on the Galápagos Islands, we can begin to piece together the historical events that led to Darwin's finches as the species they are today. Speciation in Galápagos finches occurred by founding a new population, geographic isolation, changes in the new population's gene pool, behavioral isolation, and ecological competition.

Founders Arrive A founding population of finches migrated to one of the Galápagos Islands from the South American mainland. A founder effect occurred, because these individuals would have only had certain alleles compared to the larger gene pool of the overall species back on the mainland.

Geographic Isolation Finding themselves on an island, the finches would have been geographically isolated from other populations, which would minimize the opportunity for interbreeding. If members of this founding population migrated to other islands, these new populations would become isolated.

Changes in Gene Pools Over time, each population of finch would evolve to adapt to the environment of each island. Food type and availability would be important in determining the most fit beak shape and size. Evolution continues.

Behavioral Isolation After more time, if any individuals manage to return to the original founding colony on the first island, behavioral isolation would have occurred. It is likely that courtship rituals and sexual selection would prevent birds with different-sized beaks from choosing to mate with one other.

BUILD Vocabulary

behavioral isolation form of reproductive isolation in which two populations develop differences in courtship rituals or other behaviors that prevent them from breeding

geographic isolation form of reproductive isolation in which two populations are separated by geographic barriers such as rivers, mountains, or bodies of water, leading to the formation of two separate subspecies

temporal isolation form of reproductive isolation in which two or more species reproduce at different times

Root Words The word temporal is based on the Latin word *tempus* which means "time." ☑ **Do you know any other word that has a similar root that relates to time?**

___

___

___

Competition and Continued Evolution Competition between birds with different phenotypes (beak size and shape) would result in further evolution and speciation. This process would repeat until modern times, when 13 distinct species are found among the island system.

Visual Reading Tool: Darwin's Finches Speciate

1. Fill in the diagram below with the five events that caused speciation of the finches of the Galápagos Islands.

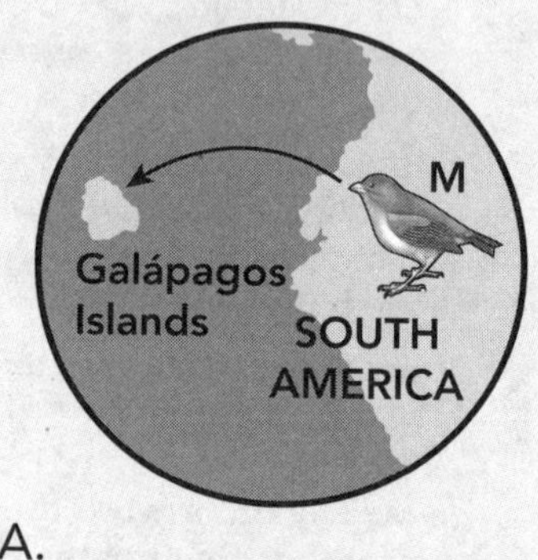

A. ______________________

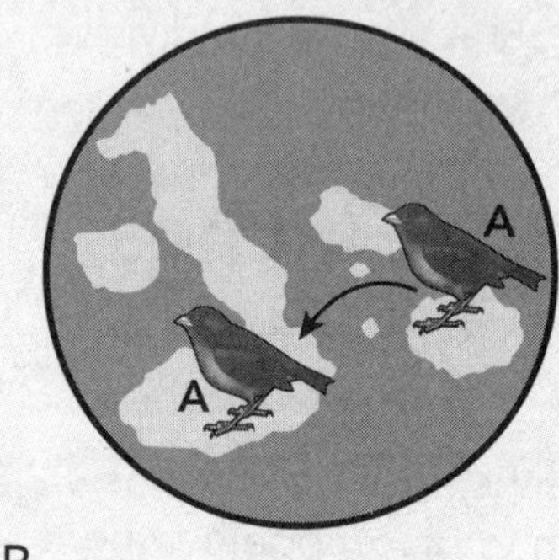

B. ______________________

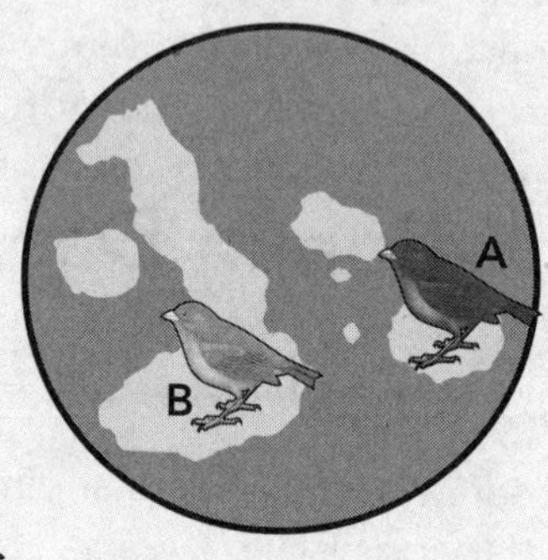

C. ______________________

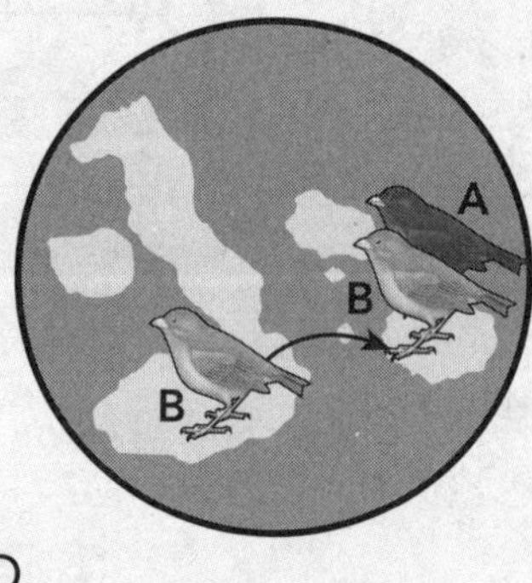

D. ______________________

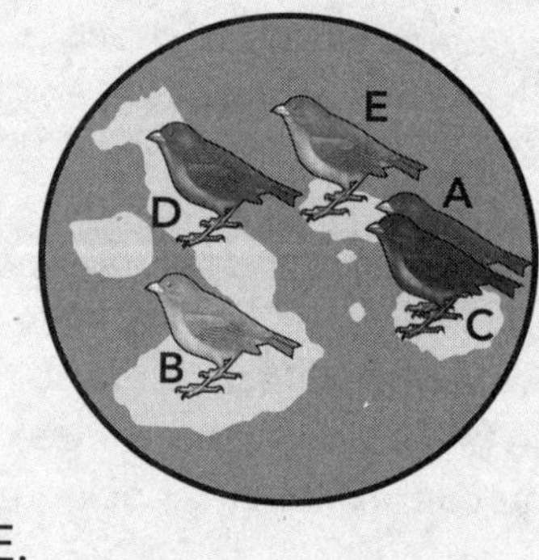

E. ______________________
____

2. Behavioral isolation occurs when one population stops breeding with another population, perhaps because of physiological differences and behaviors. In which event has behavioral isolation occurred? How can you tell?

____

____

____

3. At what stage did the founder effect take place?

____

____

____

CHAPTER 13

LESSON 4 Molecular Evolution

READING TOOL **Main Idea and Details** As you read, identify the details that describe the headings listed below.

Heading	Notes
Gene Duplication	
Genetic Rearrangement	
Hox Genes and Evolution	
Neutral Mutations	
Calibrating the Clock	

Lesson Summary

New Genes, New Functions

KEY QUESTION *Where do new genes come from?*

The human genome is made up of about 25,000 genes. How do genes change over time? One way new genes can evolve is through duplication, followed by modification, of existing genes.

Gene Duplication During meiosis, crossing-over occurs between homologous chromosomes. If extra genes get copied on to one of the chromosomes, gene duplication has occurred. If this happens without any harmful effects, these gene copies can mutate and take on new functions while one copy maintains the original function.

Genetic Rearrangement DNA sequence can be modified by insertions, deletions, duplications, and rearrangements. This changing of the DNA code can produce modified proteins, and the duplication and modification results in the formation of gene "families." These gene families allow geneticists to trace evolutionary relationships between species and groups of species.

Developmental Genes and Body Plans

KEY QUESTION *How may Hox genes be involved in evolutionary change?*

Evo-devo is a field of biology that connects evolutionary genetics with development of organisms. Studying the relationship between the two leads to better understanding of gene function.

Hox Genes and Evolution The regulatory genes that determine which embryonic parts will grow into adult body parts are known as **Hox genes**. Small changes in Hox gene activity during embryological development can produce large changes in adult animals.

Timing Is Everything When growth occurs is critical to the development of an animal. Genetic changes affecting how long or when this growth occurs will directly affect the body plan of an animal.

As you read, circle the answers to each Key Question. Underline any words you do not understand.

BUILD Vocabulary

Hox gene regulatory genes that determine which parts of an embryo develop into arms, legs, or wings.

Word Origins The word gene was coined by Wilhelm Johannsen, a Danish botanist, in 1905. It is based upon the greek word *genos* which means "race, kind, or offspring."

What other famous botanist worked with pea plants and is responsible for many important discoveries in the field of genetics?

____

____

Molecular Clocks

KEY QUESTION *How do molecular clocks work?*

Because related species should have similar genomes, the differences that do exist between their genomes will provide an estimate of how long the two species have been evolving independently.

Neutral Mutations as "Ticks" Molecular clocks are based on the relatively constant rate at which mutations occur. In particular, mutations that are not subject to selection (neutral mutations) are used as the "ticks" of the clock. More mutations, and a greater difference between the two species, means that they have been separate species for a greater amount of time.

Calibrating the Clock There are many different molecular clocks, because the rate of mutation happens differently for different DNA. If scientists already know the age of a particular species, they can use that information to calibrate the neutral mutation "ticks" in a particular gene, and determine that particular molecular clock's accuracy.

Visual Reading Tool: Gene Duplication

1. Write the sequence of events by which gene duplication occurs.

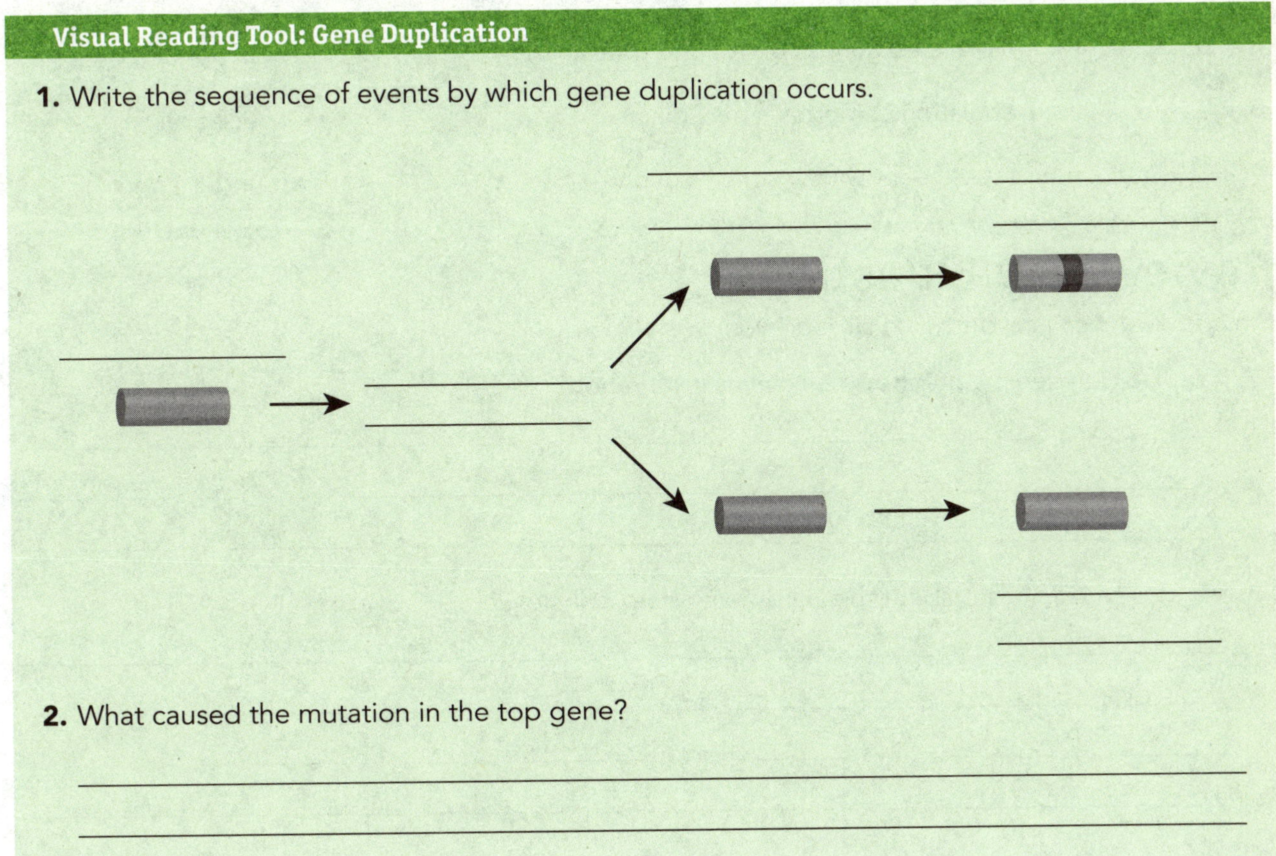

2. What caused the mutation in the top gene?

____

____

13 Chapter Review

Review Vocabulary

Choose the letter of the best answer.

1. The movement of genes in or out of a population is called:

A. gene transfer

B. gene flow

C. gene pool

D. genetic drift

2. When two populations are separated by physical barriers:

A. reproductive isolation

B. temporal isolation

C. geographical isolation

D. behavioral isolation

Match the vocabulary term to its definition.

3.	______	genes determining the development of animal body parts	a. polygenic trait
4.	______	multiple alleles/genes control one trait	b. Hox gene
5.	______	if a population colonizes a new place	c. speciation
6.	______	the process of how new species evolve	d. founder effect

Review Key Questions

Provide evidence and details to support your answers.

7. Why do polygenic traits show bell curves in variation?

____

____

____

8. What is so significant about the Hardy-Weinberg principle?

____

____

____

____

9. Why were the Galápagos Islands so significant for our understanding of evolution?

____

____

____

CHAPTER 14

LESSON 1

Human Chromosomes

READING TOOL **Apply Prior Knowledge** Before you read this lesson, think about what you have learned about human chromosomes from your study of cell division, genetics, and other biology concepts in previous chapters. Consider, too, what questions about human chromosomes you still have. Record your answers in the **Know** and **Want to Know** sections of the chart below. Once you have read the lesson, return to this page to complete the **Learned** section.

Know	Want to Know	Learned

Lesson Summary

As you read, circle the answers to each Key Question. Underline any words you do not understand.

BUILD Vocabulary

genome entire set of genetic information that an organism carries in its DNA

karyotype micrograph of the complete diploid set of chromosomes grouped together in pairs, arranged in order of decreasing size

Karyotypes

KEY QUESTION *How are human karyotypes used?*

To find what makes us uniquely human, we have to explore the human genome. A **genome** is the full set of genetic information that an organism carries in its DNA. The analysis of any genome starts with chromosomes. To see human chromosomes clearly, cell biologists photograph the chromosomes using a microscope. Scientists then arrange images of each chromosome to produce a **karyotype**. A karyotype shows the complete diploid set of chromosomes grouped together in pairs, arranged in order of decreasing size. The karyotype from a typical human cell contains 46 chromosomes, arranged in 23 pairs.

Sex Chromosomes Two of the 46 chromosomes in the human genome are known as **sex chromosomes**, because they determine an individual's sex. Females have two copies of the X chromosome. Males have one X chromosome and one Y chromosome. More than 1400 genes are found on the X chromosome. The Y chromosome, which is smaller, contains only about 158 genes.

Autosomal Chromosomes The remaining 44 human chromosomes are autosomal chromosomes, or **autosomes**.

Transmission of Human Traits

KEY QUESTION *What patterns of inheritance do human traits follow?*

Human genes follow the same patterns of inheritance as the genes of other organisms.

Dominant and Recessive Alleles Many human traits follow a pattern of simple dominance. A trait that displays simple dominance is the Rhesus, or Rh, blood group. The allele for Rh factor comes in two forms: Rh^+ and Rh^-. Rh^+ is dominant, so an individual with both alleles (Rh^+/Rh^-) is said to have Rh-positive blood. Rh-negative blood is found in individuals with two recessive alleles (Rh^-/Rh^-).

Codominant and Multiple Alleles The alleles for many human genes display codominant inheritance. One example is the ABO blood group, determined by a gene with three alleles: I^A, I^B, and *i*. Alleles I^A and I^B are codominant. Individuals with alleles I^A and I^B are blood type AB. The *i* allele is recessive. Individuals with alleles I^AI^A or I^Ai are blood type A. Those with I^BI^B or I^Bi alleles are type B. Those homozygous for the *i* allele (*ii*) have blood type O. If a person has AB-negative blood, it means the individual has I^A and I^B alleles from the ABO gene and two Rh– alleles from the Rh gene.

Sex-Linked Inheritance Because the X and Y chromosomes determine sex, the genes located on them show a pattern of inheritance called sex-linkage. A **sex-linked gene** is a gene located on a sex chromosome. Genes on the Y chromosome are found only in males and are passed directly from father to son. Genes located on the X chromosome are found in both sexes, but the fact that men have just one X chromosome leads to some interesting consequences.

In males, a recessive allele on the single X chromosome is usually expressed. In order for a recessive allele to be expressed in females, it must be present on both of the X chromosomes. This means that the recessive phenotype of a sex-linked genetic disorder tends to be much more common among males than among females.

BUILD Vocabulary

sex chromosome one of two chromosomes that determines an individual's sex

autosome chromosome that is not a sex chromosome; also called autosomal chromosome

sex-linked gene a gene located on a sex chromosome

Prefixes *Auto-* is a prefix of Greek origin that means *self* or *same*. In diploid cells, each autosome pairs with another autosome that has the same shape and the same genes.

Why are sex chromosomes not called autosomes? Use the definition of the prefix *auto-* in your explanation.

READING TOOL

Academic Words

consequence a result or an effect of a condition or an action

Explain why the presence of a recessive allele on one X chromosome often has different consequences for a man than for a woman.

BUILD Vocabulary

pedigree chart that shows the presence or absence of a trait according to the relationships within a family across several generations

Word Origins The word *pedigree* is based upon the Middle English word *pedegru*, which translates to "crane's foot." ☑ **Why do you think a pedigree is compared to the foot of a crane?**

____

____

____

X-Chromosome Inactivation In female cells, most of the genes in one of the X chromosomes are inactivated, forming a condensed region in the nucleus known as a Barr body. A special RNA molecule binds to the inactivated chromosome and keeps it in the condensed state.

Human Pedigrees

KEY QUESTION *How can pedigrees be used to analyze human inheritance?*

To analyze the pattern of inheritance followed by a particular trait, you can use a **pedigree** chart that shows the relationships within a family. A pedigree shows the presence or absence of a trait according to the relationships among parents, siblings, and offspring.

By analyzing a pedigree, we can infer genotypes and predict future outcomes by applying the principles of Mendelian genetics to humans. The information gained from pedigree analysis makes it possible to determine the nature of genes and alleles associated with inherited human traits. Based on a pedigree, you can often determine if an allele for a trait is dominant or recessive, as well as if it is autosomal or sex-linked.

Visual Reading Tool: How to Use a Pedigree

The sample pedigree below shows an example of how a dominant trait might pass through three generations of a family. Fill in the blanks to complete a key that explains how to read a pedigree.

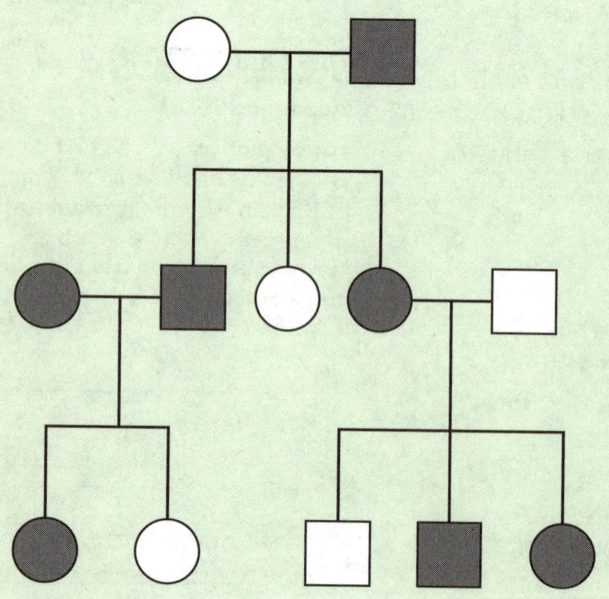

Key

1. A __________ represents a female.
2. A __________ represents a male.
3. A vertical line and bracket connect ______________________________
4. A horizontal line connecting a male and female represents ______________________________
5. Shading indicates ______________________________
6. No shading indicates ______________________________

CHAPTER 14

LESSON 2

Human Genetic Disorders

READING TOOL **Main Idea and Details** As you read your textbook, identify the main ideas and details or evidence that support the main ideas. Use the lesson headings to organize the main ideas and details. Record your work in the table. Two examples are entered for you.

Heading	Main Idea	Details/Evidence
Chromosomal Disorders	Nondisjunction, the failure of homologous chromosomes to separate during meiosis, can lead to chromosome number disorders.	
From Molecule to Phenotype		A difference of one DNA base in a single gene determines whether a person has dry earwax or wet earwax.
Disorders Caused by Individual Genes		
Genetic Advantages		

Lesson Summary

Chromosomal Disorders

KEY QUESTION *What are the effects of errors in meiosis?*

Most of the time, the process of meiosis works perfectly and each human gamete gets exactly 23 chromosomes. Every now and then, however, something goes wrong. The most common error in meiosis occurs when homologous chromosomes fail to separate. This mistake is known as **nondisjunction**, which means "not coming apart."

As you read, circle the answers to each Key Question. Underline any words you do not understand.

BUILD Vocabulary

nondisjunction error in meiosis in which the homologous chromosomes fail to separate properly

Prefixes *Non-* is a prefix meaning "not," and *dis-* is a prefix meaning "separate." When combined with the word *junction*, which comes from a Latin word meaning "to join," they make a word that indicates that something joined does not come apart. ☑ **What sorts of disorders are the result of nondisjunction?**

____

____

____

____

____

If nondisjunction occurs during meiosis, gametes with an abnormal number of chromosomes may result, leading to a disorder of chromosome numbers. For example, if two copies of an autosomal chromosome fail to separate during meiosis, an individual may be born with three copies of that chromosome. Down syndrome, a condition where an individual has three copies of chromosome 21, is associated with a range of cognitive disabilities and certain birth defects.

Nondisjunction of the X chromosomes can lead to a disorder known as Turner's syndrome. A female with Turner's syndrome usually inherits only one X chromosome. In males, nondisjunction may cause Klinefelter's syndrome, resulting from the inheritance of an extra X chromosome.

From Molecule to Phenotype

KEY QUESTION *How do small changes in DNA affect human traits?*

Genes are made of DNA and interact with the environment to produce an individual organism's characteristics, or phenotype. However, when a gene fails to work or works improperly, serious problems can result.

Visual Reading Tool: Nondisjunction

A. _______________

____

____

B. _______________

____

____

The diagram to the left shows a simplified model of meiosis.

1. On lines A and B, briefly explain what is happening during the two different parts of meiosis. Specify what structures are being separated.
2. Look at the four cells at the end of this model of meiosis. What could have caused them to have an irregular number of chromosomes? Explain this process.

____

____

____

____

____

____

____

The connection between molecule and trait, and between genotype and phenotype, is often simple and direct. Changes in a gene's DNA sequence can change proteins by altering their amino acid sequences, which may directly affect an individual's phenotype. Sometimes, however, these effects are more subtle. For example, certain alleles are associated with tendencies to develop conditions such as diabetes, heart disease, and cancer. Many other factors, such as behavior, diet, and environment, can have a profound effect on whether these conditions actually develop.

Disorders Caused by Individual Genes Thousands of genetic disorders are caused by changes in individual genes. These changes often affect specific proteins associated with important cellular functions.

Sickle Cell Disease Sickle cell disease is a hereditary disease caused by a defective recessive allele for beta-globin, one of two polypeptides in hemoglobin. The defective polypeptide causes hemoglobin to clump into long fibers that push against the membranes of red blood cells and distort their shape. Sickle-shaped cells are more rigid than normal red blood cells, so they tend to get stuck in capillaries.

Cystic Fibrosis Cystic fibrosis (CF) usually results from the deletion of just three bases in the gene for a protein. The loss of these bases removes a single amino acid, causing the protein to fold improperly. Two copies of the defective allele are needed to produce the disorder, which means the CF allele is recessive. Children with CF have serious digestive problems and produce thick, heavy mucus that clogs their lungs and breathing passageways.

Huntington's Disease Huntington's disease is caused by a dominant allele for a protein found in brain cells. The allele for this disease contains a long string of bases in which the codon for the amino acid glutamine repeats over and over again. The symptoms of Huntington's disease, mental deterioration and uncontrollable movements, usually do not appear until middle age.

Genetic Advantages Disorders such as sickle cell disease and CF are still common in human populations. Why are these alleles still around if they can be fatal for those who carry them?

CF Allele and Typhoid Typhoid is caused by a bacterium that enters the body through cells in the digestive system. The protein produced by the CF allele helps block the entry of this bacterium. Individuals who are heterozygous for CF have an advantage against typhoid. Because they also carry the normal allele, these individuals do not suffer from cystic fibrosis.

Sickle Cell Allele and Malaria Malaria is a mosquito-borne infection caused by a parasite that lives inside red blood cells. Individuals with just one copy of the sickle cell allele are generally healthy and are also highly resistant to the parasite. This resistance gives them a great advantage against malaria.

READING TOOL

Apply Prior Knowledge In previous chapters you have read about dominant and recessive alleles. Generally, the dominant allele overpowers the recessive allele and the recessive allele is not expressed. However, in some disorders, having one copy of the recessive allele gives the individual a genetic advantage.

☑ **How do scientists describe a genotype that has one copy of the dominant allele and one copy of the recessive allele?**

___

CHAPTER 14

LESSON 3

Studying the Human Genome

READING TOOL **Use Structure** As you read, fill in the graphic organizer that explains how scientists manipulate DNA to read nucleotide sequences. Fill in the boxes to explain the process as you read the text. Some examples have been filled in for you.

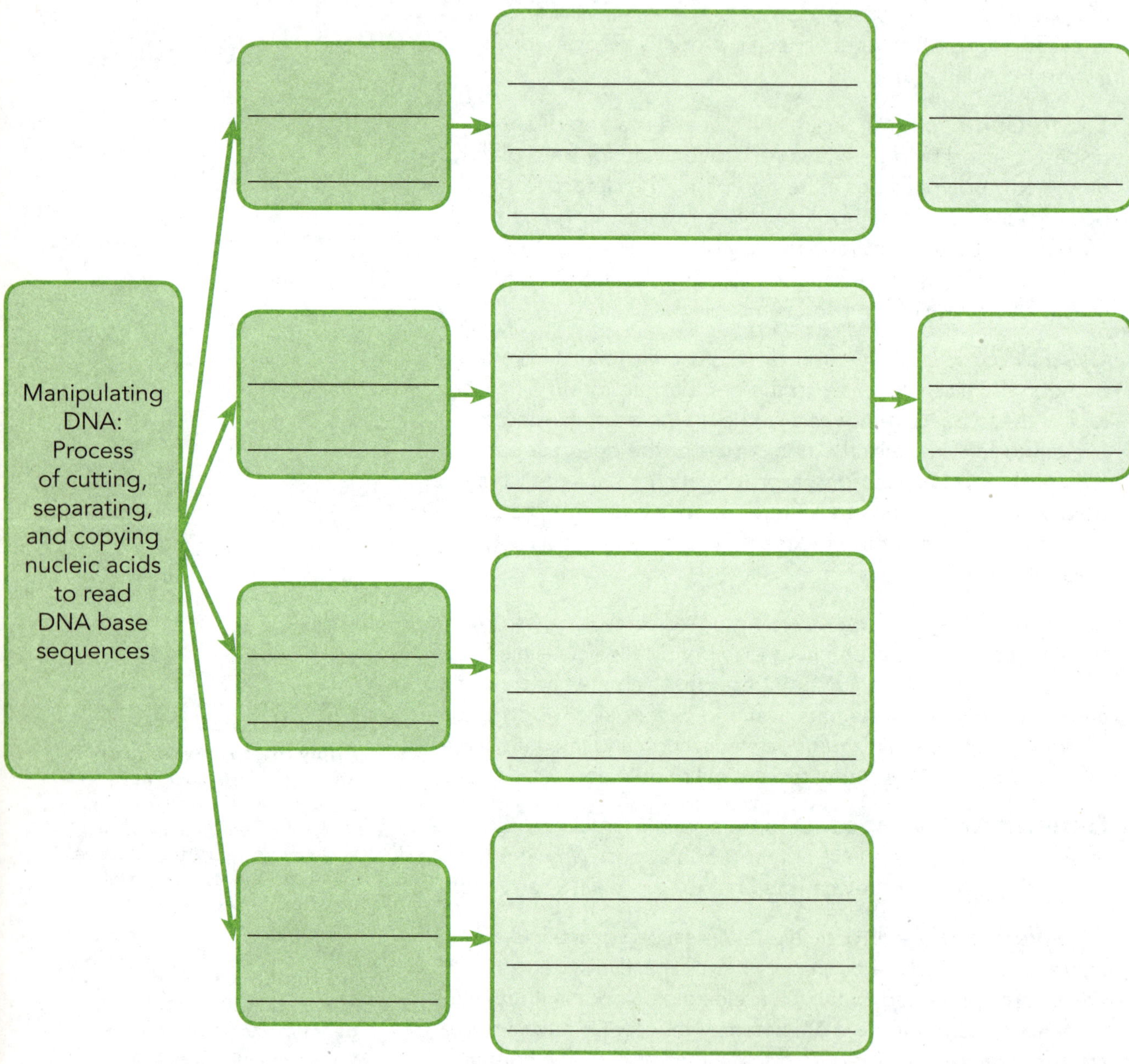

Lesson Summary

Manipulating DNA

KEY QUESTION *How can scientists read DNA base sequences?*

In the late 1960s, scientists discovered special prokaryote enzymes, called **restriction enzymes**, that could cut DNA at specific sites. By using tools that cut, separate, and copy nucleic acids, scientists can now read DNA base sequences. Such techniques have made it possible to study the genomes of living organisms, including humans, in great detail.

Cutting DNA DNA molecules must first be cut into smaller pieces for analysis. Many bacteria produce restriction enzymes that cut DNA at a very specific short sequence that is 4–8 pairs long. Each restriction enzyme can only recognize one base sequence. It cuts the strand of DNA between specific bases, leaving single-stranded overhangs. The overhangs are called "sticky ends" because they can bond, or "stick," to a DNA fragment with the complementary base sequence.

Separating DNA Once DNA has been cut by restriction enzymes, scientists can use **gel electrophoresis** to separate the fragments. DNA fragments are placed in wells on one end of a porous gel. When an electric voltage is applied to the gel, DNA molecules—which are negatively charged—move toward the positive end of the gel. The smaller the DNA fragment, the faster and farther it moves. The result is a pattern of bands based on fragment size. Researchers can then remove individual restriction fragments from the gel and study them further.

Reading DNA After the DNA fragments have been separated, researchers sequence them. The single-stranded DNA fragments are placed in a test tube containing DNA polymerase and the four nucleotide bases, A, T, G, and C. The enzyme uses the unknown strand as a template to make new DNA strands. The researchers also add a small number of bases that have a chemical dye attached. Each time a dye-labeled base is added to a new DNA strand, the synthesis of that strand stops. When DNA synthesis is completed, the result is a series of color-coded DNA fragments of different lengths. Researchers can then separate these fragments, often by gel electrophoresis. The order of colored bands on the gel tells the exact sequence of bases in the DNA.

As you read, circle the answers to each Key Question. Underline any words you do not understand.

BUILD Vocabulary

restriction enzyme enzyme that cuts DNA at a specific sequence of nucleotides

gel electrophoresis procedure used to separate and analyze DNA fragments by placing a mixture of DNA fragments at one end of a porous gel and applying an electrical voltage to the gel

Make Connections DNA is placed in gel that is *porous*, meaning that it has many small spaces or holes that air and liquids can pass through.

Why is it important that the substance DNA is placed in for electrophoresis be porous?

____

____

____

____

____

____

____

____

____

Visual Reading Tool: Separating DNA

Using the figure shown, label the different parts of a gel electrophoresis setup.

1. ______________________

____

2. ______________________

____

3. ______________________

4. ______________________

5. ______________________

6. ______________________

7. Why is a restriction enzyme important in gel electrophoresis?

____

8. Why do the DNA fragments move from the negative end of the gel toward the positive end?

____

____

Assembling the Sequence Most DNA sequencing techniques read fragments no more than a few hundred bases in length. These short "reads" of DNA are put together through a technique known as "shotgun" sequencing. Fragments are sequenced automatically, and the information is fed into a computer. A computer program analyzes the data by searching for matching sequences among the fragments, and aligns them to reassemble the fragments and complete the sequence.

The Human Genome—What's Inside?

KEY QUESTION *What research efforts have resulted from the Human Genome Project?*

In 2003, an international effort known as the Human Genome Project finished the first complete human DNA sequence. Labs around the world now study which regions of DNA are transcribed into RNA, which bind to proteins, which are marked with epigenetic tags, and which vary from one individual to the next.

READING TOOL

Make Connections After scientists had completely sequenced the human genome, it was published to the greater scientific community. **Why did the scientists share the genome with the whole world?**

____

____

____

____

____

How Many Genes? Human cells contain approximately 20,000 genes. The functions of about a quarter of human genes are unknown. The genes that we do understand fall into categories such as transcription factors, metabolic enzymes, components of the cell membrane, receptors, and regulatory factors.

The Large and Small of It The human haploid genome is larger than the genome of many other organisms. However, the cells of many organisms contain far more DNA than our cells do! Only about 2 percent of the human genome actually codes for proteins. What does the rest of the DNA code for? Some of it is involved in the regulation of gene expression. However, all of these sequences taken together account for only about 10 percent of the genome. Approximately 50 percent of the human genome is composed of highly repetitive DNA sequences. The functions of these regions remain unknown.

The Personal Genome On average, about one base in 1200 will not match between two individuals. Biologists refer to these single-base differences as single nucleotide polymorphisms (SNPs, or "snips"). Researchers have discovered that certain sets of closely linked SNPs occur together time and time again. Some of these are associated with certain traits, including the susceptibility to particular diseases or medical conditions. High-speed DNA sequencing is making it possible to rapidly pinpoint SNPs and their associated alleles, enabling physicians to tailor medical treatments to a patient's genome. In addition, many private companies now offer "personal genome" services that analyze one's DNA for a modest price.

Genome Privacy Rapid advances in the gathering and analyzing of genomic data have raised a number of ethical and legal questions. Who owns and controls genetic information? Who should have access to personal genetic information? In response to some of these issues, in 2008, the U.S. Congress passed the Genetic Information Nondiscrimination Act. This act makes it illegal for insurance companies and employers to discriminate based on information from genetic tests.

Gene Imprinting Epigenetic chemical marks can be attached to DNA and histone proteins in a way that affects gene expression by altering chromatin structure. This process is known as **genomic imprinting**. Some of these marks can be passed from one generation to the next through either the mother or the father. This means there are some genes that are only expressed if they came from a male parent and there are some genes that are only expressed if they came from a female parent. Nearly 100 known genes in humans are imprinted in this way.

BUILD Vocabulary

genomic imprinting process in which epigenetic marks affect gene expression by altering chromatin structure

Use Prior Knowledge You already know that a *genome* is all of the genetic information in the DNA of an organism. One definition of an *imprint* is an identifying marker. When you put these words together, they make a phrase that refers to marks carried on DNA. ☑ **How is genomic imprinting related to the gender of parents?**

____

____

____

____

____

14 Chapter Review

Review Vocabulary

Choose the letter of the best answer.

1. Which shows patterns of traits among members of a family?

A. genome

B. pedigree

C. personal genome

2. Which is/are used to "cut" DNA into fragments?

A. gel electrophoresis

B. restriction enzymes

C. genomic imprinting

Match the vocabulary term to its definition.

3.	________	full set of genetic information in an organism's DNA	a. nondisjunction
4.	________	process used to separate DNA fragments by size	b. genome
5.	________	when homologous chromosomes fail to separate during meiosis	c. gel electrophoresis

Review Key Questions

Provide evidence and details to support your answers.

6. How does human blood type show both simple dominance and codominant inheritance patterns?

7. Explain the difference between disorders of chromosome number and disorders caused by individual genes.

8. What steps must scientists follow in order to "read" a sequence of DNA?

CHAPTER 15

LESSON 1

Changing the Living World

READING TOOL **Make Connections** While you read this lesson, fill in the graphic organizer below. Explain the two ways that scientists carry out selective breeding practices, and the two ways they create increased variation within a population. Use examples from your text to support your explanations.

Selective Breeding

Hybridication: ______________________________

Inbreeding: ______________________________

Increasing Variation

Bacterial Mutation: ______________________________

Polypoid Plants: ______________________________

Selective Breeding

KEY QUESTION *What is selective breeding used for?*

Allowing only those organisms with desired characteristics to produce the next generation is called **selective breeding**. Selective breeding takes advantage of naturally occurring genetic variation to pass desired traits on to the next generation. This is one example of **biotechnology**, which has been practiced for thousands of years in developing animals, such as dog breeds, and plants, such as corn and potatoes. Corn was selectively bred from the wild grass teosinte nearly 10,000 years ago.

As you read, circle the answers to each Key Question. Underline any words you do not understand.

BUILD Vocabulary

selective breeding method of breeding that allows only those organisms with desired characteristics to produce the next generation

biotechnology the process of manipulating organisms, cells, or molecules, to produce specific products

BUILD Vocabulary

hybridization breeding technique that involves crossing dissimilar individuals to bring together the best traits of both organisms

inbreeding continued breeding of individuals with similar characteristics to maintain the derived characteristics of a kind of organism

Suffixes Note that the suffix *-ization* indicates "the making of."

☑ **Scientists use the process of hybridization to make what kind of organisms?**

____

____

____

Hybridization **Hybridization** is the crossing of dissimilar individuals to bring together the best of both organisms. American botanist Luther Burbank's hybrid crosses combined the disease resistance of one plant with the food-production capacity of another. This resulted in a new line of plants that led to increased food production. In fact, the Russet Burbank potato is one example of a new line of plants.

Inbreeding To maintain desirable characteristics in a line of organisms, breeders will continually breed individuals with similar characteristics. This technique is known as **inbreeding**. Inbreeding helps ensure that the characteristics that make each breed unique are preserved. Many breeds of dogs are maintained this way. Although inbreeding is useful in preserving certain traits, it also brings along some risks. Most of the members of a breed are genetically similar, which increases the chance that a cross between two individuals will bring together two recessive alleles for a genetic defect.

Increasing Variation

KEY QUESTION *How do people increase genetic variation?*

Breeders can increase the genetic variation in a population by introducing mutations, which are the ultimate source of biological diversity.

Bacterial Mutations Mutations, which are heritable changes in DNA, occur spontaneously, but breeders can increase the mutation rate of an organism by using radiation or chemicals. While many mutations are harmful, breeders can select those mutations that produce useful characteristics not found in the original population.

This technique has been very useful with bacteria. Because they are small, millions of bacteria can be treated with radiation or chemicals at the same time. This increases the chances of producing a useful mutant. This technique has allowed scientists to develop hundreds of useful bacterial strains.

For instance, it is been known for decades that certain strains of oil-digesting bacteria are effective for cleaning up oil spills. Today, scientists are working to produce bacteria that can clean up radioactive substances and metal pollution in the environment.

Polyploid Plants Drugs that prevent the separating of chromosomes during meiosis are useful in plant breeding. These drugs can produce cells that have many times the normal number of chromosomes. Plants grown from these cells are called polyploid because they have many sets of chromosomes. Polyploidy is usually fatal in animals. But, for reasons that are not clear, plants are much better at tolerating extra sets of chromosomes.

Polyploidy can quickly produce new species of plants that are larger and stronger than their diploid relatives. A number of important crop plants, such as bananas and many types of citrus fruits, have been produced in this way.

Visual Reading Tool: Mutations Timeline

Complete the timeline shown by first identifying the two plants shown, and then determining the time when they occurred. Use Figure 15-1 in the textbook to help you.

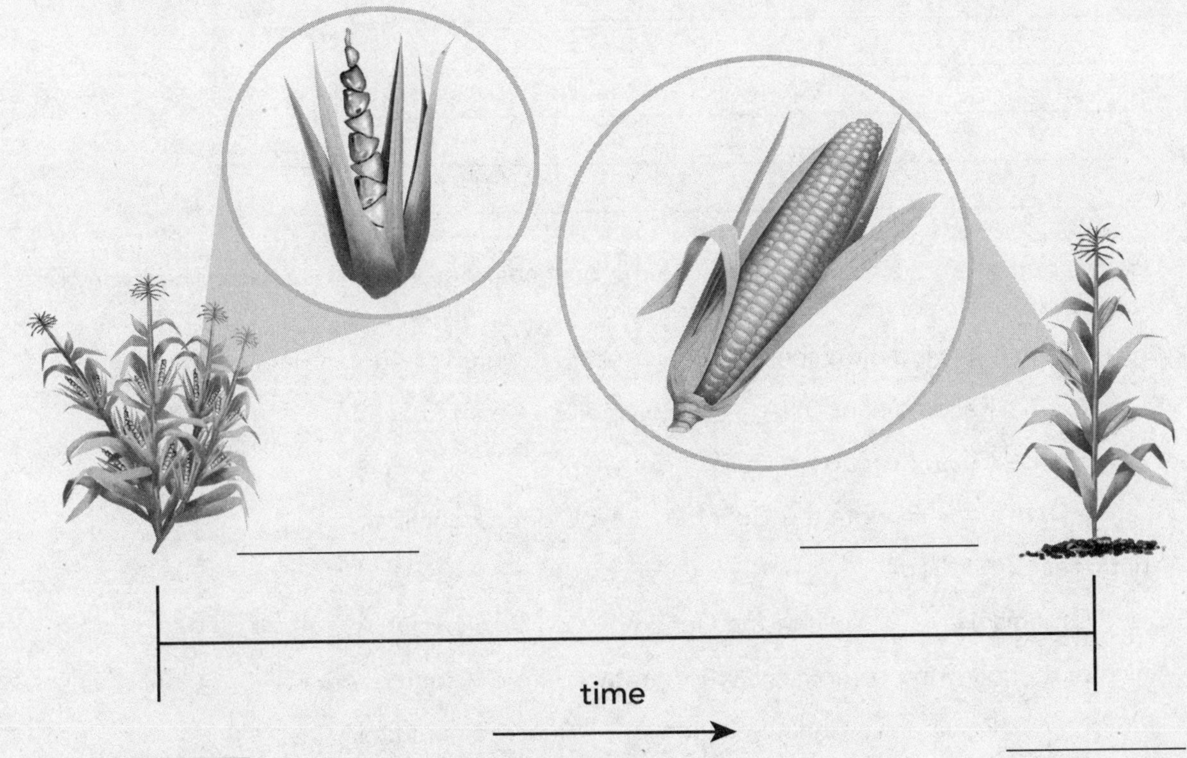

1. Describe the changes that took place between the two plants.

____

____

2. What caused these changes to occur over time?

____

CHAPTER 15

LESSON 2

The Process of Genetic Engineering

READING TOOL **Use Structure** Before you read, skim through the lesson and fill in the outline below with the section headings. The first one is shown for you as an example. Then, using your outline, answer the questions below.

I. Analyzing DNA

a. Finding a Gene

b. ______________________________

II. ______________________________

a. ______________________________

b. ______________________________

c. ______________________________

III. ______________________________

a. ______________________________

b. ______________________________

c. ______________________________

Next, Use the outline above to help you chose the best answer for each question. There may be more than one possible solution for each question.

1. Which of the following biotechnologies is used to rewrite the human genome?

CRISPR   Recombinant DNA   Polymerase Chain Reaction

2. A Polymerase Chain Reaction is used to do what?

Analyze DNA   Rewrite the Genome   Clone Organisms

3. What does CRISPR do?

Clone Organisms   Rewrite the Genome   Analyze DNA

4. Which of the following combines DNA from two different sources?

CRISPR   Polymerase Chain Reaction   Recombinant DNA

5. What do scientists call the small circular DNA sequences found in bacteria?

Markers   Plasmids   Recombinant DNA

Lesson Summary

Analyzing DNA

KEY QUESTION *How do scientists copy the DNA of living organisms?*

Genes can be engineered to change the characteristics of living organisms. Scientists can isolate single genes from among millions of fragments.

Finding a Gene Scientists analyze the nucleotide sequences of genes to screen for specific genes. The gene for the green fluorescence protein (GFP) in a species of jellyfish was isolated by a method in which DNA fragments are separated by a gel so as to isolate the fragment containing the actual gene for GFP.

Polymerase Chain Reaction Once a gene has been isolated, scientists can take a small sample and make multiple copies of specific DNA sequences using a technique known as **polymerase chain reaction**.

Rewriting the Genome

KEY QUESTION *How is recombinant DNA used?*

Recombinant DNA Not only can scientists isolate genes but they can make changes in the genome by inserting new or foreign DNA molecules into living cells. The combined molecules are known as **recombinant DNA**, and they change the genetic composition of a living organism.

Plasmids and Genetic Markers Some bacteria contain small circular DNA molecules known as **plasmids**, which are widely used in recombinant DNA studies. Plasmid DNA contains a signal for replication, but it also has a **genetic marker** that makes it possible to distinguish bacteria that carry the plasmid from those that don't. Using plasmids, recombinant DNA technology has been used to transform a bacterial cell so that it can manufacture human growth hormones.

CRISPR and DNA Editing CRISPR (clustered regularly interspersed short palindromic repeats) technology enables scientists to rewrite the base sequence of nearly any gene in a cell, transforming disease-causing genes and reengineering genes to perform new functions.

As you read, circle the answers to each Key Question. Underline any words you do not understand.

BUILD Vocabulary

polymerase chain reaction the technique used by biologists to make many copies of a particular gene

recombinant DNA DNA produced by combining DNA from two or more different sources

plasmid small, circular piece of DNA located in the cytoplasm of many bacteria

genetic marker alleles that produce detectable phenotypic differences useful in genetic analysis

Prefixes

The prefix *trans* means "across," and generally refers to things being moved from one area to another. For example: transporting goods from one side of a country to the other side. **How does this prefix express the meaning of the word *transgenic*?**

____

____

____

BUILD Vocabulary

transgenic term used to refer to an organism that contains genes from other organisms

clone member of a population of genetically identical cells produced from a single cell

Transgenic Organisms and Cloning

KEY QUESTION *How are transgenic organisms produced?*

The universal nature of the genetic code makes it possible to construct organisms that contain genes from other species. These **transgenic** organisms can be produced by the insertion of recombinant DNA into the genome of a host organism.

Transgenic Plants Plant cells can be transformed using different methods: inserting a bacterium that contains a small DNA tumor-producing plasmid, removing plant cell walls, or injecting DNA directly into the cell.

Transgenic Animals Egg cells of many animals are large enough that DNA can be inserted directly into the nucleus. Enzymes normally responsible for DNA repair and recombination may help to insert the foreign DNA into the chromosomes of the cell.

Cloning A **clone** is a population of genetically identical cells produced from a single cell. The technique of cloning uses a single cell from an adult organism to grow an entirely new individual that is genetically identical to the organism from which the cell was taken.

Cloned colonies of bacteria and other microorganisms are easy to grow, but this is not always true of multicellular organisms, especially animals.

Visual Reading Tool: Analyze a Sequence: Cloning

Use the steps listed below to explain the process of creating a cloned sheep. Label each step on the diagram with the appropriate label or description listed below.

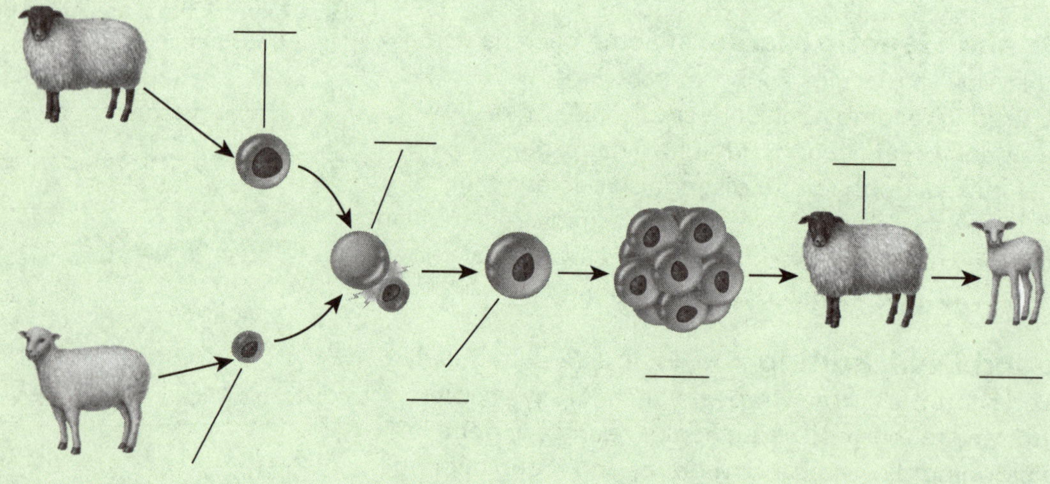

A. Egg Cell

B. Donor Nucleus

C. Nucleus of Egg Cell is Removed

D. Fused Cell

E. Embryo

F. Foster Mother

G. Cloned Lamb

Lastly, circle the two sheep on the diagram that represent two genetically identical sheep.

CHAPTER 15

LESSON 3

Applications of Biotechnology

READING TOOL **Main Idea and Details** As you read, identify the main idea and supporting details under each main heading from the text.

Main Idea	Evidence and Details
Agriculture and Industry	
GM Crops	
GM Animals	
Health and Medicine	
Genetic Testing	
Medical Research	
Preventing and Treating Disease	
Examining Active Genes	
Personal Identification	
Forensic Science	
Fallen Heroes	
Establishing Relationships	

Lesson Summary

As you read, circle the answers to each Key Question. Underline any words you do not understand.

READING TOOL

Make Connections Scientists can modify the DNA of plants or animals. **What are two ways that scientists use genetically modified animals to benefit humans?**

____

____

____

____

____

Agriculture and Industry

KEY QUESTION *How can genetic engineering benefit agriculture and industry?*

Genetic engineering can benefit agriculture by producing better, less expensive, and more nutritious foods as well as making manufacturing processes less harmful.

GM Crops Since their introduction in 1996, genetically modified (GM) plants have become an important component of our food supply. For example, corn is often modified with bacterial genes that produce a protein called Bt toxin. The Bt toxin inserted in plants makes them resistant to insects, making spraying with pesticides unnecessary, and often produces higher crop yields. Resistance to insects is just one useful characteristic being engineered into crops. Others include resistance to viral infections and herbicides, resistance to rotting, and the production of plastics.

GM Animals Transgenic animals can be made larger and faster growing, which also makes them more productive. Cows have been injected with hormones produced by recombinant-DNA techniques to increase milk production. Pigs can be genetically modified (GM) to produce more lean meat or higher levels of healthy omega-3 acids.

Health and Medicine

KEY QUESTION *How can biotechnology improve human health?*

Genetic Testing Genetic tests diagnose hundreds of disorders, such as cystic fibrosis. Because the CF allele has slightly different DNA sequences from its normal counterpart, genetic tests using labeled DNA probes can distinguish the presence of CF. Like many genetic tests, the CF test uses specific DNA sequences that detect the complementary base sequences found in the disease-causing alleles.

Medical Research Transgenic animals are often used as model test subjects in medical research, simulating human disorders, such as Alzheimer's disease and arthritis.

Preventing and Treating Disease Bioengineering can prevent and treat human diseases in a variety of different ways, from making our food more nutritious to creating strains of mosquitos that are incapable of transmitting particular pathogens.

Examining Active Genes Although each cell in a person contains the same genetic material, the same genes are not active in every cell. Scientists use **DNA microarray** technology to study hundreds or thousands of genes at once, to understand their activity levels.

Personal Identification

KEY QUESTION *How is DNA used to identify individuals?*

The variation of the human genome ensures that no individual is exactly like any other, except in the case of twins. **DNA fingerprinting** analyzes sections of DNA that may have little or no function but that vary widely from one individual to another. Because only identical twins share the same genome, DNA can be used to determine a person's identity.

Forensic Science In **forensics**—the scientific study of crime scene evidence—DNA fingerprinting has been used to solve crimes, convict criminals, and even overturn wrongful convictions. DNA forensics has also been used to conserve wildlife. Officials can use DNA fingerprinting to identify the African elephant herds where the animals were poached for their tusks to help stop the illegal ivory trade.

Fallen Heroes The U.S. military requires all personnel to provide a sample of their DNA when they begin their service. Those DNA samples are kept on file and used, if needed, to identify the remains of individuals who perish in the line of duty.

Establishing Relationships DNA fingerprinting can also be used to establish paternity and trace ancestry. For example, DNA fingerprinting makes it easy to find alleles carried by the child that do not match those of the mother. Any such alleles must come from the child's biological father, and they will show up in his DNA fingerprint.

BUILD Vocabulary

DNA microarray glass slide or silicon chip that carries thousands of different kinds of single-stranded DNA fragments arranged in a grid. A DNA microarray is used to detect and measure the expression of thousands of genes at one time

DNA fingerprinting tool used by biologists that analyzes an individual's unique collection of DNA restriction fragments; used to determine whether two samples of genetic material are from the same person

forensics scientific study of crime scene evidence

Visual Reading Tool: Compare and Contrast: DNA Fingerprints

Compare Suspect 1 (S1) and Suspect 2 (S2) to the DNA evidence sample (E). Based upon the DNA fingerprints, which suspect was likely at the crime scene and why?

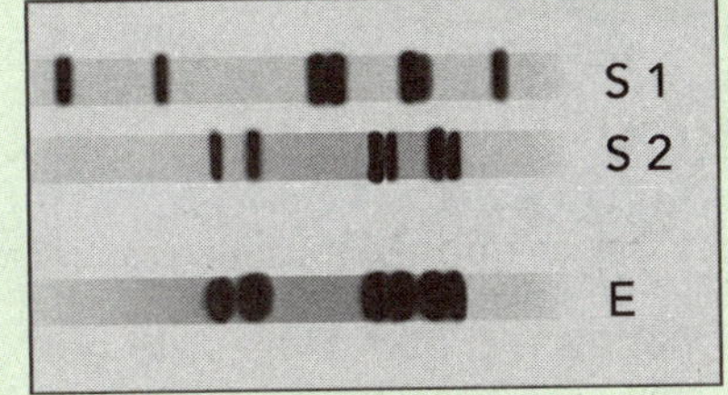

DNA fingerprint

CHAPTER 15

LESSON 4

Ethics and Impacts of Biotechnology

READING TOOL **Benefits and Drawbacks** As you read, identify the opposing views on each ethical issue. Take notes in the two-column chart shown below.

Issue	Benefits	Drawbacks
Patenting life		
Genetic privacy		
GM foods		
New biology		

Lesson Summary

Profits and Privacy

As you read, circle the answers to each Key Question. Underline any words you do not understand.

KEY QUESTION *What privacy issues does biotechnology raise?*

Private biotechnology and pharmaceutical companies do much of the research involving genetically modified (GM) plants and animals. They have often sought to protect their research by placing a patent on their discoveries. A patent is a legal tool that gives an individual or a company the exclusive right to profit from innovations for a number of years.

Patenting Life Patents have been used for years for new machines and devices. Now patents are also being used for molecules and biotechnology procedures. At times, disputes over biotechnology procedures arise—and these disputes have slowed the research of other biotechnological advancements.

One such dispute was brought to the United States Supreme Court. In 2013, the U.S. Supreme Court unanimously ruled that genes found in nature cannot be patented. Altered, or synthetic genes, however, could be patented, allowing companies to protect novel biotechnology products.

Genetic Privacy DNA can reveal personal information, including ethnic heritage, the chances of developing certain diseases, and evidence for criminal cases. The revelation of this information does raise questions of privacy. For example, it may be considered unfair for an employer to pass on a possible candidate if certain conclusions were made based on information from the candidate's DNA. As science advances, legal experts will debate ways to keep personal genetic information safe and confidential.

READING TOOL

Academic Words

novel new or unusual in an interesting way.

☑ **What type of genes are allowed to be patented?**

Safety of Transgenic Organisms

KEY QUESTION *What are some of the pros and cons of transgenic organisms?*

The presence of GM products in the marketplace has raised concerns from consumers. While nearly half of the GM crops today are grown in the United States, farmers around the world are now using GM technology. Many public-interest groups have argued that GM foods should be labeled. The U.S. Department of Agriculture is currently attempting to develop guidelines for this labeling. There are supporters and opponents of GM foods, with each side having very important points to support its opinions.

Arguments for GM Foods Those who support the use and growth of GM foods and crops argue that GM plants are actually better and safer than other crops. Farmers choose GM plants because they produce higher yield reducing the amount of land and energy that must be devoted to agriculture and lowering the cost for everyone. Supporters also argue that insect-resistant GM plants need little, if any, insecticide to grow successfully. Thus, GM crops could reduce the chance of chemical residue entering our food supply and lessen the effects of or damage to the environment. Finally, supporters point to the fact that the scientific community generally regards foods made from GM plants as safe to eat.

Visual Reading Tool: Analyzing Crop Yield Data

Below, use your own words to describe what the graph shows about the use of genetically modified crops between 1996 and 2016.

____

____

____

____

____

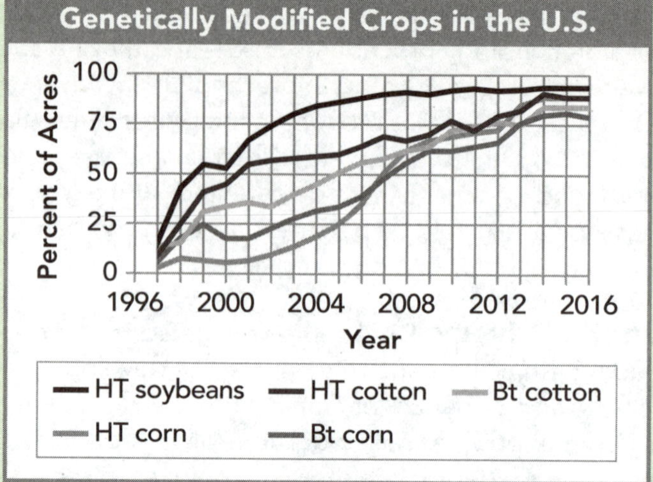

Data for each crop category include varieties with both HT and Bt (stacked) traits.
Sources: USDA, Economic Research Service using data from Fernandez-Cornejo and McBride (2002) for the years 1996–1999 and USDA, National Agriculture Statistics Service, *June Agriculture Survey* for years 2000–16.

Arguments Against GM Foods On the other hand, opponents of GM foods have raised concerns about the possible unintended consequences for agriculture of a shift to GM farming and ranching. One concern is that insect resistance may threaten beneficial insects (such as honeybees) as well as crop pests. Another concern is that patents held on GM seeds may raise the cost of seeds to the point that small farmers would go out of business, especially in the developing world.

In the United States, many public interest groups have argued that GM foods should be identified and labeled so that consumers would be fully aware of what they are eating. In 2016, Vermont passed a law that required labeling on GM foods. However, Congress later overrode that law, but did request that the United States Department of Agriculture develop rules for GM food labeling. The rules would then be implemented across all of the United States.

Ethics of the New Biology

KEY QUESTION *What are some of the ethical issues around new biotechnology?*

With the new knowledge we gain about ourselves using biotechnology, there is also a great responsibility. We can alter life forms for any purpose, scientific or nonscientific. Scientists could cure diseases such as cystic fibrosis or hemophilia. But should they try to engineer taller people or change their eye color, hair texture, sex, blood group, or appearance? The goal of biology is to gain a better understanding of the nature of life. Everyone is responsible for ensuring that the tools science has given us are used wisely.

15 Chapter Review

Review Vocabulary

Choose the letter of the best answer that defines the word.

1. Biotechnology
   A. the science of computers
   B. the evolution of animal species
   C. manipulation of organisms or cells to produce desired products
   D. computer programs for creating life

2. Hybridization
   A. creation of mutations for gene modification
   B. crossing of dissimilar organisms to combine the best traits of each
   C. development of transport using alternative fuels

Match the vocabulary term to its definition.

3. ________ small, circular piece of DNA located in the cytoplasm of many bacteria

4. ________ use of DNA in the study of crime scene evidence

5. ________ member of a population of genetically identical cells produced from a single cell

a. clone

b. plasmid

c. forensics

Review Key Questions

Provide evidence and details to support your answers.

6. Why do scientists, farmers, and animal breeders use selective breeding practices?

7. What is recombinant DNA and how is it used?

8. How is DNA used in forensics?

9. List some of the benefits and drawbacks of GM organisms.

CHAPTER 16

LESSON 1

Life Is Cellular

READING TOOL **Main Idea and Details** As you read your textbook, identify the main ideas along with details or evidence that supports the main ideas. Use the lesson headings to organize the main ideas and details. One example is entered for you. Record your work in the table.

Heading	Main Idea	Details/Evidence
The Discovery of the Cell		
Early Microscopes	The invention of the microscope led to the discovery of cells.	Microscopes show that cork consists of cells and that there are organisms present in pond water.
The Cell Theory		
Exploring the Cell		
Light Microscopes		
Electron Microscopes		
• Transmission Electron Microscopes		
• Scanning Electron Microscopes		
Prokaryotes and Eukaryotes		
Prokaryotes		
Eukaryotes		

Lesson Summary

The Discovery of the Cell

As you read, circle the answers to each Key Question. Underline any words you do not understand.

KEY QUESTION *What are the main points of the cell theory?*

The smallest living unit of any organism is a cell. Cells were unknown until the microscope was invented.

Early Microscopes Eyeglass makers in the late 1500s discovered that using several lenses in combination could magnify objects. They used their lenses to build the first microscopes. In 1665, Robert Hooke used a microscope to look at a slice of cork from a plant. The cork appeared to be made of many tiny empty chambers that Hooke called "cells." Around the same time Anton van Leeuwenhoek used a microscope to look at pond water. With the microscope, he saw many tiny living organisms in the water.

The Cell Theory In 1838, Matthias Schleiden stated that all plants are made of **cells**. In 1855, Theodor Schwann stated that all animals are made of cells. In 1885 Rudolf Virchow stated that new cells are produced only from the division of existing cells. These discoveries are summarized in the **cell theory**.

The cell theory includes three main ideas:

- All living things are made up of cells.
- Cells are the basic units of structure and function in living things.
- New cells are produced from existing cells.

BUILD Vocabulary

cell basic unit of all forms of life

cell theory fundamental concept of biology that states that all living things are composed of cells; that cells are the basic units of structure and function in living things; and that new cells are produced from existing cells

cell membrane thin, flexible barrier that surrounds all cells; regulates what enters and leaves the cell

nucleus in cells, structure that contains the cell's genetic material in the form of DNA

eukaryote organism whose cells contain a nucleus

prokaryote unicellular organism that lacks a nucleus

Root Words *Karyo* comes from the Greek *karyon*, meaning "nut" or "kernel." It is used in words that refer to the nucleus. *Pro-* is a prefix that means "before," so prokaryotes have been around since before the nucleus appeared in living organisms.

What structure distinguishes eukaryotes from prokaryotes?

____

Exploring the Cell

KEY QUESTION *How do microscopes work?*

Modern biologists still use microscopes to study the cell. Microscopes work by using beams of light or beams of electrons to produce magnified images.

Light Microscopes You may be familiar with the compound light microscope. A light microscope uses light passing through a specimen and two lenses to form an image. The first lens, called the objective lens, is just above the specimen. The second lens, called the ocular lens, magnifies the image further. Due to the nature of light, light microscopes clearly magnify an object only about 1000 times. Chemical stains or dyes are used to help make parts of cells visible. Some dyes are fluorescent, meaning they give off light of a particular color.

Electron Microscopes Electron microscopes use beams of electrons instead of light. A light microscope can view something as small as 1 millionth of a meter. An electron microscope can view something as small as 1 billionth of a meter, such as viruses or a DNA molecule.

Samples viewed on an electron microscope must be placed in a vacuum. Therefore, an electron microscope can only be used to examine nonliving samples. Images are black and white, but computers are used to add "false color" to structures.

Transmission Electron Microscopes Beams of electrons must pass through the sample, so samples of cells and tissues must be sliced extremely thin. Images appear flat and two-dimensional.

Scanning Electron Microscopes A beam of electrons scans the surface of a specimen, so samples do not have to be cut into thin slices. Images appear three-dimensional.

READING TOOL

Compare and Contrast

Transmission and scanning electron microscopy are both tools to examine biological structures. Each creates a very different type of image. **☑ How do the final images of transmission and scanning electron microscopy differ?**

____

____

____

____

____

Prokaryotes and Eukaryotes

KEY QUESTION *How do prokaryotic and eukaryotic cells differ?*

Most cells range from 5 to 50 micrometers in diameter. All cells are surrounded by a thin flexible barrier called the **cell membrane** (also called the plasma membrane). Cells fall into two categories, depending on whether they contain a nucleus. The **nucleus** (plural: nuclei) is a large membrane-enclosed structure that contains genetic material in the form of DNA. **Eukaryotes** (yoo KAR ee ohts) are cells that have nuclei. **Prokaryotes** (pro KAR ee ohts) are cells that do not have nuclei.

Prokaryotes Prokaryotic cells do not enclose their genetic material within a nucleus. They are generally smaller and simpler than eukaryotic cells. Bacteria are prokaryotes. Prokaryotes carry out all of the activities associated with living things. Prokaryotes were the first photosynthetic organisms on Earth.

Eukaryotes In eukaryotic cells, the nucleus separates the genetic material from the rest of the cell. Most eukaryotic cells contain many structures and internal membranes. Some eukaryotes are unicellular organisms called protists. Others form multicellular organisms—plants, animals, and fungi. In multicellular organisms, cells are specialized and usually work together to perform specific tasks.

Visual Reading Tool: Prokaryotes and Eukaryotes

Read the section on prokaryotes and eukaryotes to identify the similarities and differences of each cell type. Use a green pencil to circle similarities, a blue pencil to circle prokaryotic cell characteristics, and a red pencil to circle eukaryotic cell characteristics. Then complete the table below.

	Prokaryotic Cell	Eukaryotic Cell
Cell membrane		yes
Nucleus		
Cell size	smaller	
Complexity		
Example of organism with this cell type		

CHAPTER 16

LESSON 2

Cell Structure

READING TOOL **Connect to Visuals** As you read, use the figures and diagrams to help you identify and describe each part of the cell, and what the function that part performs. Complete the graphic organizer.

Cellular Structure	Form and Function
Nucleus	
Ribosomes	
Endoplasmic reticulum	
Golgi apparatus	
Vacuoles	
Lysosomes	
Cytoskeleton	
Chloroplasts	
Mitochondria	
Cell wall	
Cell membrane	

Lesson Summary

Cell Organization

KEY QUESTION *What is the role of the cell nucleus?*

Eukaryotic cells can be divided into the nucleus and the cytoplasm. The **cytoplasm** is the part of the cell outside the nucleus. The interior of a prokaryotic cell, which lacks a nucleus, is also called the cytoplasm. Eukaryotic cells also have many specialized structures that are called **organelles**, which means "little organs."

Comparing the Cell to a Factory A eukaryotic cell functions much like a factory. The different organelles of a cell are like specialized machines and assembly lines. Organelles follow instructions and create biological molecules, like the people and machines in a factory create different products.

The Nucleus The nucleus is the control center of the cell. The nucleus contains nearly all of the DNA in the cell and, with it, the coded instructions for making proteins and other important molecules. In prokaryotic cells, there is no nucleus, and the DNA is found in the cytoplasm.

The nucleus is surrounded by the nuclear envelope, which is composed of two membranes. The nuclear envelope has thousands of nuclear pores, which allow material such as proteins and other molecules to move in and out of the nucleus. The genetic material in the nucleus is found in chromosomes. Most nuclei also contain a nucleolus, which is a region of the nucleus where ribosome assembly begins.

Organelles That Build Proteins

KEY QUESTION *What organelles help make and transport proteins and other macromolecules?*

Much of the cell is devoted to producing proteins, which are responsible for the synthesis of other macromolecules such as lipids and carbohydrates.

Ribosomes Proteins are assembled on ribosomes. **Ribosomes** are small particles of RNA and protein found throughout the cytoplasm in eukaryotes and prokaryotes. Ribosomes produce proteins by following instructions that come from DNA.

As you read, circle the answers to each Key Question. Underline any words you do not understand.

BUILD Vocabulary

cytoplasm in eukaryotic cells, all cellular contents outside the nucleus; in prokaroytic cells, all of the cells' contents

organelle specialized structure that performs important cellular functions within a eukaryotic cell

ribosome cell organelle consisting of RNA and protein found throughout the cytoplasm in a cell; the site of protein synthesis

Related Words The English word *organ* comes from the Latin word "organon," meaning tool or instrument. **Using this information, explain how an organ and organelles are related.**

____

____

____

____

____

____

____

BUILD Vocabulary

endoplasmic reticulum internal membrane system found in eukaryotic cells; place where lipid components of the cell membrane are assembled

Golgi apparatus organelle in cells that modifies, sorts, and packages proteins and other materials from the endoplasmic reticulum for storage in the cell or release outside the cell

vacuole cell organelle that stores materials such as water, salts, proteins, and carbohydrates

lysosome cell organelle that breaks down lipids, carbohydrates, and proteins into small molecules that can used by the rest of the cell

cytoskeleton network of protein filaments in a eukaryotic cell that gives the cell its shape and internal organization and is involved in movement

Chloroplast cell organelle that converts energy from sunlight into chemical energy through the process of photosynthesis

mitochondrion cell organelle that converts the chemical energy stored in food into compounds that are more convenient for the cell to use

cell wall strong, supporting layer around the cell membrane in most prokaryotes and some eukaryotes

Related Words *Plasm* is a root that appears in many biological terms related to cells and living things. It comes from a Greek word that means "something molded."

☑ **What two vocabulary terms in this lesson have *plasm* as a root?**

____

____

Endoplasmic Reticulum Eukaryotic cells contain an internal membrane system called the **endoplasmic reticulum** (en doh PLAZ mik reh TIK yoo lum), or ER. The portion of the ER involved in making proteins is called the rough ER, due to the ribosomes on its surface. Proteins made on the rough ER include those that will be released, or secreted, from the cell; many membrane proteins; and proteins destined for other specialized locations within the cell. Other proteins are made on ribosomes that are not attached to membranes.

The other part of the ER is called the smooth ER because ribosomes are not found on its surface. The smooth ER produces lipids and is involved in the detoxification of drugs and the synthesis of carbohydrates.

Golgi Apparatus In eukaryotic cells, proteins produced in the rough ER move into the **Golgi apparatus**, which appears as a stack of flattened membranes. The proteins are bundled into tiny membrane-enclosed structures called vesicles that bud from the ER and carry the proteins to the Golgi apparatus. The Golgi apparatus modifies, sorts, and packages proteins and other materials from the endoplasmic reticulum for storage in the cell or release from the cell.

Organelles That Store, Clean Up, and Support

KEY QUESTION *What are the functions of vacuoles, lysosomes, and the cytoskeleton?*

Vacuoles, vesicles, lysosomes, and the cytoskeleton represent the cellular factory's storage space, cleanup crew, and support structures.

Vacuoles and Vesicles Many cells contain **vacuoles**, which are large, saclike, membrane-enclosed structures. Vacuoles store materials like water, salts, proteins, and carbohydrates. Many plant cells have a single, large central vacuole. The pressure of the liquid in the central vacuole helps plants to support structures such as leaves and stems. In addition to vacuoles, most eukaryotic cells contain smaller membrane-enclosed structures called vesicles. Vesicles store and move materials between organelles, as well as to and from the cell surface.

Lysosomes **Lysosomes** break down lipids, proteins, and carbohydrates into small molecules that can be used by the cell. Lysosomes also break down and remove organelles and other things in the cell that are no longer needed. Lysosomes are found in animal cells and in some plant cells.

The Cytoskeleton Eukaryotic cells have a network of protein filaments called the **cytoskeleton**. The cytoskeleton helps to transport materials within the cell. The cytoskeleton helps the cell maintain its shape and is involved in movement.

Microfilaments Microfilaments are threadlike structures made from a protein called actin. They form a tough, flexible framework that supports the cell. Microfilaments also help cells move.

Microtubules Microtubules are hollow structures made from proteins called tubulins. In some cells they maintain cell shape. They are important in cell division, forming a structure called the mitotic spindle that separates chromosomes. Organelles called centrioles are also made from tubulins. Centrioles help to organize cell division in animal cells, but are not found in plant cells. Microtubules also help to build projections from the cell surface such as cilia (singular: *cilium*) and flagella (singular: *flagellum*) that allow cells to swim through liquid.

READING TOOL

Academic Words

network A network is a system of connected things. In a previous chapter you learned about food webs, which are another type of network. ☑ **Based upon what you know about networks, explain why computers are more useful when they are connected to the internet.**

____

____

____

____

____

Organelles That Capture and Release Energy

KEY QUESTION *What are the functions of chloroplasts and mitochondria?*

Chloroplasts Plants and some other organisms contain chloroplasts (KLAWR uh plasts). **Chloroplasts** capture the energy from sunlight and convert it into chemical energy stored in food during photosynthesis. Chloroplasts are surrounded by two membranes and contain large stacks of additional membranes that contain the green pigment chlorophyll.

Mitochondria Nearly all eukaryotic cells, including plants, contain mitochondria (myt oh KAHN dree uh; singular *mitochondrion*). **Mitochondria** convert the chemical energy stored in food molecules into compounds that are more convenient for the cell to use. As with chloroplasts, mitochondria are surrounded by two membranes. The inner membrane is folded up inside the mitochondrion. All or nearly all of our mitochondria are inherited from our mothers.

Chloroplasts and mitochondria contain some of their own genetic information in the form of small DNA molecules. These organelles probably originated from prokaryotic cells that became part of eukaryotic cells in a mutualistic relationship. Genetic changes in human mitochondria can affect human health.

Cellular Boundaries

KEY QUESTION *What is the function of the cell membrane?*

Cell Walls The **cell wall** lies outside the cell membrane and supports, shapes, and protects the cell. Most prokaryotes and some eukaryotes, including plants and fungi, have cell walls. Animal cells do not have cell walls. Cell walls allow water, oxygen, carbon dioxide, and other substances to pass through. Cell walls provide much of the strength plants need to stand.

BUILD Vocabulary

lipid bilayer flexible double-layered sheet that makes up the cell membrane and forms a barrier between the cell and its surroundings

selectively permeable property of biological membranes that allows some substances to pass across it while others cannot; also called semipermeable membrane

Prefixes The prefix *bi-* means "two." A bicycle has two wheels, and a lipid bilayer has two layers, or sheets, of lipids. ☑ **The cell membrane is a lipid bilayer, but a cell has only one cell membrane. Which organelles in this lesson have a double membrane?**

____

____

____

Cell Membranes All cells have cell membranes. Cell membranes are made up of a double-layered sheet called a **lipid bilayer**. The cell membrane regulates what enters and leaves the cell and also protects and supports the cell.

The Properties of Lipids Lipids have oily fatty chains that are attached to chemical groups that interact with water. The fatty acid portions of the lipid are hydrophobic (hy druh FOH bik), or "water hating," while the other end is hydrophilic (hy druh FIL ik), or "water loving." When the lipids are in water, their hydrophobic "tails" cluster together while the hydrophilic "heads" are attracted to water. This results in a lipid bilayer, with the fatty acid tails forming the interior of the membrane. Many substances can cross cell membranes, but some substances are too large or too strongly charged to cross the lipid bilayer. Cell membranes are **selectively permeable** (or semipermeable), meaning that some substances can cross the membrane and others cannot.

The Fluid Mosaic Model Proteins are embedded in the lipid bilayer of most cell membranes. Carbohydrate molecules are attached to many of these proteins. The proteins in the lipid bilayer can move around, "floating" among the lipids. Scientists describe the cell membrane as a "fluid mosaic." A mosaic is a type of art made up of different materials, just as the membrane is made up of different kinds of molecules. Some of these proteins form channels and pumps that move substances across the cell membrane. Some proteins attach to the cytoskeleton, enabling cells to use their membranes to move or change shape. Many of the carbohydrate molecules help cells to identify each other.

Visual Reading Tool: Eukaryotic Cell Structure

Write the name of the numbered structures.

1. ______________________________

2. ______________________________

3 ______________________________

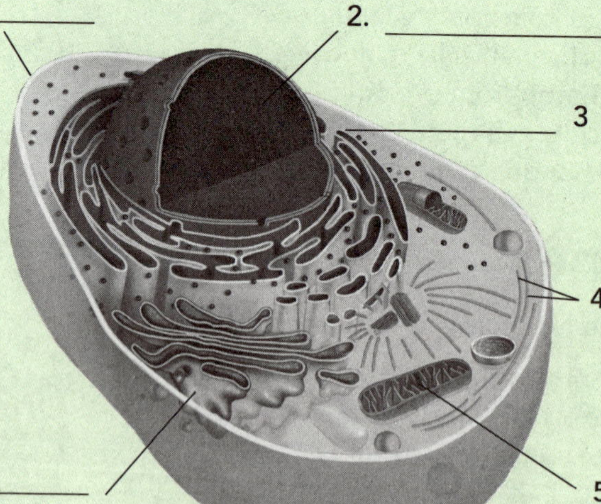

4 ______________________________

5 ______________________________

6. ______________________________

CHAPTER 16

LESSON 3

Cell Transport

READING TOOL **Compare and Contrast** As you read, compare and contrast passive and active transport. Complete the Venn Diagram by filling in the similarities where the two circles overlap, and their differences on either side. Be sure to also include the types of passive transport and active transport.

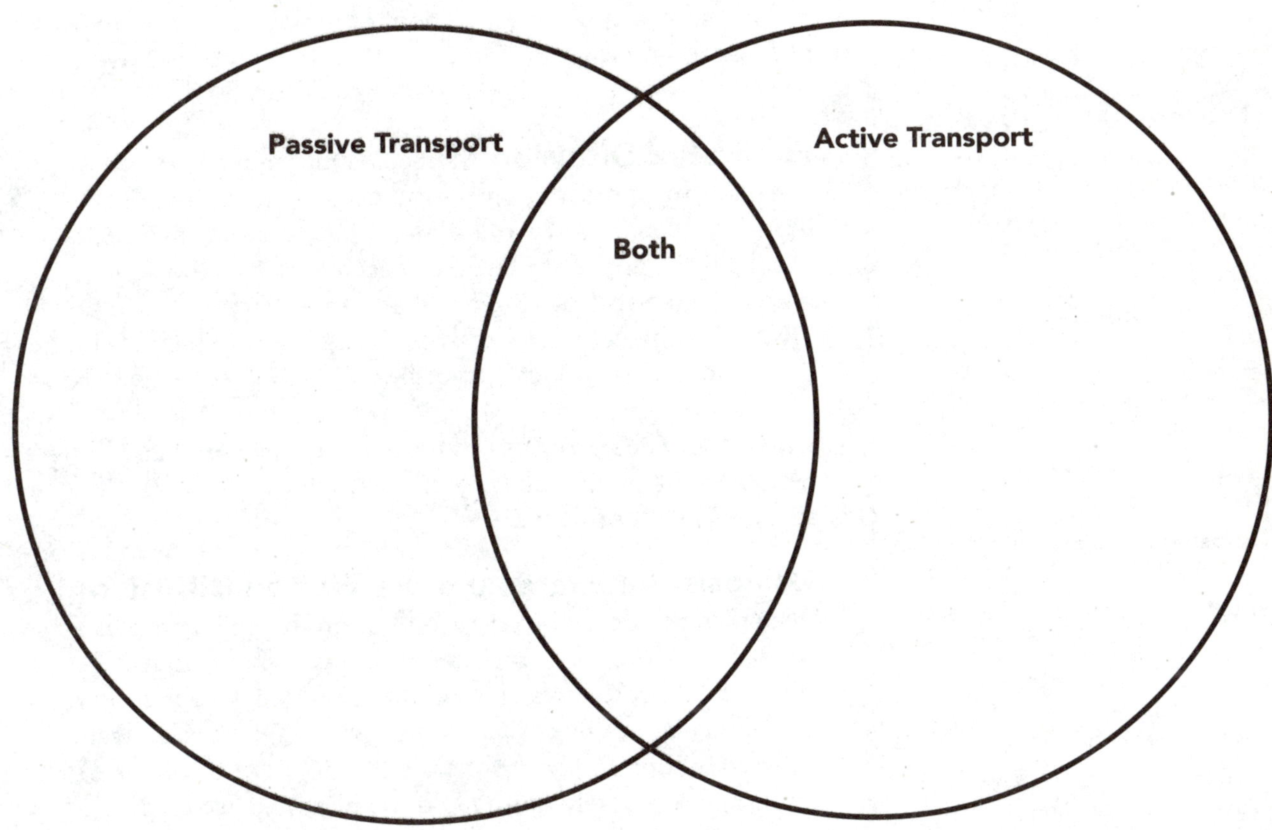

Lesson Summary

Passive Transport

KEY QUESTION *How does passive transport work?*

Living cells must stay in **homeostasis**, which is a state of relatively constant internal physical and chemical conditions. One way that cells maintain homeostasis is by controlling the movement of molecules across the cell membrane.

As you read, circle the answers to each Key Question. Underline any words you do not understand.

BUILD Vocabulary

homeostasis relatively constant internal physical and chemical conditions that organisms maintain

READING TOOL

Academic Words

passive *Passive* has multiple meanings. It can mean inactive, and it can also mean that something is unpowered, with no force behind it. ☑ ***Passive transport* does not mean that a particle is inactive or not moving. It means that the particle can move without requiring what?**

____

BUILD Vocabulary

diffusion process by which particles tend to move from an area where they are more concentrated to an area where they are less concentrated

facilitated diffusion process of diffusion in which molecules pass across the membrane through protein channels in the cell membrane

aquaporin water channel protein in a cell membrane

osmosis diffusion of water through a selectively permeable membrane

isotonic when the concentration of two solutions is the same

hypertonic when comparing two solutions, the solution with the greater concentration of solutes

hypotonic when comparing two solutions, the solution with the lesser concentration of solutes

osmotic pressure pressure that must be applied to prevent osmotic movement across a selectively permeable membrane

Prefixes *Iso-* means "equal." You may have encountered this prefix in the term *isosceles triangle* in a math class. An isosceles triangle has two equal sides. ☑ **What quantity is equal between two solutions that are isotonic?**

____

____

Diffusion In any solution, solute particles constantly move and collide with each other. The particles tend to move from an area where they are more concentrated to an area where they are less concentrated. This process is called **diffusion** (dih FYOO zhun). Diffusion is why many substances move across the cell membrane. For a substance that can cross the cell membrane, it will move to the side of the membrane where it is less concentrated. Equilibrium is reached when the concentration of the substance is the same on both sides of the membrane. Molecules will continue to move across the membrane, but the concentration will stay the same on both sides. Diffusion depends on molecular movements that do not require the cell to use energy. The movement of molecules across the cell membrane without using cellular energy is called **passive** transport.

Facilitated Diffusion Molecules that move across the cell membrane most easily are small and uncharged. Such molecules can dissolve in the membrane's lipid bilayer. But charged ions and many large molecules such as the sugar glucose can also cross the cell membrane. This is because proteins in the cell membrane act as carriers or channels for these molecules. In **facilitated diffusion**, molecules that cannot diffuse through the membrane pass through protein channels. Facilitated diffusion does not require any cellular energy. There are hundreds of different proteins that allow specific substances to cross cell membranes.

Osmosis: An Example of Facilitated Diffusion

Water molecules cannot diffuse through the cell membrane because the interior of the membrane is hydrophobic. Water enters cells by facilitated diffusion. Many cells contain proteins called **aquaporins** (ak wuh PAW rinz) that allow water to pass through them. **Osmosis** is the diffusion of water through a selectively permeable membrane, such as the cell membrane.

How Osmosis Works Think about two solutions of sugar in water separated by a membrane that is permeable to water, but not sugar. One solution has a higher concentration of sugar, which means there is a lower concentration of water. Water moves both ways across the membrane, but more water molecules will move from the side with more water and less sugar to the side with less water and more sugar until equilibrium is reached. Equilibrium is when the water and sugar concentrations are the same in both solutions. At equilibrium, the solutions are **isotonic**, meaning "same strength." Before equilibrium was reached, the solution with more sugar was **hypertonic**, or "above strength," and the solution with less sugar was **hypotonic**, or "below strength." The terms *isotonic, hypertonic,* and *hypotonic* refer the "strength," or concentration, of the sugar solute, not the water.

Osmotic Pressure The net movement of water into or out of a cell produces a force called **osmotic pressure**. Because cells contain salts, sugars, proteins and other dissolved molecules; they are almost always hypertonic to fresh water. As a result, water tends to move into a cell, increasing the osmotic pressure inside the cell and causing it to swell. This could cause the cell to burst. Most cells in large organisms are bathed in blood or other isotonic fluids, not water, so they are not in danger of bursting.

Visual Reading Tool: Passive Transport

Diffusion is the movement of particles from an area of high concentration to an area of low concentration. Osmosis is the diffusion of water through a selectively permeable membrane. Study the beakers at the right. Note changes in water levels and solute particles.

1. For both scenarios, label each of the solutions on each side of the membrane as either hypertonic, hypotonic, or isotonic.
2. Which of the two scenarios can cause cells to burst when they are placed in a hypotonic solution?

____

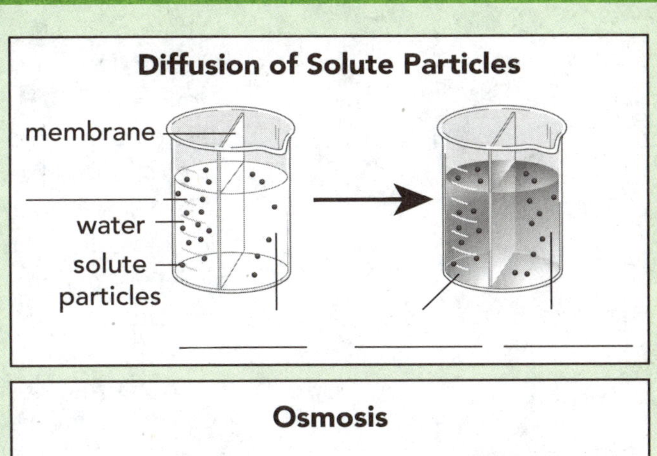

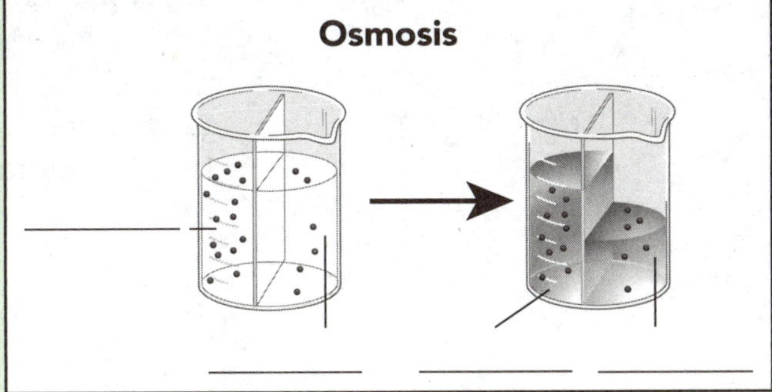

As you read, circle the answers to each Key Question. Underline any words you do not understand.

READING TOOL

Cause and Effect Small molecules have the ability to move across the cell membrane by dissolving through the lipid bilayer. This is called diffusion and it happens without any energy input.

Why do some molecules need help moving across a cell membrane in the form of energy?

____

____

____

____

____

Active Transport

KEY QUESTION *How does active transport work?*

Sometimes cells transport materials against a concentration gradient, from an area of low concentration to an area of higher concentration. The movement of materials against a concentration difference is known as active transport, and it requires energy. The active transport of small molecules or ions across a cell membrane is usually carried out by membrane proteins called protein pumps. Larger molecules can be actively transported by processes known as endocytosis and exocytosis.

Molecular Transport Many cells use protein pumps and cellular energy to move ions such as calcium, potassium, and sodium across membranes. This allows cells to store substances in a particular location even when diffusion would tend to move these substances in the opposite direction.

Bulk Transport Large molecules and even clumps of material can be moved across the cell membrane by bulk transport.

Endocytosis Endocytosis (en doh sy TOH sis) is the process of bringing material into a cell by means of parts of the membrane folding in, or forming pockets. The resulting pocket breaks away from the cytoplasmic side of the cell membrane, forming a vesicle or vacuole in the cytoplasm. Large molecules, clumps of food, and even whole cells can be taken up in this way.

Phagocytosis (fag oh sy TOH sis) is a kind of endocytosis in which extensions of the cell surround a particle and package it within a food vacuole. White blood cells use phagocytosis to destroy damaged or foreign cells. Amoebas use this method to take in food. Phagocytosis requires a lot of cellular energy.

Many cells take up liquid from the environment in a similar process called pinocytosis (py nuh sy TOH sis). Tiny pockets form along the cell membrane, fill with liquid, and pinch off to form vacuoles.

Exocytosis Cells can also release material using the process of exocytosis (ek soh sy TOH sis). In exocytosis, the membrane of a vesicle or vacuole fuses with the cell membrane, forcing the contents of the vacuole out of the cell. Cells remove water by means of a contractile vacuole and exocytosis.

CHAPTER 16

LESSON 4

Homeostasis and Cells

READING TOOL **Make Connections** As you read the text, fill in the chart below to show how each idea is related to one another.

Specialized Cells

- Definition: ______________________________________
  ____
- Example: ______________________________________

Tissues

- Definition: ______________________________________
  ____
- Example: ______________________________________

Organs

- Definition: ______________________________________
  ____
- Example: ______________________________________

Organ System

- Definition: ______________________________________
  ____
- Example: ______________________________________

Lesson Summary

The Cell as an Organism

KEY QUESTION *How do unicellular organisms maintain homeostasis?*

Unicellular organisms, like all living things, must maintain homeostasis, or relatively constant internal physical and chemical conditions. To maintain homeostasis, unicellular organisms grow, respond to the environment, transform energy, and reproduce. Unicellular organisms include prokaryotes, such as bacteria. Many eukaryotes, such as amoebas, many algae, and yeasts, live as single cells.

As you read, circle the answers to each Key Question. Underline any words you do not understand.

BUILD Vocabulary

tissue group of similar cells that perform a particular function

organ group of tissues that work together to perform closely related functions

organ system group of organs that work together to perform a specific function

receptor on or in a cell, a specific protein that receives chemical signals from molecular messengers, such as hormones

Word Origins The English word *receive* is based upon the Latin word *recipere* which means "to take back." **What do receptors in cells receive from other cells?**

____

____

Multicellular Life

KEY QUESTION *How do the cells of a multicellular organism work together to maintain homeostasis?*

The cells of humans and other multicellular organisms do not live on their own. They are interdependent. The cells of multicellular organisms are specialized for specific tasks and communicate with one another to maintain homeostasis.

Cell Specialization We each began life as a single cell. That cell grew and divided and gave rise to many other cells that became specialized to perform different roles. Each specialized cell in a multicellular organism contributes to homeostasis in the organism.

Levels of Organization In a multicellular organism, specialized cells are organized into tissues. Tissues are organized into organs, which are organized into organ systems. A **tissue** is a group of similar cells that perform a particular function. Different tissues may work together to form an **organ**. For example, the brain is an organ made of nerve and fat tissue and blood vessels. A group of organs that work together to perform a function is called an **organ system**. The brain, spinal cord, and nerves in the body work together as the nervous system.

Cellular Communication Cells in a large organism communicate using chemical signals. These signals can speed up or slow down the function of cells that receive them, or can cause the cell to change what it is doing. Some cells form connections or cellular junctions to neighboring cells. Some junctions hold cells together. Others allow molecules to carry chemical signals between cells. In order for cells to respond to a chemical signal, the cell must have a **receptor** that the chemical signal can bind to. Receptors can be on the cell membrane or inside the cytoplasm. In many animals, nerve cells carry messages from one part of the body to another.

16 Chapter Review

Review Vocabulary

Choose the letter of the best answer.

1. Proteins that will be released from the cell are assembled at the

A. central vacuole.

B. mitochondria.

C. rough endoplasmic reticulum.

2. The diffusion of water through a selectively permeable membrane is called

A. homeostasis.

B. pinocytosis.

C. osmosis.

Match the vocabulary term to its definition.

3. ________ A cell that has DNA but no nucleus.

4. ________ A complex of protein and RNA that assembles proteins.

5. ________ A protein on or in a cell that binds a chemical signal.

a. receptor

b. prokaryote

c. ribosome

Review Key Questions

Provide evidence and details to support your answers.

6. What are the three main parts of the cell theory?

7. Plants and animals are both made up of eukaryotic cells. Does this mean they have the same kinds of organelles? Why or why not?

8. A cell makes and secretes a certain protein. Explain where it is made, how it is secreted from the cell, and what kind of transport is used.

9. Why do prokaryotes not have cell specialization?

CHAPTER 17

LESSON 1

Cell Growth, Division, and Reproduction

READING TOOL **Compare and Contrast** As you read, identify the similarities and differences between sexual and asexual reproduction. Include the advantages and disadvantages of each method. Take notes in the Venn diagram below.

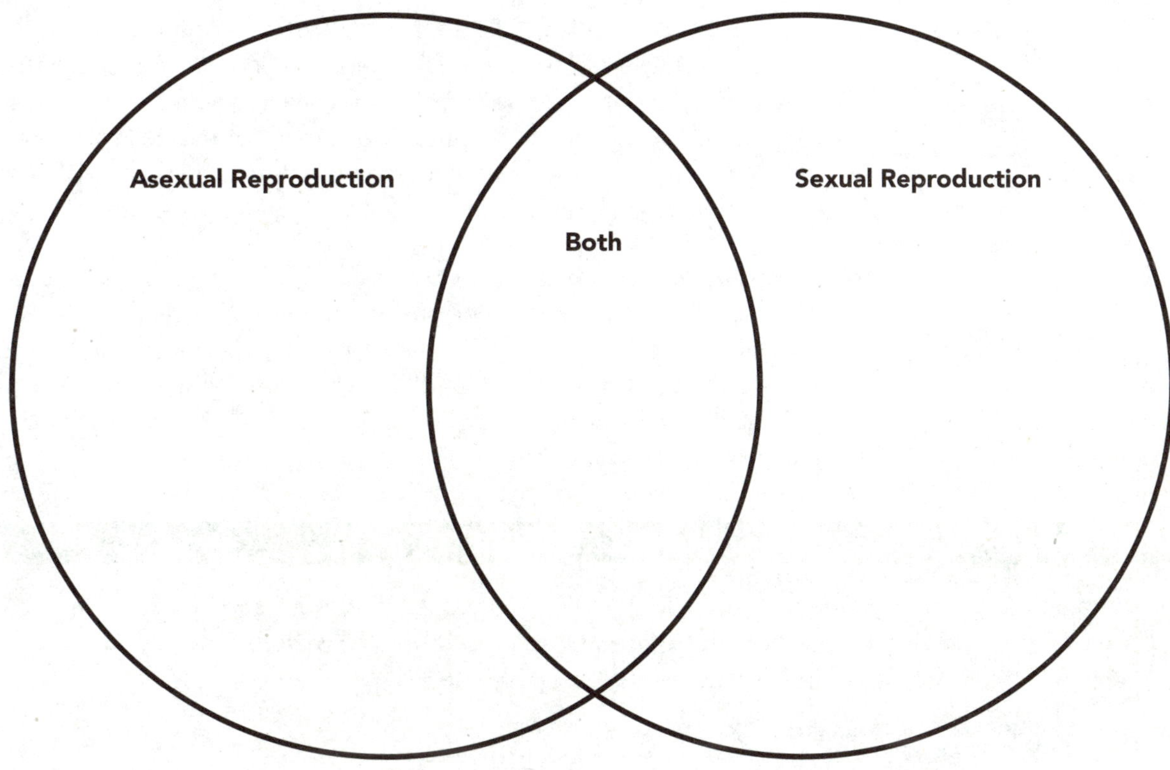

In the space provided, describe an organism that uses both asexual and sexual reproduction.

____

____

Lesson Summary

Limits to Cell Size

KEY QUESTION *What are some of the difficulties a cell faces as it increases in size?*

As a cell becomes larger, it is less efficient at moving nutrients into the cell and waste material out of the cell because the surface area does not grow as quickly as the volume. In addition, as a cell grows, it places increasing demands on its own DNA. Therefore, complex living things grow in size by producing more cells rather than by increasing cell size.

As you read, circle the answers to each Key Question. Underline any words you do not understand.

READING TOOL

Cause and Effect

Cells can only grow so big until they become inefficient. ☑ **Using a cause-and-effect statement, explain the cause of limited cell size.**

____

____

____

____

____

____

____

A Problem of Size

The larger a cell becomes, the less efficient it is in moving nutrients and wastes across its cell membrane. Food, oxygen, and water enter through the cell membrane, and waste products leave the cell the same way. The total area of the cell membrane, known as the surface area, determines how fast this transportation of materials occurs. The volume of the cell determines how much food material is needed and how much waste is produced. As the cell gets larger, both the surface area and the volume of the cell increase, but not at an equal rate.

Ratio of Surface Area to Volume Imagine that a cell is cube shaped. The surface area and volume can be calculated as the cell grows, and the surface area and volume amounts can be compared as a ratio. The growth of the cell membrane (surface area) does not increase as fast as the inside of the cell (volume) and the cell cannot function well as a result.

Traffic Problems One problem resulting from the volume increasing faster than the surface area of a cell is the decrease of "traffic flow" of nutrients and waste. The surface area of the cell membrane is the "road" into the cell. If the membrane is not large enough, proper passage of enough nutrients and wastes cannot occur.

Visual Reading Tool: Surface Area to Volume Ratio in Cells

1. For a cell to function efficiently, the surface-area-to-volume ratio needs to be large. In the table below, determine the surface area to volume ratio and write the ratio in the box provided. Don't forget units, and make sure the final ratio is in relation to 1.

Ratio of Surface Area to Volume in Cells

	1 cm × 1 cm × 1 cm	2 cm × 2 cm × 2 cm	3 cm × 3 cm × 3 cm
Surface Area (length × width) × 6 sides	___ × ___ × ___ = ___	___ × ___ × ___ = ___	___ × ___ × ___ = ___
Volume (length × width × height)	___ × ___ × ___ = ___	___ × ___ × ___ = ___	___ × ___ × ___ = ___
Ratio of Surface Area to Volume	___/___ = ___ : ___	___/___ = ___ : ___	___/___ = ___ : ___

2. What happens to the surface-area-to-volume ratio as the cell increases in size? Will the cell continue to function efficiently as the cell size gets larger and larger?

____

Information Overload Referring to the town analogy in Figure 17-3, access to information is critical to run the town efficiently. If the town grows quickly but its library stays the same, there will not be enough information to serve the population. Cells store critical information in a molecule known as DNA. The information in DNA directs all the cell's functions, but it does not increase in size as the cell increases in size. The cell solves this "information crisis" by creating a duplicate copy of the DNA and dividing it among two new cells so that each new cell has its own copy of the DNA.

Cell Division To function efficiently, the cell divides into two new daughter cells through a process called **cell division**. First, DNA is copied through a process called DNA replication, resulting in a complete set of the DNA for each new daughter cell. Then the cell splits in two. Cell division reduces the cell volume, resulting in efficient exchange of materials between the cell membrane and its environment. Cells easily obtain nutrients like oxygen, water, and food and quickly eliminate cellular waste products.

Cell Division and Reproduction

KEY QUESTION *How do asexual and sexual reproduction compare?*

Both sexual and asexual reproduction result in new individuals. Asexual reproduction produces offspring identical to the parent by cell division. In sexual reproduction, reproductive cells from two parents are fused to form a new individual.

To form new individuals, all organisms must be able to reproduce. There are two types of reproduction, asexual and sexual reproduction.

Asexual Reproduction **Asexual reproduction** is the production of genetically identical offspring from a single parent. Asexual reproduction in single-celled organisms occurs through cell division.

Sexual Reproduction **Sexual reproduction** involves the fusion of two reproductive cells from each of two parents. Offspring produced by sexual reproduction inherit some of their genetic information from each parent.

Comparing Asexual and Sexual Reproduction The advantages of asexual reproduction include quick and successful reproduction when conditions are ideal, which allows offspring to survive when in competition with other organisms. The lack of genetic diversity may prevent them from surviving if conditions change.

Sexual reproduction produces genetic diversity. If an environment changes, genetic diversity in a species may help to ensure that the individual members of the population contain the right combination of characteristics needed to survive.

Build Vocabulary

cell division process in which a cell divides into two new identical daughter cells

asexual reproduction process of reproduction involving a single parent that results in offspring that are genetically identical to the parent

sexual reproduction type of reproduction in which cells from two parents unite to form the first cell of a new organism

Word Origins The word *divide* is based upon the Latin word *dividere*, which means "to force apart or remove." ☑ **What needs to be duplicated before a cell can go through cell division?**

___

CHAPTER 17

LESSON 2

The Process of Cell Division

READING TOOL **Sequence of Events** In the cell cycle diagram below, each section represents the relative time the cell spends in each stage. In the following diagram, write in each of the following phases:

a. Interphase
b. G_1 phase
c. S
d. G_2
e. M phase
f. Mitosis
g. Cytokinesis
h. Cell division

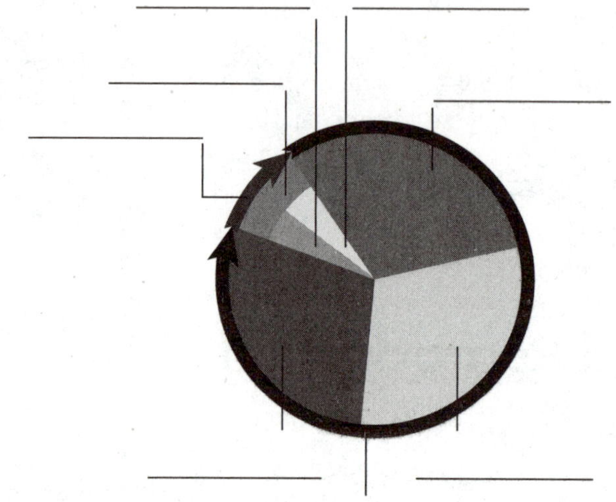

Lesson Summary

As you read, circle the answers to each Key Question. Underline any words you do not understand.

Chromosomes

KEY QUESTION *What is the role of chromosomes in cell division?*

Cells must divide to function efficiently. Each new daughter cell needs a complete set of genetic information for cell growth and function. The genetic information is bundled into packages of DNA called **chromosomes**. When DNA is organized into chromosomes, it is easier for the cell to divide the genetic material equally between the two daughter cells.

Prokaryotic Chromosomes The circular chromosome found in prokaryotic cells contains almost all of the genetic information and is not enclosed in a nucleus.

Eukaryotic Chromosomes The DNA strands in eukaryotic cells are tightly bound to proteins called histones, creating a complex called **chromatin**. Histones and DNA coil tightly together, forming beadlike structures called nucleosomes, which condense to form thick fibers called chromosomes. The X-like chromosome is actually a duplicated chromosome connected together.

BUILD Vocabulary

chromosome threadlike structure of DNA and protein that contains genetic information; in eukaryotes, chromosomes are contained in the nucleus; in prokaryotes, they are found in the cytoplasm

chromatin substance found in eukaryotic chromosomes that consists of DNA tightly coiled around histones

The Cell Cycle

KEY QUESTION *What are the main events of the cell cycle?*

During the **cell cycle**, a cell grows, prepares for division, and then divides to form two daughter cells. There are 4 main phases of the cell cycle: G_1, S, G_2, and M.

The Prokaryotic Cell Cycle The prokaryotic cell cycle takes place very quickly when conditions are ideal. As the cell grows and functions, it reaches a certain size and begins to copy its DNA. When DNA replication is complete, the cell divides by binary fission, which is a form of asexual reproduction. The two copies of the DNA attach to different regions of the cell membrane. The cell membrane then pinches inward between the two regions to divide the cytoplasm. The two resulting daughter cells have identical copies of the DNA and equal amounts of cytoplasm.

The Eukaryotic Cell Cycle The four stages of the eukaryotic cell cycle are G_1, S, G_2, and M. The longest period of the cell cycle, called **interphase**, includes the G_1, S, and G_2 phases.

G_1: Cell Growth Cell Growth is the period of cell growth in which the cell increases in size and makes new organelles.

S: DNA Replication DNA replication is the stage of the cell cycle that results in two complete sets of DNA ready to be divided between the daughter cells.

G_2: Preparing for Cell Division The preparation time for cell division is when the organelles and molecules needed to carry out cell division are made.

M phase: Cell Division **Mitosis** is the division of the cell nucleus, and the division of the cytoplasm is called **cytokinesis**.

BUILD Vocabulary

cell cycle series of events in which a cell grows, prepares for division, and divides to form two daughter cells

interphase the longest period of the cell cycle, where the stages G_1, S, and G_2 take place

mitosis part of eukaryotic cell division during which the cell nucleus divides

cytokinesis division of the cytoplasm to form two separate daughter cells

Prefixes The prefix *inter-* means "between" or "among." Interphase during the cell cycle takes place between cell divisions and is when the cell grows in preparation of cytokinesis. **What other words do you know that begin with the prefix *inter-* that describe something that is between other things?**

____

Mitosis

KEY QUESTION *What happens during the phases of mitosis?*

Mitosis is the segment of the cell cycle during which the division of the cell nucleus occurs. Mitosis is divided into four phases: prophase, metaphase, anaphase, and telophase.

During prophase, the duplicated chromosomes become visible. In metaphase, the centromeres of the duplicated chromosomes line up. In anaphase, the chromosomes separate and move to opposite ends of the cell. During telophase, the chromosomes spread out into a tangle of chromatin.

Visual Reading Tool: Mitosis

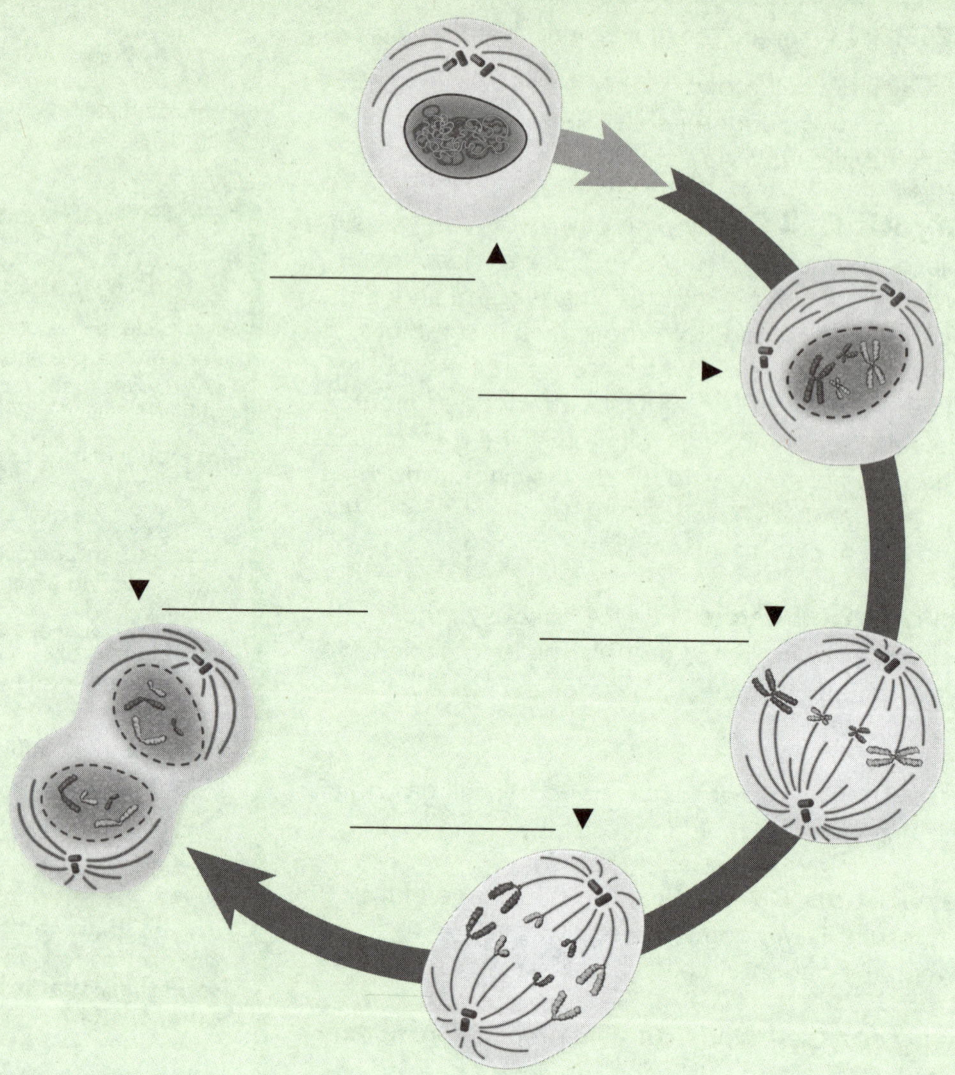

Label the diagram above with interphase and the four stages of mitosis. Then, in the space provided below, describe what happens in each stage of mitosis.

Prophase: ______________________________

____

____

Metaphase: ______________________________

____

Anaphase: ______________________________

____

Telophase: ______________________________

____

Prophase The genetic material inside the nucleus condenses and the duplicate chromosomes become visible during the first stage of mitosis called **prophase**. At the beginning of prophase, the sister **chromatids**, or strands of condensed chromosomes, become visible. They are attached to each other at a point called the **centromere**. In the cytoplasm, two tiny organelles, called **centrioles**, are involved in developing spindle fibers that span across the cell.

Metaphase During **metaphase**, the spindle fibers move the centromeres of the duplicated chromosomes to the center of the cell. These spindle fibers are connected to the two poles near the centrioles and are ready to separate the sister chromatids.

Anaphase During **anaphase**, the chromosomes separate and move along the spindle fibers to opposite ends of the cell. Anaphase ends when the sister chromatids, now considered individual chromosomes, are completely separated into two groups and the spindle fibers have almost disappeared.

Telophase During **telophase**, the chromosomes, which were distinct and condensed, begin to spread out into a tangle of chromatin. This is the final stage of mitosis. The nuclear envelope is reconstructed and the nucleolus becomes visible in each new cell.

Cytokinesis

KEY QUESTION *How do daughter cells split apart after mitosis?*

In plants, cytokinesis separates the cells by forming a cell plate between the divided nuclei. In animals, cytokinesis draws the membrane inward to separate the cells.

During the M phase of the cell cycle, mitosis forms two nuclei, each with a complete set of the DNA. The last segment of the M phase is cytokinesis. Cytokinesis completes the process of cell division by dividing one cell into two.

Cytokinesis in Animal Cells The cell membrane is drawn inward and pinched into two new daughter cells. Each cell contains the new nucleus formed during mitosis and an equal amount of cytoplasm.

Cytokinesis in Plant Cells Because of the rigid cell wall surrounding the cell membrane in plant cells, pinching from the outside inward cannot occur. A cell plate forms halfway between the two nuclei and gradually expands toward and fuses with the existing cell membranes. A new cell wall then forms to separate the two daughter cells.

BUILD Vocabulary

prophase first and longest phase of mitosis in which the genetic material inside the nucleus condenses and the chromosomes become visible

chromatid one of two identical "sister" parts of a duplicated chromosome

centromere region of a chromosome where the two sister chromatids attach

centriole structure in an animal cell that helps to organize cell division

metaphase phase of mitosis in which the chromosomes line up across the center of the cell

anaphase phase of mitosis in which the chromosomes separate and move to opposite ends of the cell

telophase phase of mitosis in which the distinct individual chromosomes begin to spread out into a tangle of chromatin

Prefixes In biology, the prefix *telo-* means "end" or "completion."

☑ **What occurs during telophase that signifies the end of mitosis?**

____

____

____

READING TOOL

Compare and Contrast

☑ **How do chromosomes differ in prokaryotes and eukaryotes?**

____

____

____

____

____

CHAPTER 17

LESSON 3

Regulating the Cell Cycle

READING TOOL **Make Connections** In the graphic organizer below, fill in each box with headings from this unit to help you understand the concepts.

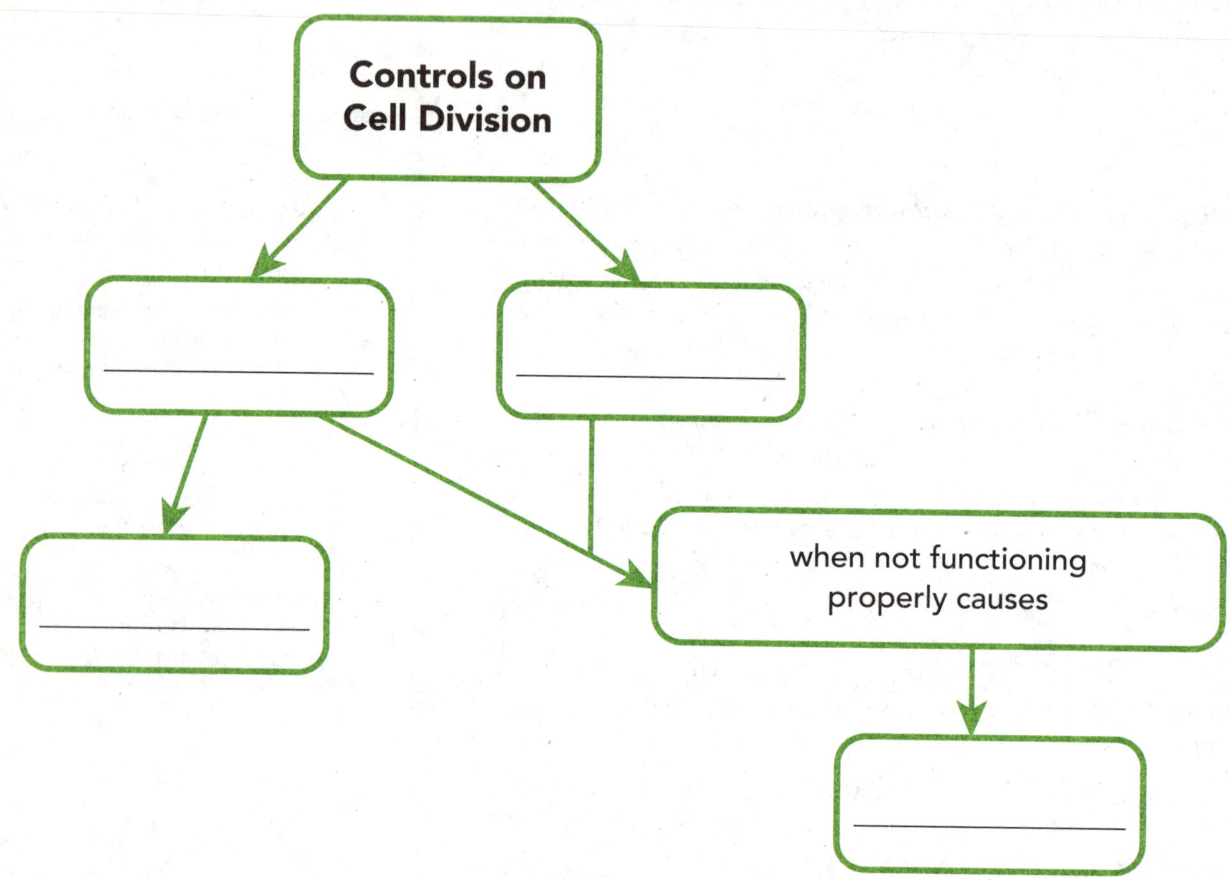

Lesson Summary

Controls on Cell Division

As you read, circle the answers to each Key Question. Underline any words you do not understand.

KEY QUESTION *How is the cell cycle regulated?*

The cell cycle is controlled by regulatory proteins both inside and outside the cell.

How do cells know when it is time to divide? Cell growth and cell division are highly controlled in multicellular organisms. Some cells grow and divide very quickly, like skin and blood cells, whereas other cells grow to a certain size and never divide, like muscle and nerve cells. Without precise regulation of cell growth and division, serious diseases like cancer can result. Controls on cell growth and division can be influenced, and scientists have identified many of these controlling factors.

Regulatory Proteins For many years, biologists searched for a signal that might regulate the cell cycle—something that would "tell" the cell when it was time to divide, duplicate its chromosomes, or enter another phase of the cell cycle. They found out that there is not just one signal, but many. Scientists have identified dozens of proteins that help to regulate the cell cycle.The cell cycle is controlled by many different regulatory proteins located inside and outside of the cell.

Internal Regulators Internal regulatory proteins control events of the cell cycle by responding to events inside the cell. These "checkpoint proteins" assure that cell activities, like DNA replication or spindle fiber production, are completed before the next phase is triggered.

External Regulators External regulatory proteins control events of the cell cycle by responding to events outside the cell. **Growth factors** are proteins that stimulate the growth and division of cells. Some regulatory proteins, found on the surface of neighboring cells, encourage slowing or even deactivation of the cell cycle to ensure that excessive growth does not occur.

Cyclins Biologists had been searching for years for the signal that regulates the cell cycle because they realized that it could help them treat diseases. Learning that there is not just one signal but many has made that job more complicated. **Cyclin** is a kind of internal regulatory protein that regulates the cell cycle. When this protein is present, the mitotic spindle forms and the mitosis phase of the cell cycle is activated.

Apoptosis The process of programmed cell death is called **apoptosis**. The steps include shrinking chromatin, cell membrane fragmentation, and cell debris clean up by neighboring cells. This process is important in growth and development because it shapes and restructures the developing parts of the organism. Uncontrolled apoptosis leads to diseases like AIDS and Parkinson's.

Cancer: Uncontrolled Cell Growth

KEY QUESTION *How do cancer cells differ from other cells?*

Cancer cells do not respond to the signals that regulate the growth of most cells. As a result, the cell cycle is disrupted, and cells grow and divide uncontrollably.

Cancer is a disorder in which body cells lose the ability to control growth. This uncontrolled growth creates a mass of cells called a **tumor**. Benign tumors, or noncancerous tumors, do not spread to surrounding tissues. Malignant tumors, or cancerous tumors, spread to surrounding tissues and destroy the healthy functioning of those tissues. As cancerous cells spread, they interfere with the other cells by absorbing necessary nutrients, blocking nerve connections, and preventing the organs they invade from functioning properly.

Build Vocabulary

growth factor one of a group of external regulatory proteins that stimulate the growth and division of cells

cyclin one of a family of proteins that regulates the cell cycle in eukaryotic cells

apoptosis the process of programmed cell death

cancer disorder in which some of the body's cells lose the ability to control growth

tumor mass of rapidly dividing cells that can damage surrounding tissue

Root Words The root of cyclin, *cycl*, is the Greek word for "circle." ☑ **How does the concept of a circle relate to cyclins?**

READING TOOL

Prefixes

The prefix *bene-* means "well" or "good," and the prefix *mal-* means "bad" or "evil." ☑ **Which type of tumor, benign or malignant, causes more damage to the body?**

What Causes Cancer? All cancerous cells have lost control over the cell cycle because of defects in the genetic material that regulates cell growth and division. The defects in the DNA can be prompted by smoking, chewing tobacco, radiation exposure, and viral infections. Some cancer cells do not respond to external regulatory proteins, and others stop responding to internal regulatory proteins.

Treatments for Cancer Some cancerous tumors can be removed by surgery, but others need to be treated with radiation and/or chemotherapy. The most severe form of skin cancer, melanoma, can be treated by surgery, especially when detected early. In radiation therapy, high-energy, carefully targeted beams of radiation are used to kill the cancerous cells because the radiation damages the genetic material of these cells. Chemotherapy is the use of chemical compounds that target and kill rapidly dividing cells, but a side effect of these drugs is the interference with division of normal, healthy cells in parts of the body such as hair or the stomach lining.

Visual Reading Tool: Cyclin Levels

The MPF (mitosis-promoting factor) enzyme is present during the entire cell cycle. When MPF cyclin is also present, mitosis occurs. View the chart and answer the questions below.

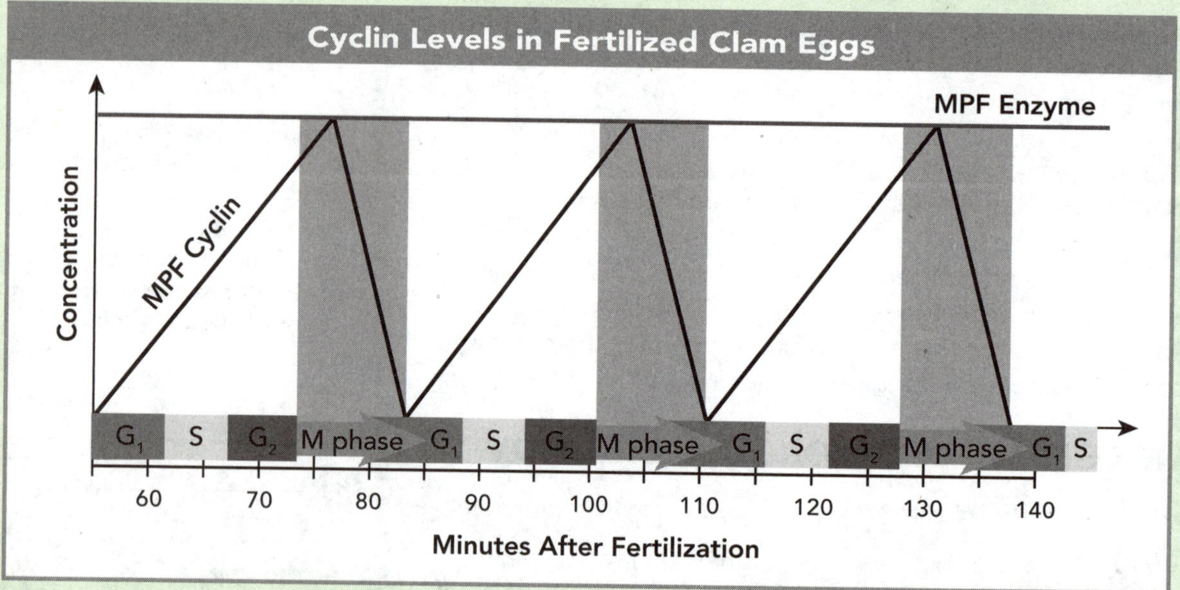

1. About how long does one cell cycle last in fertilized clam eggs?

____

2. What occurs when MPF cyclin levels are highest?

____

3. What are the four steps that occur during the M phase?

____

____

CHAPTER 17

LESSON 4

Cell Differentiation

READING TOOL **Main Idea and Details** In the chart below, fill in the details that support the main ideas from this lesson.

Main Idea	Details
From One Cell to Many	
Defining Differentiation	
Mapping Differentiation	
Differentiation in Mammals	
Stem Cells and Development	
Human Development	
Stem Cells	
Frontiers in Stem Cell Research	
Ethical Issues	
Induced Pluripotent Stem Cells	
Regenerative Medicine	

Lesson Summary

From One Cell to Many

KEY QUESTION *How do cells become specialized for different functions?*

Multicellular organisms start as one cell, and then grow through the developmental stage called an **embryo**, which gradually becomes the adult organism. As this process proceeds, cells become different from one another and perform different functions for the organism.

As you read, circle the answers to each Key Question. Underline any words you do not understand.

BUILD Vocabulary

embryo developing stage of a multicellular organism

Build Vocabulary

differentiation process in which cells become specialized in structure and function

totipotent cells that are able to develop into any type of cell found in the body (including cells that make up the extraembryonic membranes and placenta)

blastocyst stage of early development in mammals that consists of a hollow ball of cells

pluripotent cells that are capable of developing into most, but not all, of the body's cell types

stem cell unspecialized cell that can give rise to one or more types of specialized cells

multipotent cell with limited potential to develop into a certain type of cell within a tissue

Prefixes The prefix *toti-* in *totipotent* means "entirely." The prefix *pluri-* in *pluripotent* means "several." Totipotent cells can develop into *any* type of body cell. Pluripotent cells can develop into many different types of cells, but not *all* types. ☑ **There are other words that use the prefix *toti-* that mean "entirely." What is an example?**

____

Defining Differentiation During development, cell **differentiation** is the process by which cells become specialized for specific functions.

Mapping Differentiation Biologists have determined the pathway of cell differentiation in a microscopic worm, *C. elegans*. The identity of each cell from the point of fertilization to the 959-celled adult has been mapped and identified.

Differentiation in Mammals Differentiation in mammals is more complicated and influenced by many interwoven factors. However, there is a specific point in the development of the organism when cell differentiation is complete.

Stem Cells and Development

KEY QUESTION *What are stem cells?*

How the differentiated cells develop from the single cell made from the fertilized egg is one of the secrets of developing organisms that biologists are still investigating. The zygote, or the fertilized egg, is **totipotent** because it is the single cell that is able to develop into any type of cell in the body.

Human Development Human development begins as a zygote, then after a few cell divisions, the embryo is formed. The **blastocyst** is formed next, which is a hollow ball of cells with another group of cells in the center. The outer cells of the blastocyst will eventually become the tissues that attach to the placenta of the mother, and the inner cell mass will become the actual embryo. The inner cells are **pluripotent** because they can develop into any of the cell types of the body, but they cannot form the tissues surrounding the embryo like the totipotent zygote.

Stem Cells **Stem cells** are unspecialized cells from which differentiated cells develop. They are found in the developing embryo and also in specific places of the adult body.

Adult Stem Cells Adult stem cells are **multipotent** because the types of cells that they form are restricted to the tissue type in which they are found.

Embryonic Stem Cells Embryonic stem cells are pluripotent because they are able to produce any cell in the body.

Frontiers in Stem Cell Research

KEY QUESTION *What are some possible benefits and issues associated with stem cell research?*

Stem cells may be useful to repair cell damage from heart attacks, strokes, or spinal cord injuries. Human embryonic stem cell research involves ethical issues.

Basic research on stem cells takes on a special urgency in light of the importance it might have for human health. Heart attacks destroy cells in the heart muscle, strokes injure brain cells, and spinal cord injuries cause paralysis by breaking connections between nerve cells. Not surprisingly, the prospect of using stem cells to repair such cellular damage has excited medical researchers.

Ethical Issues Human embryonic stem cell research is controversial because the arguments for it and against it both involve ethical issues of life and death. Adult stem cells are harvested from people who are willing to go through the process of donating the cells. However, obtaining embryonic stem cells involves the destruction of a human embryo.

Induced Pluripotent Stem Cells Shinya Yamanaka, a Japanese Nobel Prize–winning stem cell researcher, converted human fibroblasts, cells that make proteins in skin, into induced pluripotent stem cells. These modified fibroblasts may be able to replace embryonic stem cells, potentially solving the ethical problems.

Regenerative Medicine Some organisms regenerate lost body parts. Scientists continue to study the steps of regeneration and hope to replicate the steps in the human body.

READING TOOL

Pros and Cons

People have many different opinions on stem cell research, including whether or not it is ethical. **Determine the benefits and issues regarding stem cell research.**

Benefits:

____

____

____

____

Issues:

____

____

____

____

Visual Reading Tool: Future Treatment for Heart Disease

The diagram below shows how stem cells can be used to repair damaged heart tissue. Fill in the three steps doctors would take.

❶ ____________________

❷ ____________________

❸ ____________________

17 Chapter Review

Review Vocabulary

Match the vocabulary word with the corresponding definition.

1. ________	a disorder in which cells do not respond to regulatory factors, resulting in uncontrolled growth and division	a. cell division
2. ________	the process by which cells become specialized	b. cancer
3. ________	the process by which a cell divides into two new daughter cells	c. tumor
4. ________	a mass of cancerous cells that can be benign or malignant	d. cell differentiation

Review Key Questions

Provide evidence and details to support your answers.

5. Describe the differences between asexual and sexual reproduction.

____

____

____

6. List the four phases of mitosis in the order in which they occur and describe what happens in each.

____

____

____

____

____

____

7. Describe two types of tumors, and indicate which type is harmful and which is not.

____

____

8. What are the benefits and issues regarding embryonic stem cell research?

____

____

CHAPTER 18

LESSON 1

Roots, Stems, and Leaves

READING TOOL **Make Connections** Explain how each of the listed systems works to make plants grow and thrive.

How Do These Systems Work to Help Plants	Explanations
Plant Tissue Systems	
Roots	
Stems	
Leaves	

Lesson Summary

As you read, circle the answers to each Key Question. Underline any words you do not understand.

BUILD Vocabulary

epidermis in plants, single layer of cells that makes up dermal tissue

meristem region of unspecialized cells responsible for continuing growth throughout a plant's lifetime

Plant Tissue Systems

KEY QUESTION *What are the main tissue systems of plants?*

The roots, stems, and leaves of plants include specialized tissue systems that help plants to thrive and grow.

Dermal, Vascular, and Ground Tissue In plants, dermal tissue includes a single layer of cells called the **epidermis**. The outer surfaces of these cells are covered in a waxy cuticle layer, protecting them from water loss. Vascular tissues include xylem and phloem. These tissues support the plant body and transport water and nutrients throughout the plant. Ground tissue produces and stores sugars, and contributes to the physical support of plants. Edible portions of plants are mostly ground tissue.

Plant Tissues and Growth Plant growth happens in **meristems**, or regions of unspecialized cells in which mitosis produces new cells that are ready for differentiation.

Meristems and Flower Development When the pattern of gene expression transforms apical meristems into floral meristems, flower development begins. Floral meristems produce a plant's reproductive organs and colorful flowers.

Roots

KEY QUESTION *What are the different structures and functions of roots?*

When seeds begin to sprout, they put out roots to draw water and nutrients from the soil. Rapid cell growth pushes the growing root tips down into the soil, providing the plant the raw materials to feed developing stems and leaves.

Types of Root Systems Plants have taproots or fibrous root systems. **Taproots** are large primary roots that can stretch deep into soil. Plants like grasses have branched roots growing from the base of the plant's stem, or **fibrous roots**. These help plants anchor topsoil in place.

Structure and Function of Roots Dermal, vascular, and ground tissue are all found in roots. A mature root has an outside layer, the epidermis, and contains vascular tissue and ground tissue. Roots support a plant, anchor it, store food, and absorb water and nutrients from soil.

Uptake of Plant Nutrients From soil, plants absorb inorganic nutrients, like nitrogen, phosphorus, potassium, magnesium, and trace elements. Cell membranes on the root epidermis use proteins to transport dissolved nutrients from soil into the plant.

Water Movement and the Vascular Cylinder Cells in all three tissue systems work together to transport water into roots. The vascular cylinder is enclosed by the endodermis. Where these cells meet, cell walls form a waterproof zone called the **Casparian strip**. This structure creates a one-way-only passage of water and nutrients into the vascular cylinder.

Root Pressure Water inside the Casparian strip travels upward as root pressure forces it through the vascular cylinder and into the xylem. As more water is forced up, water in the xylem is forced into the roots.

BUILD Vocabulary

taproot large primary root

fibrous roots in plants like grasses, the branched roots that grow from the base of the stem

Casparian strip waterproof strip that surrounds plant endodermal cells and is involved in the one-way passage of materials into the vascular cylinder in plant roots

node part on a growing stem where a leaf is attached

vascular bundle clusters of xylem and phloem tissue in stems

Related Words Vascular bundles contain two types of tissues, xylem and phloem, which carry different things through a plant. **☑ What does xylem carry, and where else is xylem found in the plant?**

____

____

____

Stems

KEY QUESTION *What are the functions of stems, and how does growth in stems occur?*

Stems produce leaves, branches, and flowers; hold leaves up to the sun; and transport substances throughout the plant. Stems vary in size, shape, and method of development.

Anatomy of a Stem Stems contain all three tissue systems and distinct **nodes**, where the leaves are attached. Tissue arrangement follows two patterns. In monocots, clusters of xylem and phloem tissue, called **vascular bundles**, are scattered through stem ground tissue. In gymnosperms and dicots, vascular bundles are arranged in a ring.

Apical meristem
Cork cambium
Primary Growth
Cork
Secondary Growth
vascular cambium

READING TOOL

Connect to Visuals

Figure 18-9 shows primary and secondary growth in a plant.

☑ **Explain how the parts of a plant function together during both primary and seconday growth.**

____

____

____

____

____

____

____

____

____

Primary and Secondary Growth Plant growth is carefully controlled to produce characteristic sizes and shapes in adult plants.

- **Primary growth** of stems is the result of the division and elongation of cells produced in the apical meristem.
- **Secondary growth** occurs in meristems called the vascular cambium and cork cambium; this is when older stems and roots increase in thickness and length.

Leaves

KEY QUESTION *What are the different structures and functions of leaves?*

Using energy captured in their leaves, plants make sugars, starches, and oils that feed virtually all animals.

Anatomy of a Leaf The structure of leaves is optimized to absorb light and perform photosynthesis. Leaves include blades attached to stems by petioles, and they have an outer dermal covering and inner ground and vascular tissues.

Dermal Tissue Leaf epidermis is a specialized layer of tough, irregularly shaped cells with thick outer walls that resist tearing. They are covered by a waxy layer that helps reduce water evaporation.

Vascular Tissue Vascular tissues in leaves and stems are part of the plant's fluid transport system. Xylem and phloem cells are bundled in leaf veins.

Ground Tissue The area between leaf veins is filled with specialized ground tissue cells called **mesophyll**, where photosynthesis occurs.

Photosynthesis The air spaces in mesophyll layers connect to the plant's exterior through **stomata**, or small openings in the epidermis allowing carbon dioxide, water, and oxygen to diffuse into and out of leaves.

Transpiration **Transpiration** is the loss of water through leaves, which may be replaced by water drawn into the leaf through xylem in the vascular tissue. Transpiration cools leaves on hot days, but threatens leaves if water is scarce.

Gas Exchange and Homeostasis Plants exchange gases with the air. A plant's control of gas exchange is one of the most important elements of homeostasis.

Gas Exchange Leaves take in carbon dioxide and give off oxygen during photosynthesis. Plant leaves allow for gas exchange by opening stomata.

BUILD Vocabulary

primary growth pattern of growth that takes place at the tips and shoots of a plant

secondary growth type of growth in dicots in which the stems increase in thickness

mesophyll specialized ground tissue found in leaves; performs most of a plant's photosynthesis

stomata (plural of stoma) small openings in the epidermis of a plant that allow carbon dioxide, water, and oxygen to diffuse into and out of the leaf

transpiration loss of water from a plant through its leaves

Homeostasis Plants maintain homeostasis by keeping their stomata open enough to allow photosynthesis to occur, but not so much that they lose excessive water. **Guard cells** are specialized cells regulating the movement of gases, like water vapor and carbon dioxide, into and out of leaves. When water is abundant, it flows into the leaf, raising water pressure in guard cells and opening stomata. When water is scarce, water pressure in guard cells decreases and stomata close, reducing water loss by limiting transpiration.

Transpiration and Wilting Osmotic pressure keeps leaves and stems rigid. High transpiration rates, or water loss, lead to wilting, or pressure loss in leaves.

Transport in Plants

KEY QUESTION *What are the major forces that transport water and nutrients in a plant?*

Active transport and root pressure cause water to move from soil into plant roots, then up the plant stem. Other forces are needed to lift it higher into the plant.

Transpirational Pull Force in water transport is provided by water evaporation from leaves during transpiration. As water evaporates, cell walls dry out and water is pulled from the vascular tissue.

How Cell Walls Pull Water Upward Cohesion and adhesion work together to pull water upward in plant cells. The tendency of water to rise in a thin tube is called **capillary action**. Water is attracted to the walls of plants' inner tubes and attracted to other water molecules. The thinner the tube, the higher the water will rise inside it.

Putting It All Together The combination of transpiration and capillary action lifts water upward through the xylem tissues of a plant.

Nutrient Transport The pressure-flow hypothesis states that sugars are transported through phloem via water pressure from osmosis to the places a plant needs it most. The pressure-flow system gives plants enormous flexibility in responding to their changing needs.

BUILD Vocabulary

guard cell specialized cell in the epidermis of plants that controls the opening and closing of stomata

capillary action tendency of water to rise in a thin tube

Multiple Meanings *Capillary* is a term from mid-17th-century French that means "hair." The smallest blood vessels in the human body are called capillaries. ☑ **What do the vascular cells of a plant and human capillaries have in common?**

______

______

______

READING TOOL

Apply Prior Knowledge

In earlier chapters you learned about the properties of water—specifically, cohesion and adhesion. Cohesion is the attraction between molecules of the same substance, and adhesion is the attraction between different kinds of molecules. ☑ **Explain how cohesion and adhesion work together to cause capillary action.**

______

______

______

______

______

______

______

______

______

CHAPTER 18

LESSON 2

Plant Hormones and Tropisms

READING TOOL **Compare and Contrast** Compare each of the items and how they work in helping plants grow and thrive.

Items	Comparisons
Auxins and Cell Elongation vs. Auxins and Branching	
Cytokinins vs. Ethylene vs. Abscisic Acid	
Phototropism vs. Thigmotropism vs. Gravitropism	
Photoperiods and Flowering vs. Photoperiods and Dormancy	

Lesson Summary

BUILD Vocabulary

hormone chemical produced in one part of an organism that affects another part of the same organism

target cell cell that has a receptor for a particular hormone

receptor on or in a cell, a specific protein whose shape fits that of a specific hormone

auxin hormone produced in the tip of a growing plant that stimulates cell elongation and the growth of new roots

Hormones

KEY QUESTION *What roles do plant hormones play?*

Plants respond to light, moisture, temperature, and gravity—through **hormones**, or chemical signals that affect growth, activity, and development of cells and tissues. They control development of cells, tissues, and organs, and coordinate responses to the environment. Cells affected by a particular hormone are called **target cells**. To respond to a hormone, target cells contain hormone **receptors**—usually proteins—to which hormone molecules bind.

Auxins **Auxins** stimulate cell elongation and new root growth. They are produced in the shoot apical meristem and transported to the rest of the plant.

Auxins, Cell Elongation, and Branching To elongate cells, auxins collect in shaded parts of shoots, which stimulates those cells to lengthen, bending the shoot toward the light. **Apical dominance** means the closer a bud is to the stem's tip, the more it is inhibited; the closer it is to the stem, the stronger it is. This is why plant bases grow faster than plant tops.

Cytokinins Cytokinins are plant hormones produced in growing roots and developing fruit and seeds. They stimulate cell division, interact with auxins to balance root and shoot growth, and stimulate regeneration of damaged tissues.

Ethylene Fruit tissues release small amounts of the hormone ethylene, which stimulates fruits to ripen. They also help plants to seal off and drop organs that are no longer needed, like petals after pollination.

Gibberellins Gibberellins are a type of hormones that produce growth in plants. *Gibberella fujikuroi* is a fungus that causes extraordinary growth by mimicking this hormone.

Abscisic Acid Gibberellins interact with another hormone, abscisic acid, in controlling seed dormancy by inhibiting cell division and halting growth. Abscisic acid puts seed embryos into dormancy until conditions are right for growth. Without the opposing effect of abscisic acid, the gibberellins can signal germination.

BUILD Vocabulary

apical dominance phenomenon in which the closer a bud is to the stem's tip, the more its growth is inhibited

tropism movement of a plant toward or away from stimuli

phototropism tendency of a plant to grow toward a light source

thigmotropism response of a plant to touch

gravitropism response of a plant to the force of gravity

Suffixes The suffix *-ism* comes from a Greek word and is used to form action nouns from verbs.

☑ **What action is being carried out by a plant when it goes through thigmotropism?**

____

____

____

Tropisms and Rapid Movements

KEY QUESTION *What are examples of environmental stimuli to which plants respond?*

Plants respond to the environment, just like other living things. Some movements are very slow, while others are extremely fast.

Tropisms Plant sensors that detect environmental stimuli signal elongating organs to reorient their growth. These growth responses are called **tropisms**. Plants respond to environmental stimuli such as light, touch, and gravity.

Light, Touch, and Gravity The tendency of a plant to grow toward a light source is called **phototropism**. Changes in auxin concentration are responsible for this action, which can occur within a matter of hours in seedlings. Some plants respond to touch, a process called **thigmotropism**. Examples include vines and climbing plants that exhibit thigmotropism when encountering objects like trees or trellises and wrapping themselves around them. Auxins also affect **gravitropism**, the response of a plant to gravity. Auxins migrate to lower, or shadier, sides of horizontal roots and stems, which causes stems to bend upright, but roots to bend downward.

Rapid Movements Some plant responses to environmental factors are so quick that they cannot be called tropisms. One example is the rapid response when leaves of the *Mimosa pudica* are touched. Within seconds of touching this "sensitive plant," the two leaflets fold together completely.

READING TOOL

Apply Prior Knowledge

Venus flytraps are one of a few species of plants that are carnivorous. Their leaflets can shut quickly when an insect lands on them. The plant then dissolves the insect and uses its nitrogen and nutrients to support growth.

☑ **Why is nitrogen important to plants? What important biological macromolecules require nitrogen?**

____

____

____

____

Response to Seasons

KEY QUESTION *How to plants respond to seasonal changes?*

Year after year, some plants flower in the spring, summer, or fall. Some plants flower only when daylight is short, while some plants flower only when daylight is long.

BUILD Vocabulary

photoperiodism response of plants to changing photoperiods

READING TOOL

Applying Prior Knowledge Plants need sunlight as part of their nutrients to grow properly. People also need sunlight to properly grow. ☑ **If plants don't get enough sunlight, they wither and possibly die. What happens to people who don't get enough sunlight?**

____

____

____

Photoperiod and Flowering Plants flower according to their photoperiod, or the number of hours of light and darkness received. Some plants respond to changing photoperiods, called **photoperiodism**, a major factor in the timing of seasonal activities.

Winter Dormancy As cold weather approaches, many plants prepare by turning off photosynthetic pathways, transporting materials from leaves to roots, and sealing off leaves from the rest of the plant.

Leaf Loss and Changes to Meristems Some plants lose their leaves during cold months. They absorb less light as days shorten, auxin production drops, and ethylene production increases, shutting down the leaf. Hormones also produce changes in apical meristems, stopping them from producing leaves and forming a waxy layer of cold protection. Xylem and phloem tissues pump themselves full of ions and organic compounds, which act like antifreeze to prevent tree sap from freezing.

Visual Reading Tool: Photoperiod Effects on Flowering

Effect of Photoperiod on Flowering

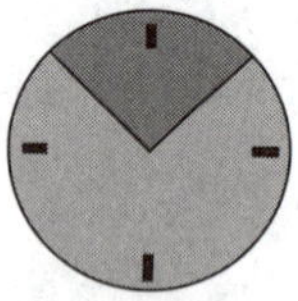

	Long Day Midnight Noon	Short Day Midnight Noon
Short-Day Plant		
Long-Day Plant		

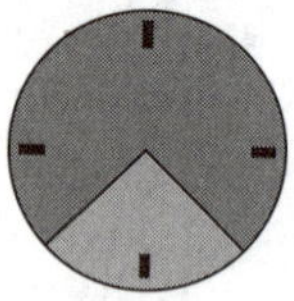

1. Explain the difference between the ways a short-day plant flowers on long days and on short days.

____

____

____

____

2. Explain the difference between the ways a long-day plant flowers on long days and on short days.

____

____

____

____

CHAPTER 18

LESSON 3 Plants and People

READING TOOL **Main Idea and Details** For each section within the lesson, identify the main idea and one to three supporting details. Several answers are already filled in for you.

Section	Main Ideas	Details
Agriculture	The systematic cultivation of plants began long before humans took part in it.	Ants harvest plant seeds, spread them around, and fertilize them.
Worldwide Patterns		
New Plants		
Changes in Agriculture		
Industrial Agriculture		
Fiber, Wood, and Medicine		

Lesson Summary

As you read, circle the answers to each Key Question. Underline any words you do not understand.

READING TOOL

Connect to Visuals
Plants do so much more than just feed humans. View Figure 18-26 in your textbook to read about different products that are made from plants. **Look around the room you're in right now and make a list of things that are made using plants.**

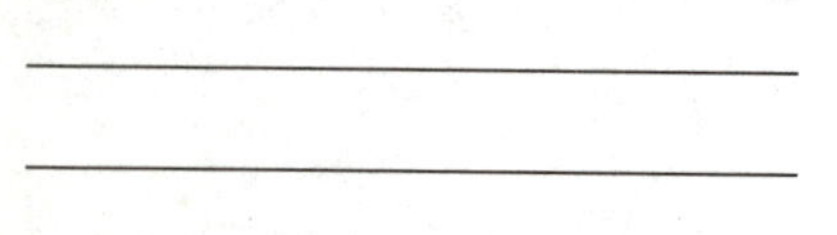

Agriculture

KEY QUESTION *Which crops are the major food supply for humans?*

Agriculture, or the systematic cultivation of plants for consumption—began with ants, who harvested seeds, spread them around, and fertilized them. Scientists believe ants had been "farming" several millions years before humans began growing food plants.

Worldwide Patterns The beginnings of human civilization can be traced back to the cultivation of crop plants about 10,000 to 12,000 years ago in multiple places worldwide. Once people discovered plants could be grown for food, they stopped migrating, which led to the establishment of social institutions. Today, agricultural pursuits occupy more humans than any other job. North America has some of the most productive cropland in the world. About 80% of U.S. cropland is used to grow wheat, corn, soybeans, and hay, three of which come from grasses.

New Plants The discovery and introduction of new crop plants has frequently changed regional agriculture. Continuing to introduce new plants into cultivation ensures strong genetic diversity in the food supply, and decreases chances that pests or disease could devastate farming.

Changes in Agriculture Between 1950 and 1970, a worldwide effort to combat hunger and malnutrition, called the green revolution, led to dramatic improvements in farming techniques and crop yields, greatly increasing the world's food supply. At the heart of this was the use of high-yield varieties of seed and artificial fertilizers.

Industrial Agriculture Improved farming methods made it possible to increase crop yields and produce food cheaply. However, the large-scale cultivation of a small number of crops has reduced genetic diversity and left our food supply vulnerable to insects and disease. As populations increase, it is necessary to safeguard genetic diversity in crop plants and address challenges caused by industrial farming methods.

Fiber, Wood, and Medicine

KEY QUESTION *What are some examples of benefits besides food that human derive from plants?*

Plants produce the raw materials for our homes and clothes, and important items like paper for printing or toilet paper. Additionally, some of our most powerful and effective medicines, like those used to fight cancer, come from plants.

18 Chapter Review

Review Vocabulary

Match the vocabulary term to its definition.

1. ______ mesophyll

2. ______ meristem

3. ______ auxin

a. unspecialized cells responsible for growth throughout a plant's lifetime

b. specialized ground tissue found in leaves that performs photosynthesis

c. substance that regulates plant growth by stimulating cells and roots

Fill in the blanks with the correct terms.

4. ______________ is where a plant's stems increase in thickness, while ______________ is where a plant's tips and shoots grow.

5. ______________ is a plant's tendency to grow toward a light source, while ______________ is a plant's response to touch, and ______________ is a plant's response to the force of gravity.

Review Key Questions

Provide evidence and details to support your answers.

6. What are the principal organs of plants and what three types of tissue do they contain?

Organs: ______________ ______________ ______________

Tissues: ______________ ______________ ______________

7. Explain how root systems help feed plants.

____

____

____

8. What would happen to a low-growing fruit bush that was infected by the *Gibberella fujikuroi* fungus?

____

9. With our current agricultural methods, what would happen if disease or insects ravaged the food crops the United States gets from grasses?

____

____

____

CHAPTER 19

LESSON 1

Feeding and Digestion

READING TOOL **Use Structure** As you read this lesson, complete the table below. Describe how different types of animals obtain food.

DIGESTION: How do each of the following obtain food?				
Filter Feeders	Detritivores	Herbivores	Carnivores	Nutritional Symbionts

Lesson Summary

Obtaining Food

KEY QUESTION *How do animals obtain food?*

All animals that obtain nutrients and energy from food are heterotrophs.

Filter Feeders Most filter feeders catch algae and small animals by using structures like modified gills as nets to filter food out of water.

Detritivores Detritus is made up of decaying plant and animal material. Detritivores feed on detritus, often obtaining extra nutrients from microorganisms that grow on and around it.

As you read, circle the answers to each Key Question. Underline any words you do not understand.

READING TOOL

Compare and Contrast

Animals have specialized digestive tracts that digest food in stages. **☑ How is chemical digestion different from mechanical digestion?**

____

____

____

____

____

____

____

____

____

Herbivores Herbivores eat plants or parts of plants, like seeds and fruits, or they eat algae. Seeds and fruits are often filled with nutrients and are easy to digest.

Carnivores Carnivores eat other animals. Mammalian carnivores use teeth, claws, and speed to hunt their prey.

Nutritional Symbionts Symbiosis is a close relationship between two or more species. Symbionts are the organisms involved in a symbiosis.

Parasitic Symbiosis Parasites live within or on a host organism, where they feed on tissues or body fluids, disrupting the health of their hosts. Some parasites cause serious diseases in humans, livestock, and plants.

Mutualistic Symbiosis Mutualistic nutritional relationships benefit both participants, and often help to maintain the health of organisms.

Processing Food

KEY QUESTION *How does digestion occur in animals?*

After food is obtained, it must be digested and absorbed to make energy and nutrients. Many invertebrates and all vertebrates digest food as it passes through a tube called a **digestive tract**, which has two openings. Food moves in one direction, entering the body through the mouth. Wastes leave through the anus.

One-way digestive tracts often have specialized structures that perform different tasks as food passes through them. Food undergoes both chemical and mechanical digestion. The intestines absorb nutrients, and wastes are expelled.

BUILD Vocabulary

digestive tract tube that begins at the mouth and ends at the anus

rumen stomach chamber in cows and related animals in which symbiotic bacteria digest cellulose

Word Origins *Digest* comes from the Latin word *digesta* which has its origins in the word *digerere*. *Digerere* means "to separate, divide, or arrange," and the suffix *-gest* means "to carry." **☑ Based on these origins, explain the term *digest* in your own words.**

____

____

____

Specializations for Different Diets

KEY QUESTION *How are mouthparts adapted for different diets?*

Animal mouthparts and digestive systems have evolved and adapted to the physical and chemical characteristics of different foods.

Specialized Mouthparts Carnivores and leaf-eating herbivores usually have very different mouthparts that are related to the foods they eat.

Eating Meat Carnivores typically have sharp mouthparts and structures that capture and break down food. Their sharp teeth, jaw bones, and muscles are adapted for up-and-down movements that chop meat into small pieces.

Eating Plant Leaves Herbivores have mouthparts that grind plant cell walls. Many herbivorous invertebrates have mouthparts that grind plants or algae. Herbivorous mammals like the giraffe have front teeth, muscular lips, flattened molars, and jawbones that pull and grind leaves in a side-to-side motion.

Specialized Digestive Tracts Carnivorous invertebrates and vertebrates have short digestive tracts that produce meat-digesting enzymes, but lack enzymes that break down plant cellulose. Animals called ruminants, like cattle, have a **rumen**, where symbiotic bacteria digest cellulose.

Visual Reading Tool: Carnivore or Herbivore

1. Analyze the figure shown. Determine which is a herbivore and which is a carnivore.

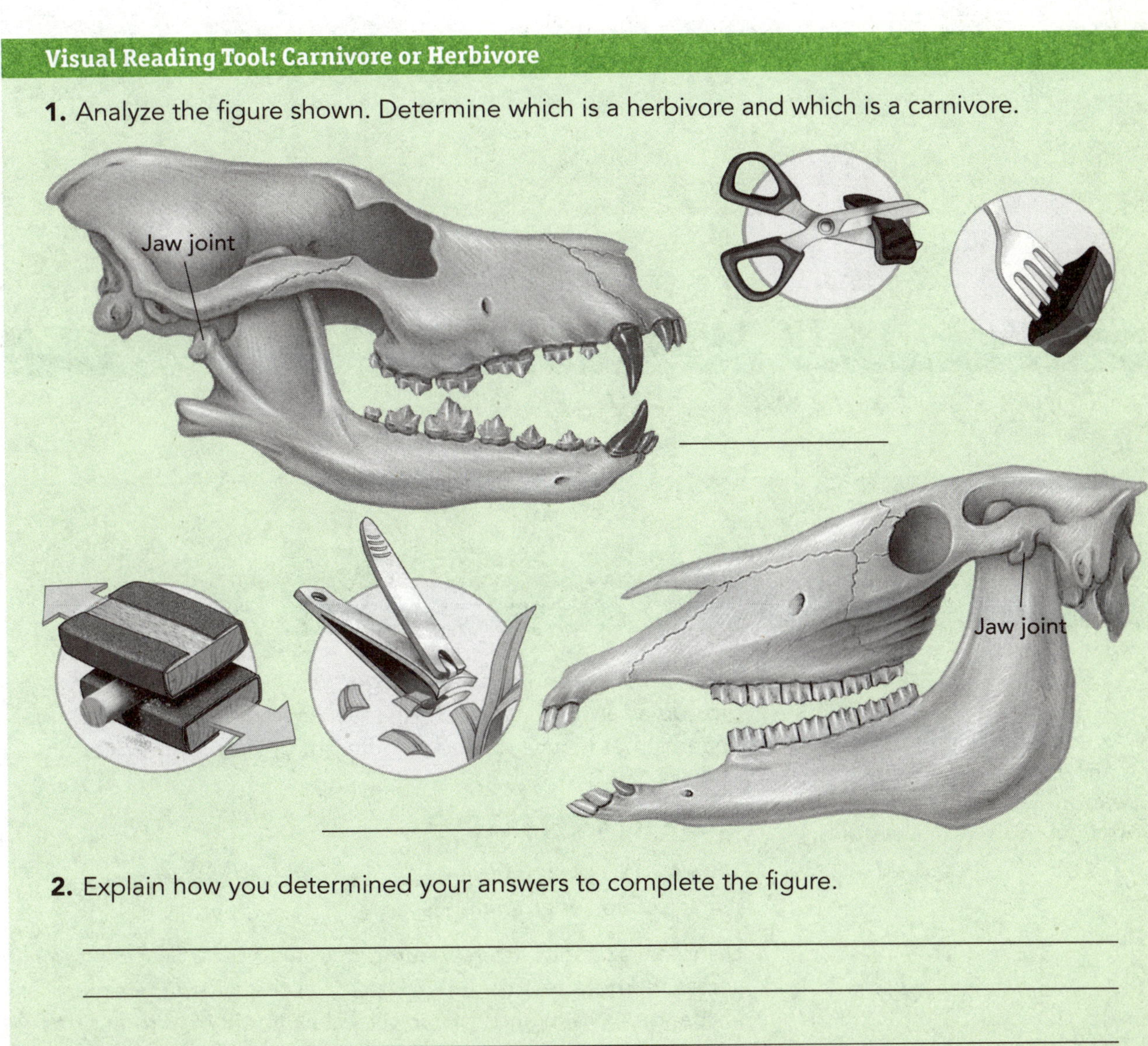

2. Explain how you determined your answers to complete the figure.

CHAPTER 19

LESSON 2

Respiration

READING TOOL **Compare and Contrast** Compare and contrast respiration in the following species.

Differences			
Amphibians	Reptiles	Mammals	Birds
Similarities			

Lesson Summary

Cellular respiration requires oxygen, and it produces carbon dioxide as a waste product. Animals have different respiratory systems that have adapted to different environments over time.

As you read, circle the answers to each Key Question. Underline any words you do not understand.

Gas Exchange

KEY QUESTION *What characteristics do the respiratory structures of all animals share?*

Living cells cannot actively pump oxygen or carbon dioxide across membranes. Yet, in order to breathe, all animals must exchange oxygen and carbon dioxide with their surroundings.

Gas Diffusion and Membranes Substances diffuse from an area of higher concentration to an area of lower concentration. Gases diffuse most efficiently across a thin, moist membrane that is permeable to those gases.

Requirements for Respiration All respiratory systems share certain basic characteristics. Respiratory structures provide a large surface area of moist, selectively permeable membrane.

Respiratory Surfaces of Aquatic Animals

KEY QUESTION *How do aquatic animals breathe?*

Some aquatic invertebrates are small and have thin-walled bodies whose outer surfaces are always wet. They rely on diffusion of oxygen and carbon dioxide through their outer body covering. A few aquatic chordates, including lancelets, some amphibians, and some sea snakes, rely on gas exchange by diffusion across body surfaces. Large, active animals that consume larger quantities of oxygen exchange gases through **gills**, which are feathery structures that expose a large surface area of thin, selectively permeable membrane to water. Inside the gill membranes is a network of tiny, thin-walled blood vessels called capillaries, which help maintain differences in oxygen and carbon dioxide concentrations that promote diffusion.

Aquatic reptiles and mammals breathe with lungs and must hold their breath underwater; they come to the water's surface to breathe. **Lungs** are organs that exchange oxygen and carbon dioxide between blood and air.

BUILD Vocabulary

gills feathery structures specialized for the exchange of gases with water

lungs respiratory organ in which gases are exchanged between the blood and inhaled air

Visual Reading Tool: Respiration through Gills

For each box shown in the figure, describe the function performed for respiration through gills.

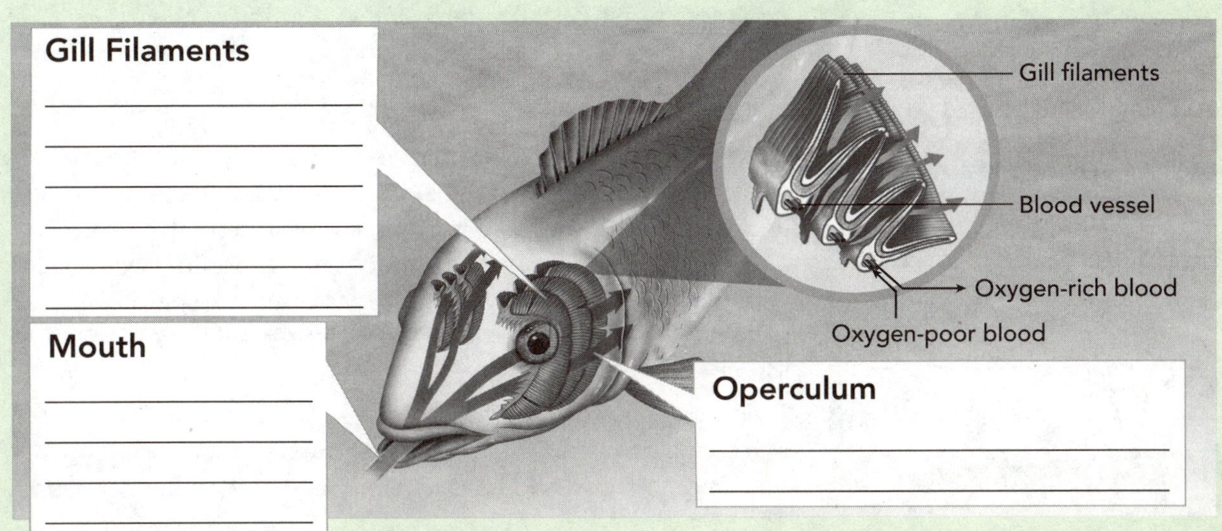

READING TOOL

Make Connections
In earlier chapters you learned that plants need certain gases to carry out photosynthesis and cell respiration. ☑ **Describe the air that humans exhale. How is it different from respiration in plants?**

Respiratory Surfaces of Terrestrial Animals

KEY QUESTION *What respiratory structures enable land animals to breathe?*

Land animals must keep their respiratory membranes moist in dry environments. They must also carry oxygen and carbon dioxide back and forth between those surfaces and the rest of their bodies.

Respiratory Surfaces in Invertebrates Respiratory structures in terrestrial invertebrates include skin, mantle cavities, book lungs, and tracheal tubes. Some land invertebrates, such as earthworms, live in moist environments and can respire across their skin if it stays moist. Other invertebrates, such as land snails, respire using a mantle cavity lined with moist tissue and blood vessels. Insects and spiders have more complex respiratory systems.

Lung Structure in Vertebrates All terrestrial vertebrates—reptiles, birds, mammals, and the land stages of most amphibians—breathe with lungs. Inhaling brings oxygen-rich air through the trachea, into the lungs. Inside the lungs, oxygen diffuses into the blood through lung capillaries, and carbon dioxide diffuses out of capillaries into the lungs to be exhaled.

Amphibian, Reptilian, and Mammalian Lungs A typical amphibian lung is little more than a sac with ridges. Reptilian lungs are often divided into chambers that increase the surface area for gas exchange. Mammalian lungs branch extensively, and air passages branch and rebranch, ending in bubblelike structures called **alveoli**. Alveoli provide a large surface area for gas exchange and are surrounded by a network of capillaries in which blood picks up oxygen and releases carbon dioxide. Mammalian lung structure helps take in the large amounts of oxygen required by high metabolic rates. When mammals and most other vertebrates breathe, air moves in and out through the same air passages, and some stale, oxygen-poor air remains.

Bird Lungs In birds, air flows mostly in only one direction. No stale air gets trapped in the system. A unique system of tubes and air sacs in birds' respiratory systems enable this one-way airflow. Thus, gas exchange surfaces are continuously in contact with fresh air. This highly efficient gas exchange helps birds obtain the oxygen they need to power their flight muscles for long periods of time.

BUILD Vocabulary

alveoli (singular alveolus) tiny air sacs at the end of a bronchiole in the lungs that provide surface area for gas exchange to occur

Word Origins *Alveolus* comes from the Latin word *alveus* which means "hollow or cavity," or from *alvus*, which means "belly or beehive." ☑ **Imagine a beehive and its honeycombs. Based on the definition of *alveoli*, what do you think a beehive and alveoli have in common?**

CHAPTER 19

LESSON 3

Circulation

READING TOOL **Compare and Contrast** Compare and contrast the four-chambered heart with the three-chambered heart. Describe their similarities in the middle column. Then provide three examples each of animals that have three-chambered hearts and those that have four-chambered hearts.

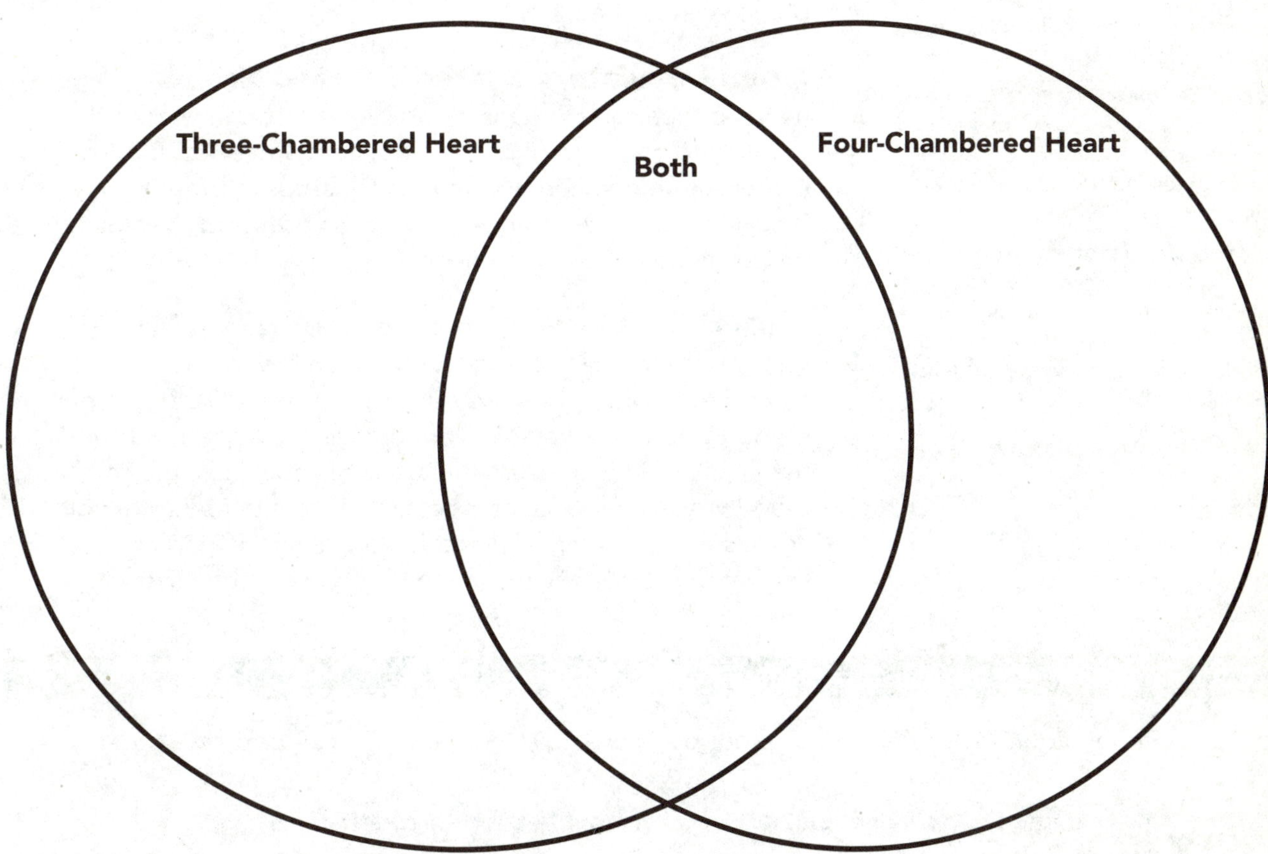

EXAMPLES	
Three-Chambered Hearts	Four-Chambered Hearts

Lesson Summary

🔑 As you read, circle the answers to each Key Question. Underline any words you do not understand.

BUILD Vocabulary

heart hollow muscular organ that pumps blood throughout the body

open circulatory system type of circulatory system in which blood is pumped into sinuses or cavities and comes into direct contact with tissues

closed circulatory system type of circulatory system in which blood circulates entirely within blood vessels that extend throughout the body; nutrients and oxygen diffuse out of vesels

Open and Closed Circulatory Systems

🔑 **KEY QUESTION** *How do open and closed circulatory systems compare?*

Many animals move blood through their bodies using one or more hearts. A **heart** is a hollow, muscular organ that pumps blood around the body.

Open Circulatory Systems In **open circulatory systems**, hearts or heart-like organs pump blood through vessels that empty into a system of sinuses, or spongy cavities. Blood comes into direct contact with body tissues in those sinuses. Blood then collects in another set of sinuses and eventually makes its way back to the heart.

Closed Circulatory Systems In **closed circulatory systems**, blood circulates entirely within blood vessels that extend throughout the body. A heart or heart-like organ pumps blood through the vessels. Nutrients and oxygen reach body tissues by diffusing across thin walls of capillaries, the smallest blood vessels. Blood that is completely contained within blood vessels can be pumped under higher pressure, and can be circulated more efficiently, than blood in an open system.

Visual Reading Tool: Single- and Double-Loop Circulation

Complete the figure by writing the different parts of single-loop and double-loop circulation.

Single-Loop Circulation

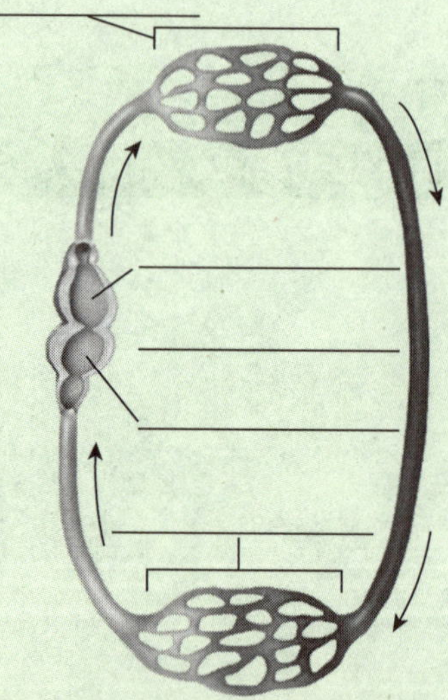

Double-Loop Circulation

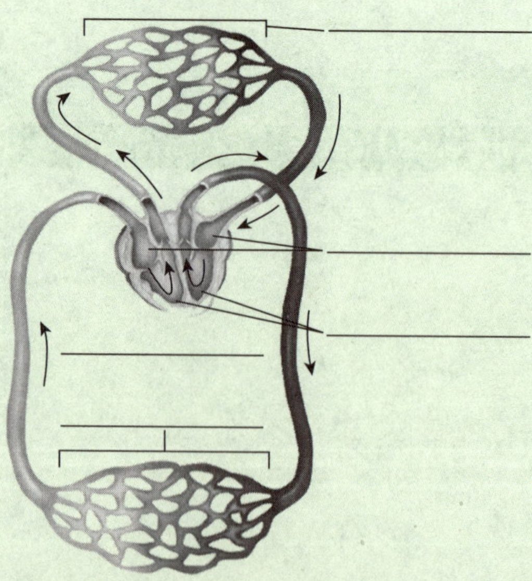

Single- and Double-Loop Circulation

KEY QUESTION *How do the patterns of circulation in vertebrates compare?*

As chordates evolved, they evolved more complex organ systems and more efficient channels for internal transport.

Single-Loop Circulation Most vertebrates with gills have a single-loop circulatory system with a single pump that forces blood around the body in one direction. In fishes, for example, the heart consists of two chambers: an atrium and a ventricle. The **atrium** receives blood from the body. The **ventricle** then pumps blood out of the heart and to the gills. Oxygen-rich blood then travels from the gills to the rest of the body; oxygen-poor blood returns to the atrium.

Double-Loop Circulation As terrestrial vertebrates evolved into larger and more active forms, their capillary networks became larger. Using a single pump to force blood through the entire system would have been increasingly difficult and inefficient. Most vertebrates that breathe with lungs have evolved a double-loop, two-pump circulatory system. The first loop, powered by the right side of the heart, forces oxygen-poor blood from the heart to the lungs. After the blood picks up oxygen and drops off carbon dioxide in the lungs, it returns to the heart. Then the left side of the heart pumps the oxygen-rich blood through the second circulatory loop to the rest of the body. Oxygen-poor blood from the body returns to the heart, and the cycle begins again.

Heart-Chamber Evolution Four-chambered hearts like those in modern mammals are two separate pumps working next to one another. During chordate evolution, partitions evolved that divided the original two chambers into four. Those partitions transformed one pump into two parallel pumps. The partitions also separated oxygen-rich blood from oxygen-poor blood.

Amphibian hearts usually have three chambers: two atria and one ventricle. The right atrium receives oxygen-poor blood from the body. The left atrium receives oxygen-rich blood from the lungs. Both atria empty into the ventricle. This undivided ventricle allows blood to be moved away from the lungs when these animals dive underwater. Some mixing of oxygen-rich and oxygen-poor blood in the ventricle occurs. However, the internal structure of the ventricle directs blood flow so that most oxygen-poor blood goes to the lungs, and most oxygen-rich blood goes to the rest of the body.

READING TOOL

Make Connections
Most fish have single-loop circulatory systems, while larger terrestrial vertebrates have double-loop circulatory systems. ☑ **What caused circulatory systems to become more complex over time?**

____

____

____

____

____

____

____

BUILD Vocabulary

atrium upper chamber of the heart that receives blood from the rest of the body

ventricle lower chamber of the heart that pumps blood out of the heart to the rest of the body

Multiple Meanings Another definition for the word *atrium* is "a central glass-roofed hall that extends through several floors in a building," such as a mall or hotel. ☑ **How is this definition similar to the atrium in the heart?**

____

____

____

CHAPTER 19

LESSON 4

Excretion

READING TOOL **Use Structure** As you read each of the sections in the lesson, briefly describe the main ideas and key takeaways in the graphic organizer below.

Section	Description
The Ammonia Problem	
Storing Wastes that Contain Nitrogen	
Maintaining Water Balance	

Lesson Summary

The Ammonia Problem

KEY QUESTION *How do animals manage toxic nitrogenous waste?*

Cellular metabolism produces wastes that are released into body fluids and must be eliminated from the body. When cells break down proteins, they produce ammonia, a toxic, nitrogenous waste. Animals either eliminate ammonia from the body quickly or convert it into other compounds that are less toxic. The elimination of metabolic wastes, such as ammonia, is called **excretion**.

Storing Wastes that Contain Nitrogen Animals that cannot dispose of ammonia as it is produced store nitrogen-containing wastes until they can be eliminated. In most cases, ammonia is too toxic to be stored in body fluids. Insects, reptiles, and birds typically covert ammonia into a sticky white compound called uric acid, which is less toxic and less water soluble. Mammals and some amphibians convert ammonia to urea, which is less toxic than ammonia, but highly soluble in water.

Maintaining Water Balance Excretory systems interact with other systems that regulate water balance in blood and body tissues. Sometimes, excretory systems eliminate excess water along with nitrogenous wastes. Other times, excretory systems eliminate nitrogenous wastes while conserving water. Many animals use **kidneys** to separate wastes and excess water from blood in urine. Kidney cells pump ions from dissolved salts in blood in ways that create an osmotic gradient. Water then "follows" those ions passively by osmosis. This process can get rid of nitrogenous wastes and retain water, but doesn't allow the kidneys to eliminate excess salts.

BUILD Vocabulary

excretion process by which metabolic wastes are eliminated from the body

kidney organ of excretion that separates wastes and excess water from the blood

Make Connections The word *excrement* means "wastes," specifically feces, and is related to excretion. ☑ **What other substances does the human body excrete?**

____

____

Visual Reading Tool: Aquatic Animal Excretion

On the diagram below, label the direction that water and salt are flowing in or out of the fish. Also label each as either freshwater or saltwater.

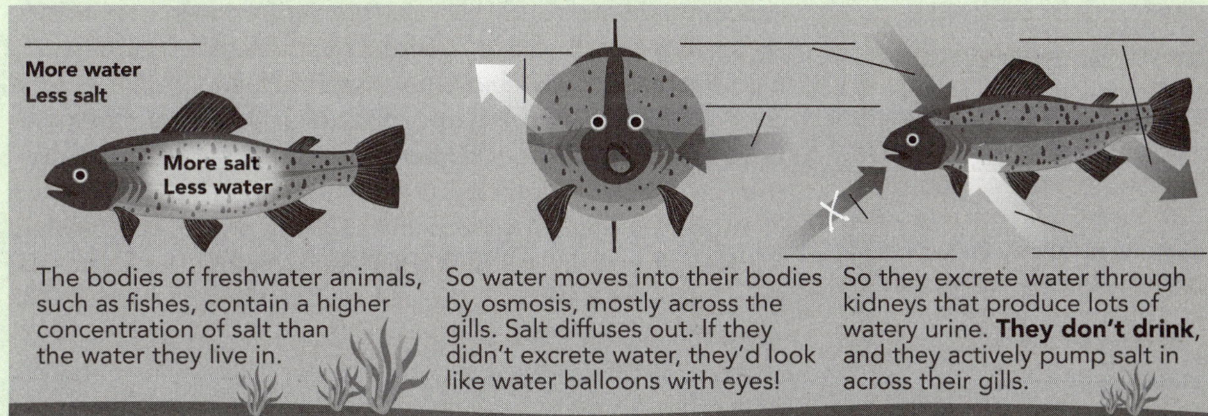

READING TOOL

Cause and Effect

Aquatic animals have to keep a certain amount of water in their cells to maintain homeostasis.

☑ **What causes water to move into invertebrates that live in freshwater?**

____

____

____

____

____

Excretion in Aquatic Animals

KEY QUESTION *How do aquatic animals eliminate wastes?*

Aquatic animals eliminate or conserve water depending on whether they live in fresh or salt water.

Freshwater Animals Many freshwater invertebrates lose ammonia by simple diffusion across their skin, and many freshwater fish and amphibians eliminate ammonia across gill membranes.

Saltwater Animals Marine animals release ammonia by diffusion. Many marine invertebrates have body fluids with solute concentrations similar to the seawater around them. Marine fish lose water to their surroundings because their bodies are less salty than the water around them, so they excrete salt across their gills. Their kidneys produce small quantities of urine, which conserves water.

Excretion in Terrestrial Animals

KEY QUESTION *How do land animals remove wastes while conserving water?*

In dry environments, land animals lose large amounts of water from respiratory membranes that must be kept moist. They must also eliminate nitrogenous wastes in ways that require disposing of water even though they may not have access to water to drink.

Terrestrial Invertebrates Some terrestrial invertebrates, including annelids and mollusks, produce urine in nephridia. **Nephridia** are tubelike excretory structures that filter body fluid. Typically, body fluid enters nephridia and becomes more concentrated as it moves through the tubes. Urine leaves the body through excretory pores. Other terrestrial invertebrates, such as insects and arachnids, convert ammonia into uric acid. Nitrogenous wastes, such as uric acid, are absorbed from body fluids by structures called **Malpighian tubules**. The wastes are then added to digestive wastes traveling through the gut. The wastes lose water, and then crystallize into a thick paste. The paste leaves the body through the anus. This paste contains little water, so these adaptations minimize water loss.

Terrestrial Vertebrates In terrestrial vertebrates, excretion is carried out mostly by the kidneys. Mammals and land amphibians convert ammonia into urea, which is excreted in urine. In most reptiles and birds, ammonia is converted into uric acid. Reptiles and birds pass uric acid through ducts into a cavity that also receives digestive wastes from the gut.

Adaptations to Extreme Environments Most vertebrate kidneys cannot excrete concentrated salt, thus they cannot survive by drinking seawater. Taking in extra salt would overwhelm the kidneys, and the animal would die of dehydration. Some marine reptiles and birds have evolved adaptations in the form of specialized glands in their heads that excrete very concentrated salt solutions.

BUILD Vocabulary

nephridia excretory structures of some terrestrial invertebrates that filter body fluid

Malpighian tubules structures in most terrestrial arthropods that concentrate the uric acid and add it to digestive wastes

Related Words A *nephron* is "the filtering and excretory unit of the kidney," which is found in most terrestrial vertebrates.

☑ **Based on the definitions of *nephridia* and *nephron*, do you think the two structures are structurally and functionally similar or different, and why?**

____

____

____

____

19 Chapter Review

Review Vocabulary

Choose the letter of the best answer.

1. Detritivores feed on which of the following?

A. animals

B. other detritivores

C. microorganisms

2. Respiratory structures in terrestrial invertebrates include all of the following except:

A. skin.

B. gills.

C. tracheal tubes.

Review Key Questions

Provide evidence and details to support your answers.

3. What would be a good way for a student studying dinosaurs determine whether a specific fossil is a carnivore or herbivore?

4. What are the benefits of a closed circulatory system over an open circulatory system?

5. Why is ammonia considered a problem that organisms need to solve?

6. What is the relationship between surface area and diffusion?

CHAPTER 20

LESSON 1

Response

READING TOOL **Main Idea and Details** As you read your textbook, identify the main ideas and details or evidence that support the main ideas. Use the lesson headings to organize the main ideas and details. Record your work in the table.

Heading	Main Idea	Details/Evidence
How Animals Respond		
Trends in Nervous System Evolution		
Sensory Systems		

Lesson Summary

Humans respond to stimuli by gathering information about their surroundings through senses, like vision or hearing. Then the brain decides how to respond to that information. However, the sensory world of animals is different from yours.

As you read, circle the answers to each Key Question. Underline any words you do not understand.

How Animals Respond

KEY QUESTION *How do animals respond to their environment?*

Animals sometimes need to respond to environmental conditions quickly, so they can survive. An animal's nervous system is made up of several kinds of nerve cells called **neurons**. Neurons allow information collected from the stimulus to be passed on to other cells like those in the brain.

BUILD Vocabulary

neurons nerve cell; specialized for carrying messages throughout the nervous system

Detecting Stimuli A **stimulus** can be light, temperature, sound, odors, vibrations, or other information in an animal's environment that causes the animal to react. **Sensory neurons** are specialized cells that allow the animal to notice the stimuli. Each type of sensory neuron responds to a particular stimulus such as light, heat, or a chemical. Humans and animals share similar types of sensory cells, and so animals react to stimuli that humans notice too, like light, taste, odor, temperature, sound, water, gravity, and pressure. However, many animals respond to stimuli that humans cannot detect, such as weak electric currents, because many animals have types of sensory cells that humans do not have.

Processing Information Once a stimulus is detected by the sensory neurons, they pass information about the stimulus to other nerve cells that also pass information. These are called **interneurons,** and they process the data to determine how the animal should respond. An animal's behavior may be more flexible and complex depending on the number of interneurons an animal has and the ways those interneurons process information. For example, worms have few interneurons and are capable of only simple responses, like swimming toward light. A more highly developed nervous system, like in a leopard, with greater numbers of interneurons, mostly in the brain, will have more complex behaviors.

Responding A **response** is a specific reaction to a stimulus. When an animal responds to a stimulus, body systems—including the nervous system and the muscular system—work together to generate the response. **Motor neurons** are nerve cells that carry directions from interneurons to muscles, which produces a response.

Trends in Nervous System Evolution

KEY QUESTION *What are some trends in nervous system evolution?*

Animal nervous systems exhibit different degrees of cephalization and specialization.

Invertebrates Invertebrates, nervous systems range from simple collections of nerve cells to complex organizations that include many interneurons.

Nerve Nets, Nerve Cords, and Ganglia A simple nervous system is called a nerve net and looks like a net. Nerve cords are interneurons grouped together. **Ganglia** are interneurons that are grouped together and that connect to each other.

BUILD Vocabulary

stimulus signal to which an organism responds

sensory neurons type of nerve cell that receives information from sensory receptors and conveys signals to the central nervous system

interneuron type of neuron that processes information and may relay information to motor neurons

response specific reaction to a stimulus

motor neuron type of nerve cell that carries directions from interneurons to either muscle cells or glands

ganglia a group of interneurons

Prefixes *Inter-* is a prefix of Latin origin that can mean "between," "mututally," or "during." ☑ **Which meaning does *inter-* have in the word *interneuron*? Explain your answer.**

____

____

____

____

____

BUILD Vocabulary

cerebrum part of the brain responsible for voluntary activities of the body; the "thinking" region of the brain

cerebellum part of the brain that coordinates movement and controls balance

Word Origins The word *cerebellum*, in Latin, means "little brain" and was introduced into the English language in the 16th century. ☑ **Why do you think the cerebellum is referred to as the "little brain?" You can use Figure 20-3 in your textbook to help you.**

____

____

____

____

"Heads" Cephalization is the concentration of sensory neurons into a "head." Some flatworms and roundworms show this characteristic. The nerves in a head are referred to as cerebral ganglia.

Brains When cerebral ganglia are organized into a complex structure, it is called a brain. Brains generally enable complex behavior and learning.

Chordates Cerebral ganglion are found in simple chordates. Most vertebrates show a high degree of cephalization and have highly developed nervous systems.

Parts of the Vertebrate Brain The **cerebrum** is part of the vertebrate brain called the "thinking" region. The **cerebellum** coordinates movement and controls balance.

Vertebrate Brain Evolution Brain evolution in vertebrates follows a general trend of increasing size and complexity from fishes, through amphibians and reptiles, to birds and mammals.

Sensory Systems

KEY QUESTION *What are some types of sensory systems in animals?*

The more complex an animal's nervous system is, the more developed its sensory systems tend to be. Sensory systems range from individual sensory neurons to sense organs that contain both sensory neurons and other cells that help gather information.

Invertebrate Sense Organs Invertebrate sense organs vary widely in complexity. Some invertebrates only sense one stimulus—like a flatworm, for example, that only detects the presence and direction of light—where others can detect several stimuli simultaneously. Invertebrates that are more cephalized have specialized sensory tissues and well-developed sense organs. Because of this complex cephalization, some cephalopods and arthropods can detect motion and color and form images through their eyes.

Other examples of different sense organs that sense the same type of stimulus are the many lenses of the eyes of an insect detecting minute changes in movement, the antennae of a midge sensing sound waves and air motion, and a garden spider detecting vibrations in its web through its legs.

Chordate Sense Organs Chordate sense organs can be simple and have few specializations. In tunicates, sensory cells in and on the siphons and other internal surfaces help control the amount of water passing through the pharynx. Lancelets have a cerebral ganglion with a pair of eyespots that detect light.

Taste, smell, and hearing are received through organs that are very sensitive to their own stimuli. Many animals can have the same parts to make up the organs, but they often have different abilities that are specialized. For example, some species, including certain fishes and the duck-billed platypuses, can detect weak electric currents in water. Some sharks use this "electric sense" to navigate by detecting electric currents in seawater caused by ocean currents moving through Earth's magnetic field. Other "electric fish" create their own electric currents and use it to communicate with one another.

Visual Reading Tool: Trends in Nervous Systems

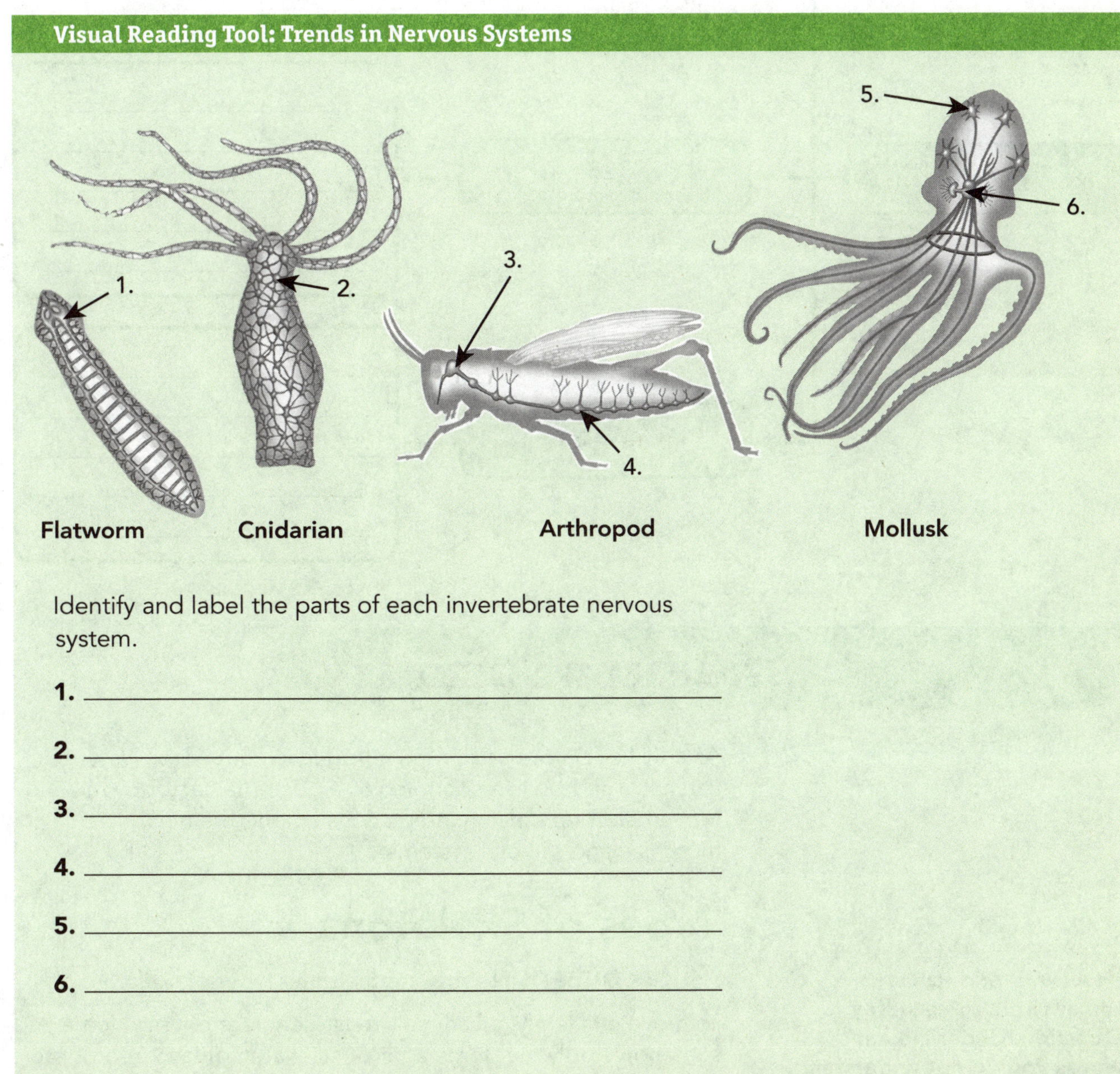

Identify and label the parts of each invertebrate nervous system.

1. ____________________

2. ____________________

3. ____________________

4. ____________________

5. ____________________

6. ____________________

CHAPTER 20

LESSON 2

Movement and Support

READING TOOL **Active Reading** As you read through this lesson, take notes on the different types of skeletons that protect and support organisms. Fill in the graphic organizer below.

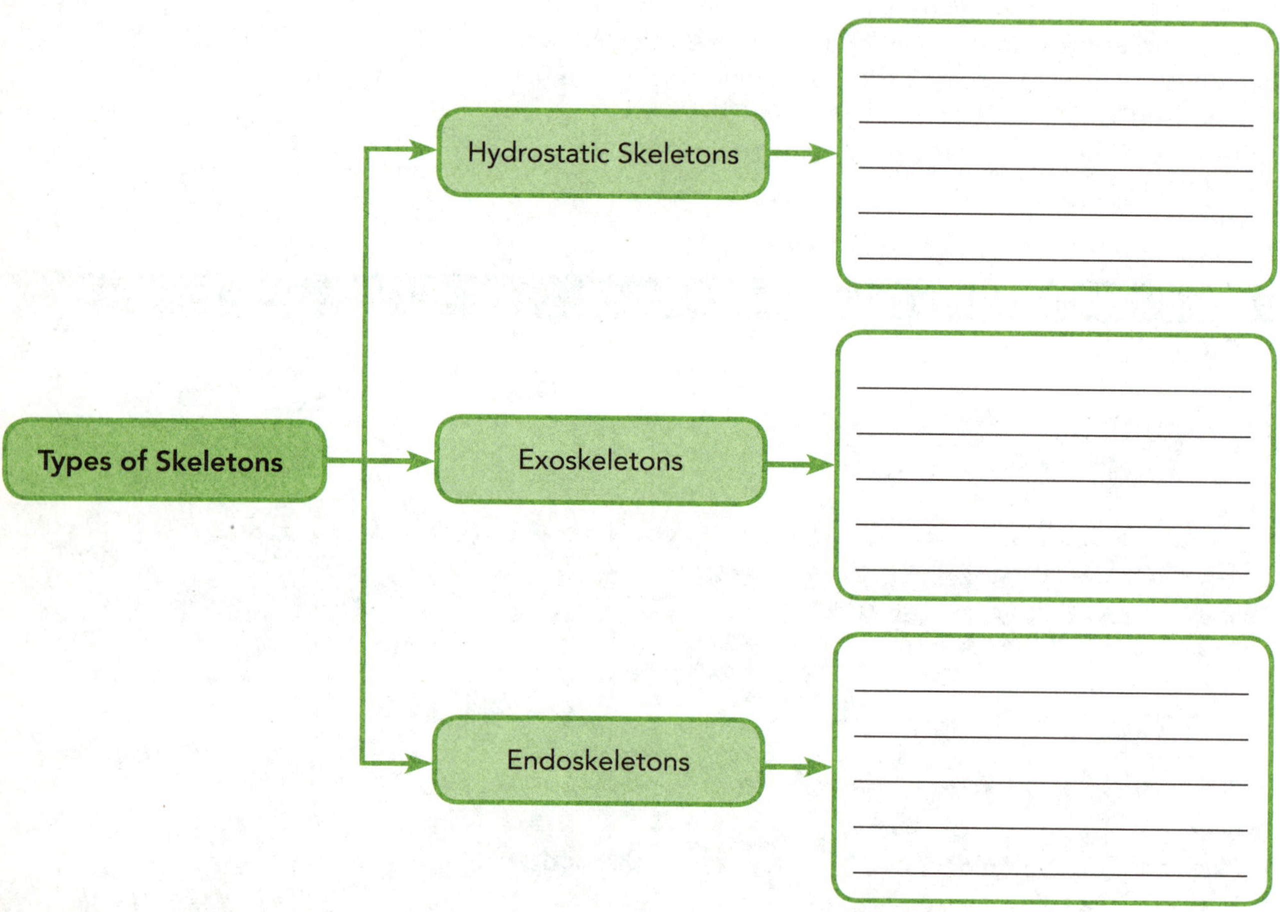

Lesson Summary

As a fly hovers over a stream, a frog leaps out of the water to catch it. The frog is responding to an external factor by moving. Movement depends on interactions among the nervous, muscular, and skeletal systems.

Types of Skeletons

KEY QUESTION *What are the three types of skeletons?*

To move efficiently, all animals must generate physical force and somehow apply that force against air, water, or land in order to push or pull themselves around.

As you read, circle the answers to each Key Question. Underline any words you do not understand.

Skeletal Support Having a rigid body part, like a skeleton, helps animals move more efficiently by applying force generated by muscles. For example, legs push against the ground, wings push against air, fins apply force against water. Hydrostatic, exoskeletons, and endoskeletons are the main kinds of skeletal systems animals can have.

Hydrostatic Skeletons An earthworm has a **hydrostatic skeleton** and consists of fluids held in a body cavity, which allows the worm to change its body shape, making it shorter and/or fatter. The earthworm has longitudinal muscles that run from one end to the other, making it shorter and fatter. The earthworm can become longer and thinner by contracting circular muscles that wrap around each body segment. By alternately contracting these two sets of muscles, the earthworm is able to move.

Exoskeletons **Exoskeletons** are external skeletons found in arthropods and mollusks. Arthropod exoskeletons are made of complex carbohydrates called chitin. Most mollusks have hard shells made of calcium carbonate. This type of skeleton provides protection from predators and acts as a watertight covering to allow survival in dry places. One disadvantage of the exoskeleton is that it doesn't grow when the animal does. An arthropod has to break out of the exoskeleton and grow a new one in a process called molting. These skeletons are also heavy and increase in weight as the arthropod grows.

Endoskeletons A structural support system found inside the body is an **endoskeleton**. Endoskeletons do not protect an animal like an exoskeleton does. However, this type of skeleton can grow as the animal grows and it can grow very large because the endoskeleton is lightweight in proportion to the body it supports.

Joints Connections that divide parts of a skeleton and allow movement are known as **joints**. Bones are connected at joints by strong connective tissues called ligaments.

Muscles and Movements

KEY QUESTION *How do muscles enable movement?*

Muscles are specialized tissues that produce physical force by contracting, or shortening, when they are stimulated by the nervous system. In many animals, muscles work together in pairs or groups that are attached to different parts of a skeleton.

Movement When one muscle group contracts and the other is relaxed, it bends the joint. Muscles can only contract, so they must be stretched back into position by the opposing muscle group.

BUILD Vocabulary

hydrostatic skeleton skeleton made of fluid-filled body segments that work with muscles to allow the animal to move

exoskeleton external skeleton; tough external covering that protects and supports the body of many invertebrates

endoskeleton internal skeleton; structural support system within the body of an animal

joints place where one bone attaches to another bone

Prefixes Both *endo-* and *exo-* are prefixes with Greek origins. *Endo-* means "inside" and *exo-* means "outside." When they are put in front of the word *skeleton*, it describes the location of the structural support for that organism.

☑ **Can you name two organisms, one with an exoskeleton and one with an endoskeleton?**

____

____

____

____

____

Vertebrate Muscular and Skeletal Systems The shapes and relative positions of bones, muscles, and joints are linked closely to the functions they perform. Paleontologists can reconstruct the habits of extinct animals by studying the joints of fossil bones and the places where tendons and ligaments once attached.

Visual Reading Tool: Muscles and Movements

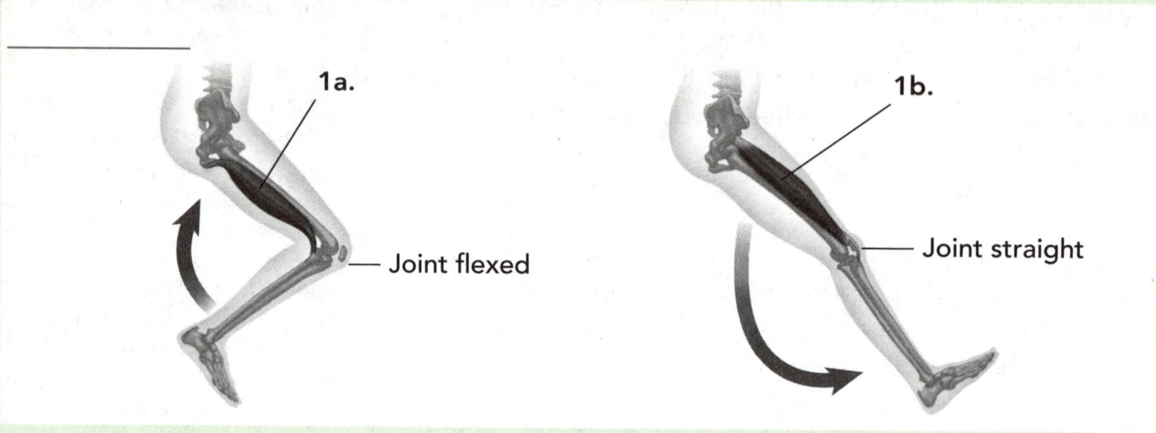

____

1a.

Joint flexed

1b.

Joint straight

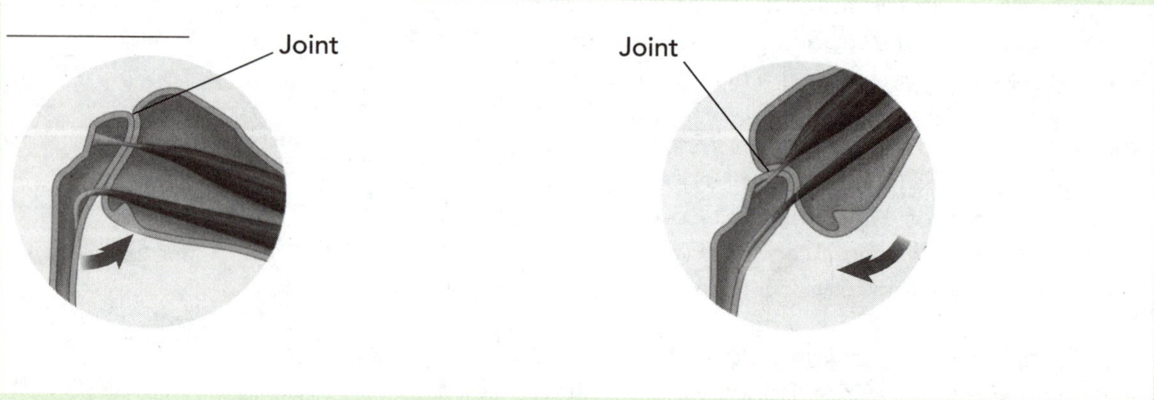

____

Joint

Joint

Identify and label the two types of skeletons seen in the pictures.

1. Determine the human leg extensors and flexors in the top diagram.

1a. ____

1b. ____

2. Explain how flexors and extensors work together to help a person kick a soccer ball.

____

____

CHAPTER 20

LESSON 3

Reproduction

READING TOOL **Compare and Contrast** As you read this lesson, keep track of the similarities and differences between sexual and asexual reproduction. Fill in the Venn diagram below.

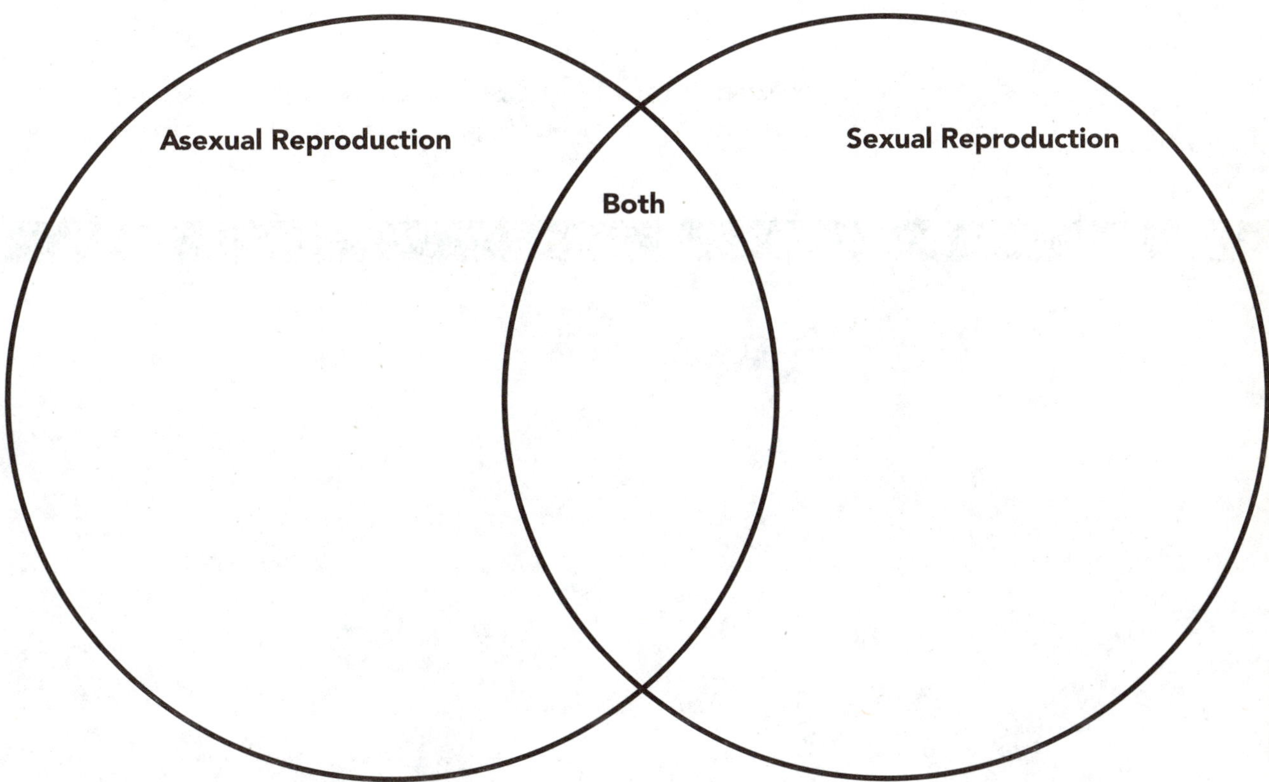

Lesson Summary

Sexual reproduction can be dangerous and can require a lot of effort for the male or female. For example, a male praying mantis will be eaten by the female after they mate, and the male peacock has to grow a huge tail in order to court the female.

Asexual and Sexual Reproduction

KEY QUESTION *How do asexual and sexual reproduction in animals compare?*

All animals must reproduce, or their populations and species become extinct.

As you read, circle the answers to each Key Question. Underline any words you do not understand.

Asexual Reproduction Asexual reproduction requires only one parent, so individuals in favorable environmental conditions can reproduce rapidly. Offspring produced asexually carry only the single parent's DNA, so they have less genetic diversity than offspring produced sexually.

Sexual Reproduction Sexual reproduction maintains genetic diversity in a population by creating individuals with new combinations of genes from both parents. Some animals are hermaphrodites and can function as both male and female for reproduction.

Reproductive Cycles Some invertebrates have life cycles that alternate between sexual and asexual reproduction.

Visual Reading Tool: Reproductive Cycles

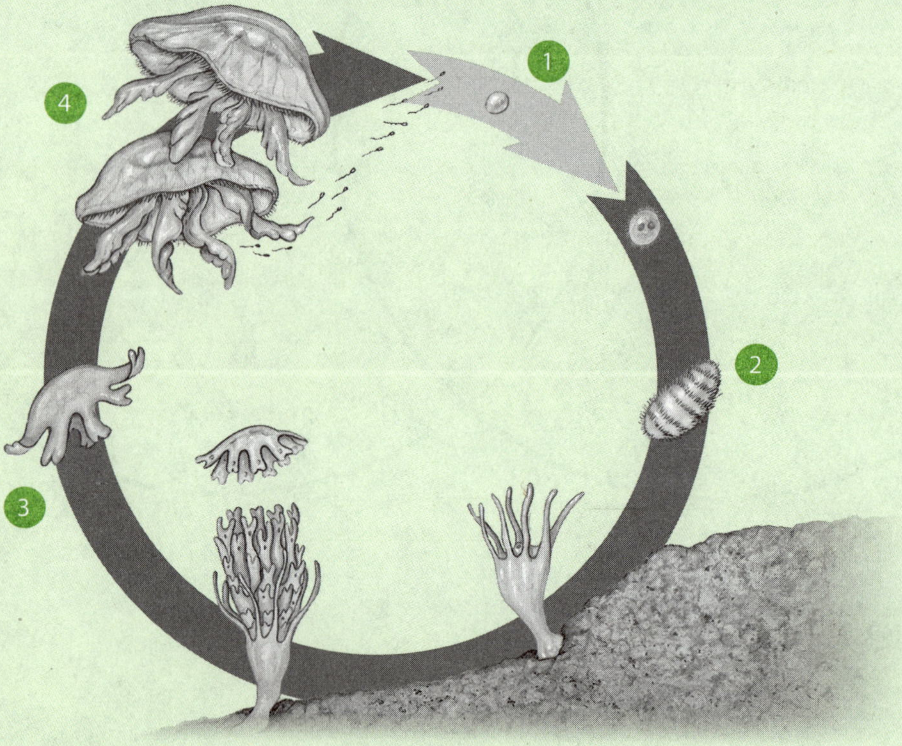

1
2
3
4

Provide a brief description of what happens at each of the four steps of the alternating reproductive cycle.

1. ______________________________
2. ______________________________
____
3. ______________________________
4. ______________________________

Internal and External Fertilization

KEY QUESTION *How do internal and external fertilization differ?*

In sexual reproduction, eggs and sperm may meet either inside or outside the body of the egg-producing individual.

Internal Fertilization During internal fertilization, eggs are fertilized inside the body of the egg-producing individual.

Invertebrates The male arthropod mates with the female and deposits sperm inside the female during fertilization. Some invertebrates, like sponges and some other aquatic animals, have eggs that are fertilized by sperm released by others of their species and taken in from the surrounding water.

Chordates In some amphibian species, males deposit "sperm packets" into their environment. Later, females will pick up these packets and put them inside their own body. Other male chordate species, like male invertebrates, mate with the female and deposit sperm inside the female.

External Fertilization Many aquatic invertebrates and vertebrates reproduce by external fertilization. In external fertilization, eggs are fertilized outside the body of the egg-producing individual.

Invertebrates Corals, worms, and mollusks release large numbers of eggs and sperm into the water. The eggs and sperm are present at the same time because gamete release is usually synchronized with tides, phases of the moon, or seasons.

Chordates In some fish species, large numbers of eggs and sperm are released into the water and the males and females spawn in schools. Other fishes and many amphibians spawn in pairs: the female releases eggs and the male deposits sperm.

Development and Growth

KEY QUESTION *Where do embryos develop?*

Mitosis, which is the cell division of the zygote, occurs after fertilization, and then the cells differentiate.

Where Embryos Develop Embryos develop either inside or outside the body of a parent in various ways. Animals may be oviparous, ovoviviparous, or viviparous.

READING TOOL

Make Connections In most species, the females choose who to mate with depending on physical characteristics and positive adaptations. This is an evolutionary mechanism to ensure that the best genes get passed down to the next generation. ☑ **In which type of fertilization is the female able to be selective about who she mates with?**

____

____

____

____

Oviparous Species Many fish, amphibians, reptiles, all birds, and few mammals are oviparous, and embryos develop in eggs outside of the parental body.

Ovoviviparous Species Guppies and some sharks are ovoviviparous. The embryos develop within the female's body, but receive no nutrients from the mother; the only nutrients they receive are in the yolk sac of their eggs.

BUILD Vocabulary

placenta specialized organ in placental mammals through which respiratory gases, nutrients, and wastes are exchanged between the mother and her developing young

metamorphosis process of changes in shape and form of a larva into an adult

Viviparous Species Viviparous species get nutrients from the mother's body. Some mammals nourish the young through a **placenta**, a specialized organ that enables the exchange of respiratory gases, nutrients, and wastes between the mother and the developing young.

How Young Develop Many groups of invertebrates will undergo **metamorphosis** as they develop, which is a process that involves dramatic changes in shape and form.

Visual Reading Tool: Metamorphosis

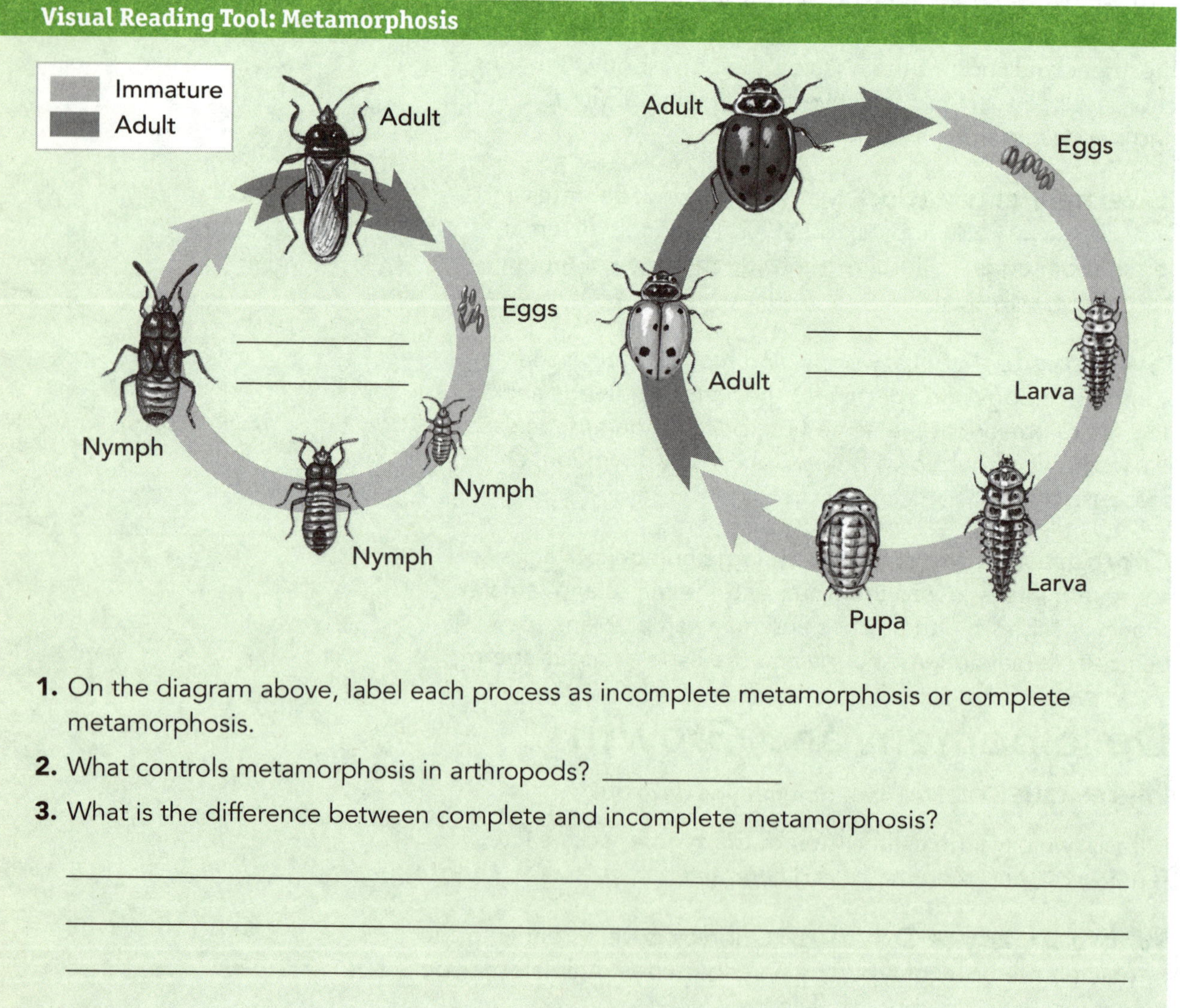

1. On the diagram above, label each process as incomplete metamorphosis or complete metamorphosis.
2. What controls metamorphosis in arthropods? ______________
3. What is the difference between complete and incomplete metamorphosis?

____

____

____

Aquatic Invertebrates Many aquatic invertebrates either have a single larval stage or pass through several larval stages to become an adult.

Terrestrial Invertebrates Insects may undergo gradual or incomplete metamorphosis, or complete metamorphosis. Hormones control metamorphosis in arthropods.

Amphibians Insects and most amphibians undergo metamorphosis that is controlled by hormones.

Care of Offspring Offspring either receive no care at all or are nurtured for years. Typically, species that provide intensive or long-term parental care give birth to fewer young than species that offer no parental care.

Reproductive Diversity in Chordates

KEY QUESTION *How are terrestrial vertebrates adapted to reproduction on land?*

Chordates first evolved in water, but some vertebrate lineages left the water to live on land. In many terrestrial chordates, reproductive strategies enable the fertilized eggs to develop somewhere other than in water.

The Amniotic Egg The **amniotic egg** is named after the amnion, one of four membranes that surround the developing embryo.

Mammalian Reproductive Strategies All three types of mammals nourish their young with mother's milk.

Monotremes Female monotremes secrete milk to nourish their young through **mammary glands**, which are pores on the surface of their abdomens. The duck-billed platypus is an example of a monotreme.

Marsupials Kangaroos are marsupials, and they crawl across their mother's fur and attach to a nipple in her pouch to drink milk when they emerge.

Placentals Placental mammals can develop the embryo for a long time inside the mother because of the placenta.

BUILD Vocabulary

amniotic egg egg composed of shell and membranes that creates a protected environment in which the embryo can develop out of water

mammary glands gland in female mammals that produces milk to nourish the young

Root Words If you break the term *metamorphosis* down into two parts—*meta* and *morph*—it may help you understand it better. From the definition, you can see that *morph* means "shape" or "form." With *meta* meaning "after," you can see the relation between the two parts of the word to mean "changing shape from a larva into an adult." ☑ **Can you name an example of an organism that goes through metamorphosis?**

____

READING TOOL

Making Connections

In this lesson you learned about reproduction, and in the previous lesson you learned about movement and support. ☑ **Provide a brief explanation of how an endoskeleton may be related to the reproduction of ovoviviparous and viviparous species.**

____

____

____

____

____

____

____

____

____

____

CHAPTER 20

LESSON 4 Homeostasis

READING TOOL **Make Connections** All of the organ systems in the human body work together to maintain homeostasis. Fill in the graphic organizer below to show how they are all interconnected.

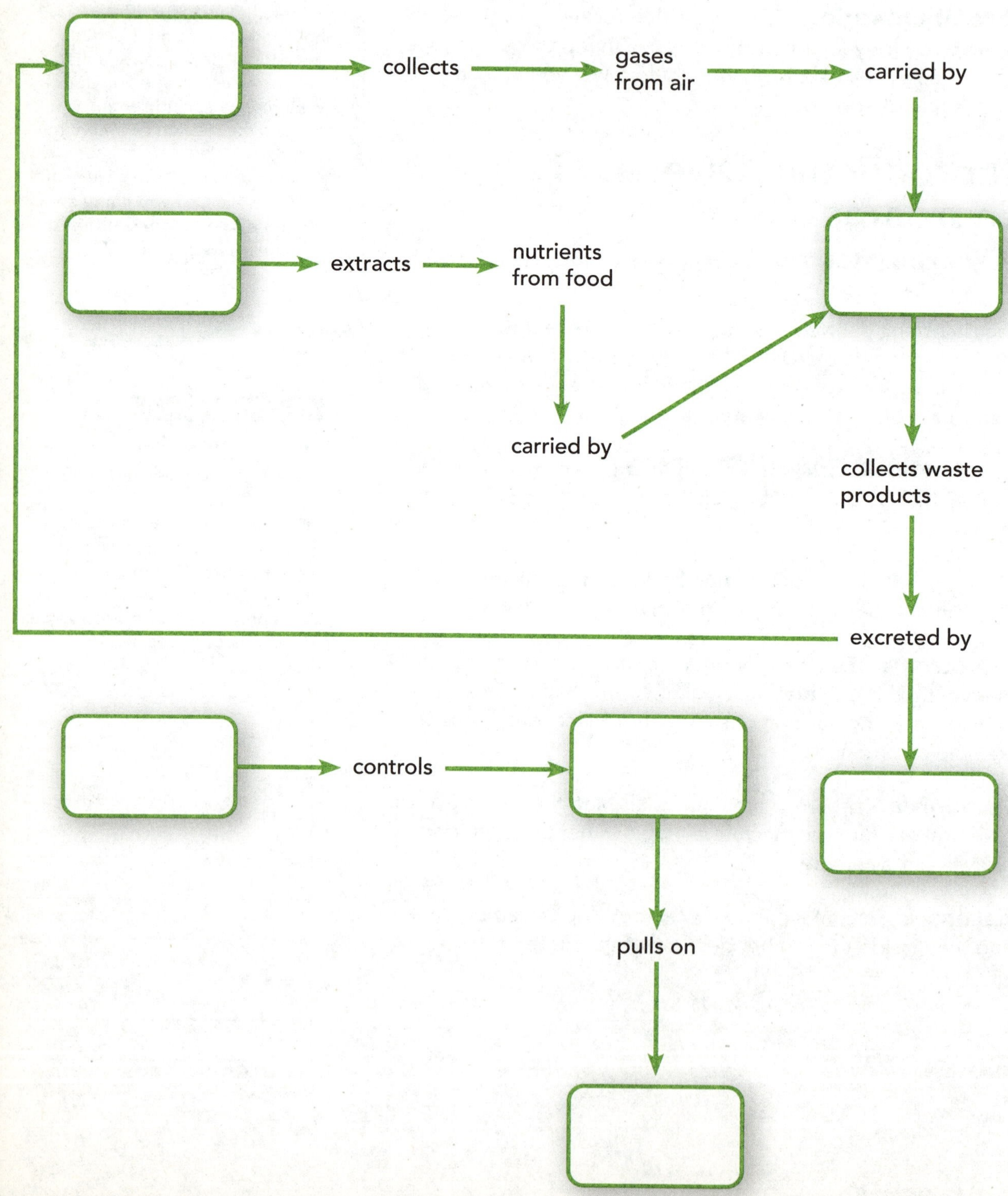

Lesson Summary

Interactions among body systems that perform the functions of regulation, nutrient absorption, reproduction, and defense from injury or illness are necessary for survival.

Interrelationship of Body Systems

KEY QUESTION *Why are interactions among body systems essential?*

The control of internal conditions is called homeostasis and is necessary for survival. All body systems interact to maintain homeostasis. For example, muscles would not work without a nervous system and skeletal system to direct and support them.

Fighting Disease Disease is caused when pathogens enter the body and grow, disrupting homeostasis. Most animals have an immune system that can distinguish between "self" and "others." The body works to restore homeostasis as soon as it discovers "others" in the body, by attacking the invaders.

Chemical Controls Endocrine glands are part of a chemical regulatory system. **Endocrine glands** interact with other body systems by releasing hormones into the blood that are carried throughout the body to regulate growth.

Body Temperature Control

KEY QUESTION *How do animals control their body temperature?*

Control of body temperature is essential to homeostasis and requires three components: a source of heat, a way to conserve heat, and a method of eliminating excess heat.

Ectotherms An example of an ectotherm is a lizard. **Ectotherms** are animals whose regulation of body temperature depends mostly on sources of heat outside its body. Most reptiles, invertebrates, fishes, and amphibians are ectotherms that regulate body temperature primarily by absorbing heat from, or losing heat to, their environment.

Endotherms An **endotherm** is an animal that regulates body temperature, at least in part, with the heat that its body generates. Endotherms, such as birds and mammals, have high metabolic rates that generate heat, even when they are resting. For example, birds conserve body heat when resting mostly with insulating down feathers.

BUILD Vocabulary

endocrine glands glands that releases their secretions (hormones) directly into the blood, which transports the secretions to other areas of the body to regulate growth and development

ectotherm type of animal whose body temperature is determined by the temperature of its environment

endotherm type of animal whose body temperature is regulated, at least in part, using heat generated within its body

Prefixes The word *endotherm* has two components: *Endo-* and *-therm*. *Endo-* is a prefix of Greek origin that means "within." **Based upon other words that contain the word part *therm*, what do you think it means? Think about a thermometer or thermal imaging.**

____

____

READING TOOL

Active Reading

Evidence suggests that endothermy has evolved among vertebrates twice. ☑ **Name a piece of evidence to support this claim.**

Comparing Ectotherms and Endotherms

Endotherms have a high metabolic rate that requires a lot of fuel. Ectothermic animals need much less food than similarly sized endotherms.

Evolution of Temperature Control Although modern reptiles are ectotherms, a great deal of evidence suggests that some dinosaurs were endotherms. Current evidence suggests that endothermy has evolved at least twice among vertebrates.

Visual Reading Tool: Endotherms and Ectotherms

	Endotherm	Ectotherm
Definition		
Examples		

1. In the table above, fill in the definitions and examples for endotherms and ectotherms.
2. How do endotherms regulate their body temperature if the weather outside is too hot?
3. How do ectotherms warm up when the weather is cold?

20 Chapter Review

Review Vocabulary

Match the vocabulary term to its definition.

1. ________ stimulus
2. ________ endotherm

a. an animal whose body temperature is regulated, at least in part, using heat generated within its body

b. a signal to which an organism responds

Fill in the blank with the correct term to complete the sentence.

3. The ____________________ is the part of the brain that coordinates movement and controls balance.

Review Key Questions

Provide evidence and details to support your answers.

4. Explain how evolution has led to increasing cephalization and specialization in animal nervous systems.

5. Explain how muscles, skeletons, and joints are related to movement.

6. Give examples and explain the difference between an insect that undergoes incomplete metamorphosis and an insect that undergoes complete metamorphosis.

7. Describe two or more body systems that work together to maintain homeostasis.

CHAPTER 21

LESSON 1

Organization of the Human Body

READING TOOL **Main Idea and Details** As you read your textbook, identify the main ideas and details or evidence that support the main ideas. Use the lesson headings to organize the main ideas and details. Record your work in the table. Two examples are entered for you.

Heading	Main Idea	Details/Evidence
Organization of the Human Body		
Organization of the Body • Cells • Tissues • Organs • Organ Systems	The levels of organization in the human body are cells, tissues, organs, and organ systems.	
Homeostasis		
Feedback Inhibition • A Nonliving Example • A Living Example		Body temperature is regulated by feedback inhibition. If the body gets too hot, it will sweat to bring the temperature back down.
The Liver and Homeostasis		

Lesson Summary

As you read, circle the answers to each Key Question. Underline any words you do not understand.

Organization of the Body

KEY QUESTION *How is the human body organized?*

The levels of organization in the body include cells, tissues, organs, and organ systems. At each level of organization, these parts of the body work together to carry out the major body functions.

Cells A cell is the basic unit of structure and function in living things. Individual cells in multicellular organisms tend to be specialized. Specialized cells, such as bone cells, blood cells, and muscle cells, are uniquely suited to a specific function.

Tissues A group of cells that perform a single function is called a tissue. There are four basic types of tissues in the human body.

Epithelial Tissue The tissue that lines the interior and exterior body surfaces is called **epithelial tissue**. Your skin and the lining of your stomach are both examples of epithelial tissue.

Connective Tissue A type of tissue that provides support for the body and connects its parts is **connective tissue**. This type of tissue includes fat cells, bone cells, blood cells, cartilage, and ligaments.

Nervous Tissue Nerve impulses are transmitted throughout the body by **nervous tissue**. Neurons, the cells that carry these impulses, are bundled together to form a nerve.

Muscle Tissue Movements of the body are possible because of **muscle tissue**. Some muscles are responsible for the movements you control, while others are responsible for movements you cannot control.

Organs A group of different types of tissues that work together to perform a single function or several related functions is called an organ.

Organ Systems An organ system is a group of organs that perform closely related functions. For example, the brain and spinal cord are organs of the nervous system. The organ systems interact to maintain homeostasis in the body.

Homeostasis

KEY QUESTION *What is homeostasis?*

Your body works constantly to maintain a controlled, stable internal environment. This process is called **homeostasis**, which means "keeping things the same." Homeostasis describes the relatively constant internal conditions that organisms maintain despite changes in internal and external environments.

Feedback Inhibition The systems of the body work to keep internal conditions within a certain range. Feedback inhibition is one way the body maintains homeostasis and prevents conditions from going too far one way or the other.

A Nonliving Example One way to understand homeostasis is to look at a nonliving system that keeps conditions within a certain range, like a home heating system.

Homeostasis is controlled by feedback inhibition. **Feedback inhibition**, or negative feedback, is the process in which a stimulus produces a response that opposes the original stimulus. Systems controlled by feedback inhibition are generally very stable.

BUILD Vocabulary

epithelial tissue type of tissue that lines the interior and exterior body surfaces

connective tissue type of tissue that provides support for the body and connects its parts

nervous tissue type of tissue that transmits nerve impulses throughout the body

muscle tissue type of tissue that makes movements of the body possible

homeostasis relatively constant internal physical and chemical conditions that organisms maintain

feedback inhibition process in which a stimulus produces a response that opposes the original stimulus; also called negative feedback

Root Words The root word *stasis* means "a state of balance or equilibrium." Organisms must maintain a state of equilibrium, or homeostasis, in order to stay alive. ☑ **Give an example of one way that the human body works to maintain homeostasis, and describe what would happen if homeostasis were not maintained.**

____

____

____

____

____

____

____

____

READING TOOL

Make Connections The liver plays a key role in maintaining homeostasis in the human body. It maintains glucose levels when blood glucose gets too high or too low. ☑ **Describe a second way in which the liver promotes homeostasis.**

____

____

____

____

____

A Living Example The body regulates temperature by a mechanism that is remarkably similar to that of a home heating system. A part of the brain called the hypothalamus contains nerve cells that monitor body temperature.

If the nerve cells sense that the core temperature has dropped much below 37°C, the hypothalamus produces chemicals that signal cells throughout the body to speed up their activities. Heat produced by this increase in activity causes a rise in body temperature, which is detected by nerve cells in the hypothalamus. If body temperature rises too far above 37°C, the hypothalamus slows down cellular activities to reduce heat production.

The Liver and Homeostasis The liver is one of the body's most important organs for homeostasis. When proteins are broken down for energy, ammonia, a toxic byproduct, is produced. The liver converts ammonia to urea, which is much less toxic. The liver also converts many dangerous substances, including some drugs, into compounds that can be removed from the body safely.

One of the liver's most important roles involves regulating the level of glucose. By taking glucose out of the blood, the liver keeps the level of glucose from rising too much. As the body uses glucose for energy, the liver releases stored glucose to keep the level of the sugar from dropping too low.

Visual Reading Tool: Body Temperature Control

In the human body, temperature is controlled through various feedback inhibition mechanisms. In each of the diagrams below, fill in the words START and STOP in the appropriate boxes. Then complete the sentences below so that each numbered sentence correctly describes its corresponding number in the diagram.

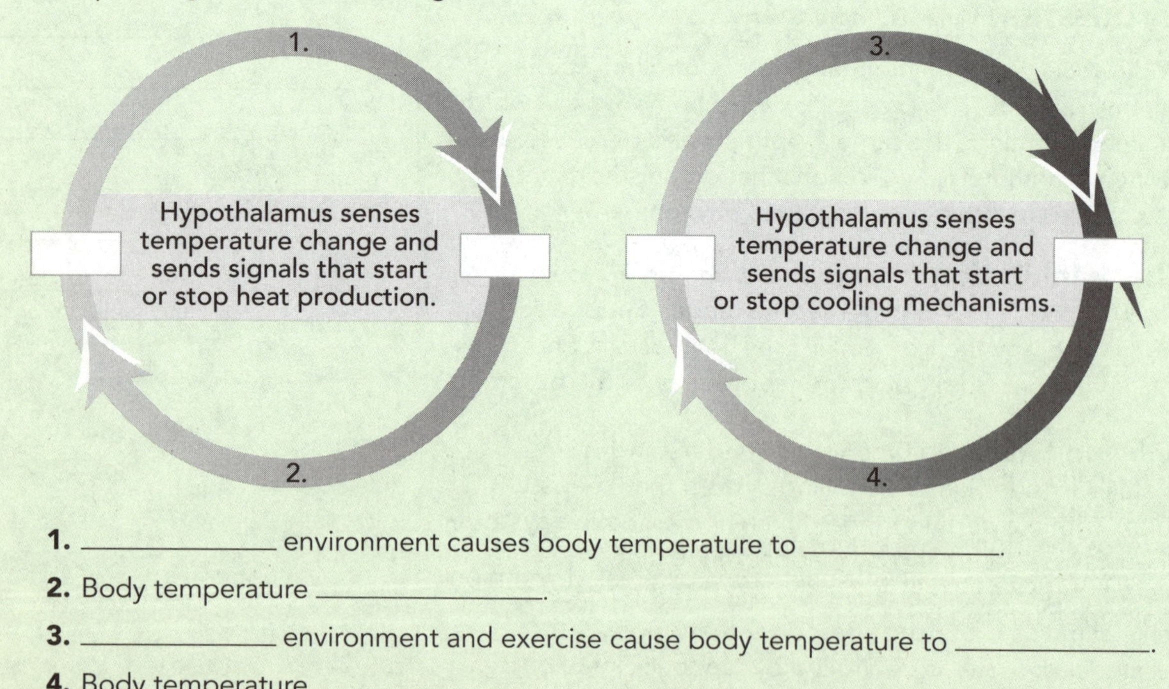

1. _______________ environment causes body temperature to _______________.
2. Body temperature _______________.
3. _______________ environment and exercise cause body temperature to _______________.
4. Body temperature _______________.

CHAPTER 21

LESSON 2 Human Systems I

READING TOOL **Sequence of Events** As you read your textbook, identify the sequence of events in which food is digested. Fill in the flowchart with details about the events that involve each main structure associated with digestion.

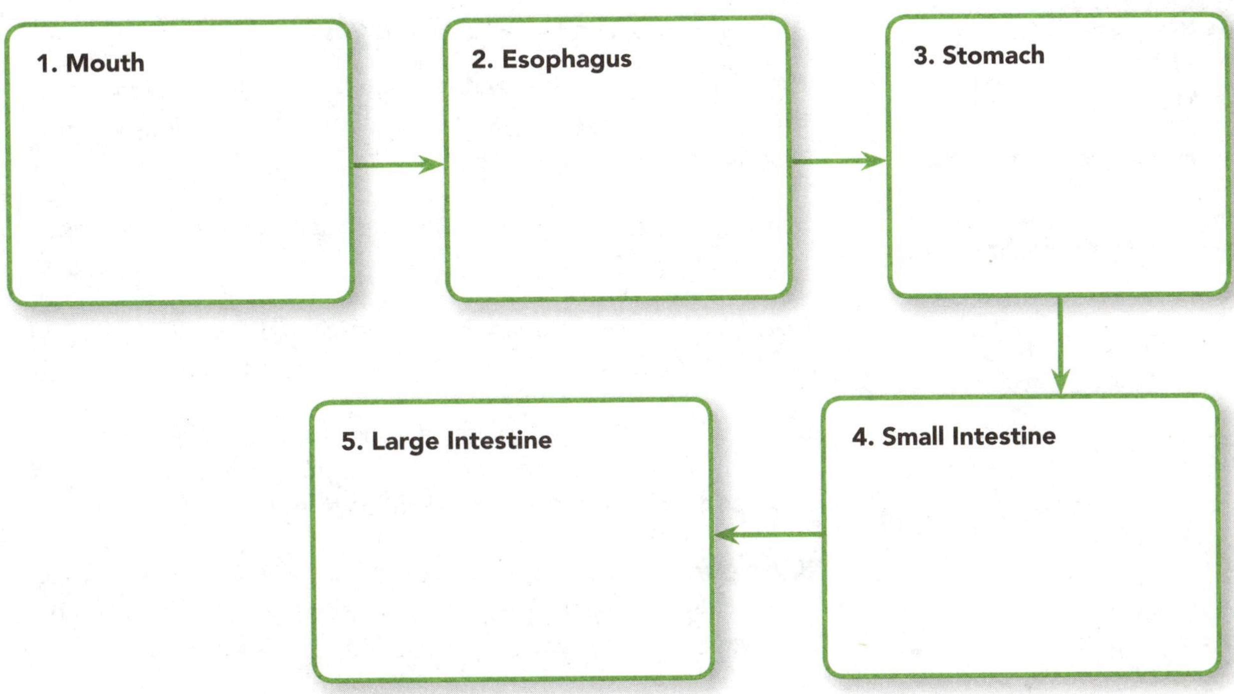

Lesson Summary

The Digestive System

KEY QUESTION *What are the structures and functions of the digestive system, excretory system, circulatory system, lymphatic system, and respiratory system?*

As you read, circle the answers to the Key Question. Underline any words you do not understand.

The digestive system converts food into small molecules that can be used by the cells of the body.

Digestion Food in the digestive system is broken down by mechanical and chemical digestion. Mechanical digestion is the physical breakdown of large pieces of food into smaller pieces by the teeth and stomach. During chemical digestion in the mouth, stomach, and small intestine, enzymes break down food into molecules that can be absorbed.

Absorption From the Small Intestine The small intestine's folded surface provides a large surface area for absorption. Its fingerlike projections, called villi, are covered with tiny projections known as microvilli, which absorb the nutrients.

Absorption and Elimination The primary function of the large intestine is to remove water from the material that is left. The concentrated waste material, called feces, forms after most of the water has been removed. Feces passes into the rectum and is eliminated from the body through the anus.

READING TOOL

Connect to Visuals

Nephrons are the functional unit of the kidneys. View Figure 21-8 to examine the complex structure that filters, reabsorbs, and excretes. ☑ **What substances get reabsorbed by the nephrons and why?**

____

____

____

The Excretory System

The process by which metabolic wastes are eliminated is called excretion. The excretory system includes the skin, lungs, liver, and kidneys.

Skin The skin removes excess water, salts, and a small amount of urea in sweat.

Lungs The blood transports carbon dioxide, a waste product of cellular respiration, from the body cells to the lungs.

Liver One of the liver's principal activities is to convert dangerous nitrogen-based wastes into urea. Urea is then transported through the blood to the kidneys for elimination from the body.

Kidneys The kidneys remove excess water, urea, and metabolic wastes from the blood. The kidneys produce and excrete a waste product known as urine.

The Circulatory System

The circulatory system transports oxygen, nutrients, and other substances throughout the body, and it removes wastes from tissues.

Circulation Blood is pumped through the body by the heart. The right side of the heart pumps oxygen-poor blood from the heart to the lungs. Carbon dioxide diffuses from the blood, and oxygen is absorbed into the blood. Oxygen-rich blood then flows to the left side of the heart. The left side of the heart pumps oxygen-rich blood to the rest of the body. Cells absorb the oxygen that they need and load the blood with carbon dioxide by the time it returns to the heart.

Arteries Large vessels, or arteries, carry blood away from the heart to the tissues of the body.

Capillaries The smallest blood vessels are the capillaries. Their thin walls allow oxygen and nutrients to diffuse from blood into tissues and allow carbon dioxide and other waste products to move from tissues into blood.

Veins After blood passes through the capillaries, it returns to the heart through veins. Many veins contain valves, which ensure that blood flows in one direction through these vessels toward the heart.

Blood Components of blood help regulate body temperature, fight infections, and produce clots to minimize the loss of body fluids from wounds. About 55 percent of total blood volume is plasma. Plasma is made up of water, dissolved gases, salts, nutrients, enzymes, plasma proteins, cholesterol, and other compounds. Plasma proteins transport substances and are necessary for blood to clot.

The most numerous cells in blood are red blood cells. The main function of red blood cells is to transport oxygen. White blood cells guard against infection, fight parasites, and attack bacteria. Platelets and plasma proteins cause blood to clot.

READING TOOL

Compare and Contrast As you read about the lymphatic system, create a Venn diagram or chart comparing and contrasting the lymphatic system and the circulatory system. ☑ **Describe how the function of the lymphatic system is related to the function of the circulatory system.**

____

____

____

____

____

____

____

____

____

____

The Lymphatic System

As blood circulates, some blood cells and plasma leak out through the capillary walls. Most of this fluid, known as lymph, is reabsorbed into capillaries, but the rest goes into the lymphatic system. The lymphatic system is a network of vessels, nodes, and organs that collects the lymph that leaves capillaries, "screens" it for microorganisms, and returns it to the circulatory system.

Role in Circulation Lymph collects in a system of capillaries that slowly conducts it into larger lymph vessels. These ducts return lymph to the blood through openings in veins just below the shoulders.

Role in Immunity Hundreds of small lymph nodes are scattered along lymph vessels throughout the body. Lymph nodes act as filters, trapping microorganisms, stray cancer cells, and debris. White blood cells inside lymph nodes destroy this cellular "trash."

Role in Nutrient Absorption A system of lymph vessels runs alongside the intestines. The vessels pick up fats and fat-soluble vitamins from the digestive tract and transport these nutrients into the bloodstream.

The Respiratory System

The respiratory system picks up oxygen from the air as we inhale and releases carbon dioxide as we exhale. The respiratory system consists of the nose, pharynx, larynx, trachea, bronchi, and lungs.

READING TOOL

Make Connections In the previous lesson, you learned that all living organisms must maintain homeostasis to stay alive. As you read about the body systems, note at least one way in which each body system supports homeostasis.

☑ **What is one way the respiratory system supports homeostasis?**

____

____

____

____

____

____

____

____

____

____

____

Air Flow Air moves from the nose to the pharynx, or throat, and then into the trachea, or windpipe. Between the pharynx and the trachea is the larynx, which contains the vocal cords. From the trachea, air moves into two large tubes called bronchi leading to the lungs. These tubes divide into smaller bronchi, and then into even smaller bronchioles. The bronchioles lead to several hundred million tiny air sacs called alveoli. A delicate network of capillaries surrounds each alveolus for gas exchange.

Gas Exchange and Transport When you inhale, a muscle called the diaphragm contracts and flattens. Atmospheric pressure fills the lungs as air rushes into the breathing passages. As air enters the alveoli, oxygen diffuses across thin capillary walls into the blood. Meanwhile, carbon dioxide diffuses in the opposite direction. These processes are reversed in the lungs before the carbon dioxide is exhaled.

Breathing The force that drives air into the lungs comes from ordinary air pressure, the diaphragm, and muscles associated with the ribs and neck. Movements of the diaphragm and rib cage change air pressure in the chest cavity during inhalation and exhalation.

Breathing and Homeostasis Sensory neurons gather information about carbon dioxide levels in the body and send the information to the breathing center in the part of the brain stem called the medulla oblongata. When stimulated, the breathing center sends nerve impulses that cause the diaphragm and chest muscles to contract, bringing air into the lungs.

Visual Reading Tool: Breathing

Fill in the blanks in the diagram below to accurately describe the events of inhalation and exhalation. Draw arrows on the diagram that show the direction of movement for air, the rib cage, and the diaphragm during each process.

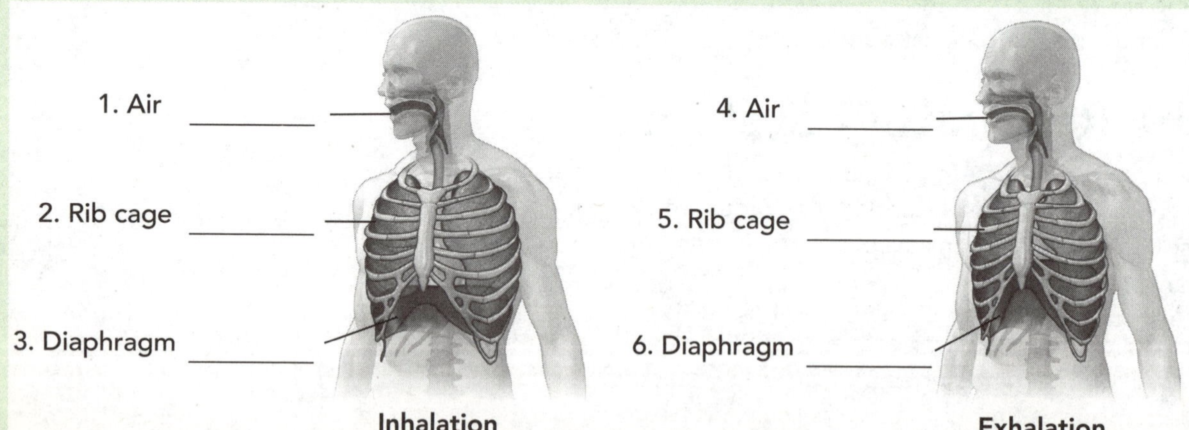

CHAPTER 21

LESSON 3

Human Systems II

READING TOOL **Connect to Visuals** As you read your textbook, examine the visuals that accompany the text. For each organ system listed, select one of the visual aids and record details you learn from the visual aid in the table below. An example has been completed for you.

Body System	Visual	Details
Nervous System	The Nervous System	The nervous system is made up of the central nervous system and the peripheral nervous system.
Skeletal System		
Muscular System		
Endocrine System		
Male Reproductive System		
Female Reproductive System		

Lesson Summary

The Nervous System

KEY QUESTION *What are the structures and functions of the nervous system, skeletal system, muscular system, integumentary system, endocrine system, and male and female reproductive systems?*

As you read, circle the answers to the Key Question. Underline any words you do not understand.

The nervous system collects information about the internal and external environment, processes that information, and responds to it. All of these messages are carried by electrical signals, called impulses, through nerve cells called neurons.

Visual Reading Tool: Neurons

The basic unit of the nervous system is the neuron, or nerve cell. Label the parts of a nerve cell in the diagram below.

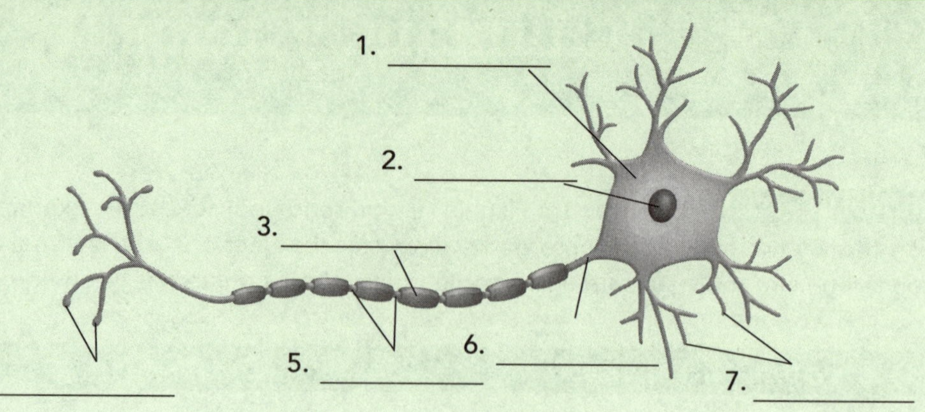

READING TOOL

Cause and Effect The peripheral nervous system sends messages in two different ways. An individual can control his or her somatic nervous system, but cannot control his or her autonomic nervous system. ☑ **Give an example of how your autonomic nervous system is working right now.**

____
____
____
____
____
____
____

Neurons Neurons can be classified into three types: sensory neurons, motor neurons, and interneurons. A neuron has a cell body, multiple dendrites, and an axon.

The Nerve Impulse Neurons carry information by creating small electrical currents. When a neuron receives a large enough stimulus, this neuron changes suddenly, producing a nerve impulse called an action potential.

The Central Nervous System The central nervous system includes the brain and spinal cord. Sensations from various body areas are "felt" by specific brain regions. Commands to muscles originate in other brain areas. The spinal cord links the brain to the rest of the body.

The Peripheral Nervous System The sensory division of the peripheral nervous system gathers information and transmits impulses from sense organs to the central nervous system. The motor division transmits impulses from the central nervous system to the muscles and glands.

Somatic Nervous System The somatic nervous system regulates activities such as the movement of skeletal muscles.

Autonomic Nervous System The autonomic nervous system regulates activities that are not under conscious control like heart rate and digestion.

The Skeletal System

The skeleton supports the body, protects internal organs, assists in movement, stores minerals, and is a site of blood cell formation.

Bones Bones are surrounded by tough connective tissue called periosteum. Beneath the periosteum is a thick layer of compact bone with nerves and blood vessels. A less dense tissue known as spongy bone may be found under the compact bone. Inside many bones are cavities containing bone marrow.

Joints A place where two or more bones meet each other is called a joint. Joints contain connective tissue that holds bones together and permits bones to move without damaging each other. Joints can be classified as immovable, slightly movable, or freely movable.

The Muscular System

There are three different types of muscle tissues that are specialized for different functions: skeletal, smooth, and cardiac muscle. Skeletal muscles are usually attached to bones. Most skeletal muscle movements are consciously controlled by the central nervous system. Smooth muscle movements are usually involuntary. Most smooth muscle cells can function without direct stimulation by the nervous system. Cardiac muscle is only found in the heart. Cardiac muscle cells can contract on their own without stimulation by the nervous system.

Muscle Contraction and Movement Muscles produce movements by shortening, or contracting. A muscle produces force by contracting in one direction. Muscles work in opposing pairs around joints. When one muscle in the pair contracts, the other muscle in the pair relaxes.

The Integumentary System

Skin and its related structures—the hair, nails, and glands—make up the integumentary system. The integumentary system serves as a barrier against infection and injury, helps to regulate body temperature, removes wastes, gathers sensory information, and produces vitamin D.

The outer layer of the skin is the epidermis. The dermis lies below the epidermis. It contains blood vessels, nerve endings, glands, sensory receptors, smooth muscles, and hair follicles. Beneath the dermis is a layer of fat and loose connective tissue that helps to insulate the body. Hair protects the skin and prevents dirt from entering the body. Nails protect fingertips and toes from damage.

The Endocrine System

The glands of the endocrine system release hormones that travel through the blood and control the actions of cells, tissues, and organs.

Hormone Action Hormones affect cells by binding to specific chemical receptors located either on cell membranes or within cells. If a cell does not have receptors for a particular hormone, the hormone has no effect on it.

Control of the Endocrine System The endocrine system is regulated by negative feedback mechanisms that function to maintain homeostasis.

READING TOOL

Apply Prior Knowledge

In the last lesson, you learned about the kidneys, which are the major organ of the excretory system. The kidneys "read" the blood that flows through them, then change their filtering and reabsorption according to the needs of the body. Hormones from the endocrine system also give the kidneys instructions. Antidiuretic hormone (ADH) causes the kidneys to reabsorb more water and return it to the blood stream. ☑ **What do you think happens to ADH levels when a person is severely dehydrated?**

____

____

____

READING TOOL

Sequence of Events As you read about the female reproductive system, create a timeline or flowchart that shows the main events of fertilization and early human development. ☑ **When does cell differentiation begin?**

____

____

____

____

Maintaining Water Balance Water balance is one example of how the endocrine system maintains homeostasis.

Blood Glucose Regulation Glucose concentration in the bloodstream is controlled by insulin and glucagon. When blood glucose concentration rises, the pancreas releases insulin. When blood glucose concentration drops, the pancreas releases glucagon.

The Male Reproductive System

In addition to producing hormones that control the development of secondary sexual characteristics, the organs of the male reproductive system produce and deliver sperm. Sperm development begins in the testes, where specialized cells undergo meiosis to form sperm nuclei. Sperm then move into the epididymis, where they mature and are stored. Glands lining the reproductive tract produce nutrient-rich seminal fluid that nourishes the sperm. The combination of sperm and seminal fluid, known as semen, is ejected through the urethra in a process called ejaculation.

The Female Reproductive System

The primary reproductive organs of the female are the ovaries. Ovaries produce hormones that control the development of secondary sexual characteristics; produce egg cells, or ova; and prepare the body nourish a developing embryo.

Fertilization and Early Development Human development begins with fertilization, the fusion of sperm and egg. The fertilized egg undergoes multiple rounds of mitosis. Cells then begin to differentiate, producing different body tissues.

READING TOOL

Make Connections

During human development, different layers of cells become different body tissues. Gastrulation creates three cell layers that make up many different organs and internal structures. ☑ **Which cell layer becomes the integumentary system?**

____

Gastrulation Gastrulation results in the formation of three cell layers called the ectoderm, mesoderm, and endoderm. The ectoderm develops into skin and the nervous system. Mesoderm cells develop into many of the body's internal structures. The endoderm forms the lining of some organs.

Neurulation During neurulation, tissue differentiates into structures from which the spinal cord, the brain, nerve cells, and other structures will later develop.

The Placenta The placenta forms the vital connection between mother and embryo.

Later Development Throughout the rest of the first trimester, the fetus continues to grow. During the second trimester, the tissues and organs of the fetus become more complex and begin to function. During the third trimester, the fetus doubles in mass and the central nervous system and lungs complete their development.

CHAPTER 21

LESSON 4

Immunity and Disease

READING TOOL **Active Reading** As you read your textbook, fill in the table with information about the different types of defenses the human body has against pathogens.

Heading	Nonspecific Defenses		Specific Defenses: The Immune System	
Subheading	**First Line of Defense**	**Second Line of Defense**	**Recognizing "Self" and "Nonself"**	**Fighting Infections**
Details				

Lesson Summary

Classifying Diseases

KEY QUESTION *What causes infectious diseases?*

A disease is an abnormal condition that harms an organism. In the mid-nineteenth century, scientists proposed the germ theory of disease, which is that **infectious diseases** occur when microorganisms disrupt normal body functions. Today, we call such microorganisms **pathogens**, meaning "sickness producers." Infectious diseases are caused by viruses, bacteria, fungi, "protists," and other pathogens.

How Infectious Disease Spreads Many bacteria and viruses are spread through coughing, sneezing, and physical contact. Other types of diseases are spread through the exchange of body fluids that occurs during sexual intercourse or through blood transfusions. Many pathogens that infect the digestive tract are spread through contaminated water.

As you read, circle the answers to the Key Question. Underline any words you do not understand.

BUILD Vocabulary

infectious disease disease caused by microorganisms that disrupt normal body function

pathogen disease-causing agent

Prefixes The prefix *patho-* comes from the Greek word *pathos*, meaning "suffering" or "disease."

What are three types of pathogens that can cause infectious diseases?

____

BUILD Vocabulary

inflammatory response nonspecific defense reaction to tissue damage caused by injury or infection

Related Words The verb *inflame* means "to make sore, red, and swollen." During the inflammatory response, the injured area of the body often becomes sore, red, and swollen due to increased blood flow. ☑ **Why is increased blood flow an important part of the inflammatory response?**

____

____

____

____

____

Disease Caused by Toxins Another important category of diseases involves toxic chemicals that may be found in food or drinking water. Chemicals found in water that can damage the body include compounds of mercury, arsenic, lead, and chromium. Some of these compounds occur naturally at low levels in streams and groundwater. However, some are released into the environment by mining or industrial activities.

Nonspecific Defenses

KEY QUESTION *What are the body's nonspecific defenses against pathogens?*

Body defenses that act against a wide range of pathogens are called nonspecific defenses. Nonspecific defenses include the skin, tears and other secretions, the inflammatory response, and fever.

First Line of Defense The skin is a physical barrier that keeps most pathogens out of the body. Saliva, mucus, and tears contain lysozyme, an enzyme that breaks down bacterial cell walls.

Second Line of Defense If pathogens do make it into the body, the second line of defense includes the inflammatory response and fever. The **inflammatory response** causes infected areas to become red and painful, or inflamed.

The immune system also releases chemicals that produce a fever. Increased body temperature may slow down or stop the growth of some pathogens and helps to speed up the immune response.

Visual Reading Tool: Inflammatory Response

Add labels to the factors involved in the inflammatory response shown in the diagram below. Then fill in the blanks in the captions to describe the main steps of the response.

1. ______________

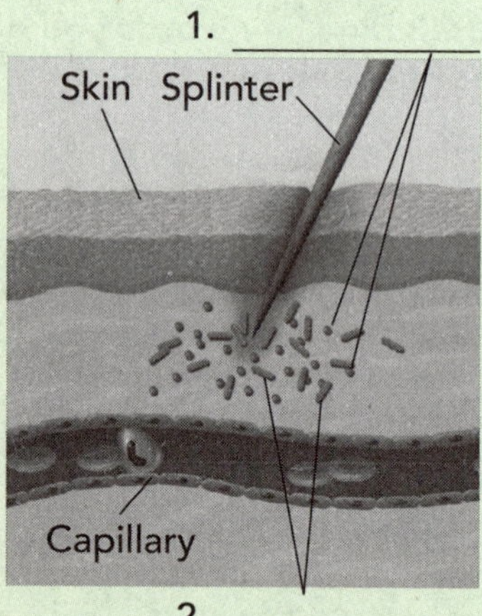

2. ______________

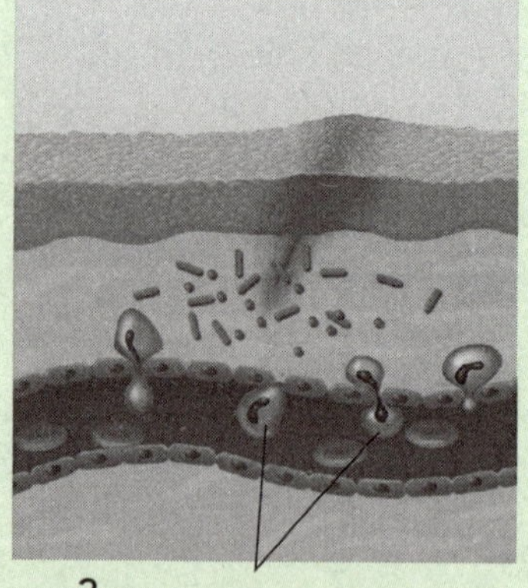

3. ______________

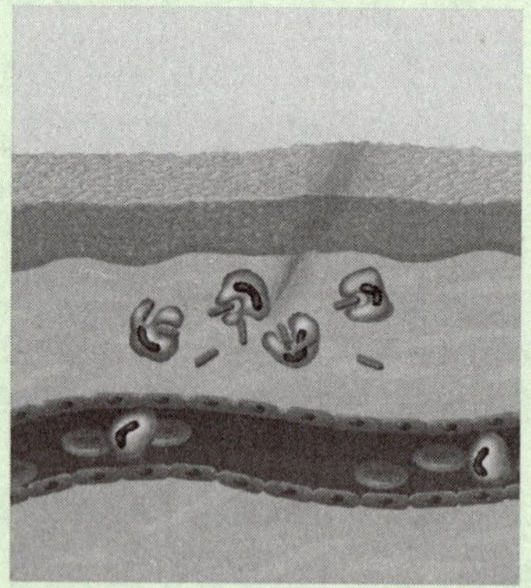

4. ______________ stimulate increased blood flow to the area.

5. ______________________________ move into the tissue.

6. White blood cells engulf and destroy ______________________________.

Specific Defenses: The Immune System

KEY QUESTION *What is the function of the immune system's specific defenses?*

The immune system's specific defenses distinguish between "self" and "other," inactivating or killing foreign substances or cells.

Recognizing "Self" and "Nonself" The immune system recognizes cells that belong in the body and treats these as "self." When the immune system recognizes a bacterium or virus as "other," it uses cellular and chemical weapons to attack it. After encountering an invader, the immune system "remembers" it. This immune "memory" enables a more rapid and effective response if the same pathogen attacks again.

Specific immune defenses are triggered by molecules called antigens. An **antigen** is any foreign substance that can stimulate an immune response.

Fighting Infections The specific immune response has two main styles of action: humoral immunity and cell-mediated immunity. **Humoral immunity** depends on the action of B cells releasing antibodies that circulate in the blood and the lymph looking for foreign antigens. **Cell-mediated immunity** uses T cells to directly attack specific foreign invaders such as viruses, fungi, and abnormal cancer cells inside living cells.

BUILD Vocabulary

antigen any foreign substance that triggers an immune response

humoral immunity immunity depends on the action of B cells releasing antibodies that circulate in the blood and the lymph looking for foreign antigens

cell-mediated immunity immune response that uses T cells to directly attack specific foreign invaders such as viruses, fungi, and abnormal cancer cells inside living cells

Related Words Antigens are often small molecules that are on the outer surfaces of bacteria, viruses, or parasites. Once the body recognizes an antigen, it begins to attack it. ☑ **What do we call the proteins that tag antigens for destruction?**

____

Immune System Disorders

KEY QUESTION *What health problems result when the immune system does not function properly?*

Problems with immune system function can result in conditions such as allergies, asthma, autoimmune disease, and AIDS.

Allergies Antigens that cause allergic reactions are called allergens. Allergens can trigger an inflammatory response. Drugs called antihistamines help relieve allergy symptoms.

Asthma In asthma, the air passages narrow, causing wheezing and difficulty breathing.

Autoimmune Disease When the immune system attacks the body's own cells, it produces an autoimmune disease.

HIV and AIDS Acquired immunodeficiency syndrome (AIDS) is caused by the human immunodeficiency virus (HIV). HIV attacks key cells within the immune system, leaving the body with inadequate protection against pathogens. Over time, HIV cripples the ability of the immune system to fight HIV itself and other pathogens, which leads to AIDS. At present, there is neither a cure for nor a reliable vaccine against AIDS.

READING TOOL

Active Reading HIV and AIDS are two different conditions that are often confused or grouped into one category. However, HIV occurs first, and then leads to AIDS. ☑ **How does HIV lead to immunodeficiency (AIDS)?**

____

____

____

____

____

____

____

21 Chapter Review

Review Vocabulary

Choose the letter of the best answer.

1. Which lines interior and exterior body surfaces?

A. muscle tissue

B. nervous tissue

C. epithelial tissue

2. Which refers to any foreign substance that triggers an immune response?

A. antigen

B. allergen

C. antibody

Match the vocabulary term to its definition.

3. ________ relatively constant internal conditions

4. ________ when a stimulus produces an opposing response

5. ________ disease-causing agent

a. feedback inhibition

b. homeostasis

c. pathogen

Review Key Questions

Provide evidence and details to support your answers.

6. Describe homeostasis.

____

____

7. What are the main structures and functions of the circulatory system?

____

____

____

8. How does the endocrine system control the actions of specific cells?

____

____

____

9. Describe a nonspecific immune defense used by the body.

____

CHAPTER 22

LESSON 1

Habitats, Niches, and Species Interactions

READING TOOL **Compare and Contrast** For each section in this lesson, you will be comparing and contrasting key elements. Fill in the graphic organizer as you read. The first one has been started for you.

Elements	Similarities	Differences
Microhabitat vs. Microbiome	Both are very small.	Microbiome is microscopic; microhabitats are larger than that.
Habitat vs. Niche		
Predator-Prey Relationship vs. Herbivore-Plant Relationship		
Commensalism vs. Mutualism		

Lesson Summary

Habitat and Niche

KEY QUESTION *What factors describe habitats and niches?*

A **habitat** is an area with a particular combination of physical and biological environmental factors that affect which organisms can live within it. Simply put, it is an organism's "ecological address."

Microhabitats Examining environmental conditions on a smaller scale will reveal the microhabitats for organisms.

Microbiomes Microbiomes are microscopic communities too small for our eyes to comprehend. The organisms existing in these tiny habitats perform various functions.

Tolerance Each species has a range of **tolerance**, or variety of environmental conditions in which it can survive and reproduce.

The Niche A species' **niche** describes where an organism lives and what it does "for a living," including the way it interacts with biotic and abiotic factors.

Resources, Physical Aspects, and Biological Aspects of the Niche A **resource** is any necessity a species needs to live. Each species needs different resources. Each niche offers a special blend of resources allowing organisms living within it to thrive. The abiotic, or physical, factors that a species needs are also included in a specie's niche. The niche also encompases the biotic, or biological, factors needed to survive. Examples of a species' biotic factors include the food it eats, the way it obtains food, and when and how it reproduces.

Competition

KEY QUESTION *How does competition shape communities?*

Competition occurs when two species try to use the same limited ecological resources in the same place at the same time. Competition among members of the same species is known as intraspecific competition, while competition between members of different species is called interspecific competition.

Competitive Exclusion Principle The **competitive exclusion principle** states that no two species can occupy exactly the same niche in exactly the same habitat at exactly the same time. When this happens, one species wins and the other dies out.

Dividing Resources Because of the competitive exclusion principle, species inhabiting the same niche within the same habitat can find success by dividing resources.

As you read, circle the answers to each Key Question. Underline any words you do not understand.

BUILD Vocabulary

habitat area where an organism lives, including the biotic and abiotic factors that affect it

tolerance ability of an organism to survive and reproduce under circumstances that differ from their optimal conditions

niche full range of physical and biological conditions in which an organism lives, and the way in which the organism uses those conditions

resource any necessity of life, such as water, nutrients, light, food, or space

competitive exclusion principle principle that states that no two species can occupy the same niche in the same habitat at the same time

Related Words As you learned previously, a biome is a large area with similar environmental conditions that houses different ecosystems. **How is a habitat related to a biome?**

____

____

READING TOOL

Make Connections

Think of the yard at your home or the sports fields at your school.

How many different microhabitats can you name?

____

____

____

____

READING TOOL

Apply Prior Knowledge

Many people think that, by definition, predators must be large, powerful carnivores. **Explain how both predators and prey can be carnivores (meat-eaters), omnivores (meat-and-plant-eaters), or herbivores (plant-eaters).**

Predation and Herbivory

KEY QUESTION *How does herbivory shape communities?*

Food webs identify which organisms feed on which other organisms, often distinguishing predator from prey. These relationships powerfully influence each other and are important in shaping communities. Any natural or human-caused environmental change that affects one population (predator or prey), will also greatly affect the other.

Predator-Prey Relationships Predators and prey powerfully affect each other's behavior. If predators can catch prey especially well in a certain area, they will spend a lot of time there. In response, prey animals will spend less time in that area.

Herbivore-Plant Relationships Herbivores and the plants they eat share a similar relationship to predator and prey, though the plants can't run away from their predators. Herbivores affect the size and distribution of plant populations in a community and determine the places that certain plants can survive and grow. When specific plants grow especially well in a location, they are sure to attract higher numbers of herbivores.

Visual Reading Tool: Analyzing Herbivore-Plant Relationships

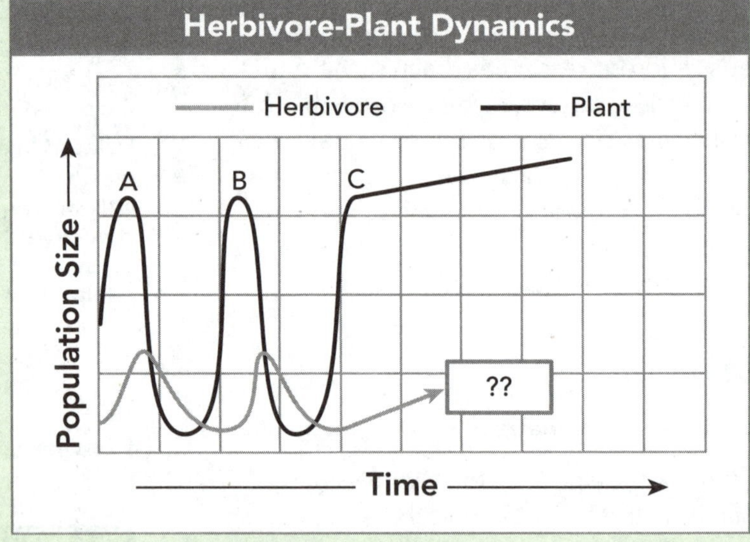

Study the graph. Using what you have learned, explain what is happening at Point C and list three things that might happen at that time.

Explain Point C:

Three Things:

Keystone Species

KEY QUESTION *How do keystone species shape communities?*

A **keystone species** plays a vital and unique role in maintaining structure, stability, and diversity in an ecosystem. These single species have a powerful influence on a community habitat. Changes in their population size can have dramatic effects on the entire ecosystem. If a keystone species is removed from an area, it can cause the ecosystem in that area to collapse entirely. Once an ecosystem has been changed in this way, returning the keystone species to the area may or may not help return it to its original condition.

Symbioses

KEY QUESTION *What are the three primary ways that organisms depend on each other?*

A particularly close, interdependent relationship between two species is called **symbiosis**. There are three types of symbiotic relationships among organisms: commensalism, mutualism, and parasitism.

Commensalism **Commensalism** is a symbiotic relationship in which one organism benefits and the other is neither helped nor harmed. This type of relationship occurs among a wide variety of large and small species. Many organisms living together in biomes share commensal relationships with each other and with larger organisms.

Mutualism **Mutualism** is a symbiotic relationship between two species in which they both benefit. Another way to say it is that the relationship is mutually beneficial to both organisms. An example is the clownfish and sea anemone. The clownfish hides among the anemone's tentacles when threatened. The clownfish is immune to the painful stings from its tentacles that kill other fish. In return for protection, the clownfish will scare away anemone-eating predators, even if they are much bigger. Mutualism is also very common in microbiomes, like the human body or Earth's soil. Their competition and other interactions help keep everything regulated.

Parasitism **Parasitism** is a symbiotic relationship in which one organism lives inside of or on another organism and harms it. A parasite gets some or all of the nutrients it needs from its host. This can weaken or even kill the host.

As you read, circle the answers to each Key Question. Underline any words you do not understand.

BUILD Vocabulary

keystone species single species that is not usually abundant in a community, yet exerts strong control on the structure of a community

symbiosis (sim by oh sis) relationship in which two species live close together

commensalism (kuh men sul iz um) symbiotic relationship in which one organism benefits and the other is neither helped nor harmed

mutualism symbiotic relationship in which both species benefit from the relationship

parasitism a symbiotic relationship in which one organism lives on or inside another organism and harms it

Using Prior Knowledge Humans have symbiotic relationships with many organisms. Some live inside of our own bodies, and some we interact with externally. **Which type of symbiosis do pets have with their humans, and why?**

CHAPTER 22

LESSON 2 Succession

READING TOOL **Cause and Effect** Identify the effects of the elements listed below. Use the headings in your text as a guide. Be specific in your explanations. The causes are filled in for you.

Elements	Causes	Effects
Primary Succession	• volcanic eruptions • glaciers retreating	
Secondary Succession	• natural disturbance • human-caused disturbance	
Succession After Natural Disturbances	• hurricane • forest fire • tsunami • flood	
Succession After Human-Caused Disturbances	• population expansion • deforestation • mining	

Lesson Summary

Primary and Secondary Succession

As you read, circle the answers to each Key Question. Underline any words you do not understand.

KEY QUESTION *How do communities change over time?*

Ecological succession is a series of somewhat predictable events that occur in a community over time. Ecosystems are constantly evolving, and they experience major change after disturbances. New species move in, populations change, and other species die out. The diversity among species in an ecosystem increases as succession progresses.

Primary Succession Succession beginning on newly-formed rock or areas with no remnants of older communities is called **primary succession**. This typically happens after volcanic eruptions or as glaciers retreat, causing new, barren rock to be exposed. Ecological succession begins when **pioneer species**, or the first species to colonize barren areas, move in. They create an environment suitable for other organisms to move in and for the area to sustain growth.

Secondary Succession Secondary succession occurs when a disturbance affects an existing community but doesn't completely destroy it. This process happens faster than primary succession because parts of the original community still exist. Possible disturbances include natural disasters like wildfires, hurricanes, and tsunamis, as well as human-created disturbances.

Why Succession Happens Succession happens in different environments in different ways. Pioneer species prepare the area for other organisms to move in. Each new species makes the ecosystem more habitable for those species already there, as well as for additional species that would benefit the area. These processes become more complex over time as species diversity increases.

Climax Communities

KEY QUESTION *How do communities recover after a disturbance?*

Scientists understand that succession follows different paths, and that the communities that are the end results of succession, or climax communities, may not always be uniform or stable.

Succession After Natural Disturbances When natural disturbances happen in healthy ecosystems, the events and processes that occur during secondary succession often, but not always, reproduce the original climax community. Since natural disasters, like fires or floods, can happen to only a small part of a community, different parts of the same community could be experiencing different stages of succession at the same time.

Succession After Human-Caused Disturbances
Secondary succession can take different paths and produce different communities. It all depends on the kind of disturbance, the season in which the disturbance occurs, and other factors. Sometimes a disturbance causes a change that prevents the regrowth of the original community. Ecosystems may or may not fully recover from some human-caused disturbances, such as clearing land for farming.

Studying Patterns of Succession Ecologists study succession by comparing different cases and looking for similarities and differences. For example, they learned that at both Mount Saint Helens and at Krakatau, primary succession proceeded through stages. Pioneer species arrived via seeds, spores, or adult stages that traveled over long distances.

The pioneer species were important because they helped stabilize loose volcanic debris. This allowed later species to take hold. Historical studies in Krakatau and ongoing studies on Mount Saint Helens confirm that early stages of primary succession are slow, and that chance can play a large role in determining which species colonize at different times.

BUILD Vocabulary

ecological succession series of gradual changes that occur in a community following a disturbance

primary succession succession that occurs in an area in which no trace of a previous community is present

pioneer species first species to populate an area during succession

secondary succession type of succession that occurs in an area that was only partially destroyed by disturbances

Using Prior Knowledge
Secondary succession is quicker than primary succession because there are still some members of a community left in the affected area.

☑ **Name two events that could cause secondary succession.**

____

____

____

READING TOOL

Applying Prior Knowledge

Secondary succession from human-caused disturbances can have a profound effect on an ecosystem.

☑ **Describe an example of an area around the world that has suffered devastating consequences from human-caused disturbances.**

____

____

____

____

Visual Reading Tool: Explaining Succession

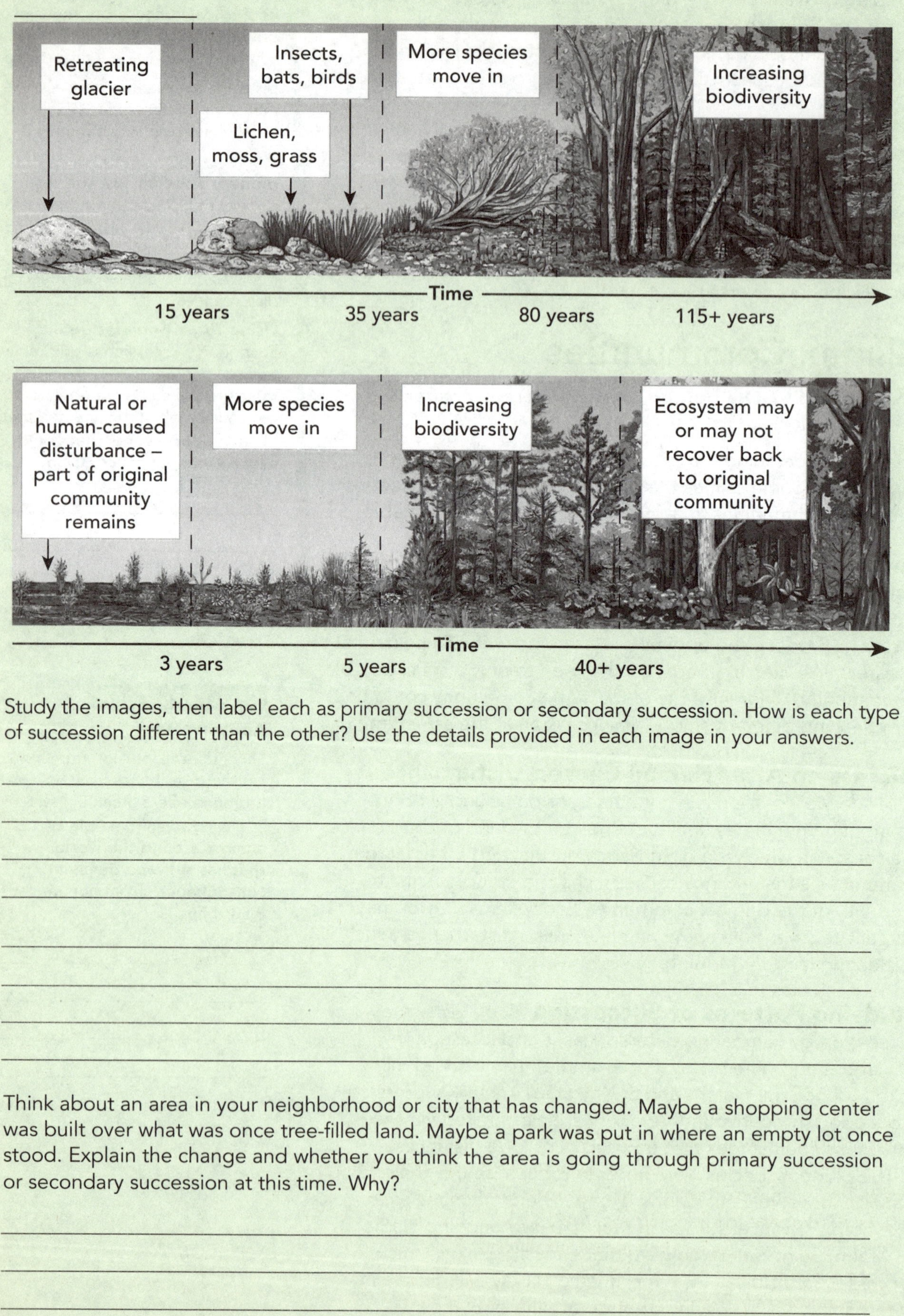

Study the images, then label each as primary succession or secondary succession. How is each type of succession different than the other? Use the details provided in each image in your answers.

____

____

____

____

____

____

____

____

Think about an area in your neighborhood or city that has changed. Maybe a shopping center was built over what was once tree-filled land. Maybe a park was put in where an empty lot once stood. Explain the change and whether you think the area is going through primary succession or secondary succession at this time. Why?

____

____

____

CHAPTER 22

LESSON 3

Biodiversity, Ecosystems, and Resilience

READING TOOL **Active Reading** As you read, list the many benefits that are gained when there is rich biodiversity within an ecosystem. Fill in the table below.

Benefit	Explanation
Biodiversity and Medicine	
Biodiversity and Agriculture	
Biodiversity and Ecosystem Resilience	

Lesson Summary

Types of Biodiversity

KEY QUESTION *What kinds of biodiversity exist?*

Biodiversity is short for biological diversity. It is the variety and variability of animals, plants, and microorganisms, including ecosystem diversity, species diversity, and genetic diversity.

Community/Ecosystem Biodiversity **Ecosystem diversity** refers to the variety of habitats, communities, and ecological processes in a biome, or in the biosphere.

Species Diversity **Species diversity** is the number of different species in a biome, ecosystem, or habitat. Biologists have identified over 1.2 million eukaryotic species. Even more diversity exists among single-celled organisms.

Genetic Diversity **Genetic diversity** refers to the total of all different forms of genes present in a particular species or population. It is responsible for variation within a species, within a single population, and among different populations and ecosystems. Genetic diversity is the raw material that enables organisms to adapt to changing external factors. Consider all the species of birds. Each one has genetically adapted based on the ecosystem in which it lives, and there is a wide selection of variations among each species.

As you read, circle the answers to each Key Question. Underline any words you do not understand.

BUILD Vocabulary

biodiversity the total of the variety of organisms in the biosphere; also called biological diversity

ecosystem diversity variety of habitats, communities, and ecological processes in the biosphere

species diversity number of different species that make up a particular area

genetic diversity sum total of all the different forms of genetic information carried by a particular species, or by all organisms on Earth

resilience a natural or human system's ability to recover after a disturbance

ecosystem services the benefits provided by ecosystems to humans

Related Words Another way to explain diversity is by calling it "variety." ☑ **Explain how biodiversity is different from genetic diversity.**

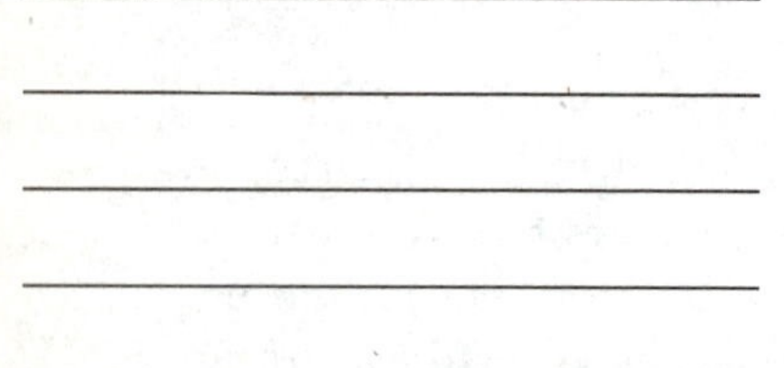

Biodiversity Benefits

KEY QUESTION *What are the benefits of biodiversity?*

Biodiversity's benefits include offering invaluable contributions to medicine and agriculture, and enabling organisms and ecosystems to adapt to environmental change.

Biodiversity and Medicine Many medicines, including aspirin and antibiotics, were discovered in wild species of plants. Other compounds from wild plants help treat diseases such as depression and cancer. These compounds offer financial and health-related benefits and uses.

Biodiversity and Agriculture Most food or crop plants have closely-related versions in the wild. These wild plants often carry genes that improve resistance to diseases, pests, or changing climate. Some of these genes could be transferred to crop plants through plant breeding or genetic engineering.

Biodiversity and Ecosystem Resilience An ecosystem's structure, stability, and function can be affected by changes to the biological diversity of an ecosystem. The loss or reduction of a keystone species can dramatically affect the biodiversity and stability of an area. Additionally, ecological models show that a decrease in species diversity in an ecosystem can also affect its **resilience**, the ability of a natural or human system to recover after a disturbance.

Ecosystem Services and Biodiversity

KEY QUESTION *What are some important ecosystem services?*

Humans depend on healthy ecosystems in many ways. **Ecosystem services** are the benefits provided by ecosystems to humans. Important ecosystem services include producing food, cycling nutrients, maintaining soil fertility, purifying water, storing carbon, regulating pests, pollinating crops, and buffering the effects of extreme weather events.

Food Production Diverse ecosystems provide resilient food plants for livestock, hold and build fertile soil, and protect water supplies. Diverse marine ecosystems provide habitat, nurseries, and feeding grounds for fish and other animals we eat. In many ecosystems, wild relatives of domestic plants and animals preserve genetic diversity.

Nutrient Cycling and Soil Structure Carbon and nitrogen cycles depend on the activities of soil microbiomes, which help maintain soil fertility and structure under changing conditions.

Purifying Water Plants and microorganisms hold soils in place and filter and clean water.

Storing Carbon Healthy ecosystems with lots of plant life help remove carbon dioxide from the air. The more resilient the ecosystem, the better it can provide this function.

Pollinating Crops and Regulating Pests Diverse and resilient ecosystems house vital pollinators and include predators that feed on plant pests.

Buffering Effects of Extreme Weather Events Diverse and resilient coastal wetlands shield shorelines from storms, while forests protect mountainsides from erosion and landslides.

Visual Reading Tool: Ecosystem Services

Review the ecosystem services listed on the left side of the chart. List two benefits for humans for each ecosystem service.

Services Provided	Benefits to Humans
Purifying water	
Buffering effects of weather	
Pollinating	
Regulating pests	
Food production and Nutrient cycling	

BUILD Vocabulary

conservation biology preserves and protects natural resources, ranging from individual species to entire ecosystems, biodiversity, and ecosystem services

Related Words Think of other words that start with *conserve*, such as conservative. The word conserve comes from the Latin word *conservare*, which means "to keep, preserve, keep intact, guard." ☑ **What is the name for an organization that seeks to preserve nature and natural resources?**

____

Measuring and Preserving Biodiversity

KEY QUESTION *What is biodiversity conservation?*

In order to study biodiversity, researchers need to measure it and describe it in numerical terms.

Measuring Biodiversity There are three basic measures of biodiversity. *Species richness* describes how many species live in an area. *Relative species abundance* measures how many individuals of each species are present. *Species diversity* is calculated by using a mathematical formula to combine species richness and relative species abundance.

Conserving Biodiversity The focus of **conservation biology** is preserving and protecting natural resources, using techniques described below.

Protecting Individual Species Captive breeding programs breed and raise young animals until they can survive in the wild. Conservationist biologists also identify endangered species and work to protect enough of their habitat to maintain the species in the wild. An *indicator species* is an organism whose presence, absence, or abundance is used as an "early warning system" to detect problems in ecosystems. Conservation biologists determine the health of ecosystems by searching for indicator species.

Preserving Ecosystems Governments and conservation groups create places like national parks and forests in an effort to protect entire ecosystems and communities.

Preventing Habitat Loss and Fragmentation Habitat loss is usually easy to see. Natural habitats are totally changed or destroyed, species emigrate or die, and communities disappear. Habitats are often lost to development, logging, mineral extraction, or agriculture.

Development and agriculture can split ecosystems into pieces. These isolated ecosystem pieces are surrounded by a different habitat. The smaller a habitat fragment is, the fewer species can live there, and the smaller the populations the fragments can support. Habitat fragmentation causes biodiversity loss.

Habitat Restoration Damaged habitats can sometimes be repaired. Ecological restoration aims to recreate conditions that resemble as closely as possible the ecosystem that existed before it was disturbed.

Identifying Biodiversity Hotspots A biodiversity "hotspot" is an area that is in immediate danger of destruction and that is home to many species found nowhere else. Conservation biologists identify hotspots so conservationists can focus their efforts on these areas. They seek to protect hotspots from habitat loss and fragmentation, as well as other human-caused changes.

22 Chapter Review

Review Vocabulary

Match the vocabulary term to its definition.

1. ________ occurs in an area that was only partially destroyed by disturbances

2. ________ occurs in an area in which no trace of a previous community is present

3. ________ where an organism lives and what it does "for a living"

a. primary succession

b. secondary succession

c. niche

Fill in the blanks with the correct terms.

4. ____________ is a symbiotic relationship in which one organism benefits and the other is neither helped nor harmed. ____________ is a symbiotic relationship in which both species benefit from the relationship.

Review Key Questions

Provide evidence and details to support your answers.

5. Explain the similarities and differences between intraspecific and interspecific competition.

Similarities:

Differences:

6. Explain how pioneer species arrive in an area undergoing primary succession.

7. Explain what happens to species with lower resilience as compared to species with higher levels of resilience.

CHAPTER

LESSON 1 Humanity, Global Systems, and Change

READING TOOL **Cause and Effect** Review Figure 23-1 and the lesson text to determine what makes up an individual's ecological footprint. For each of the items listed, identify two ways you can reduce the impact you make on the planet by decreasing your ecological footprint.

Carbon Footprint Producers	Ways to Reduce
Energy use needed to create your home	
Energy use needed to sustain your home	
Agricultural processes used to create your food	
Processes used to get fresh water for you	
Processes used to take care of your waste products (trash, sewage)	
Processes used to create products you use	
Processes used to sustain your entertainment	
Fossil fuels used to power your vehicles	

Lesson Summary

Humanity's Global Impact

KEY QUESTION *How do ecological footprints of typical Americans compare to the global average?*

As you read, circle the answers to each Key Question. Underline any words you do not understand.

For most of human history, we did not think about how human activities affected Earth. We knew that we had some effect on local ecosystems, but we thought that global systems were too big for us to change. We thought that global systems would function no matter what we did. We now know that we were wrong. Human activities are causing significant changes in global systems. We need to understand how each of us impacts the environment. We need to see how the size of our global population and technology amplify that impact.

Ecological Footprints Each person has an **ecological footprint**, which is the total area of healthy land and water ecosystems needed to provide the resources each person uses. This includes resources like energy, food, water, and shelter, as well as the production of wastes like sewage, trash, and greenhouse gases.

BUILD Vocabulary

ecological footprint total amount of functioning ecosystem needed to both provide the resources a human population uses, and to absorb the wastes that population generates

Related Words Ecology is the scientific study of interactions among organisms and between organisms and their environment.

Why would a scientist studying ecological footprints be called an "ecologist"?

____

____

____

____

____

____

National and Global Ecological Footprints There is no universally accepted formula for calculating ecological footprints. To determine a country's ecological footprint, scientists calculate an average citizen's footprint, then multiply that by the country's population. We can learn a lot about how many resources a country uses by studying their ecological footprint. We can also learn about how many resources we use ourselves. According to some calculations, the average American has an ecological footprint more than four times larger than the global average. This ecological footprint is more than twice the size of an average person living in England or Japan, and more than six times the size of the average person in China. Think about the footprints of nearly 9 billion people together. That incredible amount of human activity is what drives changes in global systems.

The Age of Humans

KEY QUESTION *What is the Anthropocene?*

Since ancient times, humans have affected local environments. Then came the Industrial Revolution of the 1800s, when we began burning fossil fuels to run machines. Since then, our actions have been changing global systems.

READING TOOL

Connect to Visuals

Examine Figure 23-4 in your textbook to learn about the different anthromes that make up the continental United States.

☑ **Find your state on the map and list the different anthromes that exist there.**

____

The Great Acceleration The 1950s was a period called "The Great Acceleration," when humans' impact on Earth began greatly accelerating. We burned more fossil fuels, used fertilizers to farm more land, and caught more fish. At the same time, medical discoveries saved millions of lives. Thanks to scientific advancements, fewer people died, and more people were born. Global population grew rapidly. Technologies advanced, and more people used them. This multiplied our impact on local and global systems.

Visual Reading Tool: The Impact of Humans

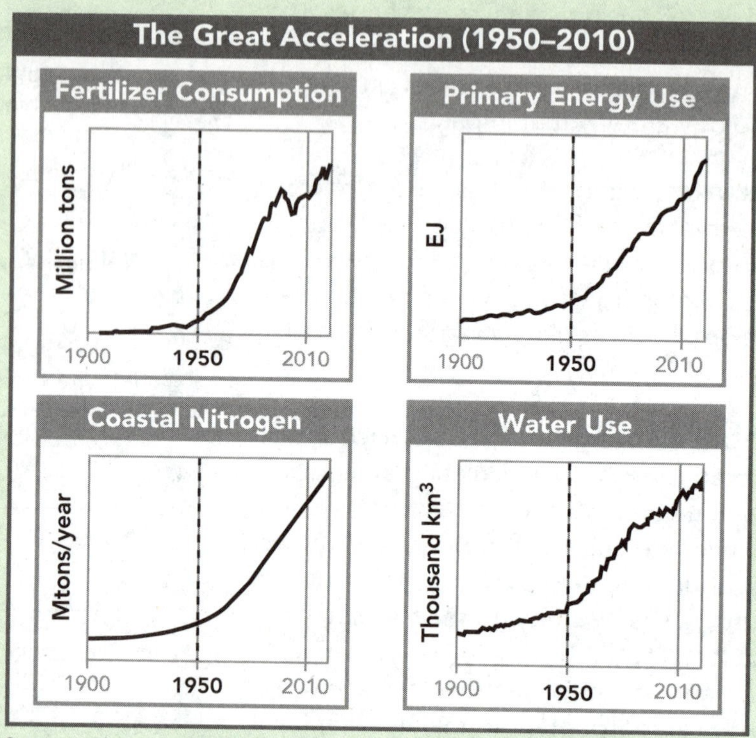

Sources: (1) Olivier Rousseau, IFA; IFA database. (2) A Grubler, International Institute for Applied Systems Analysis (IIASA); Grubler et al. (2012). (3) M Flörke, Centre for Environmental Systems Research, University of Kassel; Flörke et al. (2013); aus der Beek et al. (2010); Alcamo et al. (2003). (4) Mackenzie et al. (2002).

Review the graphs and answer the following questions.

1. Study the Fertilizer Consumption and the Coastal Nitrogen graphs. What is the connection between the trends shown on the graphs?

____

____

____

2. Study the Water Use graph. Why do you think water use began accelerating in the United States during the 1950s?

____

____

The Anthropocene Humans have altered about three-quarters of all land outside polar regions and mountain ranges. We have moved massive amounts of sediment and rock. We have dramatically altered the nitrogen cycle and vastly increased the concentrations of greenhouse gases in the atmosphere. Many scientists call the current time in which we're living the Anthropocene. This "age of humans" is the period during which human activity has become the major cause of global change.

Understanding and Modeling Global Change

KEY QUESTION *How do human and nonhuman causes of change affect Earth's systems?*

To plan for humanity's future, we need to understand the best available scientific data on how Earth systems work. We need to build a model that shows how both human and nonhuman causes of change are affecting those systems.

The full Understanding Global Change model (UGC) is shown in Figure 23.5. Imagine that this graphic is Earth's "control panel." Pushing buttons in the outer ring affects earth systems in the middle ring and causes measurable changes in the inner ring. The UGC can help us better understand the causes and effects of phenomena and how they connect to the causes and effects of other phenomena. The UGC can also help us better understand the impacts of human activities on natural systems.

Global system processes and phenomena happen in the hydrosphere, atmosphere, geosphere, and biosphere. They can also happen across two or more of those "spheres." This model includes most of what some scientists call the cryosphere. The cryosphere, or "frozen sphere," is within the hydrosphere. It is all the water on Earth that is frozen.

Biogeochemical cycles are in the model's middle ring. Plant and animal populations, communities, ecosystems, and their interactions with global systems are also in that middle ring, mainly in the biosphere. Causes of global change that affect those systems are in the outer ring. Nonhuman causes are in the lower portion, and human causes are in the upper portion. Notice that the human causes of global change occupy a larger part of the model's outer ring than nonhuman causes. Measurable changes in Earth systems are in the model's inner circle.

READING TOOL

Cause and Effect

Locate Figure 23-5 in your textbook. This diagram represents the measurable systems on Earth and how they are affected by both human and nonhuman causes.

☑ **Pick one of the red or orange icons and describe how it affects one of the four spheres on our planet.**

____

____

____

____

____

____

____

CHAPTER 23

LESSON 2

Anthropogenic Global Change and Its Effects

READING TOOL **Main Idea and Details** For each heading in this lesson, explain the main idea in the table below. Then, list details that support and explain the main idea.

Heading	Main Idea	Details
Human Causes of Global Change		
Changing the Atmosphere		
Changes in Land Use		
Direct Human Effects on Populations		
Pollution		

Lesson Summary

Human Causes of Global Change

As you read, circle the answers to each Key Question. Underline any words you do not understand.

KEY QUESTION *How do human activities change the atmosphere and climate?*

Human activities affect global systems in many ways. We change the composition of the atmosphere in ways that change climate and ocean chemistry. We changed land by overfarming. We overharvest some species and introduce species to new environments. We produce pollutants and wastes.

Visual Reading Tool: Ocean Acidification

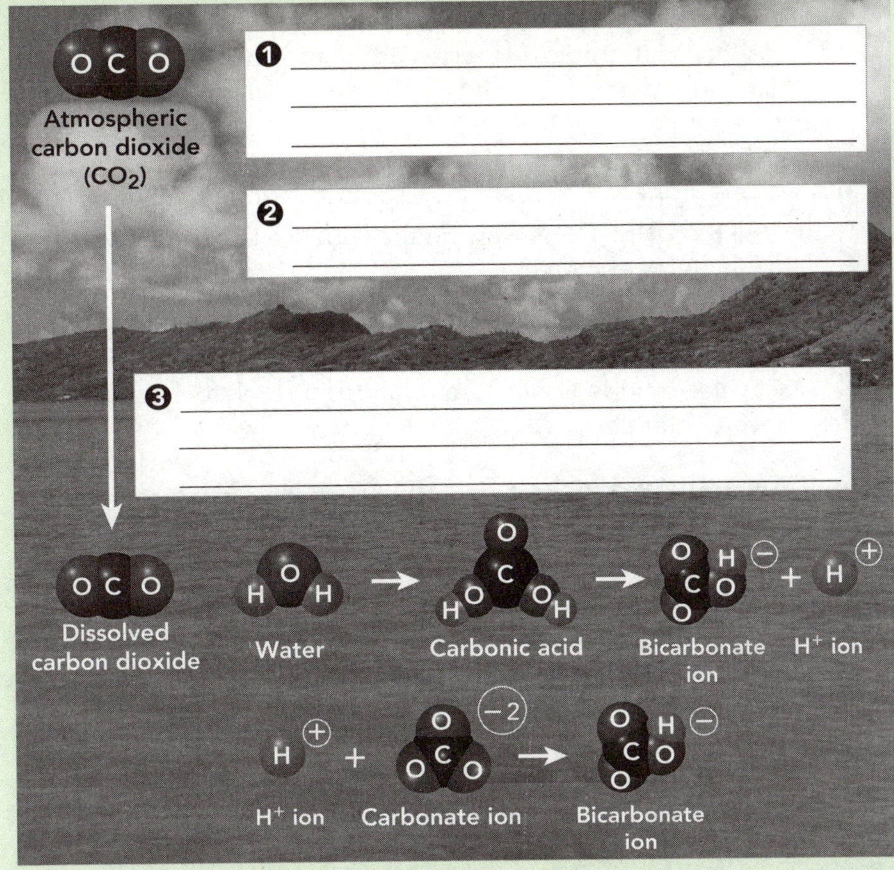

1. In each of the three steps shown to the left, describe how the diagram shows the ocean acidification process.
2. How are marine organisms affected by the change in ocean chemistry caused by ocean acidification?

Changing the Atmosphere

KEY QUESTION *How do changes in the atmosphere drive climate change and other changes in global systems?*

Human activities that affect global systems are changing Earth's atmosphere faster than it has changed historically.

Burning Fossil Fuels Scientists have confirmed that atmospheric carbon dioxide levels have been increasing since the Industrial Revolution and that the cause of the increase is the burning of fossil fuels.

Climate Change, Acid Rain, and Ocean Acidification **Climate change** is defined as measurable long-term changes in averages of temperature, clouds, winds, precipitation, and the frequency of extreme weather events. **Global warming** is the increase in average global temperatures. Acid rain damages plant leaves and root systems by releasing metals from some soils. It also interferes with bacterial decay, altering nutrient cycling. Ocean acidification is caused when carbon dioxide released from the burning of fossil fuels dissolves in seawater and turns into acid. Ocean acidification stresses marine organisms and ecosystems.

BUILD Vocabulary

climate change measurable long-term changes in averages of temperature, clouds, winds, precipitation, and the frequency of extreme weather events

global warming increase in the average temperatures on Earth

Make Connections

You have learned that the environmental conditions on our planet usually remain stable, but have been changing since humans have begun to flourish and change our planet. One of the first noticeable changes on our planet was global warming. **What is the connection between global warming and climate change?**

Agriculture and the Atmosphere Methane is produced and released through cattle farming and the cultivation of rice in flooded paddies. Methane is a more powerful greenhouse gas than carbon dioxide. Like carbon dioxide, it contributes to climate change.

BUILD Vocabulary

monoculture farming strategy of planting a single, highly productive crop year after year

deforestation destruction of forests

Prefixes The prefix *de-* indicates removal, separation, or reversal. In the case of deforestation, the *de-* indicates the removal of trees.

☑ **What other words with the prefix *de* can you think of that indicate the removal of something helpful to humans?**

____

____

____

Changes in Land Use

KEY QUESTION *How do the ways we use land drive change in global systems?*

Human activity has transformed about three-quarters of Earth's surface to provide food, housing, and energy. These activities include agriculture, monoculture, deforestation, and development.

Agriculture Today, agricultural activities cover more of Earth's land surface than any other human activity. The high-nitrogen fertilizers used on many farms are made by industrial processes that fix atmospheric nitrogen. Fertilizer manufacture and application has more than doubled the amount of nitrogen cycling through the biosphere. This has dramatically altered the nitrogen cycle.

Monoculture **Monoculture** involves planting large areas with a single highly productive crop year after year. It requires large amounts of artificial fertilizers and pesticides. When large areas are used for grazing, or to grow monocultures for long periods, fertilizers and pesticides can change soil structure and microbiomes in ways that degrade soil and prevent secondary succession.

READING TOOL

Make Connections

For many years, farmers only planted one crop type in the same field year after year. This monoculture has been shown to be harmful to the environment.

☑ **How should farmers change agricultural production methods to avoid these dangers?**

____

____

____

____

____

____

____

Deforestation/Reforestation Healthy forests hold soil in place, protect freshwater quality, absorb carbon dioxide, and moderate local climates. When forests are lost, those ecosystem services disappear.

Deforestation **Deforestation**, or the cutting of forests, can affect water quality in streams and rivers. In mountainous areas, deforestation increases soil erosion, which can cause landslides.

Natural Regrowth Through Succession Many of today's forests are secondary forests that grew back after primary forests were cut. Secondary succession makes that regrowth possible.

Reforestation Scientifically-guided reforestation, or replanting of forests, can replace areas that have been cleared of trees. Reforestation contributes to dependable, clean drinking water availability.

Development/Urbanization Today, about two-thirds of Americans live in urban areas. Large amounts of sewage caused by urbanization can disrupt nutrient cycles and stimulate growth of toxic or ecologically damaging blooms of bacteria and algae.

Habitat Loss, Fragmentation, and Restoration

Human-caused changes in natural habitats occur through habitat loss and fragmentation, or through restoration.

Direct Human Effects on Populations

KEY QUESTION *How do humans directly affect populations?*

Hunting and Fishing In the past, hunting and fishing did not have much effect on animals because human populations were small. Today, our population has grown. Our hunting technologies are more sophisticated. Because of this, many species are threatened with extinction.

Invasive Species An **invasive species** is any nonnative species whose introduction causes harm to native species. Invasive species often compete with native species for resources, driving them to extinction. There are about 3,000 invasive species in the United States.

Pollution

KEY QUESTION *What kinds of pollutants are drivers of global change?*

A **pollutant** is any harmful material created by human activity and released into the environment.

CFCs and Stratospheric Ozone Chlorofluorocarbons (CFCs) are industrially produced gases that were once widely used in many products. However, scientists found that CFCs were causing the destruction of ozone in the stratosphere, a section of the upper atmosphere. This layer, called the **ozone layer**, absorbs ultraviolet light and acts like global sunscreen.

Ground-Level Ozone **Smog** is a haze formed by chemical reactions among pollutants released by industrial processes and automobile exhaust. Ozone is one product of these reactions. At ground level, it threatens human health.

Industrial and Agricultural Pollution Many industries discard wastes from manufacturing and energy production into air, water, and soil. Chemicals used in agriculture can enter the water supply as runoff or seep into groundwater. Pollutants from industrial activity and agricultural production negatively affect air quality.

Biological Magnification, DDT, PCBs, and Heavy Metals **Biological magnification** occurs when pollutants are concentrated as they pass through tropic levels of a food chain. Due to biological magnification, the pesticide DDT, toxic chemicals called PCBs, and heavy metals such as lead and mercury have all negatively affected plants and animals.

BUILD Vocabulary

invasive species any non-native species whose introduction causes, or is likely to cause, economic harm, environmental harm, or harm to human health

pollutant harmful material that can enter the biosphere through the land, air, or water

ozone layer atmospheric layer in which ozone gas is relatively concentrated; protects life on Earth from harmful ultraviolet rays in sunlight

smog gray-brown haze formed by a mixture of chemicals

biological magnification the increasing concentration of a harmful substance in organisms at higher trophic levels in a food chain or food web

Using Prior Knowledge Pollutants are harmful materials that can enter our ecosystem through a variety of ways. ☑ **Name three substances or products you use regularly that could be considered pollutants if they got into our air, water, or soil.**

____

____

____

____

CHAPTER 23

LESSON 3 Measuring and Responding to Climate Change

READING TOOL **Cause and Effect** Complete the graphic organizer with the possible effects and possible solutions of each identified climate change. Several answers are filled in for you.

Identified Climate Changes		Possible Effects	Possible Solutions
Data shows that global temperatures are rising.	Species are forced to move to different areas to survive or face extinction.	Some species may not survive or may become extinct; species will need to adapt for survival.	Reduce rising global temperatures by reducing carbon emissions.
	Extreme weather events will occur more often.		
Data shows that global sea levels are rising.	Coastlines are receding.		
Data shows that global sea temperatures are rising.	Marine life is being negatively affected.		

Lesson Summary

When a 5300-year-old ancient human emerged from melting glacial ice, the Worldwatch Institute noted to the world that our ancestors were telling us the Earth is getting warmer. Although it was a dramatic announcement, scientists needed data to back up that claim.

Climate Change: Data

KEY QUESTION *What evidence supports the claims that the climate is changing?*

The most reliable climate data comes from the Intergovernmental Panel on Climate Change (IPCC), from the National Oceanic and Atmospheric Administration (NOAA), and from the National Aeronautics and Space Administration (NASA). IPCC data, analyses, models, and scientific consensus reports have been gathered, checked, and accepted by more than 2500 climate scientists and all participating governments.

Data from the IPCC, NASA, NOAA, and other sources all confirm that, due to human activities, emissions of greenhouse gases are the highest in history. All these data show that the atmosphere and oceans are warming; that sea levels are rising; and that Arctic sea ice, glaciers, and snow cover are decreasing.

Data also show that current warming is greater, and occurring faster, than at any other time over the last 16,000–22,000 years. It is important to remember that these numbers are not hypotheses. They are data, measured with the best scientific equipment available.

As you read, circle the answers to each Key Question. Underline any words you do not understand.

READING TOOL

Active Reading

The IPCC has concluded that the atmosphere and the oceans are warming based upon climate data that has been collected over many years. **Based upon previous data, what are scientists predicting for the future regarding the average temperature on our planet?**

____

____

____

____

____

____

____

____

____

Climate Change: Models

KEY QUESTION *What do models show about climate change?*

Computer models, based on accurate data, are vital in climate science. Researchers often compare or combine results of several models that are based on different kinds of data. Some models show predictions about climate change. Modelers compare the predictions of various models.

When the most accurate models are used to forecast future climate, they predict an increase in average global temperatures of between 0.3 and 1.7 degrees Celsius from 2000 to the end of the twenty-first century. That is *if* all nations agree on strong measures to curb greenhouse gas emissions. If emissions continue to increase as they have recently, those models predict that global temperatures could increase by as much as 2.6 and 4.8 degrees Celsius by the year 2100.

Visual Reading Tool: Sea Level Changes & CO_2 Emissions

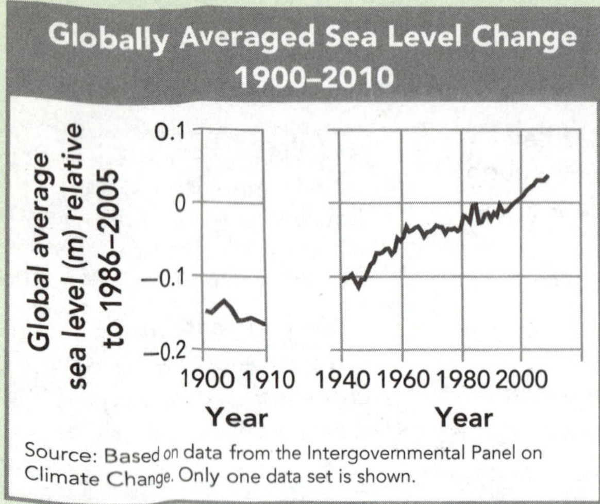

Source: Based on data from the Intergovernmental Panel on Climate Change. Only one data set is shown.

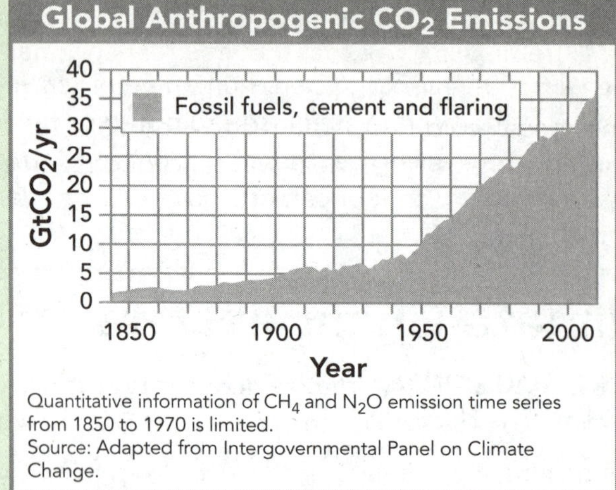

Quantitative information of CH_4 and N_2O emission time series from 1850 to 1970 is limited.
Source: Adapted from Intergovernmental Panel on Climate Change.

1. On each chart, circle the date when the measured data steeply increased. How do these two dates relate to each other?

____

2. What caused the sudden increase in CO_2 emissions?

____

3. What causes sea levels to rise?

____

4. How are CO_2 emissions and sea level rise related?

____

____

READING TOOL

Connect to Visuals

In Lesson 23.1, we saw a chart showing that America has one of the highest ecological footprints in the world. Compare that with Figure 23-17. **What connection could there be with increased temperatures in the Arctic Circle and the relative closeness of America?**

____

____

____

____

____

____

____

____

____

Climate Change: Impacts

KEY QUESTION *What are some impacts of climate change?*

The 2014 IPCC report concludes that "changes in climate have caused impacts on natural and human systems on all continents and across oceans." Climate change includes much more than just the direct effects of global warming. Total rainfall and seasonal distribution of rainfall are changing. Heat waves and droughts are expected to become longer and more intense. Many areas will experience more episodes of extreme heat and storms.

The Jet Stream and Extreme Events Temperatures are increasing faster in the Arctic than in the temperate zone and tropics. Remember, the global climate system is powered and shaped by two factors. The first factor is the total amount of heat retained by the atmosphere. The second factor is differences in temperature between polar regions and warmer areas. As the North Pole warms more than the northern temperate zone, the difference in temperature between those air masses decreases.

This temperature change affects both the speed and the behavior of the jet stream. Today, the jet stream often slows down and loops southward much further than it used to. The extremely cold air that the jet stream normally "walls in" over the Arctic extends much further south. This change can bring record cold temperatures to Florida. It can also create conditions that worsen heat waves, droughts, and floods in California.

Ecological Impacts Each organism's geographic range is determined by its tolerance to ranges in temperature, humidity, and rainfall. If conditions change beyond an organism's tolerance, the organism must adapt, move to a more suitable location, or face extinction. Some animals may soon have no place to go and may become extinct.

Life cycles of many organisms are cued by seasonal changes in both daytime and nighttime temperatures. These cues include plant flowering, animal breeding, and migration. As warming occurs, organisms respond as though spring begins earlier. Data confirms that more than 1700 species are experiencing shifts in their life cycles due to global temperature increases.

Agricultural Impacts Changes in temperature are already negatively affecting yields of corn and wheat in some places. Water availability is also changing in many areas. For instance, many farmers in California depend on water stored in winter snowpack in the mountains and the timing of summer melt. Less water available during summer spells trouble for farmers, and for all humankind.

Sea Level Rise Global warming is affecting sea levels. These levels have risen, on average, at a rate of 1.8 millimeters every year since 1961. This increase has two causes. Melting ice from glaciers and polar caps adds water to the oceans. Extra heat retained in the atmosphere is absorbed by the oceans. This makes the oceans warmer, which causes them to expand—and sea levels to rise.

Climate Change Challenge Of all the ecological challenges humanity has faced, climate change is the most complicated and difficult to fix. Since the world still depends heavily on the burning of fossil fuels and methane-producing agriculture, efforts to address climate change will require major changes in the systems supporting human life. It is up to government policy-makers around the world to use science to inform their decisions on this vital issue.

READING TOOL

Connect to Visuals

Sea level rise is caused by the melting of glaciers and polar ice caps as well as the expansion of water as it absorbs excess heat. View Figure 23-19 in the textbook to see a map of the San Francisco Bay Area and to view the areas that are at risk of flooding with sea level rise. ☑ **List some negative affects that the increase in sea level could have on the population, agriculture, and wildife in the flood zones.**

____

____

____

____

____

____

CHAPTER 23

LESSON 4 Modeling Sustainability, Resilience, and Adaptation

READING TOOL **Active Reading** For each section of this lesson, take notes on how sustainable development can be achieved.

Lesson Section	Connection to Sustainable Development
Sustainable Development	
Renewable Resources	
Nonrenewable Resources	
Innovation	
Economy and Human Needs	
Uncertainty, Models, and Resilience	
Complicated Systems and Complexity	
The Tonlé Sap Food Web	
Adding Humans	
Resilience	
Designing Solutions	
Environmental Successes	

Lesson Summary

Recent studies note that global ecosystem services are worth more than four times the total value of all the world's economies. Governments and companies must take into account ecosystem services when calculating how economies function. The value of "natural capital" must be included in development plans, because sooner or later, "ecological debt" comes due.

As you read, circle the answers to each Key Question. Underline any words you do not understand.

Sustainable Development

KEY QUESTION *What criteria can be used to evaluate whether development is sustainable?*

What happens if the stress and damage to ecosystems that we call ecological debt becomes too large? Damaged ecosystems can change their structure and function in ways that will harm humans. One strategy for avoiding loss of needed resources is **sustainable development**, which provides for human needs while preserving ecosystem services.

BUILD Vocabulary

sustainable development
strategy for using natural resources without depleting them and for providing for human needs without causing long-term environmental harm

Visual Reading Tool: Explaining Sustainable Development

Identify each link in the chain of sustainable development.

1. ____________ **2.** ____________ **3.** ____________

Explain why each link is equally important to sustainable development.

____

____

____

Sustainable development should cause no long-term harm to soil, water, or climate. It should use as little nonrenewable energy and resources as possible, and it must take into account human needs and economic systems.

BUILD Vocabulary

renewable resource resource that can be produced or replaced by healthy ecosystem functions

nonrenewable resource resource that cannot be replenished by a natural process within a reasonable amount of time

Related Words A resource is anything that is necessary for life. **☑ Name three items that are necessary to your life that are considered renewable resources.**

____

____

Renewable Resources **Renewable resources** can be produced or replaced by healthy ecosystems. Drinking water can be a renewable resource, filtered by ecosystems as part of the water cycle. But if forests and soils are degraded, cities and towns must pay for treatment to provide safe drinking water. Electricity from solar power or wind farms are also forms of renewable energy resources.

Nonrenewable Resources Resources that natural processes can't replenish are **nonrenewable resources**. Fossil fuels such as coal, oil, and natural gas are nonrenewable resources. Some resources, such as fisheries or forests, can be renewable if managed properly but nonrenewable if mismanaged.

Innovation, Economy, and Human Needs Innovation can offer new ways to provide sustainable service at reasonable cost. Solar panels are one example of human innovation that solves a problem (burning fossil fuels for energy). They've been available for over twenty years, but before now, they were too expensive for most people to buy. Engineering and manufacturing innovations of solar panels have lowered the price, and they are becoming affordable for the average consumer. We must remember, though, that innovation won't solve long-term ecological problems, unless it is guided by sustainable goals and practices. Participants in sustainable development need opportunities to use both innovation and changes in local economies that improve their standard of living.

Uncertainty, Models, and Resilience

KEY QUESTION *What are complex ecosystems?*

Life in the Anthropocene involves human-caused changes in global systems.

Complicated Systems and Complexity Communities and ecosystems are complicated. In other words, they have a lot of moving parts. Some complicated ecosystems are also complex. Complexity means that an ecosystem can change unexpectedly into a very different-looking system. A change from one condition to a very different condition can dramatically affect ecosystem services. For example, removing a predator from an ecosystem could cause it to collapse. That is a complex change that can transform an ecosystem.

The Tonlé Sap Food Web Researchers are building a mathematical model of the food web of Tonlé Sap lake in Cambodia. It is an example of a complex system. Numbers are used to show the nature and strength of interactions between organisms. Equations based on these numbers are used to build computer models that try to predict how changes in one part of the food web will affect the rest of the web.

Adding Humans Taking into account all the ways that humans interact with a complex system piles on still more complexity! Ecologists call complex systems like Tonlé Sap examples of Coupled Human And Natural Systems, or CHANS for short. In fact, in the Anthropocene, the entire world is composed of CHANS that are linked through global systems.

To guide sustainable development, researchers are trying to model this extraordinary complexity using a type of mathematical model called MIMES: Multiscale Integrated Model of Ecosystem Services. MIMES models are based on numerical data and complex calculations. They try to predict possible future outcomes of interactions between human and natural systems.

Resilience Awareness of these sorts of possible changes helps guide sustainable development towards **resilience**—the ability of a system to deal with change. Sustainable development must be resilient enough to survive environmental stresses like droughts, floods, storms, heat waves, cold snaps, and unexpected changes in the structure and function of local ecosystems.

Designing Solutions Research can help us respond to global ecological challenges by first recognizing that there is an environmental problem created by human or other causes. Next, we must gather data to document and analyze that problem and identify its cause. Finally, we must use a scientifically informed approach to guide economists, politicians, and stakeholders in creating sustainable and resilient environmental policy.

Environmental Successes Research has often guided us towards informed environmental management. Years ago, for example, ecologists discovered lead in North American streams. They conducted research that identified car exhaust as the source of that lead. Industry then designed engineering solutions that now enable cars to run efficiently on unleaded fuel. Leaded gasoline was phased out, and lead concentrations in environments across the country dropped. Addressing climate change is our next global scientific challenge.

BUILD Vocabulary

resilience the ability of a system to deal with change

Multiple Meanings The word *resilience* is often used to describe people who are able to recover from a difficulty or trauma in a fairly short period of time. These people can "bounce back" and adapt to their new life situation. *Resilience* is also used to describe an object or substance that, once stretched, quickly springs back into shape. A good example is clothing made of nylon. ☑ **Describe a situation in which a person showed resilience. Alternately, describe an object or substance that shows resilience.**

____

____

____

____

____

____

23 Chapter Review

Review Vocabulary

Match the vocabulary term to its definition.

1. ______ ecological footprint
2. ______ monoculture
3. ______ biological magnification
4. ______ resilience

a. farming strategy of planting a single productive crop in the same field year after year

b. an organism or community's ability to deal with change and successfully move on

c. the total area of healthy land and water ecosystems needed to provide the resources you use and to absorb wastes you produce

d. increasing concentration of harmful substances progressing through food chains

Fill in the blanks with the correct terms.

5. ______________ are resources that can be reproduced or replaced by natural processes, while ______________ cannot be reproduced or replaced by natural processes in a reasonable amount of time.

Review Key Questions

Provide evidence and details to support your answers.

6. Explain how the average Americans' ecological footprint compares to the average ecological footprint of people in other countries.

7. Identify two unsustainable agricultural practices currently in use in the United States.

8. Identify three ways unsustainable development practices have contributed to climate change.

9. Explain how the element of resilience affects two of the key factors needed for sustainable development: environment and society.